A History of
EGYPT

A History of
EGYPT

From Earliest Times to the Present

Jason Thompson

The American University in Cairo Press
Cairo   New York

First published in 2008 by
The American University in Cairo Press
113 Sharia Kasr el Aini, Cairo, Egypt
420 Fifth Avenue, New York, NY 10018
www.aucpress.com

Maps on pages xii and xiii by Ola Seif.

Dar el Kutub No. 3055/07
ISBN 978 977 416 091 2

Dar el Kutub Cataloging-in-Publication Data

Thompson, Jason
        A History of Egypt: From Earliest Times to the Present / Jason
        Thompson.—Cairo: The American University in Cairo Press, 2008
        p.   cm.
        ISBN 977 416 091 6
        1. Egypt—History   I. Title
        962

1 2 3 4 5 6 7 8   12 11 10 09 08

Designed by Andrea El-Akshar
Printed in Egypt

To the memory of my Egyptian mother,
Zeinab Hassan Murgan

Contents

Acknowledgments		ix
Preface		x
Maps		xii

1.	The Gift of the Nile	1
2.	The Birth of Egyptian Civilization: Predynastic and Early Dynastic Egypt	11
3.	The Old Kingdom	25
4.	The First Intermediate Period and the Middle Kingdom	43
5.	The Second Intermediate Period and the New Kingdom	59
6.	The Third Intermediate Period and the Late Period	83
7.	Ptolemaic Egypt	97
8.	Egypt in the Roman Empire	123
9.	Coptic Egypt	145
10.	The Advent of Islam	163
11.	The Fatimids and Ayyubids	173
12.	The Mamluks	189
13.	Egypt in the Ottoman Empire	207
14.	The Birth of Modern Egypt	219
15.	Mid-Nineteenth-Century Egypt	235

16. The British Occupation of Egypt 253
17. The Parliamentary Era 273
18. Nasser 293
19. Sadat 317
20. Mubarak and Beyond 341

Notes 357
Recommended Reading 360
Image Sources 362
Index 363

Acknowledgments

During the years that I have been involved with Egyptian history in one form or another I have benefited from friendship and collegiality with many scholars in almost every facet of the Egyptian past. That experience has enriched this book in myriad ways, and I am intensely grateful for it. I am particularly appreciative of Mark Linz, the director of the American University in Cairo Press, for suggesting that I write the book in the first place, then persevering when I initially declined, and to associate director Neil Hewison for encouraging me to take up the task. Valuable readers' comments and corrections on all or parts of the manuscript were provided by John Ruffle, Muhammad Williams, Angela T. Thompson, Margaret Ranger, Neil Ranger, and Jill Kamil. Jarosław Dobrowolski and Michael Jones made major photographic contributions, as did Robert K. Vincent and John Feeney, who must be acknowledged in memory. I must also express my affectionate gratitude to my Egyptian family—Baba Ahmed, Habiba, Amna, and all the rest—who allowed me to live among them in their house by the Mausoleum of Sultan Qaitbay in Cairo while I composed large portions of the book. With such valuable assistance and support, I have no valid excuse for the shortcomings that must attend a work of this scope.

Preface

Until quite recently, a one-volume survey of Egyptian history from the earliest times to the present by a single author was almost unheard of. There is an abundance of books about Egyptian history—Egypt is one of the most written-about lands in the world, an inexhaustible source of inspiration for writers and interest for readers—but they almost invariably concentrate on one particular period, as if the many phases of the Egyptian past are watertight compartments, hermetically sealed from each other. Yet few if any lands have as many threads of continuity running throughout their entire historical experience as Egypt. While the country has changed almost beyond recognition, one is repeatedly confronted by the paradox—indeed the outright contradiction—that many aspects of Egyptian culture have remained recognizably the same and can be documented across the millennia. Visible reminders of the full panoply of the Egyptian past are always available for ready reference.

Egypt's recorded history is a little more than twice as long as those of England and France, both of which have been frequently treated in one-volume formats. But mere length itself is an obstacle that can be surmounted by selectivity and adjusting the depth of field. The rich variety of the Egyptian past, the subject of so many studies by highly specialized scholars, only makes it a more fitting subject for synthesis and comprehensive presentation.

The historiographical challenge was one of my motives for agreeing to write this book. Far from being superficial, some of the problems are extremely subtle. A comprehensive generalization is often more difficult to write than a detailed description. My objectives were also to address readers who want an introduction to the major epochs in Egyptian history and the elements of continuity and transition between them, and to supply travelers to Egypt with historical background to the places they visit. Accordingly, I have attempted to allot a reasonable amount of space and attention to the full range of Egyptian history, from prehistory until the near present. Hence, nearly half of the book is concerned with the periods before the Muslim conquest. A bit more space is devoted to the past two centuries, not because they are intrinsically more important but to bring the picture into sharper focus as it approaches the present, thereby emphasizing the connectedness of this moment to the totality of the Egyptian past. The detail then dissolves around the end of the twentieth century as recent history merges into current events.

Once inducted into the vast scope of Egyptian history, readers will inevitably be drawn more deeply into its many dimensions. Although this book pays some attention to society, culture, religion, economics, and other aspects of history, its organization is primarily political in order to maintain structure and present a coherent narrative. But political history is just one way of writing history; the reader is encouraged to delve into other approaches as well. The Recommended Reading section at the end is merely a brief list of suggestions, points of departure into a vast, varied, and endlessly fascinating literary universe. Above all, the reader is encouraged to be active, to be critical, to question and test generalizations. Egyptian history is a process in which everyone can participate, a game that anyone can play. The Egyptians have their past all around them, and they generously share it with those who read about it and who visit their country. Therefore those of us from abroad should bear in mind that Egyptian history is ultimately the property of the Egyptian people, past and present, and treat it with the respect, indeed the reverence, that it deserves.

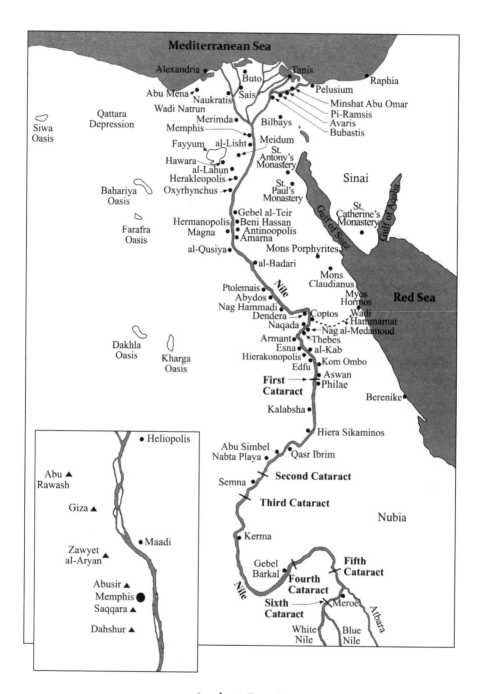

Ancient Egypt

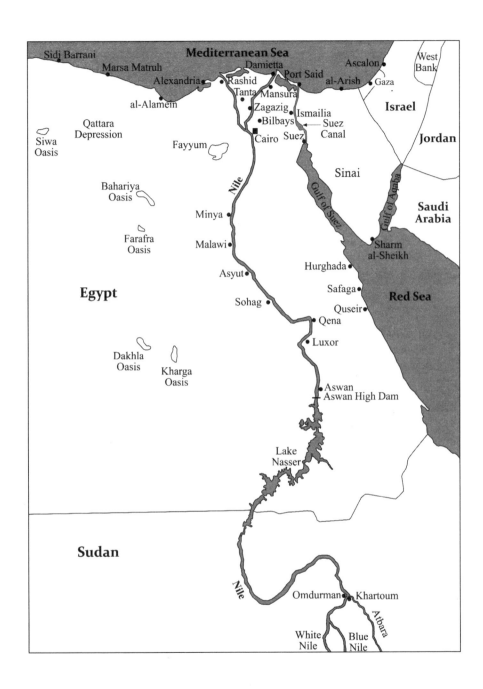

Modern Egypt

I will speak at length about Egypt
because there is no other country like it,
nor any that possesses as many wonders.
—Herodotus

1   The Gift of the Nile

Egypt is readily recognizable on the map today as an angular wedge of northeastern Africa and a chunk of southwestern Asia. It covers slightly more than a million square kilometers, and at the beginning of the twenty-first century it was inhabited by approximately seventy-five million people. The capital of Egypt, Cairo, with its population of more than sixteen million, is the largest city on the African continent.

But to envision Egypt historically, and to understand its geographical essence, one must think first about the Nile, the longest river in the world, and a river that flows through the Sahara, the largest desert in the world. When the Greek traveler Herodotus described Egypt as the gift of the Nile in the fifth century BC, he was probably just repeating what was already a well-worn phrase, but one true since long before historical memory and no less so now. Rainfall is insignificant in the valley of the Nile, and not abundant in the Delta, so that virtually all of Egypt's water comes from the Nile, and even with the amazing development during the past few decades of the Mediterranean and Red Sea coasts, 95 percent of the population of Egypt still live within a few miles of the river. Almost all of Egypt's arable land, about 34,000 square kilometers, lies in the river valley and the Delta.

The Egyptian Nile has three major sources. The longest is the White Nile. The sources of this river, until the mid-nineteenth century one of the world's great geographical mysteries, lie deep within Africa, especially in the lake region, where Lake Victoria in Uganda and Tanzania makes the largest contribution. As it flows for more than 6,400 kilometers to the Mediterranean, the White Nile passes through ten modern nations amid changing geography. In southern Sudan, it becomes mired in the Sudd, a vast swamp that slows it and causes heavy water loss through evaporation, although the Sudd also mediates the river's flow, releasing it over a longer period of time. Because of the Sudd and the fact that Lake Victoria's catchment area is fed by rainfall throughout the year, the Egyptian Nile's flow never fails entirely.

The other main sources of the Egyptian Nile are the Blue Nile, which joins the White Nile in Sudan at Khartoum, and the Atbara, which flows into the Nile farther north in Sudan. They account for the annual inundation of the Nile, the central geographical feature of Egyptian history. Their tributaries are rooted in the Ethiopian highlands, where the summer monsoon dumps vast amounts of water that runs off quickly, laden with silt and clay washed away from Ethiopia's volcanic mountains. Although popular imagination tends to associate the sources of the Nile with the White Nile and the lake region of central Africa, 84 percent of the river's water that reaches Egypt comes from Ethiopia.

In perfect harmony with the solar year, the Nile began to rise in Egypt at the midsummer solstice and peaked at the autumnal equinox, rising from a low of less than fifty million cubic meters per day in early June to over seven hundred at the inundation's height in September. When the swollen river reached the broad flood plains of Egypt, it spilled over its banks, soaking the rich alluvial soil and washing away the harmful salts that were the long-term bane of other ancient hydraulic civilizations such as Mesopotamia. As it receded, the river left behind pools of water and a fine layer of sediments and minerals. The drying earth would crack open, aerating the soil and thus completing the cycle of renewal. The shift to the past tense is because the construction of the Aswan High Dam ended the inundations in Egypt during the 1960s.

The inundation was the pulsing life force of Egypt. Everything depended on it—and that it be at the correct level. If the inundation was too low, or if it failed entirely, the fields could not be irrigated adequately.

A succession of low Niles was catastrophic, causing not only famine but also extreme general economic and political dislocation. But too high an inundation was even worse because it flooded and destroyed the homes that were built on mounds above the expected rise of the water, damaged or destroyed irrigation dams and sluices, and left the water on the land beyond the planting season.

The peculiar rhythms of the Nile created an unusual agricultural cycle in Egypt. Most rivers swell to their fullest in the spring then diminish as the weather grows warmer, but the Nile rose and crested during the summer, at precisely the hottest time of the year. Crops were sown in the fall and ripened through the winter. Harvest came in early spring; then the land was allowed to lie fallow a few weeks until the inundation again spread across it. Coming as it did at the end of June, the flood spared crops from exposure to scorching heat and people from the necessity of laboring in it. The ancient Egyptians recognized three seasons: inundation, seed-time, and harvest.

The Nile is continuously navigable for the nine hundred kilometers between the First Cataract at Aswan and the Delta, a fact that was of fundamental importance for Egypt's unification and continuing prosperity. The river is ideal for sailing vessels. Going north, they are propelled by the steady current; and, because the prevailing winds are from the northwest, boats can usually sail south up the river. If the wind fails, the crews can tow their boats from the paths along the bank. One can still get a lively sense of sail navigation on the Nile by riding on one of the ubiquitous feluccas, whose elegant triangular sails are to be seen all along the river. The Egyptians relied heavily on the Nile and continue to do so today. It was the main avenue for long-distance communication, commerce, and transportation. The Nile provided a way to move very large, heavy objects like building stone over long distances, then the annual inundation could bring the barge right next to the building site. One reason ancient Egypt was relatively late in using wheeled vehicles was lack of roads; space for roads had to come out of the limited amount of fertile land, so they were kept short and narrow. Who needed long-distance highways when the river ran the length of Egypt and was within a few kilometers of almost everyone?

A short distance north of Cairo, the Nile fans out into a wide delta. Today the river has two main channels through the Delta, the Rosetta and the Damietta; in ancient times there were seven. The Delta is Lower Egypt, Upper Egypt being the stretch of the Nile between the Delta and the First Cataract at Aswan. The distinction between Lower and Upper is determined by the fact that the river flows from south to north, not which area is higher on the map. This point is emphasized because people commonly get it backwards, thinking wrongly that Upper Egypt must be in the north and Lower Egypt in the south. Strictly speaking, it is still correct for someone traveling south from Cairo to Luxor or Aswan to say that they are "going up" to those places, although few do so today. The Delta, with twice as much arable land as Upper Egypt, was exceedingly important in early Egyptian history, but much of its material record has been concealed or obliterated by the waterlogged nature of the land, which usually makes Deltan archaeology exceedingly difficult, thereby biasing available evidence toward Upper Egypt, where conditions of preservation and access are much better.

The rocky nature of the river valley has determined the geography of Upper Egypt. After a stretch from Aswan north to Gebel al-Silsileh, where hard Nubian sandstone predominates and constricts the valley, the Nile enters a long region of softer limestone, which allowed the river to form a much wider floodplain that is highly suitable for agriculture. Between the great Qena Bend and Cairo, the hills and mountains on the west bank subside, allowing the fertile floodplain on that side of the river to become wider still while the mountains on the east push close to the river, restricting agriculture and sometimes precluding it altogether on the eastern side. This portion of Upper Egypt is sometimes referred to as Middle Egypt.

Although the border of the modern nation of Egypt lies much farther south, the land of Egypt, properly speaking, ends at the First Cataract, just above (south of) the town of Aswan. Altogether there are six of these cataracts between Aswan and the confluence of the White and Blue Niles at Khartoum. These are not so much cataracts in the dictionary sense of the word, which implies a waterfall, as they are rapids, and so they are called in Arabic. The First Cataract was formed by a band of uplifted granite bedrock and boulders that divided the Nile's waters into numerous fast-running rivulets, and that made Aswan an important source of granite. Ancient quarry marks and inscriptions still appear sharp and clear on the durable stone in the channels at Aswan. Boats could be passed through the First Cataract, but only with difficulty, so it was a barrier to navigation and became something of a cultural and political barrier as well. The First Cataract was partially obliterated by the Aswan Dam at the beginning of the twentieth century, and the Second Cataract was submerged by the waters of Lake Nasser in the middle of the century.

Nubia lies to the south of the First Cataract. Egyptian Nubia, or Lower Nubia (as in Egypt, Lower is in the north and Upper in the south), was the northern stretch of Nubia between the First Cataract and the Second Cataract at Wadi Halfa. Until it was obliterated by the waters of Lake Nasser, created by the construction of the Aswan High Dam during the 1960s, Lower Nubia was a distinct cultural and geographical area, and often politically distinct as well. The Nubians spoke different languages from ancient Egyptian and, later, from Arabic. The fate of their land vis-à-vis Egypt was heavily determined by geography, for unlike the river valley in most of Egypt, where soft limestone and other factors permitted the river to spread across a wide, fertile floodplain, Nubia was covered with much harder sandstone that allowed the river to cut only a narrow trench through it. The mountains often slanted right down into the water, resulting in steep banks along which only a slender band of cultivation was possible, and sometimes none at all. This meant that Nubia could never support a population comparable in size to Egypt's, nor could it produce the vast agricultural surplus that was the economic basis of Egyptian civilization.

A view of the Nile Valley from the air is unforgettable: a band of intense green running through a desolate desert. The contrast can also be striking on the ground, where one can literally stand with one foot in fertile fields and the other on barren sand. The band of cultivation is usually quite distinct, so that the ancient Egyptians spoke of the Black Land *(kemet)*, because of the rich mud deposited over the millennia by the annual inundation and the Red Land *(deret)*, the desert beyond the inundation's reach.

The Eastern Desert of Egypt lies between the Nile and the Red Sea. Its most significant feature is the Red Sea mountain range, which runs north–south along most of its length. The Eastern Desert's craggy peaks, resulting from both uplift and erosion, constitute some of the most memorable scenery on earth. The range is cut with numerous wadis, dry stream beds that mostly run east–west to drain into the Red Sea or the Nile. Although rain is rare in the Eastern Desert, when it comes the wadis can turn into raging torrents. Some wadis, such as the large Wadi Qena, were formed by ancient rivers. The steep walls and alluvial beds of wadis form natural passages through the difficult terrain. Of these, one of the most significant is Wadi Hammamat, which provides a line of communication between Qift on the Nile and Quseir on the Red Sea. An important source for stone and certain precious metals, the Eastern Desert has been quarried and mined since ancient times. The area has long been inhabited by Bedouin peoples, but the coastal strip began to experience intensive development in the late twentieth century.

The geography of the Western Desert, or Libyan Desert, is more varied, and it is much larger, covering two-thirds of Egypt, the entire area between the Nile and the Libyan border. Much of it consists of rocky outcrops and sandy or stony wastes. On the west is the Great Sand Sea, and the southwest is dominated by a high plateau, the Gilf al-Kebir. The Western Desert features a number of large depressions, including the enormous Qattara Depression, which descends to 133 meters beneath sea level at its lowest point. This desert also contains several fertile oases, including Siwa in the north and the Inner Oases: Bahariya, Farafra, Dakhla, and Kharga. By far the largest is Dakhla. Continuously inhabited since the Paleolithic, or Old Stone Age, Dakhla Oasis is an archaeological site of exceptional importance.

One of the depressions in the Western Desert is the area known as the Fayyum. Though often described as an oasis, it is closely connected to the Nile system and derives all its water directly from the nearby river through the Hawara Channel, a small opening in the escarpment on the western valley. The Fayyum is phenomenally fertile, its productivity enhanced by a complex system of irrigation so that water flows into it from the Nile then spreads out through ever smaller channels descending along the gentle southern slope of the depression until it reaches a large lake, Birket Qarun. The size of this lake has fluctuated greatly since the Old Kingdom with increased control over the influx of water; presently its surface is about forty-five meters below sea level. The north side of Birket Qarun is bounded by steeper infertile slopes. Sometimes a map of Egypt is likened to a lotus plant: the Nile is the plant's long stem, the Delta its flower, and the Fayyum a leaf.

The Sinai Peninsula is composed of a mountainous plateau in the south that drops sharply into the Gulf of Aqaba on the southeast and less precipitously into the Gulf of Suez on the southwest. Like the Eastern Desert, this part of the peninsula has long been a source of materials such as copper and turquoise. Northern Sinai is a wide coastal plain that provides a corridor of contact between Egypt and southwestern Asia, though one somewhat inhibited by its desert nature.

The two seacoasts of Egypt are the Mediterranean on the north and the Red Sea on the east. Although the Mediterranean coast receives slightly more rainfall than the rest of Egypt, it has historically been an area of low-density population, but it has recently been subjected to heavy development along most of its extent. It has no natural harbors, and there were no ports until the establishment of Alexandria, nor did the geography of the Delta lend itself to communication with the sea.

Only since 1869 has the Red Sea been connected to the Mediterranean, by the Suez Canal. Previously, the overland transit across the Isthmus of Suez was arduous and seldom used. To the south the Red Sea opens onto the Arabian Sea and the Indian Ocean. Through most of Egyptian history, however, this did not offer a viable, continuous link with the east, and indeed it was something of a barrier. The principal difficulty was the strong northerly wind that blows down the Red Sea for most of the year. That is why the Ptolemaic ports on the Red Sea were located as far south as possible at Myos Hormos and Berenike, not to the north at Suez where they otherwise would have been much more convenient. Although a canal linking the Red Sea and the Mediterranean was discussed in ancient times, regular, large-scale navigation through such a canal and the Red Sea was impractical until the age of steam. Despite its strategic location, many factors in Egypt's geography long tended toward isolating the country rather than integrating it with the rest of the world.

Very little is known about the earliest stages of human settlement in the Nile Valley, partly due to lack of study and partly due to the hydrology of the Nile, which concealed or washed away most of the archaeological evidence. Finds in the Eastern and Western Deserts of Egypt, especially in the latter, provide contextual and comparative frames of reference, but they have yet to be reconciled with findings in the Nile Valley. If, however, the common origin of humanity in East Africa is accepted, the Nile Valley and its surrounding areas would have been places for some people to linger as populations diffused across Africa and passed north-ward into southwestern Asia and beyond.

Human activity all along the Egyptian Nile Valley is attested by crude stone implements as early as c. 300,000 BC, far into the Paleolithic Age, and it may have been present even earlier. But the river valley was not always necessarily the most obvious or most desirable place for human habitation, for during much of the Paleolithic Age, northeastern Africa was utterly different from the way it is now. Instead of desert, the present-day Sahara was an area of wooded uplands, lush grassy plains, brimming streams, and numerous lakes, abundant in flora and fauna for food-gathering peoples. The river valley, though densely vegetated and a rich area for hunting and fishing, could present difficulties because during some periods it had raging floods, much higher than now, while at other times it almost ceased to flow.

After the last Ice Age, with the beginning of the Holocene Period, about 10000 BC, rainfall patterns shifted in northeastern Africa so that a process of desiccation set in, producing the Sahara Desert over the next several thousand years. The process was not steady, interrupted by several 'wet phases,' so that a dry savannah covered much of the area before eventually being replaced by desert. These climatic changes were roughly contemporary with cultural and technological advances from the Paleolithic Period, with its chipped stone tools and hunter-gatherer lifestyle, to the Neolithic or New Stone Age Period around the end of seventh millenium BC, when animal husbandry, cultivation of crops, and more permanent settlements developed. Increasingly regular behavior by the Nile would have made the river valley an obvious location for agriculture.

It was not in the Nile Valley, however, but in the southern part of the Western Desert that the earliest major Neolithic site so far found in Egypt was recently discovered. This is at Nabta Playa, located on the shore of what was once an ancient lake about a hundred kilometers west of Abu Simbel. Dating from 6000 BC or earlier, the Nabta Playa site consists of several hundred Stone Age camps, numerous sepul-chral mounds (tumuli), standing stones (monoliths), some as high as 2.75 meters, and megalithic structures. The excavators of the site are likely justified in concluding that "at least some of the roots of ancient Egyptian beliefs, magic and religion" are present at Nabta Playa. These are evident in the cosmic alignment of many of the monoliths, which could be interpreted as making them proto-temples; the anthropo-morphic (human-shaped) nature of others, suggesting monuments commemorating dead individuals; and burial practices that emphasize preservation of the body. The presence of goods imported from the Nile Valley indicates interaction with the more agricultural dwellers along the river. The culture associated with Nabta Playa collapsed around 3350 BC when it was overwhelmed by increasing desertification.

The wet phases of the Holocene Period were punctuated by hyperarid spells that steadily forced both people and animals out of the Sahara to seek more hospitable regions in the south or to the east, where the Nile provided abundant water and good soil. It was once naively but reasonably assumed that this concentration of the population in a small place like the Nile Valley, with its enormous agricultural potential, created a sort of critical mass that exploded into civilization. Such a simplistic view is no longer accepted, but by the beginning of the Predynastic Period around the end of the sixth millennium BC, most of Egypt's population had moved to the Nile Valley, where it began to display characteristics that clearly differentiated it from surrounding peoples and eventually developed into ancient Egyptian civilization.

2 The Birth of Egyptian Civilization: Predynastic and Early Dynastic Egypt

Ancient Egyptian Chronology

Before delving into ancient Egyptian history, something must be said about the structure of its chronology, a system largely devised by modern scholars during the past two centuries. Though unsatisfactory in many respects, the system is so firmly established that it is impossible to navigate the byways of ancient Egyptian history without at least basic familiarity with its distinctive features. It is based on the work of the third-century BC historian Manetho (see chapter seven) who presented the Egyptian past as a series of kings and dynasties, thirty-one in all, ranging from Menes, the supposed first king of the First Dynasty, to Alexander the Great. Unfortunately, Manetho's *Ægyptiaka*, which drew upon many crucial sources that no longer exist, survives only in epitomes, brief abstracts or synopses that were prepared by later writers like Flavius Josephus, who adapted portions of it in the first century AD for his work *Contra Apionem* in order to refute exaggerated claims for Greek antiquity. The result is often ambiguous and incomplete, and sometimes demonstrably wrong, but there is no alternative.

Modern scholars took Manetho's dynastic framework and organized it into a series of periods, resulting in the following pattern:

11

Predynastic Period c. 5300–2950 BC
Early Dynastic Period c. 2950–2613 BC
Dynasties 1–3
Old Kingdom c. 2613–2160 BC
Dynasties 4–8
First Intermediate Period c. 2160–2055 BC
Dynasties 9–11
Middle Kingdom c. 2055–1640 BC
Dynasties 11–14
Second Intermediate Period c. 1640–1550 BC
Dynasties 15–17
New Kingdom c. 1550–1069 BC
Dynasties 18–20
Third Intermediate Period c. 1069–715 BC
Dynasties 21–25
Late Period c. 715–332 BC
Dynasties 25 (continued)–31

Even in outline there is room for individual preference as well as scientific judgment in ancient Egyptian chronology. The Third Dynasty, for example, is often assigned to the Old Kingdom, and the Twenty-fifth Dynasty to the Third Intermediate Period. A more fundamental problem is the way the validity of most of these periods has become increasingly questioned as knowledge has increased; but like Manetho's dynastic framework, they have become canonical. The ancient Egyptians, of course, were unaware of such periodization and likely would have thought it unreflective of the times in which they lived.

An additional important word about ancient Egyptian chronology is that almost all of its dates before and even into the Late Period are approximate, there being no absolute basis for fixing them, hence the frequent use of c. (circa = approximately) in Egyptological literature. Also, there is more than one system for dating, notably the so-called high and low chronologies. These are some of the reasons why dates in Egyptological works often differ, but the differences are usually no more than a few decades, a relatively insignificant bit of the colossal span of the ancient Egyptian past.

Predynastic Egypt

The Predynastic Period, stretching from about 5300 to 2950 BC, is the least-known time in all of ancient Egyptian history, yet it was the most creative. The Egyptians emerged from the general matrix of North African material culture and developed many of the distinctive features of ancient Egyptian civilization—political unity, kingship, writing, monumental architecture, agriculture, large-scale irrigation, modes of artistic expression, and social organization.

Modern scholars were unaware of the very existence of Predynastic Egypt until the late nineteenth century, when it was revealed by the energetic work of the Egyptologist Sir Flinders Petrie. There is no written evidence from the Predynastic Period until the very end, and then mostly in terse bits whose precise meaning is usually far from clear. However, through an ingenious classification of pottery in graves, Petrie devised a system of relative dating and classification that still provides the basis for the chronology of Predynastic Egypt. Since the political organization of the period is unknown, its peoples and societies are categorized according to 'cultures' that are named for important archaeological sites that became identified with them.

Of the several Predynastic cultures, two are essential for understanding the development of ancient Egyptian civilization. The first is the Badarian, so called because it was identified at al-Badari, near the town of Sohag in Middle Egypt. It appeared at least by 4400–4000 BC, and perhaps even earlier. Although some Badarian settlements have been excavated, the most compelling information about the Badarian culture comes from its cemeteries, as with all other Predynastic cultures. These show little differentiation in grave goods, indicating a fairly egalitarian social order. Badarian settlements appear to have been impermanent, but remains of larger, more enduring settlements on natural levees on the banks of the Nile may have been covered by accumulated silt or scoured away by the river. Within their dwellings, the inhabitants of Badarian settlements made significant advances in furniture, and they practiced agriculture and animal husbandry. They fished the Nile extensively. The plastic arts began to be practiced, most notably in human figurines. Badarian pottery features exceptional thinness of its walls, unequaled in subsequent periods of Egyptian history. The extent of Badarian culture is unclear, but it probably ranged from just above Asyut in the north to al-Kab in the south, with trading and cultural contacts ranging somewhat farther afield.

The Naqada culture, the other major culture of the Predynastic Period, is divided into three phases. The first, Naqada I (also called Amratian), flourished from about 4000 to 3500 BC. Naqada I sites resemble the Badarian but are generally larger and more prosperous. Grave goods were still simple, though more diverse, a development that has been interpreted as signifying increasingly complex social organization. Metalwork advanced little beyond Badarian techniques for making small, hammered objects, but notable improvements are obvious in the working of hard stone, rudimentary in Badarian times, such as granite, porphyry, and limestone. This is evident in the appearance of stone mace heads and slate cosmetic palettes, which clearly had ritual and status significance far beyond mere accessories for makeup.

Naqada I pottery, though of no finer material quality than Badarian, began to be decorated, sometimes with geometrical patterns or representations of plants, animals, or people. When people are depicted, two motifs predominate: the hunt and the victorious warrior, perhaps signifying the presence of dominant hunter-warrior groups. The motif of the victorious warrior resonated throughout ancient Egyptian history in depictions of the pharaoh smiting his enemies.

The Naqada I culture appears to have been more sedentary than the Badarian. It was essentially a subsistence economy, relying heavily on cultivated crops, primarily barley and wheat, and domesticated animals such as goats, sheep, cattle, and pigs, although wild game and fish remained important parts of the diet. Like the Badarian, the Naqada I culture was centered in Upper Egypt along the great Qena bend in the Nile, but it was more widespread than the Badarian.

The next major phase, Naqada II (c. 3500–3200 BC), has been described as the turning point in the development of Predynastic Egypt. Also known as Gerzean, Naqada II was a time of change. A simple, egalitarian community evolved into a stratified society with an exploitative elite increasingly distinct from the rest of the population. Along with this stratification of wealth and power, the institution of chieftainship emerged. This is evident in differences in the shapes and sizes of dwellings and in the cemeteries, where the trend, incipient in Naqada I, was for more elaborate tombs with richer burial goods for a few individuals. Most burials remained simple, but funerary rituals became more complex.

The material culture of Naqada II was also marked by developments in metallurgy, with copper implements becoming more common; but flint working continued to develop, producing ripple-flaked knives of exquisite quality. Stone working techniques also continued to advance, laying the groundwork for pharaonic achievements in stone architecture. Increasing craft specialization indicates the emergence of a proto-artisanal class whose members were able to devote at least a substantial part of their time to their crafts instead of the production of food because they were supported by a redistributed agricultural surplus. Division of labor increased social stratification, but those two elements may have resulted in the great surge of creativity and innovation during the Late Predynastic and Early Dynastic Periods that produced the elite culture of pharaonic Egypt.

Astonishing developments occurred in Naqada II visual arts, including sculpture in the round, executed in exuberant, free-flowing forms that bear little resemblance to the art of pharaonic times. Palettes were fewer in Naqada II than Naqada I, but were decorated with complex reliefs that later recorded narrative or commemorative information and that make them of great value as historical documents for the later Predynastic Period, even though their interpretations are highly speculative. Mace-heads, also decorated, became important symbols of the political power of chieftains and incipient kings. New types of pottery appeared on which the predominant decorative motif was the boat, evidence of increased trade and wider contacts. By the end of the Naqada II phase, the indigenous material culture of Lower Egypt had been replaced by Naqada artifacts, a cultural prelude to political unity.

Most people probably lived in a string of small villages along the Nile during the Naqada II phase, but large population centers also developed, principally at Naqada, Hierakonpolis, and Abydos, serving as political, religious, and trading centers. The economic role is evident in Naqada's Egyptian name of Gold Town, indicating its proximity to the precious metal mines in the Eastern Desert and its situation near the western end of Wadi Hammamat, the way from the Nile Valley through the mountains to the Red Sea and the trading opportunities it offered. The growing populations of Naqada II's villages and towns were supported by cereal agriculture, practiced with increasing success on the Upper Egyptian floodplain where emmer wheat and barley did especially well, providing larger agricultural surpluses. Naqada II sites are found along the Nile from the Delta to Aswan. Virtually nothing is known about the political organization of Egypt at this moment, but archaeological evidence suggests separate and competing centers of power.

The reader may have noticed that the foregoing has focused almost exclusively on Upper Egypt. The impetus toward civilization does indeed appear to have come from that part of the country, but the picture is heavily biased by the preponderance of Upper Egyptian evidence because of the peculiarities of Deltan geography and the difficulties it presents to archaeological work, as noted earlier. Even so, exciting Predynastic discoveries are being made in the Delta, with the examination or re-examination of sites such as Maadi south of Cairo, Minshat Abu Omar in the Eastern Delta, Merimda on the west, and Tell al-Fara'in (ancient Buto) in the north central Delta. Ongoing work encourages hope for more, in the expectation that Egyptian prehistory will continue to be modified by more universally representative information.

The accelerating pace of change during Naqada III (c. 3200–3000 BC), the last Predynastic phase, culminated in the unification of the Egyptian state and the creation of ancient Egyptian civilization. When nineteenth- and twentieth-century scholars first attempted to account for the appearance of pharaonic Egypt, a major area of speculation was whether it developed internally or came from outside; Sir Flinders Petrie, for example, posited an Asiatic "new race" that invaded Egypt, conquered it, and imposed civilization. Other invasion theories also used to be popular because they seemed an obvious way to account for momentous changes over a short period of time. As archaeological evidence accumulated, however, a continuous process of development within Egypt became apparent, showing that the ancient Egyptian achievement was an indigenous one, although some foreign conquest, interaction, and stimulation are still possibilities, so little being known about the overall process.

There are, in fact, indications that stimulus from Mesopotamia in present-day southern Iraq, where civilization and many of its associated arts had developed slightly earlier, may have affected Egypt at just the crucial moment during the late Naqada phase. The possible areas of cultural borrowing are writing, boat design, artistic conventions, metallurgy, and construction of monumental buildings in brick. The evidence includes several vessels and cylindrical seals, objects already long in use in Mesopotamia, which may have been directly imported into Egypt. A number of artistic motifs on late Naqadan luxury goods bear striking resemblances to Mesopotamian ones. Naqadan tombs, with their niched brick architecture, could have been taken from Asian prototypes. And although Mesopotamian and ancient Egyptian scripts look very different, they contain a number of underlying similarities. Naqada's location at the western end of Wadi Hammamat, which led to the Red Sea, may well have provided contact with Mesopotamia, then in an expansionist phase and equipped with seaworthy ships. Naqadan gold and trading opportunities would have been powerful attractions for Mesopotamian goldsmiths and merchants. If there was a period of Mesopotamian stimulation, however, it was brief, and the late Predynastic Egyptians took any ideas that they may have imported and made them uniquely their own.

Another area of borrowing—interaction or diffusion might be better words—was the pattern of subsistence economy that was developed in southwestern Asia and featured the domestication of certain plants and animals by people in permanent agricultural settlements. Here the avenue of contact was through the Delta. It occurred over a relatively long expanse of Predynastic time, and in this, as in other things, the ancient Egyptians adapted it to their own circumstances and in innovative ways. By the Naqada III phase, the hydraulic irrigation infrastructure that sustained ancient Egyptian civilization was far advanced, with the construction of canals and levees with perpendicular dikes. Where the inundation had once lingered in natural pools, large basins were dug to retain it for release over time as needed. The invention of basin irrigation was traditionally attributed to King Menes at the beginning of the First Dynasty, but it probably existed long before his reign, which may have been mythical in any case. According to one interpretation of a scene on the mace-head of King Scorpion of Dynasty Zero, it shows the king with a hoe, preparing to open a dike in late Naqada III times.

The development and maintenance of such large, complex irrigation systems obviously required correspondingly large, complex administrative organizations, giving rise to an inconclusive 'chicken or the egg' debate about whether organization stimulated irrigation or vice versa.

But once in place, the two developments were mutually reinforcing as the irrigated society produced much greater and more predictable agricultural surpluses. These in turn sustained a growing exploitative elite, provided for increasing differentiation of non-agricultural skills, and supported the ambitions of regional chiefs who sought to extend their control over areas with more resources in an ever expanding process.

It will never be possible to write a political history of the Naqada III phase, but some of its outlines can be discerned. In an increasingly complex society such as Egypt had become, the growing demands of chiefs could only be met by enhancing social organization yet further. As local communities grew larger, they came into conflict, leading to ever larger political units. Hierakonpolis, a major religious center in Upper Egypt, played a significant role. It may be that the early kings of Hierakonpolis moved their capital to Abydos, another important cult center about forty kilometers south of present-day Sohag; or Hierakonpolis could have fallen under the control of kings from Abydos. However it happened, at an early stage of the Naqada III phase, most of Upper Egypt was probably unified under a single king who ruled from Abydos.

Advances in material culture corresponded to rapid social and political development. Conventions appeared that would become integral to ancient Egyptian art, such as depiction of scenes in registers, use of ground lines, relative size of figures, and recurring motifs. As in the Naqada II phase, this material culture spread throughout Egypt. Its direction apparently was from the south to the north, but that assumption is based on an incomplete archaeological record and inferences from traditions about the Predynastic kings.

That territorial consolidation was accompanied by military conquest is indicated in evidence, especially palettes and mace-heads, found at Hierakonpolis. The fragmentary Libyan Palette may depict towns under siege, and the Scorpion Mace-head contains scenes of fighting, though interpretation of these is a matter of dispute among Egyptologists. Other palettes depict the standards of gods over bound captives and slain enemies trodden underfoot to be eaten by vultures and wild beasts. The process reached its conclusion when one ruler acquired control of most of the land along the river. This political unification of Egypt occurred at the very latest around 2950 BC under King Narmer of the

First Dynasty, whose palette is the best-known source for the process, but it had probably already been accomplished, at least to a substantial degree, by the kings of the late Naqada III phase. For that reason, scholars have placed the odd-sounding Dynasty Zero at the beginning of Manetho's dynastic scheme.

The achievement that we call unification must not be interpreted in the traditional, simplistic view of a struggle between two competing political entities, Upper Egypt and Lower Egypt, with the eventual triumph of Upper Egypt. That notion, which was largely based on myth and an ancient Egyptian penchant for duality, is no longer believed by scholars and is not supported by archaeological evidence, although the initiative did come from Upper Egypt. The concept of the two lands, however, was of paramount importance in ancient Egypt. The king wore double crowns, one representing each land, and adopted a royal title that combined symbols of Upper and Lower Egypt.

The Early Dynastic Period

The time of the first three dynasties of the unified Egyptian state is referred to as the Early Dynastic Period (c. 2950–2613 BC), or sometimes as the Archaic Period.* It was a period of continued development, experimentation, and innovation, much as the Late Predynastic Period had been. The fixed political, artistic, and religious standards that characterized ancient Egyptian civilization were still being formalized, though once that was done they were established to such a degree that they retained strongly recognizable similarities for several thousand years so that they seem almost static. Such conservatism is a strange outcome for a process of intense creativity, but it indicates that the ancient Egyptians had developed forms with which they were supremely comfortable. Also, it might be borne in mind that things were not always as static as they outwardly appeared. As one Egyptologist perceptively observed, "a changing ideology was disguised by being presented always in conservative terms."

Although Egypt was unified during Dynasty Zero, it was under the First Dynasty that the center of development and political power switched from the south to the north, and the city of Memphis was

---

* Some classifications confine the Early Dynastic Period to the first two dynasties.

established at the apex of the Delta, on the west bank of the Nile south-west of present-day Cairo. It became the administrative center of the Egyptian state. The Egyptian name of Memphis was Ineb-hedj, "White Wall"; its monumental architecture, strategically sited at the juncture of Upper and Lower Egypt, must have been a powerful political statement, especially with the development of the imposing mortuary monuments on the desert plateau immediately behind. Memphis retained its administrative importance for the next two and a half millennia.

The paramount importance of Memphis might well be emphasized, for little remains to be seen of it today apart from fragments and mounds of rubble. It has never been properly excavated, but the vast adjacent cemeteries at Saqqara tell some of the city's story. Abydos lost its political function with the rise of Memphis, but it long continued to be a major cult center. The tombs of all the First Dynasty kings are at Abydos, as are those of some of the Second Dynasty kings, although their high officials were probably buried in the large, niched tombs on the edge of the plateau at Saqqara.

The 'historic' period is considered to begin with the First Dynasty, but the task of sorting out the history of the Early Dynastic Period is one of great uncertainty. The tombs of the First Dynasty kings at Abydos are major sources, for although they were plundered extensively in ancient times, then devastated by inept archaeological excavators in the nineteenth century, later work extracted valuable information from them. These tombs were a continuation of the Late Predynastic Period's trend toward larger, richer burials for powerful individuals. Huge rectangular superstructures of sun-baked mud brick stood above subterranean burial chambers and store rooms. Widely used for elite burials during the Old Kingdom as well as the Early Dynastic Period, tombs of this type are known today as *mastaba*s. Pairs of stone stelae affixed to the tombs at Abydos proclaimed the identities of their occupants. The contents of the store rooms were often recorded in archaic hieroglyphic labels. Some of the stelae and labels have been recovered.

Archaeologists were shocked to discover that the First Dynasty kings practiced human sacrifice. When they died, they took whole households with them: guards, officials, women, dwarfs (for whom the early kings had a fascination), and even their dogs, to serve them in the afterlife. King Djer was accompanied by approximately six hundred sacrificed retainers who were buried in satellite tombs arranged in rows around his tomb. Death was apparently inflicted by strangulation so as to leave the body intact. Human sacrifice was discontinued after the First Dynasty. People were replaced with *shabtis*, small model figures, which were designed to provide eternal service. A magical spell to empower *shabtis* for that function was later described in the *Book of the Dead*, a practical guide for travelers into the next world that appeared toward the end of the Middle Kingdom.

The best known of the First Dynasty kings was Den, who must have come to the throne at a young age, considering his long reign. The unusually large number of tombs of his elite (located principally at Saqqara, not Abydos) attests to a growing administration, while his census of the land indicates a more systematic exploitation of its resources, human as well as agricultural, made possible by rapid development of the art of writing, which had appeared by the end of the Late Predynastic Period. There is evidence of military operations against enemies in both Asia and Libya. A much higher degree of craftsmanship is discernible in the artistic production of Den's reign. Two rolls of uninscribed papyrus found in Den's tomb are the earliest evidence of paper manufacture.

Contrary to the general tendency of evidence and knowledge to increase with time, the First Dynasty is fairly well sorted out, at least in the sequence of rulers, but the Second Dynasty is much more obscure. While the First Dynasty burials at Abydos are well known, the locations of many Second Dynasty royal tombs have not been established. It is likely, but by no means certain, that most of its kings were buried at Saqqara, although the tombs of the last two monarchs of the dynasty, Peribsen and Khasekhemy, are at Abydos near those of the First Dynasty. There is some indication of a troubled transition between the First and Second Dynasties, and much stronger, though still indefinite, evidence for a time of disorder during the Second Dynasty. Perhaps the forces of regionalism, not yet firmly subdued by centralizing kings, reasserted themselves and had to be suppressed in a civil war.

If anything, the obscurity grows even deeper with the Third Dynasty (c. 2686–2613 BC). Its second ruler, Netjerykhet, better remembered as Djoser, was the most renowned of all Early Dynastic kings, but even the alleged facts associated with his reign are mostly legends that arose during later periods of Egyptian history. One fact about Djoser that cannot be disputed, however, is his Step Pyramid at Saqqara, the first great stone building in the world, a source of awe from ancient times to the present. It was one of many indications that unified Egypt had attained the levels of technical mastery, economic power, and centralized control that enabled it to undertake projects in monumental architecture that no other ancient civilization could match in magnitude.

In its original concept, the Step Pyramid was just another royal mastaba, though one exceptional in size and material, being made of stone instead of mud brick. As construction proceeded, however, successive modifications transformed the original design into something quite different from its predecessors, with profound consequences for the rest of the pharaonic era and beyond. The size was expanded and, in effect, one mastaba was stacked onto another, finally resulting in a pyramid of six steps that rose to a height of sixty meters and covered a ground area of 121 by 109 meters.

The superstructure of the Step Pyramid was but one of its many remarkable features. Underground passages had become progressively more complex in royal tombs during the Second Dynasty, but nothing like the labyrinthine maze that underlay the Step Pyramid, with its numerous corridors that eventually found their way to an immense central shaft containing a granite burial vault. Described by one Egyptologist as a "subterranean palace," the underground dimension of the Step Pyramid was never equaled in subsequent pyramids. The pyramid was surrounded by an enormous niched stone enclosure wall, much of which has been restored and reconstructed.

The Step Pyramid conferred immortal fame not only on Djoser but also on his vizier Imhotep, the pyramid's architect. Such was Imhotep's reputation for wisdom that during the Late Period he came to be worshiped as a god of learning, writing, and medicine. The Egyptians linked him to Thoth and Ptah; the Greeks equated him with Asclepius. Pilgrims who came to his cult center at Saqqara for healing left mummified ibises, the symbol of Thoth, inscribed with Imhotep's name as votive offerings. Imhotep must have been buried at Saqqara, but so far his tomb has not been identified, and it may yet be discovered.

None of the kings who followed Djoser in the Third Dynasty were able to replicate his monumental accomplishment, though not for lack of trying. His successor Sekhemkhet began a step pyramid, but it literally never got off the ground. Known as the "Buried Pyramid," Sekhemkhet intended it to be taller than Djoser's, but he completed little more than the subterranean passages and foundation, probably because his reign was brief. Another dismally failed step pyramid is the "Layer Pyramid," perhaps belonging to Khaba, at Zawyet al-Aryan between Saqqara and Giza. Brevity of rule was likewise the probable cause of its incompletion. Several small, unfinished step pyramids have been tentatively assigned to Huni, the last king of the Third Dynasty. These are at various sites in Egypt, one as far south as Aswan.

Innovative as it was, Djoser's Step Pyramid looked behind as well as ahead. Its basic concept was still that of the mastaba, multiplied and amplified. And although it was the world's first great building in stone, the material was used much as mud brick had been, not with stone's peculiar qualities in mind. Apparently the techniques for quarrying and moving large blocks were not yet fully developed. The true Pyramid Age would begin in the next dynasty.

The later years of the Third Dynasty are as obscure and confused as is the dynasty as a whole. Modern scholarship assigns five or six kings to the Third Dynasty with combined reigns of about seventy-five years, while Manetho lists several more kings and a total of two hundred years. Manetho's time span is too long, and his transition from the Third to the Fourth Dynasty raises questions because Huni, the last king of the Third, was the father of Sneferu, the first king of the Fourth. There is no apparent reason for a change. Yet, although Manetho was mistaken about chronology, it is also possible that he knew things we do not. With the beginning of the Fourth Dynasty, which may also be taken as the beginning of the Old Kingdom (c. 2613–2160 BC), ancient Egyptian civilization seems suddenly to come to life in its distinctively recognizable forms, forms so firmly fixed and so enduring—and yet so versatile and adaptable—that many of them continued to function as long as three thousand years later.

3   The Old Kingdom

Egypt of the Old Kingdom was to an exceptional degree a world of its own, stable and self-sufficient. It could be regarded as a cultural oasis. To the north was the sea to which the Delta was a barrier, not a connection, for it was difficult for a seagoing vessel to sail into its branches. Ancient Egypt had no sea port. On both the east and the west lay vast desert barriers. Only from the northeast was it possible to approach the land with any real facility, but no powerful enemy threatened from that direction. To the south the First Cataract hindered further navigation and offered some protection. Self-sufficiency was provided by the extraordinary produce of the land—grain, fruit, plants for oil, flax, papyrus, domesticated animals, hunting, and fishing. The one basic deficiency, construction timber, could easily be supplied by trade with Lebanon, a trade that was carefully regulated on Egyptian terms. The land's productivity was assured by fairly stable inundations throughout most of the Old Kingdom. A Fifth Dynasty papyrus reads, "The order is great; its effectiveness endures. It has not been disturbed since the time of Osiris."

With the partial exception of Nubia, to which the ancient Egyptians always felt a proprietary right in any case, Old Kingdom Egypt was not an expansionist society. Elephantine Island, located just below the First Cataract at Aswan, was fortified in the Early Dynastic Period; and Egyptian control was extended into Lower Nubia during Dynasty Zero and the First Dynasty, with military operations documented as far as the Second Cataract. It is unclear whether permanent military and trading installations were established in the Early Dynastic Period, but at least one was present by the early Old Kingdom. No effort was made to establish a provincial administrative system in Nubia, where the native population was devastated by repeated Egyptian incursions. In Asia, fortified settlements had been established in Palestine during the Late Dynastic Period, and these continued through the First Dynasty but lapsed thereafter. Not until the Sixth Dynasty were extensive military operations conducted there, and then primarily for frontier security against the 'sand dwellers.' Even the northeastern Delta was apparently not a formal part of the Old Kingdom provincial system because it was not worth the expense and effort of maintaining it.

The ancient Egyptian state was embodied in the king, also called the pharaoh, a term meaning 'big house' that originally referred to the royal palace and was later applied to the king himself. The king ruled a united Kingdom of Upper and Lower Egypt as a god, one endowed with certain supernatural powers; he was worshiped as a god and obeyed as one. The function of this god-king was to mediate between the gods and humankind, especially in dispensing and regulating *maat*, a concept of supreme importance in ancient Egypt. *Maat* can be variously translated as 'truth,' 'order,' 'proper behavior,' and 'justice'; above all, it was the Egyptian way of doing things. Kings continued to serve that function even after death, and for all eternity, hence the importance of their tombs and the mortuary cults associated with them.

The authority of the king was immense. In theory, and to a large degree in practice, he owned the land of Egypt and was entitled to its produce. A state system of taxation was in place by Early Dynastic times. During the Old Kingdom, this was rigorously applied, and measures were taken to make the land even more productive to meet the growing demands of the court. Taxes were collected in kind, i.e., in a portion of the produce; money did not appear in Egypt until the Ptolemaic Period, well after the pharaonic era was finished. The king's ability to appropriate the vast agricultural surplus and redistribute it as he wished was the basis of his power. Through the institution that came to be known as the corvée—compulsory labor—the king could assemble huge numbers of workers for his projects. All economic and political institutions were subject to royal control. The central government was the employer and commissioner of everyone whose services or production of goods benefited the king and the social elite. It was the driving force of the economy. Relatively little of what we would call commerce existed in Old Kingdom Egypt. Common people produced most of what they consumed; other necessities such as salt, oil, and clothing were provided by the estates on which they worked and to which they were bound. Local markets were small and limited in their distributive capacity.

The increasing magnitude of the state's operations required a highly organized bureaucracy manned by professional administrators. Royal relatives held most of the highest offices during the Fourth Dynasty, but large numbers of commoners began to occupy administrative posts as well. The highest office was that of the vizier. Directly responsible to the king, his authority extended over all areas of state administration with the exception of religious affairs. Certain departments received and stored the agricultural surplus taken by the king's collectors. The Master of the Largess supervised its distribution. Another powerful official was the Overseer of Royal Works. The relationship of the kings and their senior administrators is demonstrated at the Pyramids of Giza where the pyramids are surrounded by orderly rows of the mastabas of the high officials who served the kings in life and were to do so in death.

The Kingdom of Upper and Lower Egypt was divided into provinces, twenty-two in Upper Egypt and twenty in Lower Egypt. These provinces are called nomes, although that term did not come into use until Ptolemaic times. The governors of the nomes, or nomarchs, were headquartered in provincial capitals. A higher regional office, the Overseer of Upper Egypt was created during the Fifth Dynasty. The nome system proved exceedingly durable, lasting into Roman times.

It is difficult to overstate the importance of the institution of kingship and the court culture in ancient Egyptian civilization, especially during the Old Kingdom. The development of writing was closely connected with the need of the royal administration to coordinate and supply large groups of workmen, maintain tax records, identify and distribute products, and record Nile floods. This stimulated the development of a scribal bureaucracy. Perhaps as little as one or two percent of the population could read and write, but for that tiny minority literacy provided the means for advancement and access to power. Consequently, even the highest government officials took pride in their scribal origins and had themselves portrayed in traditional scribal poses, writing equipment in hand. The desirability of the scribal profession is extolled in the Middle Kingdom *Satire on the Trades*:

> See, there's no profession without a boss,
> Except for the scribe; he is the boss.
> Hence if you know writing,
> It will do better for you
> Than those professions I've set before you,
> Each more wretched than the other.[1]

In one of the Old Kingdom *Pyramid Texts*, the king assumes the place of the divine scribe of the gods.

Contact with Mesopotamia may have initially stimulated ancient Egyptian writing, though it is unclear in which area writing first began. But if someone else provided the idea, then the ancient Egyptians transformed it into something utterly original and thoroughly Egyptian. The best known form of their writing is hieroglyphs (never 'hieroglyphics'!), which means 'priestly writing,' a term applied by the ancient Greeks to the decorative Egyptian script used for formal applications such as inscriptions on standing monuments or exceptionally important texts the paper-like material called papyrus that was made from the stems of plants that grew in Egyptian marshes. Although they appear to be pictographic, ancient Egyptian hieroglyphs are primarily, though by no means entirely, phonetic in nature; in other words, they were usually combined to make sounds to form words, like the Latin alphabet, although individual hieroglyphs could function as ideograms that signified the object that they resembled or some closely related concept. By the end of the First Dynasty, hieroglyphs had lost much of their pictorial function and were being used to write complete sentences.

Over time, two other scripts were developed for writing ancient Egyptian. Hieratic was a highly simplified, more cursive form of hieroglyphs that was in use by the end of the Early Dynastic Period. It could be written with pen instead of chisel or brush and on materials other than papyrus, especially *ostraka*, or potsherds, that were available in abundance around any settled site. The script known as demotic was devised during the Late Period. Even more cursive than hieratic, to the uninstructed eye demotic resembles rows of scarcely distinguishable commas, but its uses ranged from the monumental to the everyday. It is one of the scripts on the famous Rosetta Stone, a key element in the decipherment of the hieroglyphs in the early nineteenth century.

Despite their clumsiness and their many shortcomings as an 'alphabet,' however, hieroglyphs did not go out of fashion. Mysterious and awe-inspiring even in ancient times, they served a decorative as well as communicative function. Also, they were gifts to humankind from the god Thoth, so there were religious reasons for keeping them, and their magical efficacy was considered to be much more powerful than other scripts. Hieroglyphs continued to be used throughout the pharaonic periods and far into Roman times.

The names of kings were written in hieroglyphs and set in distinctive forms that made them instantly recognizable as statements of royal power whether the viewer could read or not. During the first three dynasties the king's name was placed inside a *serekh*, a palace-façade design that was surmounted by a falcon, the symbol of the god Horus who was closely associated with the kings. In later dynasties the two principal names of the kings (they had five altogether) were enclosed in oval-shaped forms called cartouches. Tuthmosis III went so far as to have his burial chamber in the Valley of the Kings shaped like a cartouche. Even after the pharaonic era, the names of Ptolemaic kings and Roman emperors were presented within cartouches to emphasize that they too were legitimate god-kings of Egypt.

The language spoken and written in ancient Egypt is a member of the so-called Afro-Asiatic or Semito-Hamitic family of languages. Other members of this large family include the Semitic languages, such as Hebrew and Arabic, the Berber languages of North Africa, and several African languages. Anyone who has studied both Arabic and ancient Egyptian is struck by a number of shared characteristics. During the long span of ancient Egyptian history, the Egyptian language underwent many basic changes, much more drastic than the change from Chaucerian or Shakespearian English to modern English, including changes in pronunciation and vocabulary, and the introduction of loan-words from other languages. Even during the same time period, there might be differences, depending on what was being expressed and who was saying it; religious texts, for example, used archaic language while personal letters were written in a more colloquial one, and there is evidence for dialects based on geographical and social distinctions.

The court culture was also the driving force in ancient Egyptian art. By the beginning of the Old Kingdom, basic patterns of Egyptian culture had formed. These patterns, adapted and changed over the next two thousand years or so, remained recognizably the same, so that even an uninformed observer might glance at objects from the Old Kingdom or the New and instinctively identify them all as 'ancient Egyptian.' This distinctive appearance was in part the result of strict artistic conventions that modern scholars call the *canon*. For example, human figures were represented in certain ways. When men were depicted in profile, their shoulders were turned squarely to the front, while their hips and legs, like their heads, returned to the profile, an unnatural and indeed impossible position. Likewise, standing statues of kings were rendered with seldom varying attributes such as gaze fixed resolutely ahead, clenched fists, and left foot thrust forward. Alongside the king, almost unnoticeable at first, might be the diminutive figures of his wife and daughters, their relative size reflecting their relative importance in Egyptian society.

The canon was strictest during the Old Kingdom. While many of its tenets remained in force thereafter, patrons and artists in succeeding centuries proved themselves capable of startling innovations, even while working within the overall conventions of the prevailing artistic idiom. The most dramatic point of departure is to be found in the art of the New Kingdom, particularly in the work patronized by the nobility of that period and in the short-lived Amarna interlude, which featured a strong element of naturalism. During the Late Period, when the great days of ancient Egypt were long gone, there was a return to the strict models of what even then was remote antiquity as artists produced works modeled on those of the Old Kingdom in an effort to evoke the greatness of the past.

Because of its prodigious demand for artistic productions to adorn palaces and temples, to reward members of the administration, and above all for funerary purposes, the state was by far the greatest patron of art in ancient Egypt, and to such a degree that art could be described as a function of the state. So vast was the scale that it required a high degree of bureaucratic organization and a substantial portion of the state's resources to supervise and maintain production in many different specialties such as ceramics, jewelry, goldsmithing, woodworking, painting, and statuary. To take the specialty of sculpture alone, it was necessary not only to maintain the sculptor and his workshop but also to see to the quarrying and transportation of the stone or other materials, and to setting the finished object in place. Standards had to be understood and enforced, for art served important functional purposes, leading some to suggest that bureaucratic supervision may have accounted for the relatively static nature of ancient Egyptian art.

Art was not practiced for art's sake in ancient Egypt, nor did artists enjoy the special status they acquired in early modern times from the Renaissance onward. They were craftsmen like any others, as is clear from their burials, which are undistinguished apart from sometimes including the tools of their trade. For the most part they labored in anonymity, although a few managed to leave marks of their individuality, such as Niankhptah, the Overseer of Sculptors, who had himself depicted in a relief in the chapel of Ptahhotpe at Saqqara. Personal obscurity did not prevent a high degree of technical mastery, however, and many surviving pieces from the Old Kingdom are not those of mere craftsmen but master sculptors. The life-sized statues of Prince Rahotpe and his wife Nofret from an early Fourth Dynasty mastaba at Meidum, now in the Egyptian Museum at Cairo, project a powerful sense of immediacy across a temporal gulf of more than four and a half millennia.

As with so many aspects of the Old Kingdom, the king played a paramount role in religion; indeed, he was a functional part of the religion which permeated every aspect of ancient Egyptian life. A god himself, only the king could communicate with the gods. He was the chief religious official. In theory, the king conducted all services in all temples; the priests acted in his name. Only in later periods with the development of phenomena such as 'personal piety' did access to the gods cease to be the exclusive prerogative of the king.

Ancient Egyptian religion contained so many elements, some contradictory and all changing over time, that it is a daunting task to describe it in a systematic way or to provide a comprehensive Egyptian pantheon that would be meaningful for any particular period. One of the most fundamental qualities of the religion during its early stages of development was its localism, with tutelary gods for various places—Bastet at the town of Bubastis in the Delta or Thoth at Hermopolis Magna, to provide just two of many possible examples. Sometimes gods were organized into triads of father, mother, and son at major cult centers. Amun, Mut, and Khonsu were the triad associated with Thebes; the triad at Memphis consisted of the gods Ptah, Sekhmet, and Nefertem; and other centers had their own triads. When towns increased in political importance, their gods extended their sway, as with Ptah at Memphis or Amun at Thebes. In the earliest times, the gods were visualized as animals: Bastet as a lioness (and later as a cat), Thoth as an ibis, Hathor as a cow, Sobek as a crocodile, and so forth. Artistic convention sometimes represented them as combinations of human and animal features, hence Horus would be depicted as a man with a human body and the head of a falcon while Sekhmet was shown as a lion-headed woman. The gods were also depicted in fully anthropomorphic forms, that is, as normal men and women, albeit highly idealized. Over time the gods changed through the process of syncretism as the characteristics of two or more gods were fused into one. An exceptionally important instance of this was the combination of Amun and Ra into the transcendent Amun-Ra in the New Kingdom.

An important distinction should be made between what might be termed 'state' religion on the one hand and 'household' or 'popular' religion on the other. The former was primarily concerned with matters of kingship and conduct of the state. The latter focused on the immediate cares of the individual and family, especially averting misfortunes through domestic disasters such as death in childbirth. Household religion undoubtedly touched the lives of the vast majority of people much more directly than the state religion, but it is less represented in the archaeological record. Bes and Tauret were important protective household gods.

With such a profusion of gods and religious concerns, the ancient Egyptians developed a rich mythological tradition. Many of the myths are represented in the religious iconography, but rarely is there enough surviving textual evidence to interpret them fully and understand what they actually meant to the people of the time. One that fortunately was preserved in a coherent form, though at a very late date by the Roman writer Plutarch, is that of Osiris, Isis, and Horus, a myth deeply rooted in primordial times and of fundamental importance to the institution of kingship in ancient Egypt.

According to this myth, the divine Osiris, who was married to his sister Isis, was the first king of Egypt, who brought his people out of savagery and taught them the arts of civilization. But his brother Seth, who envied him and coveted the kingship, killed him and scattered his body in pieces along the Nile. The grieving Isis reassembled the pieces, thereby making the first mummy, and breathed life back into Osiris. In the process she became pregnant with their son Horus. When Horus grew to manhood, he defeated Seth in desperate, bloody combat. Horus became the ruler of the living and the resuscitated Osiris the king of the dead. When Horus died, he became Osiris and his son the next Horus in a continuing process of life, death, resurrection, and afterlife.

In like manner, the pharaoh was identified with Horus in life and with Osiris in death, exercising his kingly functions in both realms. The importance of the latter connection is shown in the frequent mummi-form representations of the king, such as those of Ramesses II on the columns of the Ramesseum or inside Abu Simbel where he appears tightly wrapped, clutching the symbols of rule against his chest, wearing the distinctive Osirian crown. In early times this Horus–Osiris progression was exclusively the king's, but with the 'democratization of the afterlife' that began after the Old Kingdom, any person could aspire to be resur-rected as Osiris.

Ancient Egyptian religious beliefs placed enormous emphasis on an eternal afterlife. Preparation for it was a matter of such intense concern and consumed such a large proportion of the country's resources that one Egyptologist described the building and equipping of funerary monuments as "the single largest industry" of the Old Kingdom. Most people were interred in simple graves at the desert's edge, but for the elite the ideal was a fine tomb. Many individuals obviously devoted a great portion of their lives to preparing their habitations in death. One way kings could ensure their subjects' loyalty was to promise them good tombs. Much more than mere monuments, tombs were effectively mechanisms that preserved the body in such a way that the deceased's *ka* and *ba*—ancient Egyptian concepts of personality, soul, and spirit were fairly complex—could interact in the ways necessary to form an *akh* so as to enjoy eternal comfort and happiness. If people could afford it, they endowed their tombs so a priest and his descendents would make regular presentations of food and drink to sustain the *ka* and perform prescribed rites in perpetuity. This is one of those customs that has endured in Egypt from pharaonic times, perhaps even earlier, right down to the present, for even today people often visit the tombs of departed relatives, carrying baskets of food and drink to be consumed on site, accompanied by recitations from the Qur'an.

Eternal existence required not only a suitable spiritual habitation but also the preservation of the body, therefore mummification was devised to prevent decay and maintain the body in as recognizable a state as possible. After weeks of preparation, the body was wrapped in linen bandages and placed in a coffin which might in turn be put into an outer coffin. The process was performed by a highly specialized guild, supervised by men who held priestly rank, and accompanied by elaborate magical rituals. Cheaper methods were available to accommodate the less affluent. But most people were buried without mummification in the sand where natural desiccation often preserved their bodies to a remarkable degree, sometimes better than mummification.

Although the point has been made many times before, it bears repeating that the inordinate amount of attention that the ancient Egyptians devoted to death and the afterlife was not an expression of morbidity. Quite the contrary. They enjoyed life and wanted to experience it for all time, but without worrying about hunger, fatigue, sickness, loss, and old age. The embalming ritual ends with the priest reciting: "You are alive; you are alive forever. Behold, you are young again and forever!"

The area where royal administration had the greatest impact on Egypt during the Old Kingdom was the construction of pyramids, the quintessential symbols of ancient Egypt. In order to build them, the economy of the country had to be organized and expanded to its full capacity. The fact that the king and an exploitative elite could command nearly all the available surplus resources of Egypt through taxation and assembly of royal corvée labor and apply it to pyramid building is testimony not just to the power of the central government and the efficiency of its highly developed bureaucracy but also to a widely shared ideology about the nature of society and how it should function.

Sneferu (c. 2613–2494 BC), the first king of the Fourth Dynasty, was the greatest of pyramid builders. The pyramid that his son Khufu built at Giza was the largest ever constructed, but Khufu only built one; Sneferu built at least two and probably three pyramids whose combined mass far exceeds that of any other pharaoh. Sneferu was also remarkable for design as well as magnitude. Unlike his predecessors in the late Third Dynasty with their fitful attempts to build step pyramids like Djoser's, Sneferu made the transition to the true pyramid, a monument with a square base and smooth sides that meet at a point on the summit.

The transition was not immediate. Sneferu's first pyramid, located some sixty kilometers south of Memphis at Meidum, began as a step pyramid, like Djoser's at Saqqara. When it was completed—or when what turned out to be its first phase was finished—Sneferu moved north to Dahshur, much closer to Memphis, where he built not one but two pyramids, the Bent, or Rhomboidal, Pyramid and the Northern Pyramid, also called the Red Pyramid because of the rosy appearance of its stone in certain shades of light. The Bent Pyramid was the first to be constructed, but when it had reached somewhat more than half its intended height, the angle of its outer faces was noticeably reduced from 55° to 43°, giving it its curious shape. The reason for the alteration is unknown, but was likely the result of structural concerns. Sneferu completed the Bent Pyramid, but began the Northern Pyramid, whose unusually low incline of 43° may have resulted from the experience with the Bent Pyramid. Toward the end of his reign, Sneferu then returned to Meidum for additional construction that transformed his step pyramid into a true pyramid. At some point, however, its outer layers collapsed, so that the pyramid at Meidum now has the appearance not of a pyramid but of a tower standing on a hill. Precisely when this happened is hotly debated by Egyptologists, some asserting that it occurred during construction (and influenced the Bent Pyramid) while others believe that it did not happen until the New Kingdom or even medieval times.

Sneferu's successor Khufu (c. 2589–2566 BC), also known as Cheops, chose a prominent site on the plateau at Giza for his pyramid, an example that was followed by two later Fourth Dynasty kings, Khafra (c. 2558–2532 BC) and Menkaura (c. 2532–2503 BC), whose pyramids stand in loose alignment with Khufu's, creating the best-known of Egypt's several pyramid fields. The Great Pyramid of Khufu originally stood 147 meters high (it has since lost about three meters of its height) with a base that measured 230 meters on each side. The accomplishment becomes even more staggering when one considers that like all Old Kingdom pyramids, the Great Pyramid was just one part of a much larger complex, another Fourth Dynasty innovation. Besides the Great Pyramid, there was a satellite pyramid, three queens' pyramids, at least seven boat pits containing vessels for solar journeys across the sky, a mortuary temple adjacent to the pyramid, a long causeway leading to the river valley, a valley temple, and two extensive cities of the dead to the east and west of the pyramid where the king's high officials were buried in large stone mastabas, arranged in regular rows like modern city streets.

The pyramids were certainly designed as royal tombs. Doubts that any society would devote so much of its resources to such a purpose are based on misunderstandings of the Old Kingdom and its driving ideology. The methods for constructing the pyramids, once a great mystery, have largely been worked out by Egyptologists, though some areas of uncertainty remain. Much of the stone was quarried nearby with finer limestone for finishing work brought from across the river at Tura. Most likely the stone blocks were dragged into place along huge earthen ramps. Much of the work would have been done during the inundation when the river, whose bed ran much closer to Memphis and Giza than now, spread across the floodplain, providing ready access to the worksites, and the workers were not required in the fields. Even so, the process is mind-boggling. It has been estimated that for the Great Pyramid to have been completed during Khufu's reign, as it apparently was, one of its stones had to be moved into place, and done with phenomenal precision, about every two or three minutes of the working day. These stones weigh an average of two and a half tons, and some are much heavier. The overall process—quarrying, transportation, construction, assembling the workers then providing them with food and shelter—must have stressed the country's economy to the limit. Recent discoveries near the pyramids have provided new insights into the lives of the workers.

The pyramid complex was not just a commemorative monument to a dead king. It was a thriving, continuing institution of which the pyramid itself, though the dominating centerpiece, was just one component among many and not necessarily the most important from a functional point of view. All temple complexes were endowed for the maintenance of the royal cult, usually by extensive grants of land, sometimes in close proximity to the pyramid although they could lie some distance away from it; or they were supported by ongoing contributions from the state treasury. Each of Sneferu's two pyramid cults, for example, was a separate operation, directed by a staff of priestly bureaucrats who supervised their cult's extensive economic activities. Although the ideology motivating the temple cults was observation of the prescribed rites for the departed king and providing the necessary material offerings to sustain his *ka*, the cults became some of the most important institutions in the overall economic organization of the land.

It is impossible to say just how much land the temple cults controlled, but it was large and constantly increasing with the establishment of each new pyramid and with new donations to local cults. Combined with the cult endowments of local temples, temple cults were a major force in the exploitation and redistribution of Egypt's resources. The offerings that were gathered for the deceased god-king were not, of course, materially consumed by him. Some were kept by the temple staff; some were redistributed to the temple's many clients. Official posts in the temples became highly coveted because they provided salaries either in a share of the proceeds from the temple lands or the right to cultivate a portion of those lands. Control of most of the remaining land lay in two other categories: the royal farming estates, administered directly by the central bureaucracy, and what might be termed private property, mostly large estates controlled by individuals who had been rewarded with land by the king.

The lives of the people who lived and labored on these lands, by far the bulk of Egypt's population, are poorly documented. Their poor graves contained little information; their houses have rarely been excavated; they left little impression on the literary record. Glimpses of them are seen through the eyes of the elite, for scenes of agricultural life were favorite subjects in private tomb chapels. These are frequently captioned with the words people might say as they go about their chores, speaking directly from remote antiquity. "Watch what you are doing," an ox-driver warns. The overseer announces, "I am telling you, men, the barley is ripe, and he who reaps well will get it." "Hey! my darling, eat the bread," a kind herdsman tells an ox lying by his side.[2]

Insufficient evidence survives to determine the legal status of the peasantry, but it appears that they were regarded virtually as part of the land. They were not free to leave it, but neither were they property to be bought and sold apart from it. Serfdom, not slavery, could characterize their situation from our remote point of view, but simple connectedness to the land might be a better way of looking at it. Their lives were often harsh, sometimes not far above bare subsistence even in good times, but they lived in a society suffused by *maat*, in which all of its members experienced a sense of place, of belonging, and felt they had some stake, however small. Our popular impression of the pyramids being constructed by gangs of slaves working under the lash has long ago been shown to be insupportable. Coercion was assuredly necessary to make the system work—the king ceremonially held a whip as well as a shepherd's crook—but so was committed participation by the Egyptian people, otherwise the projects could never have been completed, nor could the stability of the Old Kingdom have been maintained for so many centuries. Slavery was a relatively unimportant factor in ancient Egypt. Occasionally droves of captive workers might be brought in after successful military expeditions to supply the chronic shortage of labor, but over time these people were absorbed into the society as a whole instead of forming a distinct class.

Returning to the apex of society, and looking behind the massive monumental façade of the Fourth Dynasty, one finds a historical void. Little is known about the kings for whom the pyramids were made, and that little is more the stuff of legend and hypothesis than demonstrable fact. Sneferu was said to be benevolent and loved. Khufu and Khafra were renowned for their cruelty. Menkaura was notable for his kindness, so much so that he offended the gods, who inflicted punishment on the kingdom. The relatively small size of Menkaura's pyramid at Giza, which contains about one-tenth the mass of the Great Pyramid of Khufu, naturally prompts speculation of dynastic decline, reinforced by the even more diminutive mortuary construction of his successor Shepseskaf, but there are other possible explanations. Perhaps sheer size was no longer the primary consideration. Resources could be put elsewhere. Even as the size of pyramids declined, their associated temples grew more elaborate and their endowments larger. Also, Menkaura made extensive use of granite in his pyramid although it was a much more expensive building material. He is by far the best represented Fourth Dynasty king in statuary remains.

Menkaura died before finishing his pyramid, leaving it for his son Shepseskaf (c. 2503–2498 BC) to complete. Shepseskaf did so, albeit hastily. All too aware of the uncertain span of human life, kings were eager to get on with their own pyramids, not spend time and resources on the unfinished business of others. In a major departure from Old Kingdom practice, however, Shepseskaf chose not to build a pyramid for himself but instead had a very large mastaba erected at Saqqara. Reasons for this are entirely conjectural, but a plausible guess is that it represented a crisis, perhaps associated with the religious developments that became manifest during the next dynasty. Shepseskaf was followed by a two-year rule by another king whose name has been lost. The obscurity of that brief, anonymous reign conceals the reasons for the shift from the Fourth to the Fifth Dynasty.

According to a legend preserved in the Papyrus Westcar, which dates from the Middle Kingdom, the kings of the Fifth Dynasty (c. 2494–2345 BC) originated in a union between the sun god Ra and Radjedet, the wife of one of his priests. Whatever reality underlay that story, the religious policy of the dynasty was certainly an expression of the sun god's emergence to a status that could almost be described as the state god, his importance attested by the fact that most of the dynasty's kings, beginning with the first, Userkaf (c. 2494–2487 BC), built temples to him. These were similar in plan to royal pyramid complexes and located close to them, emphasizing the kings' relationship to the paramount god Ra, the supreme creator and the moving force in nature. Although the first king of the dynasty, Userkaf, built his pyramid at Saqqara, as did the last, Unas (c. 2375–2345 BC), the site most closely associated with the Fifth Dynasty is Abu Sir, between Saqqara and Giza.

The political history of the Fifth Dynasty is obscure, but some general trends are fairly clear. One is the withdrawal of the royal family from the highest offices of the state. Princes frequently served as viziers during the Fourth Dynasty and staffed other important positions; their tombs often stand in close proximity to the king's pyramid. But it is their general absence from the administration and their unassuming tombs that become notable by the Fifth Dynasty; in fact, it becomes increasingly difficult to identify male royal relatives at all, a trend that continues through the Middle Kingdom and beyond. This was probably because of the need to prevent a profusion of rival claimants for the succession and to preclude the formation of mini-dynasties, though it is curious to note that as princes become less prominent in the funerary record, princesses assume a much more conspicuous role than before. Perhaps the explanation lies in the ever increasing complexity of administration, which could no longer be maintained through the force of family ties. However it came about, commoners obtained the highest offices, including the viziership, during the Fifth Dynasty.

At the same time, priests and government officials were becoming less dependent on the king. The institution of temple cults may have enhanced royal authority in the short run, but over time the cults developed interests of their own. Meanwhile their wealth and power grew steadily with increased royal donations and exemptions from taxation, which were often granted exemptions from taxation and corvée levies. At the termination of each reign, a new royal cult had to be established, and the creation of sun temples, of which there were at least seven major foundations during the Fifth Dynasty, required yet more endowments. Grants of royal land were also used to pay important officials.

The system fed on itself. The king's power ultimately rested on his control of the land's resources. As this passed to temples and locally based lords—with the distinction between the two becoming progressively less sharp—royal authority was steadily undermined. To make matters worse, many newly empowered individuals used their personal bases to gain high positions in the government, therefore further weakening the king, for in those instances he depended more on them than they did on him. Provincial control was also attenuated as the office of nomarch, which had been conferred by the king for a limited period, or perhaps for the lifetime of the holder, became hereditary during the Fifth and Sixth Dynasties, creating a class of provincial nobles whose interests were local and who owed their places to birth, not to the king. This is evident in the increasing size and richness of the tombs of provincial nobles. More priests and high officials were able to make tombs on their own instead of relying on the favor of the king in what they truly viewed as a matter of life and death.

Yet, even as their foundations eroded underneath them, the kings of the Fifth Dynasty were still powerful rulers. Their pyramids were much smaller than those of the previous dynasty, but that was at least partly a result of the trend toward downsizing already evident in the later Fourth Dynasty. The overall pyramid complex of Unas, the last ruler of the Fifth Dynasty, though modest in size, was a masterpiece of exquisite workmanship, especially its causeway and temples. Unas's pyramid is also notable for the first appearance of the *Pyramid Texts*, a complex assemblage of religious utterances or spells designed to ensure the king's eternal survival and well-being. This innovation may have been prompted by a desire to be less dependent on the permanent services of a priesthood that was proving less reliable with time.

Unas may have left no successor, causing a spell of dynastic instability that was resolved by the accession of Teti (c. 2345–2323 BC), the first king of the Sixth Dynasty. Significantly, Teti chose as one of his royal names "He Who Pacifies the Two Lands." But all cannot have been well. Manetho states that Teti was killed by his bodyguard, and there was a reign by a usurper, Userkara (c. 2323–2321 BC), before Teti's son, Pepy I (c. 2321–2287 BC), could claim the throne. Then Pepy had to confront a conspiracy by one of his queens. Although the plot was thwarted, Pepy felt it necessary to strengthen his position by marrying two daughters of a powerful official at Abydos. Meanwhile, the power of nobles outside the court and in the provinces continued to increase, compounding the problems of decentralization already evident in the Fifth Dynasty.

The Sixth Dynasty enjoyed some successes. The kings were extensive builders. A channel was cut through the First Cataract to facilitate communication with Nubia. Military expeditions were sent into the northeastern Delta and into southern Palestine to counter Bedouin incursions. Resurgent problems in Nubia were also met. Pepynakht Heqaib, one of Pepy II's military commanders, recorded that "His Majesty of my lord sent me to hack up the countries of Wawat and Irtjet. I did as my lord praises. I killed there a large number, including chief's children and commanders of elite troops. I brought a large number from there to the Residence as captives while I was at the head of a large and mighty army as a hero."[3] Clearly these were energetic measures, but the fact that they were necessary indicates that the frontiers had been neglected, and they did not result in permanent security in either Nubia or the Delta.

After the brief reign of his older brother Merenre, Pepy II (c. 2278–2184 BC) came to the throne at the age of six and began the longest reign in ancient Egyptian history, ninety-four years altogether, so that his rule included the baleful effects of both a child-regency during times of difficulty and an extended dotage during even worse days. Secure in their local holdings, many nomarchs extended their influence further. Unprecedented numbers of rock-cut tombs in Middle and Upper Egypt show that local administrators were becoming local rulers. Once things began to fall apart, the process accelerated because of the geography of Egypt. Concentration of the population in the Nile Valley and the function of the Nile as an artery of communication could work for decentralization as well as centralization because of the country's great length. Interruption at any point disrupted the functioning of the whole.

Already depleted by grants to cult temples and individuals, royal finances, as well as the land in general, were devastated by a series of low inundations resulting from a fundamental change of climate. Famine and even cannibalism are attested. Royal taxes were assessed in relation to the height of the flood, so during the latter part of Pepy II's reign, there was little to collect. Deprived of resources, the king could no longer perform his proper function. The condition of the kingdom is evident in the tombs of the officials huddled around Pepy II's pyramid at south Saqqara. Those mud brick mastabas can best be described as impoverished.

After the very brief reign of Pepy II's son, Merenre II, came something most unusual in ancient Egypt: rule by a woman (who may have been Merenra II's wife). According to Manetho, Queen Nitiqret (c. 2184–2181 BC) was "braver than all the men of her time, and the most beautiful of all the women." But no amount of bravery or beauty could retrieve the situation. With Pepy II's death, the period we define as the Old Kingdom had effectively come to an end.

4   The First Intermediate Period and the Middle Kingdom

The collapse of the Old Kingdom was not caused by external factors. It came from within and was associated with—and at least partly resulted from—the decentralization of power as various regional powers disregarded central authority. Egypt became much as it had been before political unification at the end of the Predynastic Period. This condition, which persisted for about a century and a half, is termed the First Intermediate Period (c. 2160–2055 BC).

Some pretense of overall pharaonic authority had been maintained for a time at Memphis by the kings of the Seventh and Eighth Dynasties (c. 2181–2160 BC), but these were ephemeral, ineffectual rulers. According to Manetho, the Seventh Dynasty consisted of seventy kings who reigned for a total of seventy days, but that probably reflects a confusion of sources as well as dynastic instability. The Eighth Dynasty was slightly more substantial, but only one of its kings, Hakare-Ibi, enjoyed the resources and longevity—a rule of perhaps two years—to construct a pyramid, a small affair compared to the great pyramid complexes of the Old Kingdom. It is unlikely that any of these kings exerted authority far beyond the boundaries of Memphis, and after a couple of decades or so, the Eighth Dynasty was extinct.

The real northern center of power shifted to Herakleopolis, near the entrance to the Fayyum. Its rulers are the kings of Manetho's Ninth and Tenth Dynasties. But their sway extended only into Middle Egypt, and they were unable to prevent extensive Asiatic infiltration of the eastern Delta. Even in the areas they controlled, the Herakleopolitan kings never succeeded in developing an effective centralized system similar to the one that later emerged in the south, instead relying on the loyalty of powerful local magnates.

Upper Egypt was a patchwork of autonomous nomes and less distinct areas ruled by local leaders, some of whom paid outward allegiance to the nominal central authority at Memphis. But this was merely a cloak for asserting their independence as they competed fiercely with each other, marshaling their resources and hiring foreign mercenaries, probably from Nubia. The tomb of Ankhtifi, nomarch of al-Kab, records how he "sailed downstream with my strong and trustworthy troops" to conduct a campaign against the Theban nome. In marked departure from previous practice, there is not even a nominal reference to the king; instead, Ankhtifi proclaims, "I was the beginning and the end of mankind, since nobody like myself existed before me nor will he exist . . . I am the hero without equal."

A dominant southern power center developed at a later date than the northern one. Its kings, who were based at Thebes, hitherto an obscure provincial town, are those of the Eleventh Dynasty, which runs at the same time as the Ninth and Tenth Dynasties, lending further confusion to dynastic chronology. As their authority extended northward, they inevitably clashed with the northern kings in a prolonged conflict that eventually resulted in a victory for the south and the reunification of Egypt at the end of the First Intermediate Period.

Early Egyptologists generally presented the First Intermediate Period as a time of chaos, anarchy, and widespread misery, contrasting starkly to the orderly Old Kingdom and the resurgent Middle Kingdom. This dismal picture was supported by a body of ancient Egyptian literary sources so numerous as almost to form a genre in themselves, bewailing the disastrous state of affairs. The sage Ipuwer wrote how "the land spins around as does a potter's wheel," and Neferrohu complained that "this land is helter-skelter, and no one knows the result." Long litanies of wrongs follow: the byways are unsafe, fighting can break out anywhere, murders are everyday occurrences, a person can be killed in his own house, servants are impudent, social order is overturned, those who were rich are now poor and vice versa, exploitative lords impose extortionate taxes, robbery is commonplace, and so on to the point that life becomes unbearable. "Would that it were the end of men, no conception, no birth!" The predominant theme is a catastrophic failure of *maat*. The king was not performing his proper functions.

That conditions were often difficult during the First Intermediate Period is beyond doubt. With no effective central authority to mediate local disputes and prevent armed competition between local polities, the land's resources were wasted, people suffered needlessly, and property was devastated. "Indeed, the ship of the southerners had gone adrift," Ipuwer lamented. "Towns are destroyed and Upper Egypt has become empty wastes." The period can be interpreted as a prolonged civil war with resulting loss of order and security. Old ideas were inevitably called into question. Nostalgia for a distant, idealized past was a normal reaction.

But some of the longstanding notions about the First Intermediate Period have been questioned. Scholars recently noticed that many of the most pessimistic accounts were composed not during the First Intermediate itself but during the succeeding Middle Kingdom when the prevailing ideology that emphasized restoration of *maat* by the kings would have encouraged horrific descriptions of a time when central authority was weak or nonexistent. Also, the political fragmentation of the period could be interpreted not as collapse but as continuity, for it was the logical extension of a trend that began during the Sixth and Sixth Dynasties when the nomarchs became increasingly self-sufficient. Historians have an inclination to evaluate unification as intrinsically good and disunity as inherently bad.

Looking at the evidence actually generated by the First Intermediate Period, many problems and peculiarities become readily apparent. For the Herakleopolitan kingdom in the north, the most striking thing about the evidence is its absence. We know that the kings changed fairly frequently, suggesting some kind of political instability, and the fact that there was little construction of funerary monuments is probably significant, but it is impossible to establish sound historical generalities on such negative foundations. Despite loosening of control in parts of the Delta, no large-scale invasion came from southwestern Asia, and the Herakleopolites were able to confront their rivals to the south while maintaining the appearances and indeed some of the realities of the old Memphite monarchy throughout the territories they controlled. An end to the long series of low inundations that afflicted the last decades of the Old Kingdom provided additional resources for governmental exploitation and perhaps alleviated some of the hardships that the general population endured.

In the south, the state of the evidence is just the opposite: there is much more of it than before and of a much more varied nature. But that does not necessarily make it easier to interpret. Several factors account for the profusion, including the usual tendency for evidence to be better preserved and easier to access in Upper than in Lower Egypt because of geographical conditions, although improved methods in the archaeology of northern Middle Egypt and the Delta are casting new light on Deltan settlements. More significantly, perhaps, was the existence of local magnates like Ankhtifi who had the means to prepare elaborate tombs that recorded their alleged deeds and personal might. Then, once the rulers of Thebes established their regional kingship and extended their authority, they enjoyed longer, more stable reigns, therefore left a richer record, both monumental and written.

By the time Intef II (c. 2112–2063 BC) came to the southern throne, the Theban monarchy ruled much of Upper Egypt where the nomarchs had been suppressed, giving the king firm personal control over his territories without relying on local magnates. This secure power base enabled Intef to take the offensive in the north, where he captured Abydos and ranged even farther north to Asyut, which held firm in its allegiance to the Herakleopolitan kings. Thus began a period of hostilities between the northern and southern kingdoms that lasted on and off for several decades.

Details of the war are scanty. A Herakleopolitan counteroffensive may have recaptured Abydos at one point, but any such northern successes were fleeting at best because the initiative returned to the Thebans. The decisive push came under Mentuhotep II* (c. 2055–2004 BC). The Tomb of the Warriors at Deir al-Bahari, which contained sixty soldiers who were killed in battle, may be a result of this final phase of the conflict. The northern kingdom was defeated, its funerary monuments smashed, and its

---

* Mentuhotep II is numbered as I by some writers, and that numerical decrease also affects Mentuhotep III and IV.

capital probably sacked. Egypt was reunited, although violence continued for some time before order could be fully restored. With the reunification of Egypt began the period known as the Middle Kingdom.

The first part of the Middle Kingdom was marked by an unusually large number of energetic, able rulers. The precise lengths of their reigns are matters of debate because of problems peculiar to Middle Kingdom chronology, but most were long enough to implement ambitious programs. There is a marked difference between the kingship of the Old and Middle Kingdoms, one that is apparent in the royal portraiture. For one thing, statuary portrayals of kings become much more lifelike. The statues of the Old Kingdom monarchs are idealized figures that probably bore little or no resemblance to the actual individuals. But looking at Middle Kingdom statues of men like Senwosret III or Amenemhet III, it is difficult to believe that one is seeing anything other than accurate representations of the kings themselves.

But there was more to Middle Kingdom portraiture than realism, for that realism is a deliberately contrived effect designed to convey an impression of a king who is closely involved in the business of the kingdom—and paying a human price for it. In place of the serenity of the Old Kingdom, where the pharaoh is blissfully detached from the everyday world, the Middle Kingdom monarch is strong but sometimes a bit haggard, as if careworn in the conscientious performance of his duties. He is a 'good shepherd,' a formulation used in the literature of the time. The king also acquires a personal voice in the Middle Kingdom. Instead of the inscrutable remoteness of the Old Kingdom, he begins to make statements, purportedly composed by himself, about his accomplishments in government.

Mentuhotep II's reign of fifty years was long even by Middle Kingdom standards. Active in every area of kingship, he increased the size of the bureaucracy and created new offices in the central government. Recognizing the dangers posed by the nomarchs, he reduced their number and took steps to ensure their personal loyalty that he reinforced by frequent visitations. Revenue was regularized through collection of taxes in kind and in the corvée by which labor was provided for his many public works projects. Mining and quarrying resumed in the Nile Valley and in the Eastern Desert and Sinai. Frontier security was guaranteed by numerous military campaigns. Mentuhotep's interest in Asia, however, was primarily commercial. Trade was reestablished with Syria, where the ruler of the Lebanese trading city of Byblos became known as the "servant of Egypt." Likewise, Mentuhotep campaigned in Nubia, but his interest there was also trade, not conquest. The southern military garrison was established at Aswan. The country that Mentuhotep II bequeathed to his successor was powerful, peaceful, and prosperous. His role as restorer of Egypt became so renowned that it was still being commemorated hundreds of years later at the end of the New Kingdom.

Following such a long reign as his father's, Mentuhotep III (c. 2004–1992 BC) was relatively old when he came to the throne, but he used his twelve years of rule well, continuing his father's energetic policies of building and maintaining strong frontier defenses. He was particularly active in the south in promoting trading contacts. But Mentuhotep IV (c. 1992–1985 BC) presents a historical enigma. On the ancient king lists he is missing, his reign being merely recorded as seven blank years. Recorded details are insufficient for a reconstruction of events, but they indicate that his vizier Amenemhet somehow seized the throne, inaugurating the Twelfth Dynasty.

Once Amenemhet I (c. 1985–1956 BC) had consolidated his position, he moved the capital from Thebes to an entirely new fortified town of Itjtawy, somewhere between Memphis and the Fayyum at a site that has not been discovered but was probably near al-Lisht. This offered a number of advantages: a clean break with the past, detachment of the royal court from individuals' local power bases in Upper Egypt, proximity to the rich resources of the Fayyum, readier access to the Asiatic frontier, and above all a commanding position from which to control both Upper and Lower Egypt, as is obvious in the meaning of the name Itjtawy, "Seizer of the Two Lands." Itjtawy was the capital of Egypt for the next three hundred years.

Another point of departure for Amenemhet I was his construction of a pyramid at al-Lisht. The kings of the Eleventh Dynasty had been buried in tombs at Thebes, of which that of Mentuhotep II at Deir al-Bahari is the most notable example. Amenemhet I reintroduced the royal pyramid complex, and his successors followed his example. But it had been nearly two centuries since a pyramid was constructed; techniques had been lost, and times had changed, so that Middle Kingdom pyramids had a number of features unlike those of the Old Kingdom. The major difference was that Middle Kingdom pyramids were not constructed with well-laid blocks of stone throughout. Amenemhet I's pyramid had an inner fill of unbaked mud brick, rubble, and sand which was cased with finely dressed, carefully joined Tura limestone to provide a smooth exterior. Because of subsidence problems, later Middle Kingdom pyramids were stabilized with interior stone cross walls, but their cores were of mud brick. In either case, once the casing stones were robbed, as they invariably were, the inner cores deteriorated, giving surviving Middle Kingdom pyramids their slumped, ruinous appearances; but they were impressive monuments in their day. Amenemhet I's pyramid at al-Lisht, like the nearby pyramid of his successor Senwosret I, is little more than a low, indistinct mound now, often unnoticed by passing travelers, but it originally stood fifty-five meters high, and it had a causeway and mortuary temple. A Middle Kingdom pyramid complex was an imposing statement of power.

Amenemhet I also switched over to a more aggressive military posture. He used his army against Asiatic settlers in the Delta and built the great fortified system known as the Walls of the Ruler to protect the northeastern approaches to Egypt. Fortified posts were established elsewhere in Egypt. In Nubia, he reversed earlier Middle Kingdom policy, which had mainly consisted of sending trading and quarrying expeditions into the region, by undertaking campaigns of conquest and permanent settlement. These were conducted with great brutality. At the time of his death, he had dispatched a major expedition to the west against the Libyans.

In the twentieth year of his reign, Amenemhet I associated his son Senwosret with him as king, establishing a co-regency, another innovation that was followed by his successors—and that has complicated ancient Egyptian chronology because official documents were dated not by any absolute system but by regnal years. This was probably intended to safeguard the succession, about which Amenemhet I may have felt some insecurity, and to provide a helping hand, for Amenemhet must have been getting on in years; he was almost certainly a middle-aged man when he seized the throne. As co-ruler, Senwosret took an active role as military leader, conducting campaigns on all of Egypt's frontiers. Amenemhet I's dynastic precautions proved justified, for he was murdered during his thirtieth regnal year, when Senwosret was in the west on a Libyan campaign. Apparently the succession was disputed, but Senwosret returned and successfully asserted his claim to the throne.

During his sole rule of thirty-five years, Senwosret I (c. 1956–1911 BC) exhibited the qualities of continuity, adaptation, and incremental innovation that were hallmarks of the Middle Kingdom. In Nubia he continued his father's policies through expansion and fortification. Lower Nubia became a fully organized Egyptian province. But his Asian policy emphasized establishment of commercial and diplomatic connections, not territorial expansion. Extensive mining and quarrying provided the wealth and materials for a comprehensive program of monumental construction throughout Egypt. Most of that is gone now, but the reconstruction of his exquisite little alabaster temple at Karnak provides an example. In yet another lengthy reign, Amenemhet II (c. 1911–1877 BC) consolidated his predecessors' accomplishments.

The reign of Senwosret II (c. 1877–1870 BC) was brief by the standards of the early Middle Kingdom, but it was peaceful and prosperous, featuring expanded commerce with southwestern Asia and Nubia, enabling him to undertake a public works project of momentous importance, the Fayyum irrigation system. An enormous dike was constructed along with a system of canals to connect the Fayyum with the long waterway known as Bahr Yussuf, which runs parallel to the Nile through much of Middle Egypt. These provided control over the amount of water entering the fertile depression so that the level of the lake at its bottom could be lowered, freeing more land for cultivation, watered by the improved canal system. The productivity of the Fayyum, and consequently the power of the Middle Kingdom monarchy, was thereby vastly increased. The Fayyum's enhanced importance is evident in the fact that Senwosret II sited his pyramid complex at al-Lahun, overlooking the channel from the Nile Valley into the Fayyum basin. Amenemhet III, the greatest builder of the Middle Kingdom, later followed his example a short distance farther west at Hawara.

Long reigns resumed with Senwosret III (1870–1831 BC), who exploited his opportunity both administratively and militarily. The power of the nomarchs of Middle and Upper Egypt, which had done so much to undermine the Old Kingdom, had never been entirely broken and indeed was resurgent. Nowhere is this more apparent than in the magnificent rock-cut tombs overlooking the Nile at Beni Hasan that belonged to the "Great Overlords of the Oryx [Sixth] Nome" of the late Eleventh and early Twelfth Dynasties. These remarkable monuments, decorated with scenes of sieges, Asiatic traders, funeral rituals, and the famous rows of wrestlers, are unmistakable statements of wealth and status. The means by which he accomplished it are unclear, but Senwosret III curtailed the influence of his powerful governors, as is indicated by a subsequent decline in provincial tombs. To enhance royal control of the kingdom, he divided it into three administrative units—one for the north, another for the south, and a third for Aswan and Nubia—each headed by a vizier who supervised all areas of administration and was directly responsible to the king.

As a war leader, Senwosret III conducted at least one expedition into Syria, but the primary focus of his military activity was in the south, where Nubian settlement had been steadily encroaching northward as Nubia recovered from the devastation it had suffered during the Old Kingdom. His Nubian campaigns were marked by exceptional brutality, as he boasted on a commemorative stela: "I carried off their women, I carried off their subjects, went forth to their wells, smote their bulls: I reaped their grain, and set fire thereto." Senwosret III extended Egypt's southern frontier, establishing it beyond the Second Cataract at Semna, secured by a series of strong fortifications with vigilant garrisons, and sternly admonished his successors to maintain it there. To facilitate communication with the south, he enlarged the Old Kingdom channel at the First Cataract, near Aswan. So great was Senwosret III's impact on Nubia that he was worshiped there as a god during the New Kingdom.

The political and military achievements of the Middle Kingdom were matched, and often expressed, by accomplishments in literature, art, and architecture. This is not readily appreciated, in part because of a tendency to view the Middle Kingdom as an interlude between the stately Old Kingdom and glorious New Kingdom, and partly because so much of the Middle Kingdom's monumental record was erased in a process of effacement that began in ancient times. The alabaster temple of Senwosret I at Karnak, to return to that example, was demolished and used for fill in an Eighteenth Dynasty pylon. Fortunately enough of its blocks remained for it to be reconstructed.*

---

* A notable exception to the effacement of Middle Kingdom monuments by later construction is the obelisk of Senwosret I at Heliopolis, where the other monuments, of both earlier and later date, at that great cult site have vanished, leaving the obelisk standing alone.

Far from being mediocre, Middle Kingdom culture was of an exceptionally high standard and exerted a profound influence over the rest of ancient Egyptian history.

Elegant simplicity and symmetry characterized the monumental architecture of the Middle Kingdom. While paying conscientious attention to Old Kingdom models, Middle Kingdom architects could be astonishingly innovative. The much-admired New Kingdom temple of Hatshepsut at Deir al-Bahari was obviously inspired by the adjacent terraced temple of the Middle Kingdom monarch Mentuhotep II, with its dramatic avenue and wedge-shaped ramp, set against one of the most thrilling geological backdrops in all of western Thebes. The failure of Middle Kingdom pyramids to hold their forms over the millennia is not an indication that workmanship was poor during the Middle Kingdom but that resources were judiciously applied. Middle Kingdom pyramids served the purposes of their builders during their times and long afterwards before slumping into ruin. Also, as in the later Old Kingdom, more attention was paid to the pyramid complex's temples, the most famous example being the mortuary temple of Amenemhet III at Hawara, which, like so much Middle Kingdom architecture, has been obliterated. Many more temples were constructed in the provinces during the Middle Kingdom than in the Old Kingdom, such as Senwosret III's temple of the war god Montu at Nag al-Medamoud, north of Thebes, built with wealth from Senwosret's Nubian campaigns. It, too, has been destroyed.

Middle Kingdom painting and sculpture sometimes pale in comparison to those of the Old Kingdom because one of the results of the regionalism of the First Intermediate Period was to weaken the central government's control over artistic production. That meant discontinuity in training, less access to high-quality materials, and lack of supervision to ensure standards, sometimes resulting in relatively clumsy work during the early part of the period. But it also meant new approaches to artistic representation and innovative use of available materials. Recognizable regional styles emerged, rendered with greater originality and representing a much wider range of subjects. Influences from the outside world made themselves felt in Egyptian art. Over time, the court culture at Itjtawy established standards that extended throughout the kingdom, introducing new techniques such as grid patterns to produce uniformity in the representation of the human figure. Sculptured raised relief work from the time of Senwosret I onward is of especially fine quality; the unique ability of Middle Kingdom royal sculpture to convey personality as well as power has already been noted.

A particular area of excellence in Middle Kingdom artistry was jewelry. The finely wrought examples from the tombs of royal women at Dahshur and al-Lahun are among the best ever produced in ancient Egypt. The burial of the Twelfth Dynasty Princess Khemet at Dahshur included the famous 'bull mosaic' pendant, influenced by Cretan design. Technique, design, and motifs were all combined in elegant ways to achieve breathtaking aesthetic effects. One of the most remarkable qualities of Middle Kingdom jewelry is artistic restraint. Precious materials were used with delicacy instead of reliance on sheer mass.

Like their Old Kingdom predecessors, the artists of the Middle Kingdom were regarded more as 'technicians' and 'craftsmen' than what we would understand as 'artists' today. Almost always they worked to order, applying accepted forms with well-established techniques, knowing that they were likely to be little remembered as creators of their works after they passed on to the next life. But this did not preclude pride in technical proficiency. The Middle Kingdom sculptor Irtisen proclaimed on his stela at Abydos:

> I was an artist, accomplished in my art, preeminent because of my knowledge of it. I knew the rules of relief, both sunken and raised, so that everything fell into place. I knew how to represent the movement of a man or the walk of a woman, the position of a snared bird, the bending of a captive while one of his eyes winks at his companion; how to show fear in an enemy's face, the poise of an arm about to spear a hippopotamus, the action of a runner. I knew how to make inlaid paints that water cannot wash away.[4]

It would have been an immense source of satisfaction to people like Irtisen to know that some of their works have survived and are much admired today, for they believed their works had eternal value.

One of the brightest facets of Middle Kingdom culture was a literary efflorescence unlike any other in ancient Egypt. Here again the influence of the central government was a vital force, as scribal training was emphasized to support the reestablishment of a countrywide bureaucratic tradition. Many training texts exist from the time; one of their recurring themes is loyalty to the king. But a broader literary tradition also developed with works of great complexity in different genres, including fiction. The *Tale of the Eloquent Peasant* has a framing device worthy of the *Arabian Nights*. Robbed of his goods by a well-connected official named Dehuti-necht, the peasant Hunanup petitions the chief steward, Meruitensi, but in terms so eloquent that Meruitensi keeps him talking through nine appeals so he and his colleagues, and even the king, can enjoy his rich metaphors and compelling poetic imagery. The papyrus breaks off, but not before one learns that it has a happy ending: Hunanup receives not only his own property but is also awarded that of the evil Dehuti-necht. *The Shipwrecked Sailor*, a story about a castaway on a remote island who encounters a giant talking snake, is reminiscent of Sindibad the Sailor. The *Tale of Sinuhe* might be classified as historical fiction, with its references to Twelfth Dynasty court life, the Walls of the Ruler, and Sinuhe's adventures in Syria. Like other literature then and now, the *Tale of Sinuhe* contains many standard but ever popular dramatic devices, including an exciting fight scene between Sinuhe and a formidable Syrian adversary.

Another genre well represented in the Middle Kingdom was Wisdom Literature, the notable example of which is the *Instruction of Amenemhet I*. In that work, the king purportedly tells his son Senwosret I how he was murdered and gives practical advice about the art of kingship. The fact that it is clearly a clever propaganda tool for Senwosret does not diminish the effectiveness of the narrative device of having the dead king speak from beyond the grave. The language and literature used in the Middle Kingdom was so influential that it remained standard for the rest of pharaonic history. More than a thousand years later, students were still being taught how to read and write by copying its texts.

While ancient Egyptian artists were relatively anonymous craftsmen, their literary counterparts often achieved significant and lasting levels of individual recognition. In the words of an ancient text:

> As to those learned scribes,
> Their names have become everlasting,
> While they departed, having finished their lives,

And all their kin are forgotten.
Man decays, his corpse is dust,
All his kin have perished;
But a book makes him remembered
Through the mouth of its reciter.
Better is a book than a well-built house,
Than tombchapels in the west;
Better than a solid mansion,
Than a stela in the temple![5]

As in all periods of ancient Egyptian history, the art, literature, and monumental architecture of the Middle Kingdom were heavily biased toward the elite, as is the archaeology, but they nevertheless shed light on conditions within ancient Egyptian society as a whole, and in more ways than earlier periods. Documentary evidence, though still sketchy, is more abundant. Insight into rural life and family affairs comes from the letters written by the Twelfth Dynasty farmer Hekanakhte, who was away from home for extended periods and had to make his concerns about estate and household management explicitly clear to people who otherwise might pay little attention to him. Tomb murals, as always, contain vivid background snapshots of the social setting, but the Middle Kingdom practice of putting models in tombs provides the most poignant pictures of daily life. These models might be of houses, shops, and boats, complete with inhabitants, workers, and crews. The cattle census model in the tomb of Meketra at Thebes consists of dozens of models of the scribes seated under their columned portico, the herdsmen driving their charges, and the dappled, horned cattle walking by to be counted. Marching ranks of Twelfth Dynasty armed common soldiers come from the tomb of Mesehti at Asyut.

While the evidence allows some meaningful inferences to be drawn about the quality of ancient Egyptian society, quantitative measurements of it are impossible. The historical demography of ancient Egypt is merely guesswork within the broadest of parameters. Very low numbers have been posited for the population of Late Predynastic Egypt, as low as one or two hundred thousand. It was certainly much larger in the Early Dynastic Period with development of agricultural resources, perhaps two million or more. For exceptionally prosperous times, such as the great days of the New Kingdom, reasonable estimates reach as high as three and four and a half million. The great majority of people, as during most periods in Egyptian history, lived in the countryside and worked the land. The elite groups and those closely connected to them, the ones who dominate the surviving evidence, were a very thin layer on the overall population.

The cultural apex of the Middle Kingdom came under Amenemhet III (c. 1831–1786 BC). Egypt was peaceful and prosperous, at least during the first part of his reign of forty-five years. He completed Senwosret II's irrigation system in the Fayyum, where he constructed several major temples and two colossal seated statues that once stood nearly twenty meters high. Like so many Middle Kingdom monuments, the colossi were entirely destroyed, leaving only their bases, which modern travelers initially mistook for small pyramids. For his pyramid, Amenemhet III followed the examples of his predecessors Amenemhet II and Senwosret III, and chose a site on the eastern edge of the pyramid field at Dahshur. As its construction advanced, however, serious problems developed with the foundation and interior spaces.

Recognizing the problems at Dahshur, Amenemhet III turned to the Fayyum and began another pyramid at Hawara, a short distance north-west of his grandfather's pyramid at al-Lahun. The problems that had afflicted the previous pyramid were avoided, but the Hawara structure was also much more ambitious than the one at Dahshur; even in ruin, stripped of its limestone mantle, it is an impressive structure that stands more than thirty meters above the surrounding plain, about half its original height. Its adjacent mortuary temple, the so-called Labyrinth, was one of the wonders of the ancient world. "I have seen this building," the Greek traveler Herodotus wrote more than 1,300 years after its construction, "and it is beyond my power to describe; it must have cost more in labour and money than all the walls and public works of the Greeks put together. . . . The pyramids, too, are astonishing structures, each one of them equal to many of the most ambitious works of Greece; but the labyrinth surpasses them."[6] Nothing of that surpassing monument remains except fragments in the sand, because it was relentlessly quarried over the centuries to extract lime from its stone.

Fissures may have spread through the glorious edifice of Amenemhet III's regime before its end. His building program was so extensive as to prompt conjecture that it overstrained the economy. Also, there are indications of low inundations during his last years. Because of the exceptional length of his reign, that of his son (possibly his grandson) and successor was short. Little is known about the nine years of Amenemhet IV's rule (c. 1786–1777 BC) apart from some temple construction, including the unusual temple at Qasr al-Sagha on the north side of the Fayyum. He was probably married to his sister Sobekneferu who ruled in her own right for four years after his death. Sobekneferu may have been able enough; she undertook some building projects and asserted her authority through use of masculine as well as female titles. But female rule was almost always a sign of dynastic trouble in ancient Egypt, and with her brief reign the Twelfth Dynasty came to an end.

Although the Thirteenth Dynasty lasted less than a century and a half, it had some seventy kings (more if one counts the Fourteenth Dynasty, which was probably at least partially contemporary with it), an indication that the kingship was not particularly effective. This is reflected in the dynasty's royal burials, which indicate an impoverished monarchy. Several Fourteenth Dynasty kings built pyramids, but they are small affairs, and some cannot even be assigned to a particular monarch. King Awibra Hor (c. 1720 BC) was buried in a mere tomb shaft. Some continuity was provided by the administrative system that had been developed by the great rulers of the Middle Kingdom after a strong, capable family assumed the viziership, maintaining central government and a degree of internal stability, but this final phase of the Middle Kingdom was mostly an exercise in decay.

A fleeting revival of royal fortunes around the reign of Sobekhotep III (c. 1744 BC) and his two successors promised better things, but could not be sustained. In the eastern Delta, the kingdom could no longer maintain tight frontier security, resulting in a steady infiltration of settlers from southwest Asia. These were the forerunners of the movement that would result in Hyksos rule during the Second Intermediate Period. Obviously the Walls of the Ruler system was not being maintained. The same was true in Nubia, where the once vigilant fortress garrisons were left to their own devices, allowing them to become virtually independent and ineffective against native revolts. Beyond the frontier, a powerful state had developed, the Kingdom of

Kush with its capital at Kerma near the Third Cataract. Having grown wealthy by exploiting their strategic location between rich sources of materials to the south and a voracious market to the north, the rulers of Kerma seized the opportunity to extend their control northward as far as the First Cataract. And once again climate intervened, this time with inundations that were too high, with all the damage and disruption they could cause.

The final collapse of the Egyptian central government was likely associated with the abandonment of Itjtawy in favor of Thebes, from which the last king of the Thirteenth Dynasty reigned. The end of that dynasty around 1640 BC marks the end of the Middle Kingdom.

5   The Second Intermediate Period and the New Kingdom

At the end of the Middle Kingdom, Egypt again fell apart politically, inaugurating the Second Intermediate Period (c. 1640–1550 BC). This might appear similar to the decentralization that characterized the First Intermediate Period, but a new factor, an outside force, was involved this time. It is described by Manetho in the epitome of Josephus:

> I do not know why, but God was angry with us, so that men of low origin came from the east without warning and boldly invaded our country, conquering it without a battle. After they defeated our leaders, they savagely burned our cities, leveled the temples of the gods, and treated the population with great cruelty, killing some and taking their wives and children as slaves. . . . They wanted to exterminate the Egyptian people. They were generally called Hyksos, or Shepherd Kings, for in the sacred language of the hieroglyphs, 'Hyk' means a king, and in the common speech 'sos' is a shepherd.[7]

Manetho must always be used with care, especially when filtered through Josephus. Even his etymology is wrong, because 'Hyksos' does not mean 'Shepherd Kings'; it is a composite of two Egyptian words meaning 'Rulers of Foreign Countries.' Yet Manetho is correct overall, for taking advantage of the absence of central authority and the relaxation of the northeastern frontier, an immigrant population from west Asia settled in Lower Egypt, where some of their leaders set themselves up as kinglets over small areas around the Delta. Within a couple of generations, these Hyksos leaders grew strong enough to gain control of the entire Delta, as well as the Fayyum and much of Middle Egypt. The Hyksos kings, major and minor, are the pharaohs of Manetho's Fifteenth and Sixteenth Dynasties, which ran contemporaneously.

The main Hyksos base was in Avaris in the eastern Delta. Manetho, as epitomized by Josephus, states that it was held by a garrison of nearly a quarter of a million warriors. That number can safely be dismissed as nonsense, but the Hyksos were undeniably formidable soldiers. The Egyptians could not stand against their superior weapons and dazzling tactics, featuring swift-striking attacks with horses and chariots, that the Egyptians had not encountered before. Even on the few occasions when the Egyptians managed to get the better of them, the Hyksos could retreat quickly and take refuge in their fortified camps, another innovation that the Egyptians did not know how to overcome at first.

But in a process reminiscent of the later First Intermediate Period, a native Egyptian dynasty emerged in the Theban area, where local leaders consolidated their positions, and extended its power both toward the north where the Hyksos claimed hegemony and toward the south against the expanding Kushite kingdom. In the opening rounds the Hyksos may have enjoyed the upper hand, for their king wrote contemptuously to the Theban king, complaining of the noise that the hippopotami were making in their pool at Thebes and commanding that it cease. The rambunctious hippos to which the Hyksos king referred were the Theban king and his court.

Soon, however, the Theban kings had to be taken more seriously, as they began a hard-fought but ultimately successful offensive against the Hyksos, recorded in the monuments of the kings and the nobles who fought alongside them. It began under the Theban Seventeenth Dynasty king Seqenenre Tao II, whose mutilated mummy looks as if he was killed in combat. The makeshift burial of Seqenenre's son Kamose suggests that he also died suddenly and unexpectedly. The process was completed by an experienced military commander named Ahmose (c. 1550–1525 BC), founder of the Eighteenth Dynasty. Capturing Memphis and then the Hyksos capital of Avaris, Ahmose drove the detested foreign invaders back into Palestine and Syria. With the reunification of Egypt begins the period known as the New Kingdom (c. 1550–1069 BC).

Although the Egyptians later referred to the Hyksos with loathing, Hyksos rule benefited Egypt in many ways, including technological innovation, an area in which Egypt had lagged behind some of the societies of western Asia. The Hyksos brought better techniques for metalworking; improvements in the potter's wheel and the loom, as well as superior strains of plants and animals; also new weapons such as the horse-drawn chariot, the curved sword, the compound bow, and body armor—all of which the Egyptians learned to use against the invaders.

Hyksos rule in Egypt also altered Egypt's attitude toward the outside world, resulting in expansionist policies during the early New Kingdom that were notably more ambitious than those of the Middle Kingdom. The Kingdom of Kush in the south had not only become a significant regional power, but also established control over Lower Nubia, formerly an Egyptian province. There had even been a strong possibility of concerted action between the Kushites and the Hyksos, which would have compelled the Thebans to fight on two fronts. Now the New Kingdom pharaohs reasserted Egyptian hegemony in Nubia, where they rebuilt the forts at the Second Cataract and established Egyptian colonies far upriver as they rampaged through the full extent of the Kushite dominions. With the relish for brutality that characterized Egyptian campaigns in Nubia, Tuthmosis I boasted, "The Nubian bowmen fall by the sword and are thrown aside on their lands; their stench floods their valleys. . . . The pieces cut from them are too much for the birds carrying off the prey to another place."

Operations in Nubia were framed in terms of recovering Egyptian possessions; likewise, when the Egyptians returned to Asia they used the pretext of chasing away the Hyksos, but they were really carving out an Egyptian empire, or at least a sphere of political/military domination in an area where an assortment of independent and semi-independent city-states offered easy pickings to a centralized power like Egypt. Under Tuthmosis I, Egyptian control reached as far as the Euphrates River, where he set up a commemorative stela. The kings of the early Eighteenth Dynasty, and again in the early Nineteenth, were true war leaders who directed and often personally participated in military campaigns.

The Egyptians maintained control over their Asiatic dominions through annual raids and small garrisons, but they primarily relied on the rulers of the individual city-states, often taking their sons to be educated in Egypt, thereby holding hostages who were Egyptianized before being returned to rule their homelands after their fathers' deaths. This approach worked well enough early on, but the region's balance of power politics eventually turned Syria into a diplomatic and occasionally military battlefield, as constant changes of allegiance and shifting alliances caused continuous confusion.

The pressing priority during the early New Kingdom, though, was internal reform. A strong central government with a hierarchical structure was reestablished with two viziers, one for Upper and one for Lower Egypt. Directly answerable to the king, the viziers oversaw all offices and administration within their spheres. Another official with the title "King's Son of Kush" managed Nubia, including its important gold mines. He too was directly under the king. Beneath them was a bureaucracy that fell into three general parts: military, religious, and civil. These were not kept completely separate, since officials often moved between them as their careers advanced, but the military, now influential for the first time in Egyptian history, was growing in wealth, power, and prestige. In the Middle Kingdom, the school texts from which student scribes learned to read and write had been about leading a good life and loyalty to the king, whereas the New Kingdom texts included warnings about the hardships of the soldier's life, suggesting that military careers were luring too many promising young men away from civilian jobs.

True to their origins, the New Kingdom monarchs lived and ruled from Thebes at first, but within a couple of generations the king was usually to be found living in the north, where he could better control both Upper and Lower Egypt while managing operations in Asia. Memphis therefore continued its venerable function as Egypt's administrative center, as it had been since the beginning of pharaonic times and would continue to be until their end. Because of Asian concerns, a third capital was established during the Nineteenth Dynasty in the eastern Delta at Pi-Ramesses, near the old Hyksos base of Avaris. Progressions from one capital to another must have been great occasions that enabled the king to project his authority publicly and obtain information through personal inspection and contact instead of having it filtered through his high officials. Thebes became Egypt's religious capital; no other city had as many temples.

The early Theban kings attributed their successes to the god Amun, who amalgamated with the god Ra, the major deity around Memphis, to become supreme in the Egyptian pantheon: "the king of the gods," the god "who exists in all things." Drawing on the wealth from tribute and booty from successful military campaigns, they built and rebuilt temples to Amun-Ra throughout the land and richly endowed them. By far the greatest of these temples was Karnak on the east bank at Thebes. The largest temple in Egypt, indeed in the world, Karnak Temple is actually a complex of temples that covers more than a hundred hectares and includes chapels and precincts to other gods, principally Mut, Montu, and Khonsu. Almost every major New Kingdom monarch sought to enhance his (or her, in the case of Hatshepsut) glory by adding some major feature to it. A sphinx-lined processional way led to the other imposing temple on the east bank, Luxor Temple. Every year, the statues of Amun and the other gods of Karnak would be taken along it to visit the gods who resided in Luxor Temple during the great Opet festival that celebrated the identity of the king as the earthly manifestation of Amun.

As the religious capital, Thebes was also the burial place of the kings of the New Kingdom. Unlike their predecessors in the Old and Middle Kingdoms, however, they were buried not in pyramids but in tombs cut into the rock of the large wadi in the western hills that became known as the Valley of the Kings. The royal tombs are long corridors that descend gently far into the hillside, opening into halls and chambers that were often sumptuously decorated with bright paintings depicting the afterlife and the relationship of the divine kings to the gods. The burial chambers were filled with fabulous supplies of grave goods. Security at the Valley of the Kings was maintained by regular patrols and guard stations at the mouth of the wadi and on the cliffs overhead. Although their tombs were largely out of sight from the general public, the kings' mortuary temples stood in prominent locations along the edge of cultivation on the west bank. With their large endowments, these imposing temples became important local foci of secular power.

Thebes was also the favored burial place of the New Kingdom's highest officials. The prime location was the hill of Sheikh Abd al-Qurna, a spectacular site overlooking the wide Theban plain. Whereas the royal paintings in the Valley of the Kings generally conformed strictly to the traditional artistic canon, those in the Tombs of the Nobles at Qurna took a very different turn, resulting in some of the most exciting developments in all of ancient Egyptian art. Here one finds an extraordinary degree of artistic innovation, resulting in more fluid lines, experiments in perspective, sensuousness, and, above all, naturalism. More scenes of daily life were depicted than ever before, providing a wealth of information about ancient society, as workers were shown going about their chores in the fields or workshops. Hunting scenes were a favorite subject, as were banquets, accompanied by music and dance, and with plenty of food and drink (perhaps too much drink, as some pictures show, so that a lady might throw up or a man be carried away unconscious). The tomb-owner and his wife are depicted observing it all happily, companionate, content—and forever young.

The men who built and decorated the tombs in the Valley of the Kings and at Sheikh Abd al-Qurna were a special group of scribes and artisans. They and their families lived in the workmen's village of Deir al-Medina, a well-preserved site and one so well documented that in many instances we know which artist lived in a particular house. Their tombs in the nearby hillsides provide numerous insights into their lives and work, as do the abundant finds of ostraka, inscribed with notes and rough plans. These were highly skilled, specialized craftsmen who prized their professions and strove to pass them on to their sons.

Because of the profusion of its glorious artistic and monumental remains—despite all that has been lost and continues to disappear—and because of its relative proximity in time, much of our picture of ancient Egypt is strongly conditioned by the New Kingdom. But the gaps in the period's historical record are, if anything, even more monumental than the remains. That is why historians often disagree so widely in their interpretations, and not just in descriptions of general trends, but also in statements of the most fundamental facts.

Consequently, it is impossible to write a full narrative history of the New Kingdom or of any other period in ancient Egyptian history.

After driving the Hyksos from Egypt, Ahmose continued his military activities without interruption, campaigning extensively in Palestine, where he may have been pursuing the Hyksos and destroying their Asiatic bases, and in Nubia. His Nubian operations were completed by Amenhotep I (c. 1525–1504 BC), who continued his father's ambitious building program that asserted the power and wealth of the restored kingdom and its monarchy. Loyal courtiers were well rewarded, as is evident in large numbers of beautifully decorated tombs.

Amenhotep I had no children, but the succession passed without problem to Tuthmosis I (c. 1504–1492 BC), whose father is unknown and who was related to Amenhotep I only by marriage, causing one to wonder why there is no break in Manetho's dynastic scheme at that point. Tuthmosis I built upon the accomplishments of Ahmose and Amenhotep I with extensive campaigns. In Asia he advanced the frontier to the Euphrates; in Nubia he reached the Fourth Cataract and beyond. Such expansion required a standing army of unprecedented size. Egypt became the most powerful state in the Near East, countered only by the Kingdom of Mitanni in northern Syria. Unlike Amenhotep I, Tuthmosis I had several children, including Hatshepsut, his daughter by his chief wife, and his son and successor by a lesser wife, also named Tuthmosis.

Tuthmosis II (c. 1492–1479 BC) may have been a sickly man, judging from the condition of his mummy. During a reign of thirteen years he left little monumental record, and his only known military expedition was in Nubia, where he committed the usual atrocities. He was married to his half-sister Hatshepsut, a measure likely designed to strengthen his claim to the throne, for her lineage was much more exalted. She had already received conspicuous attention during her father's reign, and during her husband's she enjoyed the high status of both Great Royal Wife and God's Wife of Amun. Tuthmosis II and Hatshepsut had a daughter, Neferure. With one of the women of his harem, Tuthmosis II had a son, another Tuthmosis, whom he designated as his successor.

When Tuthmosis III (c. 1479–1425 BC) came to the throne, he was just a child, so it was natural that his illustrious aunt and stepmother Hatshepsut (c. 1473–1458 BC) should act as regent for him. In the words of Ineni, who had been a high official during the previous reign, she "executed the affairs of the Two Lands according to her counsels. Egypt worked for her, head bowed." But during the seventh year of Tuthmosis III's reign she discarded the role of regent and became a ruling queen—or to put it another way, a female king of Egypt.

This was an innovative and dangerous experiment. There had been ruling queens before Hatshepsut, one at the end of the Sixth Dynasty and another at the end of the Twelfth, but both were exceptional, and both had presaged disaster, marking not only the end of their dynasties but also the beginnings of the First and Second Intermediate Periods. But as the daughter of one king and the wife of another, Hatshepsut knew what she was doing and the risks she was running. Her assumption of the throne was a carefully planned coup for which she had a supportive constituency among the nobility who were well rewarded with fine tombs. The individual that is best known, however, is a commoner named Senenmut, who obviously was an important man in her administration. Speculation, supported by little evidence, has assigned him the role of power behind the throne, and even that of her lover.

Hatshepsut's motives are also matters of speculation, not fact. Did she consider herself entitled to the kingship? New Kingdom royal women were often powerful people within the regime, so she may have decided that becoming a pharaoh herself was a logical next step. Some have wondered if she intended to establish a matriarchal succession. The titles she bestowed on her daughter Neferure could be interpreted to that end. Or she may have intended to marry Neferure to Tuthmosis III, but if that was the case then it is strange that she did not do so during her years of rule. (One line of speculation holds that Neferure was married to Tuthmosis III, which in turn raises sinister questions about her disappearance at about the time he began his sole rule.) A plausible hypothesis is that Hatshepsut took the throne as a dynastic self-defense measure. It is significant that she did not have Tuthmosis murdered, nor did she push him out of the political picture; on the contrary, although she was the senior partner, he was a co-regent king whom she entrusted with increasing responsibilities, military as well as civil, as he grew older. Had he been mistreated, it seems likely he would have used his power against her.

What is unmistakably clear is that Hatshepsut's was one of the outstanding reigns of the New Kingdom. The government was stable and well run; the country was prosperous. It was also militarily strong, for there is evidence for at least four campaigns of conquest during her reign. The Egyptian position in Syria may have slipped a bit, but that was probably more because of growing Mitanni strength than Egyptian negligence. Her most celebrated foreign adventure, however, was a peaceful one: a trading mission to the land of Punt in eastern Africa.

In building, Hatshepsut surpassed all her New Kingdom predecessors. Her monuments can be found throughout the country, including Middle Egypt where the small temple known as the Speos Artemidos records her restorations of damaged temples in that area. Her most memorable construction projects were at Thebes, including several important works at Karnak Temple, such as the Eighth Pylon and four obelisks, one of which is the tallest standing obelisk in Egypt. The architectural masterpiece of her reign is her visually stunning mortuary temple at Deir al-Bahari. She was the first king to have a tomb prepared in the Valley of the Kings.

One of the most frustrating things about Hatshepsut's story is that the ending is unknown. What happened to her after twenty-one years of rule? Was she overthrown by Tuthmosis III? Murdered? Or did she die powerful and honored? There is no evidence. Even the effacement of her monuments is mysterious. After her reign, her cartouches were obliterated, usually by being replaced with or adapted to those of other monarchs, although the odd inscription was missed. But this did not occur until near the end of Tuthmosis III's reign, raising yet more questions about his precise motives. Did he resent his powerful stepmother/aunt? If so, why did he wait so long to strike at her memory? Or was he erasing any rival familial claims that might jeopardize the succession of his son Amenhotep, which he was preparing during his last years? Perhaps on careful consideration it was decided that her reign violated *maat* and needed to be removed from the record, having served its stopgap purpose. These and other conjectures have been advanced, but none can be substantiated. Whatever the reason, the reign of Hatshepsut was largely forgotten until she was rediscovered in the nineteenth century.

Tuthmosis III entered his period of sole rule around 1458 BC when his reign still had twenty-three years to run. Almost immediately he embarked on a series of campaigns in Palestine and Syria that established him as the greatest conqueror in ancient Egyptian history. Quite likely he felt he needed to prove himself, but there was also danger that the region's city-states would fall into the orbit of the Kingdom of Mitanni, Egypt's major rival in the Near East. These campaigns were immensely rewarding in spoils, as is attested in detail on his monuments and by the tombs of his military commanders—another indication of the growing presence of the standing army. But in the long run, the Mitanni Kingdom was able to hold its own against Tuthmosis III, and he could not maintain his deepest penetrations into their sphere of influence. The conflict was unresolved at the time of his death. His most memorable construction project is the Festival Temple behind the central court in Karnak.

It might have been expected that the next king would follow in his father's martial footsteps. Amenhotep II (c. 1425–1400 BC) was an athletic young man, renowned for his skill at shooting a bow from his war chariot. He did indeed begin his reign with two Syrian campaigns from which he returned laden with spoils, but he saw that the advantages of peace could outweigh those of war. Once the situation in the north was stabilized, he concluded a lasting peace with the Kingdom of Mitanni that allowed him to devote the rest of his reign to internal affairs. He strengthened the administration by retaining tried and proven men from his father's time while infusing it with good new personnel of his own choosing. Where the arts of war had been most highly esteemed before, culture came to be valued as well. Texts from the Middle Kingdom, already regarded as a classical period in Egyptian literature, were copied and read, while standards rose in art where individual expression became noticeably more pronounced. It was a peaceful, wealthy country that Amenhotep II bequeathed to Tuthmosis IV (c. 1400–1390 BC), who reinforced the alliance with Mitanni by marrying a princess from that land.

The reign of Amenhotep III (c. 1390–1352 BC) was even more dazzling. Egypt ruled a widespread empire; it stood preeminent among other powers in the Near East; the country was at peace; prosperity reached new heights. Just what all that meant to most Egyptians of the time can never be known, but for Amenhotep III it provided a court culture of unequaled opulence and the opportunity to embark on a building program throughout Egypt matched by few ancient Egyptian kings. His major works at Thebes included the Third Pylon at Karnak and the great processional colonnade in Luxor Temple. On the west bank he built a palace and had a large artificial lake excavated far into the floodplain.

Yet the greatest of Amenhotep III's buildings has mostly vanished. Visitors to the Colossi of Memnon on the west bank at Thebes see two enormous seated statues that tower more than twenty meters above the level plain stretching all around them. Those two immense monuments are not statues of the Homeric hero Memnon but of Amenhotep III. They stood on each side of the main entrance to his cult temple, a structure that was much greater than the nearby Ramesseum or Medinet Habu, or than any other royal cult temple in ancient Egypt. Amenhotep III recorded that it was made of "white sandstone, wrought with gold throughout, its floor covered in silver, its doors with electrum." Unlike the other royal cult temples at Thebes, this one was built on low-lying land so that the waters of the inundation washed through its courts and colonnades, and around the bases of its numerous statues, of which only fragments remain.

Amenhotep III paid careful attention to diplomacy, as many surviving archival texts attest. His relations were especially close to the king of Mitanni, with whom he arranged marriages with not one but two Mitanni princesses, but he also maintained contact with other power centers like Babylonia, Mycenaean Greece, and Crete. When Amenhotep III died, the king of Mitanni wrote to his chief wife, Queen Tiye, and asked her to remind her son just how close relations had been between Egypt and Mitanni. Problems may have lurked beyond the shimmering horizon, but Amenhotep III's reign can be regarded as the high noon of the New Kingdom, the culmination of several generations of hard, constructive work.

Then the continuity was broken in a most unexpected and in some respects bizarre fashion. Amenhotep IV (c. 1352–1336 BC) was not originally intended to be king. He does not appear on monuments during his father's reign and may have been kept in the background. He would have had little training for the kingship, for only the death of an elder brother put him in line for the succession. There was also something distinctly strange about his appearance—a long gaunt face with unusually full lips, distended belly, wide hips, weak legs. Psychologically, he may have been consumed with resentment; he certainly had some new ideas. His reign was an aberration from which Egypt largely though never fully recovered, but since it continues to attract a disproportionate amount of attention, and since it had undeniable effects on the rest of New Kingdom history, it is worthwhile to linger over some of its aspects.

Amenhotep IV ruled in a more or less orthodox manner until the fifth year of his reign, when he instituted a radical change in religious policy that shook ancient Egyptian government and society to their foundations. Rejecting the traditional gods of Egypt, and above all the worship of the powerful god Amun-Ra, he replaced them with one god—more a universal force than a deity—the Aten, the solar disk itself. Unlike other gods, the Aten was not represented in human form, and never in animal form. He was simply shown as the sun, from which rays emanated downward. The only anthropomorphic touch was human hands at the ends of the rays, holding out *ankh*s, the looped crosses that symbolized life, to Akhenaten and his family. The Aten was "central, one, indivisible, and unique. . . . No one can escape its power, claims, or obligation." The supremacy of the Aten was emphasized by writing his name in cartouches, as if he were a king.

Amenhotep IV ostentatiously signaled his break with the past by changing his name from Amenhotep ('Amun is Content') to Akhenaten ('He Who Acts Effectively for Aten'). Favoring one god or group of gods over another was not necessarily a new thing in Egypt, nor were tendencies toward monotheism; also, there had been increasing solarization in religion during the preceding reigns. What was different about Akhenaten's religious policy was its exclusivity. There was no place in it for any of the traditional gods. He declared Amun anathema and sent troops of craftsmen to erase his name from the monuments. Revenues from Amun's establishments were diverted to the new temples for the Aten.

Akhenaten had no intention of remaining in Thebes, the center of the worship of his enemy Amun. Nor was he inclined to move to Memphis, for that place was also intimately identified with the old religion and its gods. Instead, he chose a location about halfway between Thebes and Memphis, where a broad, barren plain opens into the mountains that crowd close to the river on the east bank along that stretch of Middle Egypt. There he established an entirely new town, his capital, which he named Akhetaten ('Horizon of Aten'). We know it today as Amarna. Consecrated to the Aten, Akhenaten marked out its boundaries with a series of stelae, several of which survive.

Built quickly, the town of Amarna soon had some thirty thousand inhabitants. It was the result of both central planning and haphazard development. The main features were a palace complex in the north and a great temple of the Aten toward the center. Unlike most ancient Egyptian temples, which were dark, mysterious places, the Aten temple was unroofed, open to the sky. Administrative buildings, offices, workshops, stables, and other support buildings were constructed. Several clusters of private homes arose along the axis of the Royal Road down which Akhenaten and his chief wife Nefertiti rode in their chariots in great state. Because the town was built on barren ground above the reach of the inundation and abandoned soon after Akhenaten's death, it is the best preserved example of an ancient Egyptian city and has yielded a number of major discoveries. From the Hall of Records came the Amarna Letters, hundreds of baked brick tablets inscribed with cuneiform that record Egypt's relations with the other powers of the ancient New East. The house and yard of the sculptor Tuthmosis were scattered with unfinished pieces and models, including the famous painted limestone bust of Nefertiti, now in Berlin's Egyptian Museum (much to the annoyance of some Egyptians, who resent the way it and many other antiquities have been exported from their country).

Of course, an ancient Egyptian town had to make provision for its dead as well as its living. For the high officials, tombs were cut into the hills to the north and south, in clear sight of town. Their walls were decorated with scenes of the royal family and of the Aten bestowing his *ankh*-bearing rays. There also are found the only surviving texts of the *Hymn to the Aten*. In a variation on the Valley of the Kings, Akhenaten chose a wadi east of town for the royal tombs. Several were planned, but just one came anywhere near completion. "If I die in any town of the north, south, west, or east, in the multitude of years," Akhenaten commanded, "I will be brought, and my burial be made in Akhetaten." The only securely attested burial there, however, is that of his second daughter Meketaten, poignantly documented by murals showing her grief-stricken family, the only such royal depictions in all of ancient Egyptian art. Strangely enough, none of the commoners' graves have been located at Amarna, leading to conjecture that they may have been transported by river to traditional cemeteries in their homelands.

Akhenaten's chief wife Nefertiti occupied a powerful position in the regime. Much more than a chief wife, she became Akhenaten's official coregent in the later years of his reign. Her extraordinary status is shown in her distinctive crown, and she is even depicted in the traditional royal pose of a king smiting his enemies. Akhenaten, Nefertiti, and their six daughters are frequently and prominently displayed as an intimate, informal family group in Amarna art. Nefertiti may have been eclipsed for a time by a lesser wife named Kiya who received the special title of "Greatly Beloved Wife of the King." It was probably with Kiya that Akhenaten had a son whom a contemporary source describes as "the King's bodily son, his beloved, Tutankhaten." This Tutankhaten was the future king Tutankhamun. But after a few years, Kiya suddenly disappears from the record, her names erased from the monuments, and Nefertiti reemerges transcendent. Clearly Nefertiti was not a woman to trifle with.

The innovations in Amarna art are as astonishing as those in religion. Naturalism had been developing for some time in New Kingdom art, but it had never been applied to the royal family. Now the highly developed skills of court artists depicted Akhenaten, Nefertiti, and their daughters in the most charmingly unaffected poses. In one scene, Akhenaten cradles and kisses his eldest while two of the others clamber over Nefertiti, one of them pointing at her father and saying something unheard to her mother about him, a family moment caught forever, as is another in a depiction of Nefertiti sitting on Akhenaten's knee. Akhenaten is almost always depicted not in idealized form, but as he really was, though sometimes the strange shapes of his body are exaggerated and stylized, and even applied to other individuals. Deprived of much of their traditional repertoire, such as kings in the company of gods, artists paid closer attention to the human form and attempted new techniques, including experiments in conveying impressions of depth. Akhenaten was also an ambitious builder, especially of temples to the Aten, and perhaps a hasty one as well, for his engineers used smaller blocks of stone, called *talatat*, that could be set in place quickly. Unfortunately, that also meant they could be dismantled more easily and recycled into other buildings after Akhenaten's death.

Naturalism found new expression in literature as well as art. The best-known work to emerge from Amarna is the *Hymn to the Aten*, a series of poems to the god that some scholars believe was written by Akhenaten himself.

You rise beautifully on the horizon,
Oh Aten, living creator of life.
You fill the land with beauty
When you rise in the east.
Your are beautiful, mighty,
Shining high over the earth.

Unlike earlier New Kingdom works, which were composed in the somewhat archaic classical language that was formalized during the Middle Kingdom, Amarna literature was written in Late Egyptian, which was much closer to the everyday speech of that moment.

Remote though Akhenaten was at Amarna, he was by no means isolated from affairs of state. Close by the northern palace was a harbor on the Nile through which communication was maintained with the country's other administrative centers and the capitals of the nomes. Foreign envoys came to present their compliments and gifts. Among the Amarna Letters is a complaint from the king of Assyria that his delegation had been kept standing too long in the sun. Nor was Akhenaten, as has sometimes been assumed, a pacifist. A rebellion in Nubia was firmly suppressed during the twelfth year of his reign. But when the expanding Kingdom of the Hittites defeated Egypt's ally, the Mitanni kingdom, weakening Egypt's control over her northern tier of client states, Akhenaten did not mount an expedition against the new power in the north. The Amarna Letters contain hysterical appeals for help—just three hundred Egyptian soldiers, the prince of Byblos pleaded—and the Egyptian deputy at Jerusalem warned that the situation was deteriorating rapidly, but Akhenaten responded cautiously by maintaining a regular military presence in northern Syria to prevent anyone else from switching sides. Evidence suggests that his lack of more energetic action against the Hittites may have caused unease within the army, hitherto a strong base of support, but considering subsequent Syrian events, Akhenaten's restraint may have made a wise adjustment to changing realities.

Just how deeply Akhenaten's innovative experiment affected Egypt as a whole is unknown. At the lower levels of society, among the great masses of the people, it may have made little difference. Even among the remains of the workmen's village at Amarna there are plenty of signs that traditional cults were observed, at least privately. For the common folk, the new religion cannot have been satisfying—no more of the great festivals like Opet, no mythology, no imagery, not much of an afterlife. As for the established priesthood, their acceptance of the new religion can only have been grudging at best. One thing is certain. The fact that Akhenaten was able to institute his religious reforms is unmistakable evidence of a powerful monarchy that rested on strong foundations. But the way he exercised his power eroded those very foundations while building no substantial new ones. During the later years of the reign there are hints of trouble and evidence that he took initiatives of reconciliation with the old cults.

The Amarna experiment is another intriguing episode in ancient Egyptian history where the ending is not fully known. Akhenaten died around 1336 BC and would have been buried in his tomb at Amarna, according to his wishes. Unfortunately the tomb was carelessly cleaned out after its discovery so that remaining evidence was lost, and there is a good deal of debate about whether he was actually buried there or at Thebes. No evidence remains to tell us what happened to Nefertiti. It is possible that she died a few years before her husband and was buried in his tomb. Akhenaten's daughter Meritaten was married to a mysterious, ephemeral king named Smenkhkare (c. 1338–1336 BC). It is debated whether Smenkhkare ever had an independent reign, and even who he was—or who *she* was, because Smenkhkare may well have been Nefertiti, who depicted her daughter Meritaten as the Great Wife in the surviving iconography. Another daughter, Ankhesenpaaten, was married to Tutankhaten, who was probably her half-brother, the son of Akhenaten by Kiya. The familial connection is reinforced by a recent analysis of clothing in his tomb which shows the same distorted body shape as Akhenaten's.

Because Tutankhaten (c. 1336–1327 BC) was a child when he ascended to the throne, a regency was assumed by Ay, a senior official in Akhenaten's government, and Horemheb, the army's commander-in-chief. The Amarna experiment came to an abrupt halt. Tutankhaten moved from Amarna, which ceased to be the political and religious capital of Egypt and soon turned into a ghost town. The administration returned to Memphis, and Thebes was again the religious center. Akhenaten's religious innovations were not merely abandoned but actively expunged, with such success that Akhenaten vanished from human memory until he was recovered from oblivion by nineteenth-century scholarship. The temples of the old gods were restored, and the ascendancy of Amun reestablished, and with a vengeance; Akhenaten's palaces and temples were demolished, his cartouches defaced. When it was absolutely necessary to mention him in official documents, he was referred to as "the Enemy." Tutankhaten's name changed to Tutankhamun (and Ankhesenpaaten's to Ankhesenpaamun). Akhenaten's restrained policy in northern Syria was also reversed, but perhaps unwisely because the Hittites defeated the Egyptians at Amqa, leaving the situation on the northern frontier much as before.

When he was about seventeen years old and in the tenth year of his reign, Tutankhamun died unexpectedly. Many hypotheses have been advanced about his demise, including natural causes, murder, a chariot accident, and mortal wounds sustained in combat. He was buried not in the tomb originally intended for him, but in a lesser one that happened to be almost ready for occupancy. The rediscovery of his tomb by Howard Carter in 1922 was a major event in the history of Egyptology and exerted a powerful effect on the popular imagination. "Gold—everywhere the glint of gold," was what Carter saw when he first peered inside. Yet, it is well to remember that the boy-king was an insignificant monarch whose burial was hastily improvised, as is suggested by the disorder of the precious goods crammed into his small tomb. The accoutrements in the tombs of some of the great kings were probably much more magnificent, just as their tombs were much larger and more elaborate.

Tutankhamun was succeeded by Ay (c. 1327–1323 BC) during whose brief reign a curious incident occurred that is recorded in the Amarna Letters. Tutankhamun's young widow, Ankhesenpaamun, wrote to the Hittite king Shupiluliuma to ask for a prince to marry her and become king of Egypt. "My husband has died and I have no son, but of you it is said that you have many sons. If you would send me one of your sons, he could become my husband. I will on no account take one of my subjects and make him my husband. I am very much afraid." Suspicious at first, Shupiluliuma finally agreed to send one of his sons, Zanzanza, to Egypt, but the prince was murdered on the way, likely on the orders of Horemheb who succeeded the aged Ay.

Under Horemheb (c. 1323–1295 BC) the campaign against the material remains and indeed the very memory of Akhenaten's heresies reached its maximum. His commitment to Amun is manifest in the Great

Hypostyle Hall at Karnak Temple which was begun during his reign. But his efforts to recover the advanced Egyptian position in northern Syria, where conflict with the Hittites had resumed after the murder of Zanzanza, were unsuccessful. Horemheb's death ended the Eighteenth Dynasty according to Manetho's scheme, although the Nineteenth Dynasty kings regarded him as their founder.

After the short reign of Ramesses I (c. 1295–1294 BC), who had been Horemheb's vizier and was well advanced in years, Ramesses' son Seti I (c. 1294–1279 BC) became king. An energetic ruler, Seti I reopened the mines and quarries in Sinai and the Eastern Desert, and in Nubia where he sent raiding expeditions, bringing new wealth into the land. To the north he brought the rebellious vassal city-states of Palestine back into line and pushed back the Hittite sphere of influence in northern Syria, although the Hittites were able to recover most of the lost ground and remained as Egypt's major rival in the Near East. On the west, he countered incursions by the Libyans, who were to plague Egypt for the remainder of the New Kingdom.

Seti I was also a notable builder. He continued the monumental campaign against Akhenaten's memory, but in a more positive way, by commanding droves of chiselers to restore the inscriptions of Amun and the pre-Amarna pharaohs that had been altered by the heretic king. Most of the restoration of the traditional temples begun by his predecessors was completed by Seti I. His own temples at Thebes and Abydos both display unusually fine taste and expert workmanship, maintaining the high standard set in the reign of Amenhotep III and incorporating some of the artistic innovations of the Amarna experiment. He continued work on Karnak's Great Hypostyle Hall, where his exploits are carved on the outside wall. After a successful reign, Seti I was buried in the most magnificent tomb in the Valley of the Kings.

Ramesses II (c. 1279–1213 BC) was an ancient Egyptian king who became a legend in his own time—and of his own making. Everything about his reign was stupendous in scale, or presented as if it was. He ruled for an extraordinary sixty-six years, during which he and his seven wives plus his harem of beautiful women produced at least forty-five daughters and forty sons. He outlived twelve of those sons and prepared a vast tomb for them in the Valley of the Kings in addition to his own.

The building program of Ramesses II was staggering in size. The best known of his temples are the Ramesseum at Thebes, immortalized in Percy Bysshe Shelley's "Ozymandias," and Abu Simbel in Nubia with its four colossal seated statues; but there were many more scattered along the length of Egypt and Nubia, though several of these were usurped from previous rulers, especially Amenophis III. Some of these buildings, like the Ramesseum, were architectural masterpieces, but others were not as good, suffering from an emphasis on quantity at the expense of quality. Perhaps in continued reaction to the Amarna innovations, there was a return to classicism in architecture, a trend reflected in a revival of great classical literary works; but contemporary literature was composed in the modern language, like Amarna productions. Statues of Ramesses II were so ubiquitous that they must have kept armies of sculptors busy, although many of the statues were appropriated from earlier kings. Recycling of royal monuments was a well-established practice in ancient Egypt.

As a military leader, Ramesses II acquitted himself well early in his reign in Nubia, where affairs often needed putting in order. His temple at Beit al-Wali, which has been resited just above the Aswan High Dam, attests to this. But by far his most sensational exploits were in Syria, where the Hittite Empire posed a continuing threat to Egypt's possessions and allies. Taking the field in personal command of his forces, Ramesses met his adversary, the Hittite king Muwatalli, at Qadesh. Inadequate Egyptian reconnaissance allowed the Hittites to catch the Egyptian army on the march and quickly destroy part of it, leaving Ramesses isolated. According to his accounts, boldly proclaimed on the pylons of the Ramesseum, Luxor Temple, and many other places, Ramesses single-handedly charged the enemy six times, routing a total of 3,500 chariots, and "made the plain of Qadesh turn white" with corpses while Muwatalli "stood averted, shrinking, and afraid." The reality, as one might suspect, was somewhat different. Ramesses probably did fight vigorously, not that he had much choice, but he was saved by the timely appearance of his bodyguard and the rest of his army. The battle itself was an indecisive encounter in which neither side performed particularly well. The situation in the north was finally stabilized not by fighting but by diplomacy, in a treaty that is preserved in both Egyptian hieroglyphs and Hittite cuneiform, and was sealed with a marriage alliance.

In contrast to the apparent splendor of the reign of Ramesses II, the later years of the Nineteenth Dynasty are obscure but were frequently troubled. Ramesses' son and successor Merneptah (c. 1213–1203 BC) was probably already in his sixties when he came to the throne (Ramesses II was over ninety when he died) and reigned less than ten years. The great event of his reign occurred in the Delta, where Libyan infiltration, long a problem, escalated into a full-fledged invasion. Merneptah responded effectively, meeting his foes near the modern town of Bilbays and crushing them. In a gruesome detail, he boasted that 6,200 of the slain enemies' severed penises were carried away as trophies. The survivors were settled in military colonies, chiefly in the Delta, where they would become significant factors in Egyptian political life.

Merneptah therefore acquitted himself well enough, but much of the reign of Seti II (c. 1200–1194 BC) was complicated by a struggle against a usurper named Amonmessu, perhaps a son of one of Merneptah's lesser queens, who was overcome only with great difficulty. When Seti II was succeeded by his only son Siptah (c. 1194–1188 BC), a crippled boy, the young king's stepmother Twosre acted as regent, supported by a powerful official named Bay who was described as the "chancellor of the entire land" and whose status was such that he was accorded a tomb in the Valley of the Kings. After Siptah's death, Twosre (c. 1188–1186) ruled openly as a pharaoh, as Hatshepsut had done in the Eighteenth Dynasty, long before.

Twosre's death ended the Nineteenth Dynasty. How the Twentieth Dynasty came to power is unknown but the propaganda of its first king, Sethnakht (c. 1186–1184 BC) spoke of a time of anarchy and illegitimate rule by a Syrian upstart, possibly Chancellor Bay, that was settled by Sethnakht's resolute actions. His enmity toward the preceding regime is apparent in the appropriation of Twosre's tomb in the Valley of the Kings for his own.

After a short reign Sethnakht was succeeded by his son Ramesses III (c. 1184–1153 BC). The problems this king encountered were manifold, including a plot on his life from within the palace known as the Harem Conspiracy. Administrative difficulties resulted in the first recorded strike in history when the craftsmen from the workmen's village at Deir al-Medina protested that they had not been paid and staged a sit-down in front of the temples. Ramesses III twice had to take the field to counter resurgent Libyan problems in the Delta, and although he was victorious in each instance—again with grisly body-part counts—raids by smaller bands of Libyans reached as far south as Thebes, forcing the royal workmen of Deir al-Medina to interrupt their work and take refuge behind the nearby temple walls at Medinet Habu, demonstrating the kingdom's inability to maintain internal security. But the greatest crisis of the reign, the invasion of the Sea Peoples, was met and overcome.

The Sea Peoples were not a nation but a mass migration of desperate displaced peoples. They were also a mighty force, bent on plunder and destruction, as well as settlement, and they wrought havoc throughout the eastern Mediterranean and the Near East. Formidable on both land and sea, they smashed the mighty Hittite Empire and overran Anatolia, Cyprus, and northern Syria, where they razed the ancient city of Ugarit to the ground. The Egyptian sources spoke of the Sea Peoples with awe: "They laid their hands upon the countries as far as the circuit of the earth, their hearts confident and trusting: 'Our plans will succeed!'" In the eighth year of Ramesses III's reign, they turned their full attention toward Egypt, presenting one of the gravest dangers the country ever faced, for invasion and occupation by the Sea Peoples undoubtedly would have been a far worse catastrophe than the Hyksos.

Fortunately Egypt had time to prepare. The eastern approaches to the Delta were fortified, and an army moved into southern Palestine. When the hosts of the Sea Peoples appeared on the frontier by land, they were soundly defeated. But the enemy also attacked by water, as their terrifying warships with distinctively curved rams penetrated the Delta. It is an understatement to say that the ancient Egyptians were not great sailors, but Ramesses III used an innovative combination of land and marine tactics to repulse this attempt as well. His victories are boldly proclaimed in pictures on the first pylon of his temple at Medinet Habu. Because of them, Ramesses III is sometimes referred to as the last great pharaoh of Egypt, so it was perhaps appropriate that he was buried in a grand tomb in the Valley of the Kings.

The rest of the Twentieth Dynasty was a continuous series of kings named Ramesses, so that the dynasty is also known as the Ramessid era. Historical details about the individual kings are scanty, but the general outline is a time of steady decline. Egypt had been spared invasion by the Sea Peoples, but the onslaught so damaged Egyptian imperial and diplomatic arrangements in Syria and Palestine that those areas were lost. After Ramesses III, no major temples were built within New Kingdom Egypt. Administration continued to falter, as is again shown by the experiences of the workmen of Deir al-Medina, whose problems with pay became so bad that their chief workman and scribe finally found it necessary to collect government taxes themselves to support the community. A breakdown of order is also evident in an epidemic of tomb-robbing on the west bank at Thebes. Robbing tombs was nothing new in ancient Egypt, but this was on such a scale, implicating people ranging from common workmen to high officials, that a strong government should at least have been able to curb if not eliminate it.

The political and religious authority of the kings eroded. In theory, the king was the ultimate head of every part of the government; his was the wealth of the land; indeed, he owned the land itself. In practice, however, the old tendency toward heredity in both property and position reasserted itself, so that lands and government posts were passed on from father to son, resulting in the formation of firmly established families whose wealth and power were largely independent of the king, leaving him with little influence and no direct control over them.

By the same token, temples progressively accumulated wealth to the extent that by the end of the reign of Ramesses III it is estimated that they owned about one-third of the cultivable land and one-fifth of the people in Egypt. The most dangerous concentration of this sacred power was in the office of the High Priest of Amun at Karnak, who was the virtual ruler of Upper Egypt. Like other important positions, the priesthood became hereditary, therefore largely independent of the king, and it eventually developed an institutional power that rivaled the king's. The restoration of Amun-Ra had gained too much momentum, shifting power away from the king into the hands of the priests of Amun.

The restoration of Amun-Ra also undermined royal authority in more insidious ways, such as the development of what is termed personal piety. Previously the king alone had mediated between the gods and humankind: he was the earthly representative of the gods, therefore obedience was due him because he was executing their wishes, and only through him could the favor of the gods be obtained. After the Amarna period, however, Amun-Ra came to be perceived not only as a supremely powerful deity, but also as an omnipresent one. "Far away he is as one who sees, near he is as one who hears," reads one hymn to Amun. An individual could pray directly to Amun-Ra, and the god would hear. Among the many depictions of this divine attentiveness is the Nineteenth Dynasty stela of a man named Mai, showing him kneeling, praying to Amun-Ra, "He Who Listens to Prayers." To make the point explicit, the stela portrays three giant sets of listening ears. As the religious function of the king diminished, his political authority declined accordingly.

Contrary to what might be expected, the army played no major role in the decline; only right at the end of the Ramessid era can anything like a naked grab for power by the military be seen. Garrisons were too widely dispersed to take concerted action. Also, colonists and other militia-like elements were not ordinarily armed. When the need arose, they were served with arms from arsenals in the major royal cities where, as a text explicitly states, they were armed "in the presence of Pharaoh."

The reign of Ramesses XI, the last king of the Twentieth Dynasty and of the New Kingdom, was unusually long by Ramessid standards, twenty-eight years, and is well documented compared to the shadowy ones that went before, but the documentation has few good things to tell. The most eloquent testimony to the hard times on which Egypt had fallen is preserved in the misadventures of Wenamun, whom Ramesses XI dispatched to Byblos to obtain cedar for the divine boat of Amun-Ra. Previously such missions were well financed and conducted in great state. Wenamun, however, traveled alone with only a small amount of gold and silver, and had to book passage on a foreign merchant vessel. He was robbed on the way so when he reached Byblos he had neither money nor credentials. The prince of Byblos, once styled as the "servant of Egypt," received the pathetic emissary with contempt, pointing out that in bygone days as many as six ships laden with precious metals were sent to purchase his cedar. He was not subject to the king of Egypt, the prince declared, and refused to give Wenamun anything without payment.

Egypt had already lost its Asiatic possessions in earlier Ramessid times; under Ramesses XI, Nubia and Upper Egypt fell away as well. After several years of confusion in which Ramesses XI ineffectively tried to intervene, a general named Piankh staged a military coup at Thebes and took the offices of southern vizier, King's Son of Kush, and High Priest of Amun, effectively establishing himself as an independent ruler. Piankh was succeeded by his son-in-law Herihor, who made his position explicit by assuming royal titles after Ramesses XI died.

Ramesses XI was the last king for whom a tomb was cut into the Valley of the Kings, but even this monument bears sad witness. It was never completed, and Ramesses XI was buried elsewhere. During the Twenty-first Dynasty, when Pinudjem I was High Priest of Amun, it served as a chop shop where royal mummies and other objects from neighboring tombs were stripped of their valuables, a shabby ending for the glorious New Kingdom monarchy.

6 The Third Intermediate Period and the Late Period

The concept of the Third Intermediate Period (c. 1069–715 BC) fits uncomfortably into the established periodic format of ancient Egyptian history. For one thing, it is disproportionate for an 'intermediate' period to be some 360 years long, a span much greater than both of the previous intermediate periods combined, longer than the Middle Kingdom, and nearly as long as the Late Period. Also, persistent thematic threads ran through the Third Intermediate Period, giving it much more coherence than the ensuing Late Period.

The strong central authority and administrative unity that had characterized much—though by no means all—of the Old Kingdom, Middle Kingdom, and New Kingdom were certainly absent during the Third Intermediate Period, as Egypt was divided between two political centers of gravity, one in the Delta and the other in Upper Egypt, with territories in Middle Egypt oscillating between them as the fortunes of the polar regimes waxed and waned. But the period was by no means a return to the lawlessness and regionalism that characterized earlier times of disorder. Indeed, during much of the period, a working *modus vivendi* was achieved that enabled Egypt to function on a reasonably stable basis, even though its weight in the Near East's balance of power was greatly diminished from the imperial days of the New Kingdom.

In the north, Smendes, the first king of the Twenty-first Dynasty, transferred the capital from Pi-Ramesses, whose harbor had become silted, to Tanis, approximately twenty kilometers to the north in the Delta. The remains of Tanis have a distinctly thrown-together look about them, with assorted statues, columns, and building blocks, some dating as far back as the Old Kingdom, taken from various sites and not always assembled in orderly, logical fashion. But it was a large town, enclosed within walls ten meters high and fifteen thick. The royal tombs of the Twenty-first and Twenty-second Dynasties were in the middle of town, beside the great temple of Amun-Ra. Some of the coffins were of silver, a metal more precious than gold in pharaonic times. The discovery of these undisturbed tombs in 1939 rivaled that of Tutankhamun's in importance, but was overshadowed by the outbreak of the Second World War. The control of the northern kings extended through the Delta and into Middle Egypt to the town of al-Hiba, fifty miles beyond the Fayyum.

Farther south was the domain of the High Priests of Amun, who ruled as kings in all but name, and occasionally in name also. Their government functioned as a theocracy in that the edicts of the High Priest had the force of commands from the god. When necessary, these could be confirmed by oracles. One source of revenue for the priestly regime in the early Third Intermediate Period was mining the wealth of the Valley of the Kings, which had been largely preserved from the wave of tomb robbing at the end of the Twenty-first Dynasty. Fortunately the tomb of Tutankhamun escaped notice at this time because it was located on the floor of the valley, where it had long ago been covered by rubble and forgotten. As the royal tombs were cleared of their valuables, the mummies of the kings were stashed in other places. One such cache in a reused Eleventh Dynasty shaft tomb at Deir al-Bahari was discovered by local antiquity dealers in 1871 and excavated by Egyptologists four years later. It contained forty royal mummies, including those of Ahmose I, Tuthmosis I, II, and III, Seti I, and Ramesses II. A second cache was later discovered, and there may well have been yet another. The workmen's community at Deir al-Medina was disbanded, there being no further need of its inhabitants' services.

The southern extremity of the Theban realm of the High Priest of Amun did not extend far beyond the First Cataract. As at the close of the Middle Kingdom, the Nubians had taken advantage of Egyptian weaknesses and reasserted their control of Lower Nubia. Little is known about the process, which was probably gradual, but it worked greatly to the advantage of a resurgent Kingdom of Kush, this time with its capitals much farther south, around Gebel Barkal near the Fourth Cataract. Over time, the Kushite Kingdom filled the void left by the collapse of Egyptian authority in the region. Although titles like "King's Son of Kush" persisted for some time in governmental nomenclature, the Egyptians left the south alone militarily, apart from a short-lived intrusion as far as the Second Cataract in the mid-ninth century BC, and engaged in trading and diplomatic relations with the Kushites.

Thebes made token acknowledgments of northern supremacy, but the political division of Egypt was complete. Unlike the preceding separations of the country into competing northern and southern centers, however, relations between the two kingdoms were generally tolerant, cemented by diplomatic interchanges. The High Priest Pinudjem I had married a daughter of Ramesses XI, and one of their sons became Psusennes I (c. 1039–991 BC), the third king of the Twenty-first Dynasty. In turn, Psusennes I married his daughter to the Theban High Priest Menkheperre; their son eventually became the High Priest Pinudjem II. But the period was nevertheless one of extensive internecine fighting, particularly in the south where rebellions persisted, and later among the competitive fiefdoms that developed in the Delta, in a contest for control of the diminished resources of an impoverished country.

Another factor was the Libyans, whose numbers were swelled by steadily increasing immigration. Once despised intruders, they had become part of the Egyptian system with the practice of settling them in military colonies begun by Ramesses III. Their presence in the army increased to the point that it may have been almost entirely composed of them by the end of the New Kingdom. Many Libyans rose to high offices in the administration. Shoshenq I, for example, was very much an establishment figure by the time he took the throne. Many retained a strong sense of ethnic identity, however, and their settlements provided power bases for local dynastic families.

The founder of the Twenty-second Dynasty, Shoshenq I (c. 945–924 BC), came from a Libyan family in the Delta city of Bubastis. Exploiting his position as army commander and close ties by marriage to Psusennes II, he assumed the throne with a minimum of opposition and proved himself the outstanding king of the Third Intermediate Period. Whereas the Twenty-first Dynasty had accepted the division of the country, Shoshenq I strove to restore its integrity. He installed his son Iuput, who was already army commander, as High Priest of Amun and developed bonds of loyalty with regionally influential families.

Returning to a forward policy in the Levant, where Egypt had been inactive for over a century, Shoshenq I took advantage of the division of the short-lived unified Kingdom of Israel following Solomon's death in 930 BC into the Kingdoms of Judah and Israel. Leading a strong army that included 1,200 chariots, he defeated them both and laid siege to Jerusalem. Only a heavy price paid by the city's defenders saved it from capture. The First Book of Kings in the Bible states that that Shoshenq "took away the treasures of the house of the Lord, and the treasures of the king's house; he even took away all: and he took away all the shields of gold which Solomon had made." The restored Egyptian presence in Palestine was evanescent, however, and quickly diminished after Shoshenq I's reign. When he returned to Egypt, Shoshenq I undertook several notable building projects, including a new court at the Second Pylon at Karnak.

Shoshenq I's son and successor Osorkon II* (c. 924–889 BC) continued his father's building programs, most notably in the family's base at Bubastis, and maintained control in the south by making his son High Priest of Amun as well as his co-regent in the north. This son duly succeeded as Shoshenq II (c. 889 BC), but any impetus toward reintegration of the two parts of the country in his person died with him a few months later. Under his half-brother, Takelot I (c. 889–874 BC), the tendency toward political fragmentation resumed though his authority, despite a reign of fifteen years, and the fact that Takelot I left no major monuments indicates a weak rule. Over the following decades, the post of High Priest of Amun once more became hereditary, as did other high offices, increasing provincial independence at the expense of royal control.

---

* According to some series, he is numbered Osorkon I.

Northern attempts to reimpose authority were violently resisted by Thebes, where the High Priest Hariese declared himself king. Many local rulers, particularly in the Delta, achieved so much autonomy that several of them also proclaimed their kingship. Some of these may be members of Manetho's Twenty-third Dynasty, but that is not certain. By 730 BC, according to the count of one modern historian, "there were two kings in the Delta (at Bubastis and Leontopolis), one at Hermopolis, and one at Herakleopolis in Upper Egypt; besides those in the Delta, and virtually independent, were a 'Prince Regent,' four Great Chiefs of the Ma, and a Prince of the West in Sais. This last, Tefnakht, had taken over all the territories of the western Delta and Memphis, and was expanding into the northern reach of Upper Egypt."[8]

Such a political hodge-podge presented a golden opportunity for the kings of Kush, who had consolidated their control over Lower Nubia and made themselves major players on the Egyptian political scene as well. When Kashta (c. 770–747 BC), the first king of the Twenty-fifth Dynasty of Nubian kings of Egypt, marched north, he probably encountered little resistance from the Theban state. A stela at Aswan proclaims him "King of Upper and Lower Egypt," though his authority is unlikely to have extended north of Thebes. Kashta soon returned to his capital at Napata, far to the south near the Fourth Cataract, where he was succeeded by his son Piye (c. 747–716 BC).

Control of Thebes was exercised through the remarkable institution of the Divine Adoratrices of Amun. That venerable office, dating back to the reign of Hatshepsut, had been put to new purposes by Osorkon V* (c. 730–715 BC) of the Twenty-third Dynasty, who hoped to prevent the reemergence of a hereditary high priesthood of Amun with all its associated problems. He appointed his daughter Shepenwepet I as Divine Adoratrice of Amun and, as such, the supreme religious figure at Thebes. The Divine Adoratrice henceforth could not marry; her office would be passed on through a process of adoption through which the royal family could choose the adoratrice and therefore control Thebes. But it was Piye who made the choice by compelling Shepenwepet to adopt his sister Amenirdis I.

---

* Sometimes numbered Osorkon IV.

The political situation in Lower Egypt remained unstable because of the competing local centers of power, of which Sais, a town on a main branch of the Nile in the western Delta, was emerging as the most powerful. When Tefnakhte of Sais began to extend his power into the Valley of the Nile, infringing on the Theban sphere, Piye responded vigorously. Campaigning as far north as Memphis, which was taken by storm, Piye compelled Tefnakhte and the local dynasts who had allied with him to submit, although they were allowed to retain their positions. His achievements are recorded on a remarkable stela at Gebel Barkal that shows just how Egyptianized he was. Piye is presented as the exemplar of a pure Egyptian civilization that had been sullied by unworthy rulers. His conduct in Egypt, at least according to surviving records, was much more humane that that of the pharaohs who had ravaged Nubia so many times before.

After showing due homage to the gods and celebrating his coronation, Piye returned to Napata, but what he had seen in the north obviously made a deep impression on him, for he had a pyramid constructed for himself near Gebel Barkal and became the first king of Egypt to be buried in a pyramid in eight hundred years. His example was imitated during the next thousand years with the result that about twice as many pyramids were constructed in Nubia as in Egypt. The Nubian pyramids are not as tall as the Egyptian ones and have a noticeably steeper angle, but they were well made of good stone so that most of the damage or destruction that many of them have suffered has been from human activity, not natural forces. Thus an ancient Egyptian idea, one of a great many, was transplanted far up the Nile and took firm root.

Sais had been suppressed, but its power was not broken. Under Tefnakhte's successor Bocchoris (c. 720–715 BC), whom Manetho assigns to a brief Twenty-fourth Dynasty, there was another bid for Saite power in the north, so that conflict resumed just as Piye's brother Shabaka (c. 716–702 BC) succeeded to the throne. (Here it might be noted that Kushite succession, in a pattern similar to others in the East to this day, gave priority to the late king's brothers over his sons, and then moved down to the next generation. Hence, Shabaka was in turn succeeded by his nephews, Piye's sons, Shebiktu and Taharqa.) Again the king marched north to war from Nubia. Bocchoris paid for his ambition by being killed in battle or, according to one account, burned alive, but even so the Saite principality was still not destroyed.

It is at about this point (some put it a bit earlier, others slightly later) that modern chronological organization dates the beginning of the Late Period, which continues until Egypt was incorporated into the empire of Alexander the Great. Of all the periods imposed on ancient Egyptian history, this one seems the least satisfactory as a coherent concept, beginning as it does with a spell of Nubian rule that was followed successively by Assyrian domination, establishment of a native Egyptian dynasty, conquest by the Persians, reestablishment of native rule, and finally reassertion of Persian control. It has also been disparaged as a time when Egypt was merely a "broken reed." As one distinguished Egyptologist said in the mid-twentieth century, "The inner dynamic power was dead in the organism." Yet, Egypt was still to show an extraordinary degree of creativity and adaptability while preserving many of the values most important to it. Also, whoever was in charge, the land was more or less united.

After Shabaka's victory over Sais, the kings of the Twenty-fifth Dynasty took a much closer interest in Egypt. Instead of returning promptly to Napata as his predecessors had done, Shabaka and his Nubian successors ruled from Thebes and from Memphis, paying particular attention to the latter in a deliberate effort to legitimize their rule, as well as to exploit the strategic advantages of the ancient capital. They expressed their desire to be accepted as proper Egyptian pharaohs in a deliberate appeal to the past that affected almost every aspect of court culture during the Late Period. A trend toward archaism, already evident under the Libyan monarchs, was accelerated in religion, literature, art, and architecture, as models from the Old Kingdom and Middle Kingdom were closely imitated. In an active building program, old temples were restored and new ones built. Egypt was more united and vital than it had been in centuries. Far from being a stagnant period of foreign domination, the Twenty-fifth Dynasty was a time of Egyptian revival.

Unfortunately Egypt no longer enjoyed the relative isolation that had long protected it from the vicissitudes of Near Eastern affairs. The Assyrian Empire was in the ascendancy. The first clash with that ruthless state came in 701 BC when the Egyptians fought alongside the Kingdom of Judah against the Assyrian king Sennacherib. The result was inconclusive, but the Assyrians were provoked, making it just a question of time and opportunity before they turned on Egypt. The first attack came under their king Esarhaddon in 674 BC. He was repulsed at the frontier, but a second attempt three years later captured Memphis, forcing Taharqa (c. 690–664 BC) to flee to Nubia. According to their practice, the Assyrians entrusted the government to local authorities, in this case rulers of the Delta principalities, including Sais, and departed to intimidate other portions of their restive empire, enabling Taharqa to return and recover control of Egypt. Esarhaddon died before he could mount another Egyptian expedition, but his successor Assurbanipal, with Saitic collaboration, defeated the new Twenty-fifth Dynasty king Tantamani (c. 664–656) in two devastating campaigns that reached as far south as Thebes and forced Tantamani out of Egypt altogether, never to return. But Sais proved to be an unreliable Assyrian vassal, for when Assurbanipal had to return to Mesopotamia to deal with a rebellion, the Saite ruler, Psammetichus I (664–610 BC), made himself independent, instituting the Twenty-sixth Dynasty. At this point, it might be noted, dating is no longer approximate but absolute.

Psammetichus I eliminated all remaining local rulers in Lower Egypt and installed his daughter as the successor to the Divine Adoratrice of Amun at Thebes, uniting Egypt much more thoroughly than the Kushites had done. Prosperity quickly returned to the land, indicating that the Assyrians had done little lasting damage and that the Kushites had laid a good foundation for recovery. Egypt also benefited from fuller integration into the overall economy of the Eastern Mediterranean. As might be expected of a time of recovery, Psammetichus built extensively, especially at Sais. Nothing of that remains above ground now, but the massive brick enclosure walls of Sais were noted with wonderment by European travelers well into the nineteenth century. The archaizing trend in art and architecture reached its fullest flowering during the Saite period, as models from the distant past continued to be copied. So close at times was the imitation that it often takes an expert to discern whether a particular object was made during the Old Kingdom or the Late Period; but this was more than merely mindless reproduction, for Saite art also shows great creativity and innovation.

In foreign affairs, Psammetichus I had to play a careful, shifting game. Fearful of yet another Assyrian invasion, at first he threw his support behind Assyria's enemies. But as Assyrian power declined, it became obvious that other dangerous players had entered the game, such as the Medes and the Chaldeans with their capital at Babylon. In 629–627 BC, he had to beat back a Chaldean attack at the Egyptian frontier. Realizing that the balance of power in the Near East was tilting, he actively intervened on behalf of the hard-pressed Assyrians, even to the point of sending troops to Mesopotamia to help them fight the Chaldeans, but Egyptian aid was insufficient to prevent the final collapse of the Assyrian Empire in 612 BC, leaving Egypt to confront the Chaldeans and ongoing diplomatic turmoil in the Levant.

Necho II (610–595 BC) had no choice but to continue Psammetichus I's policies in the north. He strengthened his forces with Greek mercenaries, just as his father had done, but he also recruited Greek sailors and deployed a fleet of triremes in the Mediterranean, the first time Egypt, a nation with a longstanding aversion to the sea, had such a navy. Necho began a canal between the eastern branch of the Nile and the Red Sea, probably so he could switch his warships between the Mediterranean and the Red Sea as needed, while also facilitating trade.

Necho's foreign adventures began well. He occupied Palestine, defeating and killing Josiah, King of Judah, as he went, and established an Egyptian presence on the Euphrates, only to be disastrously defeated by the Chaldeans at Carchemish in 605 BC. He was at least able to defend the frontier against the subsequent attack by Nebuchadnezzar II in 601 BC, and some of the ground was recovered by Psammetichus II (595–589 BC), who conducted a minor expedition into Palestine and fomented a troublesome revolt against the Chaldeans in the Levant. This, however, merely caused Nebuchadnezzar to respond in greater force. He laid siege to Jerusalem, captured it in 587 BC, and carried away thousands of its people in the famous Babylonian Captivity. Many others found their way to Egypt, forming the basis of the large Jewish population that became an important factor in Egypt during Greco-Roman times. Fortunately for Egypt, Nebuchadnezzar apparently contented himself with a limited punitive expedition in its direction.

The next king, Apries (589–570 BC), continued operations in Palestine and Lebanon with mixed results, but his downfall came from the west, where he dispatched an army in 570 BC to aid the Libyan ruler of Cyrenaica in a struggle against the Greek colonists who were gaining control of the area. The army was defeated, then it mutinied. When Apries sent his general Amasis to restore discipline, Amasis joined the mutiny, declared himself king, and overthrew Apries. A few years later Apries attempted to reclaim the throne, supported by Nebuchadnezzar II, but was killed in the unsuccessful attempt. The Chaldeans, soon busy with internal problems, never had the opportunity to threaten Egypt again.

Amasis (570–526 BC) developed closer diplomatic relations with the Greek world that resulted in a growing Greek presence in Egypt. He granted increased civic privileges to the Greek trading post and port at Naukratis that had been founded the century before in the western Delta near his home town of Sais and showed other favors to Greek merchants. Greek mercenary garrisons were stationed at Memphis and around the Delta, though Amasis carefully restricted contact between Greeks and Egyptians to prevent ethnic conflict. The Hellenization of Egypt was already well under way two centuries before the arrival of Alexander.

The reign of Amasis's successor, Psammetichus III (526–525 BC), was cut short by the appearance of another new power in the East that finally upset all the Saites' balance of power diplomacy. Through a rare combination of military skill, administrative genius, and shrewd diplomacy, Cyrus the Great created the mightiest empire the world had yet seen, extending from India on the east, through Iran and Mesopotamia, to Asia Minor and Syria on the west. Only his death on a campaign deep in Central Asia prevented Cyrus from turning his attention to Egypt, which had vainly lent support to his adversaries, fearful of his growing strength.

It was Cyrus's son Cambyses (525–522 BC) who invaded Egypt and defeated Psammetichus III at Pelusium in 525 BC. According to an ancient account, Cambyses won by placing dogs and cats at the head of his army so that the Egyptians held back, fearing to harm animals they regarded as sacred, but the Persians had no need of such stratagems. Cambyses encountered little effective opposition as he proceeded to occupy Memphis and extend his control over the rest of the country, initiating the First Persian Period, or the Twenty-seventh Dynasty. But things did not go smoothly for Egypt's new ruler. He lost an entire army, the so-called Vanished Army, when he sent it on an ill-equipped, poorly guided expedition to Siwa Oasis. It disappeared without a trace in a sandstorm, but left a strong mark in legend, as many have dreamed of finding its bleached bones, weapons, armor, and treasure among the western dunes. The Persians do seem to have been rather improvident when it came to logistical planning in Egypt. In 373 BC they attempted a major military operation in the Delta in July, just as the annual inundation was turning the entire area into a large swamp. It too was a complete failure.

Cambyses acquired a reputation for great cruelty and devastation. It was said that he destroyed many temples and ridiculed the gods, and that he first showed mercy to Psammetichus but later had him killed. His successor Darius I (521–486 BC) took a more conciliatory approach by displaying profound respect for local religion and encouraging temple restoration and construction, most notably with the Hibis Temple at Kharga Oasis. His efforts to stimulate prosperity were successful, and he conducted major public works such as completion of Necho II's canal. Even so, there was a serious Egyptian revolt during the last year of Darius's reign that was suppressed by his successor Xerxes I (486–466 BC) with such severity as to provoke yet another revolt when Xerxes died. The latter revolt was led by Amyrtaios of Sais and Inaros of Heliopolis, a son of Psammetichus III. Aided by the Greeks, the conflict fizzled on until it was finally suppressed in 454 BC.

During the ensuing period of relative tranquility, the Greek historian and traveler Herodotus visited Egypt. It was once fashionable to dismiss Herodotus, the 'Father of History,' as the 'Father of Lies,' but this misconception arose from a failure to understand that Herodotus recorded accurately not only what he saw but also what he heard, and that he usually took care to distinguish between the two. His account has been largely confirmed by archaeological discoveries and remains an important source for ancient Egypt. He could also write with humor, as in his description of the Egyptian people:

> The Egyptians, along with having their own peculiar climate and a river with a nature different from all other rivers, have established many habits and customs which are almost the complete opposite of the rest of mankind. For example, the women go to market and keep shop, while the men stay home and weave. Meanwhile, others push the woof upward when they weave, but the Egyptians pull it down. It is the

men who carry burdens on their heads, while the women carry them on their shoulders. Women urinate standing up; men do it squatting down. They relieve themselves in their own homes, but they eat out in the street. The logic behind this is that one must perform shameful necessities secretly and those that are not shameful openly. There are no priestesses whatever, for either male or female gods; only male priests for gods of both sexes. Sons never have to take care of their parents if they don't want to, but daughters must, whether they like it or not. In other places, the priests of the gods wear their hair long, but in Egypt they shave their heads. Among other people, it is the custom for those most touched by grief to shave their heads, but the Egyptians honor the dead by letting the hair on their heads and their faces grow. The rest of the time, they shave it all off. Other people live apart from their animals, but Egyptians live among their animals. Others live on wheat and barley, while it is the greatest disgrace for an Egyptian to make his food from these things—instead, they make bread with horse fodder, a grain some call zeia. They knead flour with their feet, but they pick up mud and dung with their hands. Other people (except those who learned from the Egyptians) leave their genitals in their natural state; the Egyptians practice circumcision. Every man has two garments, but every woman only one. Others tie the ringbolts and reefing ropes to the outside of the ship, but the Egyptians tie them inboard. Greeks write and work the abacus by moving their hands from left to right, the Egyptians from right to left; but they call that writing forward, while the Greeks call it writing backward.[9]

And so on. Book Two of Herodotus's *History*, which deals with Egypt, can be regarded as the first of a long series of travelogues written by Western travelers in Egypt.

All things considered, Persian rule in Egypt was not particularly harsh though it was often inept. Egypt was expected to contribute to the Persian Empire in a number of ways—through manpower, taxes, and material contributions. The Persian fleet at the Battle of Salamis in 480 BC, for example, contained two hundred Egyptian triremes. But these exactions were not heavy, nor did the Persians generally rule with an iron fist. In fact, the Persian approach to provincial government was to allow local customs, laws, and institutions to function as much as possible under the overall supervision of a Persian satrap, or governor. Clearly many Egyptians found the imperial regime altogether compatible, but others were never reconciled to it, suggesting a sort of eternal antipathy between the Egyptian and Persian peoples, one that developed into deep hatred as it was stoked by the ambitions of local Egyptian dynasts, never fully suppressed, who longed to be kings in their own right in their own land.

It was largely because of these unreconciled families that revolt rekindled early in the reign of Darius II (424–404 BC). Sais was, as before, a particular center of resistance with its proximity to inaccessible swamps and a ready supply of Greek mercenaries from Naukratis. Deadly dissension within the imperial family so weakened the Persian response that Amyrtaios of Sais (404–399 BC), grandson of the earlier Amyrtaios, drove the Persians out of the Delta and freed the entire country from their rule. This Amyrtaios is the single member of Manetho's Twenty-eighth Dynasty, but he was overthrown by the usurper Nepherites I (399–393 BC) with whom the Twenty-ninth Dynasty begins. Unfortunately, usurpation and deposition were recurring features of that brief dynasty, which ended when Nepherites II was deposed in a military coup staged by Nectanebo I (380–362), the first king of the Thirtieth Dynasty. The country enjoyed great prosperity under the three kings of this dynasty, as is evident in building and artistic expression, and in its attempts to influence events in the Near East to regain some of Egypt's former stature and to ensure safety from the Persians.

But Egypt was playing out of its league in world affairs. Persia was determined to restore control over this former province, whose meddlesome diplomacy was a constant irritant, and only Persian internal problems, Egyptian good luck, and Persian incompetence—such as the abortive midsummer invasion of 373 BC—prevented it from succeeding sooner than it did. After several failed attempts, Artaxerxes III Ochus reconquered Egypt in 343 BC, beginning the Second Persian Period, or the Thirty-first Dynasty. The last king of the Thirtieth Dynasty, Nectanebo II (360–343 BC), fled south, apparently fulfilling Ezekiel's prophecy that "there shall be no more a prince of the land of Egypt," because more than two thousand years would pass before Egypt was again ruled by its own people.

This short restoration of Persian domination was not a happy time. The Persians were even more hated than before and resorted to exceptionally oppressive measures, plundering temples and demolishing town walls. The Egyptians responded with rebellion. One insurrection led by Khababash, who became something of a folk hero, managed to gain control of Lower Egypt for a couple of years. So detested was the Persian yoke that when Alexander the Great arrived in Egypt, he was welcomed as a savior.

7   Ptolemaic Egypt

A lexander the Great, having conquered other Persian possessions in
Asia Minor and Syria, entered Egypt without resistance at the end
of 332 BC. After establishing himself at Memphis, he and a small
escort made the long trek west through the desert to Siwa Oasis, where the
oracle recognized him as the son of Amun (and therefore a rightful pharaoh
of Egypt), destined to rule the world. He also traveled north to the
Mediterranean coast. There, by the fishing village of Rhakotis, he ordained
the construction of a new city, Alexandria, and personally marked out some
of its basic features. This could be seen as visionary, and indeed the inspiration for the foundation came to Alexander in a dream, but it was also
based on practical experience. He had recently captured some of the major
commercial cities of the East; now, having just visited Naukratis, which was
more a trading-post than a commercial center and too far from the sea, the
desirability for a Greek port located directly on the Mediterranean must
have been obvious. After a stay of just a few months, Alexander left Egypt
to complete the conquest of the vast Persian Empire and beyond, but the
course of Egyptian history was profoundly affected for centuries to come.

Alexander's death at Babylon in 323 BC was followed by a struggle in
which his generals attempted to gain control of the new empire or

establish themselves as masters of parts of it. Egypt fell to Ptolemy, a boyhood friend of Alexander's, and participant in many of his most memorable adventures. Like many of his descendants, Ptolemy was of a literary bent. He wrote what was said to be the best biography of Alexander, now lost, that drew on his own experiences and Alexander's personal journal. Having accompanied Alexander on that brief visit to Egypt, he had seen for himself the riches of the land and knew what a powerful base it could be. At first he ruled as satrap of Egypt, but he intended from the outset to establish a viable independent state and a dynasty. When the fiction of maintaining Alexander's empire intact had worn thin, he arranged to be acclaimed king of Egypt by his soldiers in 306 BC. Two years later he celebrated his coronation as an Egyptian pharaoh. He ruled as Ptolemy I Soter. The grandiose epithet Soter ('Savior') would prove typical of Ptolemaic style.*

Egypt was the basis of an extensive Ptolemaic Empire. Even before becoming king, Ptolemy I exploited an internal power struggle in Cyrenaica to install a Ptolemaic garrison. This fertile coastal area around the present-day city of Benghazi, though surrounded by desert, was readily accessible to Alexandria through coastal communication, as is attested by ample piles of potsherds at bays and inlets along the way where ships put in for the night. The focus of centuries of Greek colonization, Cyrenaica was already thoroughly Hellenized; by 320 BC it had become a major component of the Ptolemaic Empire. Ptolemy I also moved quickly to take control of Phoenicia and southern Syria, an area known as Coele Syria that was rich in agricultural products and served as the terminus of lucrative caravan routes to Arabia. Coele Syria became an ongoing bone of contention between the Ptolemies and the Seleucids, another dynasty founded by one of Alexander's generals who had taken northern Syria when the conqueror's empire was divided. In 295/294 BC Ptolemy I added the island of Cyprus to his empire and extended his control into southern Anatolia. Ptolemaic influence, as well as direct

---

* Ptolemaic kings are often referred to in literature by their epithets or in other ways. Hence Ptolemy II Philadelphus might be called simply Philadelphus. Ptolemy VIII Euergetes II can appear as just Euergetes II. Here the simplest forms of dynastic names and numbers are used.

rule, eventually reached areas far into the Aegean Sea and even onto the Greek mainland. South of Aswan, control of northern Nubia fluctuated between the Ptolemaic Empire and the remote Kingdom of Meroë, with its capital beyond the Fifth Cataract, where the successors of the kings of Kush were still building pyramids and would continue to do so for several centuries more. Through its Red Sea ports in the southeast at Myos Hormos (just north of the modern town of Quseir) and Berenike, and through a canal from the Delta to the Red Sea, Ptolemaic Egypt maintained trading contacts with East Africa, Arabia, and beyond. Drawing on the abundant resources of Egypt, augmented by their other possessions, the Ptolemies were able to maintain strong standing armies and navies. When they suffered losses, of which they had their share, they could quickly recover. The Ptolemaic Empire was a force to be reckoned with in the Eastern Mediterranean, both on land and at sea. Seleucid Syria and Macedonia, the third center of power in the Hellenistic world, were repeatedly compelled to combine against it in order to maintain an often uneasy balance of power.

The century following Ptolemy I's assumption of power was the zenith of the Ptolemaic Empire. The first three kings of the dynasty were able, energetic men, each of whom enjoyed a long reign. When Ptolemy I died in 283 BC, he was succeeded by his son, Ptolemy II Philadelphus, who furthered his predecessor's accomplishments. Ptolemy II extended Egyptian possessions in the Aegean. He fought two wars with the Seleucids (there were six Syrian Wars altogether during the Ptolemaic Period), emerging victorious in the first and holding his own in the second. A six-year contest with Antigonus Gonatus of Macedon was unsuccessful, but losses were slight, and Ptolemy II could even claim some small gains. Establishment of coastal garrisons in East Africa and south Arabia facilitated trade in those areas and guaranteed access to the African war elephants that were an important factor in the Ptolemaic army, though no match for the Indian elephants used by the Seleucids. Large-scale construction programs and institutional foundations in Alexandria turned many of Ptolemy I's visions into realities. Ptolemy III Euergetes ('Benefactor') also proved himself worthy by restoring the situation in Cyrenaica, where things had gone awry, and fighting a Third Syrian War, gaining additional towns in Syria and Asia Minor. But his greatest accomplishment was the long period of peace during much of his reign. The Ptolemaic empire had reached its greatest extent when Ptolemy III died in 221 BC after a twenty-five year reign.

Military victories and territorial expansion were not the only ways the Ptolemies demonstrated their power in the Hellenistic world: they also sought to excel their Macedonian and Syrian rivals in wealth, pageantry, culture, and material achievements. Alexandria became the greatest city in the Eastern Mediterranean. Its Museum was not only intended to preserve and promote learning but also to do it bigger and better than anyone else, and to be the undisputed center of Greek culture. Exorbitant sums were spent on festivals and processions; the magnificent Panhellenic Games were designed to impress foreign visitors as well as the local population. Even the excesses of the royal family served the practical purpose of displaying the godlike lifestyles of the Ptolemies. When Rhodes was devastated by the earthquake that toppled its wondrous Colossus, Egypt sent a massive relief effort, a gesture motivated less by generosity than desire to outdo the contributions of Macedonia and Syria. The Ptolemies easily surpassed their competitors, at least during the third century BC, because they could always outspend them.

Ptolemaic kings emphasized their dynastic connections, as is apparent in the epithets they took for themselves such as Philopater: 'father lover'; Philomater: 'mother lover'; and Philadelphus: 'sibling lover.' Another appropriate epithet would have been 'sister lover,' for Ptolemy II married his full sister Arsinoe II, and several of his successors followed suit. The reasons for this are unclear. It was certainly not a custom of their Macedonian ancestors; indeed, such consanguineous unions were taboo in Macedonia, and Ptolemy II's marriage provoked some mockery at the time, although a poet who expressed it paid for his temerity with his life. It has been conjectured that the Ptolemies sought to emulate their pharaonic predecessors, but if so they were misinformed, for the Egyptian pharaohs did not practice full sister marriage. A more plausible assumption is that marriage to their brothers kept these princesses from becoming dangerously independent players in diplomatic and political fields, but the unions often created dissonant power relationships within the royal court, especially when the numerous royal mistresses and polygamous liaisons—for which the Ptolemies also had a penchant— were factored into the situation. Whatever the reasons, full brother-sister marriage became a normal practice within the Ptolemaic dynasty.

By 311 BC, Ptolemy I had moved his residence from Memphis to Alexandria, which became one of the greatest cities in the world and brought about a complete change of orientation for Egypt. A causeway, the Heptastadion, was built from the mainland out to Pharos Island; over the centuries it accreted into the substantial peninsula covered by the present-day al-Gumruk neighborhood. Breakwaters running from each end of the island to the mainland formed two fine harbors. A land that previously had no Mediterranean port now had one of the best, closely connecting it to the Hellenistic world. The Pharos, or Lighthouse, built of white stone to a height of 135 meters, became one of the wonders of the ancient world. At the top, an ingenious set of mirrors both reflected and magnified a fire that burned at night so that mariners could see it even from a great distance out at sea. The Pharos stood until the fourteenth century, when its sturdy structure was finally undone by two earthquakes. Its location is now occupied by Fort Qaitbay, some of whose stones may have been recycled from the ruins of the ancient Pharos.

Alexandria grew quickly, stimulated by commerce and government, and by the deliberate policy of the Ptolemies to surpass all other Greek cities, a goal they soon attained, as each king sought to add to its splendor. The palace quarter, near the southeastern corner of the present Eastern Harbor, became ever more magnificent as successive kings built new residences for themselves, vying to excel their predecessors in opulence. A short distance to the west, also near the waterfront, stood the Museum and the Great Library. Two great avenues, more than thirty meters wide, formed the axes of a regular grid of lesser but by no means insignificant streets. At their intersection was the glass tomb of Alexander the Great, whose body Ptolemy I had hijacked when it was being conveyed to its intended burial place in Macedonia. The city was filled with great public buildings such as the gymnasium, the hippodrome, and theaters; with ostentatious private residences, extensive porticoes, taverns, and a vast number of temples. The greatest of the temples was the Serapeum, actually a large complex in itself, which stood on a commanding location. At the end of the Ptolemaic Period, the Roman historian Diodorus Siculus accurately described Alexandria as "the first city of the civilised world, certainly far ahead of all the rest in elegance and extent and riches and luxury."

With its international connections, Alexandria was a cosmopolitan city, attracting visitors and permanent residents from all over the Mediterranean and beyond. At its greatest, it probably numbered about half a million inhabitants. The dominant group was the Greeks, who enjoyed special rights of citizenship that were denied to other ethnic groups, but native Egyptians were to be found in substantial numbers, concentrated around the old fishing village of Rhakotis, which was subsumed into the city. A large number of Jews also settled in Alexandria. Found primarily in two of the city's several quarters, they were ineligible for Alexandrian citizenship, but they had many privileges of their own and were presided over by their own ethnarch whose power was, according to one historian of the Ptolemaic Period, "like that of the highest magistrate of an independent state." Though Hellenized to a considerable degree, the Jews of Alexandria retained their cultural distinctions, and relations between them and the Greek population were often marred by mutual animosity.

Preeminent in population, splendor, wealth, and power, Alexandria also became the leading cultural center of the Hellenistic world. The Museum, literally 'Shrine of the Muses,' was a concept of Ptolemy I that Ptolemy II brought into institutional being. Modeled on the great schools of Plato and Aristotle, opulently furnished, and staffed with some of the greatest scholars of the age in nearly every field of intellectual endeavor, the Museum was generously supported by the state. A list of the luminaries reads almost like a *Who's Who* of the ancient intellectual world, for the Ptolemies sought the most distinguished talent wherever it could be found. The renowned mathematician Euclid taught at the Museum and famously told Ptolemy I that there was no royal road to geometry when the king asked for an easy course of instruction. Archimedes also passed some time there and may actually have invented the Archimedean Screw, an ingenious device for raising water, while he was in Egypt. The Museum's polymathic scientist Eratosthenes of Cyrene calculated the circumference of the earth with a high degree of accuracy and propagated his heliocentric theory, suggesting that the earth was not the center of the universe. Medicine was always strong at Alexandria, with people such as Praxagoras of Cos, considered by the great Galen to have been one of the greatest physicians of antiquity, followed by his student Herophilus of Chalcedon, who made dissection a regular practice. The poets Theocritus and Apollonius of Rhodes were among the distinguished representatives of Alexandrian *belles lettres*. Several historians worked at the Museum, some of whom wrote about Egypt, including Hecataeus of Abdera, who posited Egypt as the source of civilization. The most intriguing historian, however, was Manetho, probably active early in the reign of Ptolemy II, who was unique in being a native Egyptian high priest. His three-volume work in Greek about Egyptian history from mythological times until 323 BC, which survives only in those inadequate but invaluable epitomes, was based on careful archival work and personal observation and experience. This is to name only a few of the superstars of the Alexandrian intellectual firmament. There were numerous other worthy scholars; all made their contributions to the greatest intellectual institution of the classical world.

Close by the Museum was the Great Library of Alexandria. No other library in antiquity came close to it in size and organization. Estimates vary, but the Library at Alexandria is said to have contained from five to seven hundred thousand rolls, and one roll often contained more than one work. Ptolemy I sent searchers to all parts of the Greek world to buy texts to fill its shelves, and Ptolemy III wrote "to all the world's sovereigns" to borrow texts to have them copied. He even had ships in the harbors searched for texts that were seized for copying—then the copies, not the originals, were returned to the owners. Nor was it merely a matter of acquisition, for the Library also devoted a prodigious amount of work to cataloging, collating, arranging, editing, interpreting, critiquing—all the manifold aspects of working scholarship. The Library's mission was furthered by energetic directors, some themselves accomplished textual scholars like Aristarchus of Samothrace. The poet Callimachus of Cyrene, highly esteemed during antiquity, worked at the Library and cataloged its contents in 120 volumes. A major Jewish contribution to Alexandrian scholarship associated with the Library was the translation of the Old Testament into Greek. This version, known as the Septuagint because it was supposedly the work of seventy scholars, was later accepted as the Old Testament of Greek-speaking Christians. The Great Library was complemented by a second library that was established at the Serapeum by Ptolemy II.

Alexander initially left the governmental and the financial systems— though taxes were diverted into the Macedonian war chest—in the hands of native Egyptians, which must have made the transition of rule from the hated Persians to the Greeks much easier. But as soon as they could, the Ptolemies created an elaborate Greek bureaucratic state, perfected under Ptolemy II, whose layers of officials reached directly from the king right down to the villages. One of the primary objectives of this system—indeed, its essential point—was maximization of revenue, an objective assiduously pursued though strict administrative oversight. Many areas of commercial activity such as glassware, textiles, various luxury goods, and export of papyrus were conducted by government monopolies, and businesses in private hands were carefully regulated and taxed. A mint was established at Alexandria, and a strict policy of monetarism was enforced. Only Ptolemaic coins were permitted to circulate within the Empire; foreign currency was exchanged in markets owned or supervised by the state, and at rates fixed by the state. A country that had hitherto relied almost entirely on barter quickly developed into the most monetized in the Mediterranean, transforming the Egyptian economy and facilitating its interaction with the wider world, often on terms favorable to Egypt.

Egypt's greatest source of wealth by far, of course, was the produce of the land, which was considered to be in royal ownership with tenure granted to individuals under varying conditions. The Ptolemies carefully surveyed Egypt, assessed its productivity, and devised a means of local administration designed to extract the maximum amount of revenue. It is often said that the Ptolemaic system was so thorough that the Romans left it mostly intact when they took control of Egypt, a statement that does not quite hold up under detailed examination, but that is nevertheless indicative of the efficiency of Ptolemaic exploitation.

The Ptolemies also sought to increase Egypt's agricultural productivity. In part this was accomplished by innovation, especially the *saqiya*, or waterwheel, introduced into Egypt during Ptolemaic times. Since the early New Kingdom, the primary device for raising water from the river or canals to higher ground had been the *shaduf*, a counterweighted, levered pole by which its operator could lift one bucketful at a time. The *saqqiya*, powered by yoked oxen, could irrigate about five hectares of land, more than three times the amount a *shaduf* could water, and could lift the water four times higher. New areas were brought into cultivation, particularly in the Fayyum where the Ptolemies greatly increased productivity by building a dam at al-Lahun so the level of the Birket

Qarun, the large lake in the Fayyum, could be lowered farther than the Middle Kingdom hydraulic system allowed, greatly extending the amount of cultivable land. Construction of an artificial lake in the southern Fayyum provided for intensive irrigation of marginal lands. New crops were introduced, increasing variety as well as quantity. Much of the produce was collected in kind by the government and redistributed within the country according to policy, but there was almost always a large amount that could be exported in return for foreign exchange. Ptolemy I had chosen shrewdly when he selected Egypt as his portion in the division of the spoils at Alexander's death. It provided an annual revenue that any ancient king would have envied.

With such productivity, Egypt could support a large population, one that has been estimated as high as 7.5 million, exclusive of the half million or so who lived in Alexandria. A lower figure somewhere between four and a half or five million seems more plausible, but Diodorus Siculus, writing in the first century BC after a prolonged period of hardship in Egypt, may have been drawing on authentic information when he asserted that the country's population was at least three million but had been about seven million "in antiquity." Whatever figures are preferred, there can be little doubt that the Egyptian population increased dramatically during the Ptolemaic Period and maintained high levels well into Roman times.

The population of Ptolemaic Egypt consisted of a comparatively small number of relatively privileged Greeks superimposed onto the great masses of native Egyptians, most of whom lived around subsistence level but whose back-breaking labor supported Ptolemaic society and government. The Hellenistic Period is generally characterized as a time of cultural mixing, interchange, and fusion, but that notion must be treated with caution when dealing with Egypt, for although there were many points of contact between Greeks and Egyptians, these points were often barriers, not portals; indeed, one of the striking features of the Ptolemaic Period is the degree to which the two cultures remained separate. The Ptolemaic dynasty was purely Macedonian throughout, with the possible exception of the last ruler, Cleopatra VII, who may have had an Egyptian mother. She was also the only member of the dynasty who learned to speak Egyptian, and it was just one of several languages she spoke. Greek was the exclusive language of government, and high posts within the administration were not opened to Egyptians until the later days of the Ptolemaic Period. Separation is also evident in the official designation of the city of Alexandria which was "Alexandria *beside* Egypt," not "Alexandria *in* Egypt." A Greek who traveled from the city to the Delta or Upper Egypt spoke of "going to Egypt."

In addition to a considerable Greek presence already established during the Late Period, immigrants from all over the Greek world streamed into Egypt under the Ptolemies. Greek governmental agents and merchants penetrated every corner of the kingdom. Veteran Greek soldiers, known as *cleruchs*, were rewarded with grants of land in return for their military service, creating a class of Greek peasantry. The Ptolemies established many new Greek towns within Egypt. There is evidence within these of cultural interaction, as some Greeks inevitably became more Egyptian in their lifestyles while many Egyptians adopted Greek ways, but strong elements of separation remained. The rights and privileges of Greek citizenship were scrupulously maintained and seldom granted to outsiders. In one town, intermarriage between Greeks and Egyptians was expressly prohibited. This legal—and cultural—divide persisted far into the Roman Period. The Greeks were always a small minority in Egypt, but a highly influential one.

Beneath the Hellenic veneer, Egyptian culture and society retained its vitality. The old Egyptian aristocracy was never destroyed, and though initially excluded from the central administration, many of its members continued to hold high military and civil offices at the regional level. The documentary evidence also indicates the presence of numerous Egyptian scribes who performed temple duties and served as secretaries, and later as civil servants. If they learned Greek, they could become interfaces between the Greek elite and the Egyptians because demotic continued to be widely used during the Ptolemaic Period. Egyptian law persisted alongside Greek law, but the court system almost invariably favored Greeks. Egyptians were generally excluded from the regular military, although the native *machimoi*, or militia men, served as policemen and auxiliary soldiers, but with fewer privileges than the Greek *cleruchs*. There were also plenty of Egyptian artisans and craftsmen as well as small businessmen, but most people were, as they had been since time immemorial, agricultural workers.

Ptolemaic rule was readily accepted at first, perhaps because it was a change from the detested Persians, but it became highly resented over time. There were numerous rebellions, especially during the second and third centuries BC. Most may have resulted from economic desperation or lax central control because of dynastic infighting, but some were accompanied by pharaonic trappings that expressed a longing for the glorious past when Egyptians ruled Egyptians. A distinctly 'nationalistic' literature appeared, such as the pseudo-historical *Demotic Chronicle* of the mid-third century BC and the apocalyptic late second-century *Oracle of the Potter* that prophesied: "And the belt-wearers [i.e., the Greeks] will destroy themselves. . . . These things will come to pass when all evils have come to an end, when the foreigners who are in Egypt disappear as leaves from a tree in autumn. And the city of the Belt-wearers [Alexandria] will be deserted . . . on account of the impieties they have committed. And the Egyptian statues which were carried thither will be restored to Egypt, and the city by the sea will be transformed into a drying-place for fishermen . . . so that passers-by will say: 'This was the all-nurturing [city], that was inhabited by all races of men.'"[10]

It might be reasonably assumed that imposition of Ptolemaic rule did not greatly increase the heavy burdens that the Egyptian people already bore, at least during the first century of the dynasty, but as the political situation outside Alexandria deteriorated from the reign of Ptolemy IV onward, the masses suffered from the disorder and factional fighting. Government officials extorted everything they could from the peasantry, frequently leaving them insufficient means to sustain themselves. Famine, inflation, banditry, and flight are all too abundantly attested during the later Ptolemaic Period, though some individual Egyptians were able to exploit the chaotic conditions to improve their lot as powerful positions in government finally opened to them.

It is significant that the Ptolemies, despite their ever-present concern for increasing revenue, left the Egyptian priesthood undisturbed in its properties, endowments, and revenues, and indeed enhanced them. This is evident in the Canopus Decree of 238 BC which declared: "Since King Ptolemy, son of Ptolemy and Arsinoe, the Brother-sister Gods, and Queen Berenike his sister and wife, the Benefactor Gods, constantly confer many great benefactions on the temples throughout the land and increase more and more the honours of the gods . . . be it resolved by the priests in the country to increase the honours which already exist in the temples for King Ptolemy and Queen Berenike."[11] During times of crisis, royal favor of the priesthood tended to increase, as is attested by several major documents, including the famous Rosetta Stone from Ptolemy V's reign. Its text, written in hieroglyphs, demotic, and Greek, refers to "King Ptolemy, the ever-living, beloved of Ptah, the god Manifest and Beneficent" who "has conferred many benefits on the temples and those who dwell in them and on all the subjects in his kingdom, being a god born of a god and goddess. . . ." Strong support for the Egyptian priesthood can be explained in part by the function of the native religion in the Ptolemaic monarchy: the kings were pharaohs; they were the divine, rightful rulers of Egypt, just as their predecessors had been for thousands of years. But there must also have been a practical political calculation that the priesthood and their institutions could help keep the Egyptian people under control.

Support for the traditional Egyptian religious establishment was just one aspect of Ptolemaic religious policy. Alexander was deified at the outset by Ptolemy I, who in turn was recognized as a god. Ptolemy II established a cult for himself and his wife/sister Arsinoe II as living gods. Arsinoe II was posthumously elevated to the status of an individual god, and her cult statue was assigned a place in all Egyptian temples beside the local gods. Other royal women, notably Berenike II, were accorded cults. Over time, a collective dynastic cult developed so that the priest of Alexander, already the highest ranking in the land, became "the priest of Alexander and of the brother-sister gods." The Ptolemaia, a lavish festival even by Ptolemaic standards, celebrated the dynasty's divinity and proclaimed it to the world. Dionysus, whom the Greeks associated with Osiris, occupied a special place in the Ptolemaic pantheon, as did Isis. Previously worshiped with Osiris and Horus, Isis now acquired temples and chapels of her own, and was considered by Greeks to be the Egyptian counterpart of Aphrodite. Male rulers became identified with Dionysus and females with Isis.

The most original Ptolemaic religious innovation was the introduction of a new god, Serapis, whose name represents the merging of the sacred Apis bull with the god Osiris, but who also incorporated elements of the Greek gods Zeus, Hades, Dionysus, and Asclepius. His consort was Isis. The magnificent Serapeum in Alexandria contained an imposing statue of the god. Although Serapis might seem a particularly appropriate syncretism of Egyptian and Greek elements, he is best interpreted within a Hellenic context, and his worship was consciously contrived to appeal to the wider Greek world. Statues and portraits of Serapis bear an unmistakable resemblance to depictions of Olympian Zeus, king of the gods in the classical Greek pantheon. The cult of Serapis spread widely. By Roman times his temples were to be found in places as remote as York in the north of Britain.

Ptolemaic religious policy was profusely expressed in art and architecture. Old religious centers were restored. The Sphinx at Giza received a major face-lift and was painted red. Substantial additions were made to existing complexes like Luxor Temple and Karnak Temple, and many new temples were erected. Much of our impression of what ancient Egyptian temples were like comes from the Ptolemies because the remaining ancient temples that are most intact were built by them: Dendera, Edfu, Kom Ombo, and above all beautiful Philae. Esna Temple, another monument in a high state of preservation, was also a Ptolemaic foundation, but most of what is readily apparent there today is of Roman origin.

Under its first three rulers, the Ptolemaic Empire enjoyed over a century of stability, growth and consolidation, and ever-increasing sophistication made it the preeminent power in the eastern Mediterranean. But with the accession of Ptolemy IV Philopater ('Father-Lover') in 221 BC, the Ptolemaic dynasty entered a period of decline that, upon his death, exploded into a series of crises that removed Egypt from the ranks of the world's leading powers, and at precisely the moment when new challenges were emerging, especially the one posed by the growing power of Rome.

The threat of Rome, however, was scarcely a cloud on the Egyptian horizon when Ptolemy IV came to the throne. Around twenty years of age at his accession, he emulated his grandfather by marrying his full sister, Arsinoe III, an intelligent, able woman. He too had talents, for he was a great patron of the arts and something of a writer; during the crisis of the Fourth Syrian War, he acquitted himself reasonably well on the battlefield. But he was basically indolent, loved festivals, and gave himself over to the sumptuous luxury that the Ptolemaic state bestowed on its rulers, leaving much of the government in the hands of a powerful courtier named Sosibus. Skilled in manipulation and the uses of power, Sosibus had the leading members of the royal family murdered early on. Thus perished the king's uncle, his younger brother, and even his mother.

When the Seleucid king Antiochus III began the Fourth Syrian War, Sosibus reacted well to initial reverses, ably buying time through subtle diplomacy while accumulating a powerful force so that at the decisive Battle of Raphia in 217 BC, the Ptolemaic army, led by the king, forced Antiochus to withdraw and make a peace favorable to Egypt. For the last time, a Ptolemaic king returned in triumph from a Syrian War. In later crises, however, Ptolemy IV reacted ineffectively, for example in sending aid too late to an allied king in Asia Minor when the latter was attacked by Antiochus.

There also were new problems within Egypt itself. Part of the victorious force at Raphia had contained a large contingent of native Egyptian soldiers. That experience may have increased their discontent at their subordinate place within their country. According to the Roman historian Polybius, "Elated with their victory at Raphia they refused any longer to receive orders from the king; but looked out for a leader to represent them, on the ground that they were quite able to maintain their independence. And this they succeeded in doing before very long."[12] The result was a series of native revolts that broke out along the Nile; in Upper Egypt a de facto state emerged and sustained itself for decades, with two native kings ruling in succession. These problems probably never engaged the full attention of Ptolemy IV, who was mostly given over to sumptuous pleasures. Since Ptolemaic kings were identified as gods—especially as Dionysus, who was closely associated with wine and revelry—fantastic drunken parties were a function of Ptolemaic divine kingship, making them a religious duty that Ptolemy IV took very seriously indeed. Arsinoe III, a prudent woman, watched with dismay as her brother/husband became ever more extravagant, but she was marginalized by the Royal Mistress, a sister of Agathocles, another powerful minister and ally of Sosibus, who used her as his instrument to control the king.

When Ptolemy IV died in 204 BC at less than forty years of age, his heir was his six-year-old son, Ptolemy V Epiphanes ('Manifestation of God'). Ordinarily Arsinoe III would have acted as regent for the boy king, but Sosibus moved quickly and ruthlessly. Concealing the king's death, he had Arsinoe III murdered. The members of the extended family who might have protected the boy king's interests (while serving their own), or taken the throne themselves, were all long since dead. The dynasty was helpless. Sosibus quickly gathered the reins of power into his hands, supported by Agathocles and some fellow ministers.

For all his evil ways, Sosibus was a skilled diplomat, effective military leader, and master of court intrigue. He might have steered the Ptolemaic state through the troubled waters it had entered, but he soon died, and Agathocles, always intensely loathed by almost everyone, had become even more hated after Arsinoe III's murder, for she was much loved by the people. At the end of 203 BC, Agathocles and his family were torn to pieces by the Alexandrian mob, which emerged as a recurring and often fatal factor in Alexandrian politics. A series of unstable regencies and guardianships ensued, as did a run of disasters, foreign and domestic, that accelerated a decline already well under way.

Seleucid pressure mounted under Antiochus III, who had recovered from his defeat at Raphia; Rome interfered diplomatically more and more; problems continued in Upper Egypt. Coele Syria was lost during the Fifth Syrian War at the Battle of Panion in 200 BC, as were the Ptolemaic possessions in Asia Minor, reducing the empire to Cyrenaica, a few Aegean islands, and Cyprus, the last of which the Seleucids probably would have snatched as well had their fleet not been stopped by bad weather. Ptolemy V showed signs of initiative when he attained manhood. Upper Egypt was reconquered in 187/6 BC, and a dangerous native revolt in the Delta suppressed. He talked of recovering Coele Syria. One wonders what kind of military leader he might have made— he was said to be very athletic, and a good horseman and swordsman, though of unsavory character—but he lacked the financial means to undertake an expensive military campaign. Hints that he might confiscate his friends' fortunes prompted his generals to have him poisoned. When he died in 180 BC, Ptolemy V left another child king in his place, his son, the six-year-old Ptolemy VI Philometor.

With the accession of Ptolemy VI, the dynasty entered an especially confused and sordid stage. The empire now possessed few resources for recovery, and any favorable trends were offset by dynastic rivalry. Even so, the beginning of the new reign was smoother than the previous one's as Ptolemy VI's mother, Cleopatra I, became guardian and regent. It may have been because she was a Seleucid princess that Cleopatra I firmly stopped plans for another Syrian war, but she may also have realized that the empire needed time to recover before attempting any such thing. When she died in 176 BC, however, two incompetent courtiers, a former Syrian slave Lenaios and the eunuch Eulaios, seized control. They married the boy king to his sister, Cleopatra II, in 175 BC; five years later they proclaimed a triple joint rule, that of Ptolemy VI, Cleopatra II, and their younger brother Ptolemy VIII*, a move that was to prove disastrous, as did their imperial policy. Lenaios and Eulaios were determined to recover Coele Syria, but their inadequate preparations only served to alert the Seleucid king Antiochus IV Epiphanes, who decided that Egypt was ripe for the taking with its wretched government and nominal monarchs (who were his nephews and niece).

When hostilities opened in 170/169 BC, Antiochus seized the offensive and defeated the Egyptian forces in the Delta. Ptolemy VI went to his uncle's camp and agreed to peace terms, but the Alexandrians angrily disavowed them and proclaimed Cleopatra II and Ptolemy VIII as joint kings, although Ptolemy VI later made his way back to the city, and the triple monarchy was reinstated. Antiochus advanced to Alexandria but was thwarted by the annual inundation of the Nile and a determined defense that compelled him to withdraw to Syria. He resumed the offensive in 168 BC, capturing Cyprus and occupying the northern part of Egypt. As he prepared to attack Alexandria again, he had good reason to expect success. It was not Ptolemaic strength that prevented him but the threat of Roman intervention.

The Ptolemaic Empire had come into contact with Rome in 273 BC after Rome's victory in the Pyrrhic War, which consolidated Roman hold over the Italian peninsula and made Rome a major Mediterranean power. Egypt and Rome exchanged embassies, making one wonder what the rustic Roman delegates thought when they saw cosmopolitan Alexandria. Relations were equal and cordial, though distant, throughout the third century BC. Egypt was much closer to Rome's rival, Carthage, with which it had many commercial dealings, although Egypt remained strictly neutral during the First Punic War (264–241 BC)

---

* Ptolemy VIII was born before Ptolemy VII, who was the son of Ptolemy VI and Cleopatra II. Ptolemy VII was proclaimed as joint ruler with his father in 145 BC but was killed on the orders of Ptolemy VIII the following year.

between Rome and Carthage. Rome emerged from the Second Punic War (218–201 BC) as the leading power in the Mediterranean and quickly displayed its strength by defeating Macedonia as punishment for aiding the Carthaginians. A few years later, Rome clashed with Syria and decisively defeated it, imposing a restrictive peace treaty in 188 BC.

Rome was cautious at first about becoming involved in a conflict between Syria and Egypt because it was busy fighting another war with Macedonia, but it had no intention of tolerating a unitary Syrian-Egyptian state under Seleucid domination, especially since the Seleucids had violated the terms of their treaty with Rome by maintaining a navy and employing war elephants. As soon as the Macedonians were decisively defeated at the Battle of Pydna in June 168 BC, a Roman embassy, headed by the former consul Gaius Popillius Laenus, traveled to Egypt. Popillius confronted Antiochus in Eleusis, a suburb of Alexandria, demanding immediate cessation of the war and prompt and full withdrawal from Egypt. Antiochus asked for time to consider. Polybius, an excellent source for this period, described the ensuing scene.

> Popillius did a thing which was looked upon as exceedingly overbearing and insolent. Happening to have a vine stick in his hand, he drew a circle around Antiochus with it, and ordered him to give his answer to the letter before he stepped out of that circumference. The king was taken aback by this haughty proceeding. After a brief interval of embarrassed silence, he replied that he would do whatever the Romans demanded.[13]

The Romans also compelled Antiochus to return Cyprus to Egypt. Thus Egypt survived the Sixth Syrian War, but there could be no doubt who the real power was in the Mediterranean world, east as well as west.

Before departing, Popillius exhorted the three monarchs to rule harmoniously, but soon the two brothers were fighting each other, and their feud was echoed by disorder within the kingdom. Ptolemy VIII drove Ptolemy VI out of Alexandria and assumed the epithet 'Euergetes,' but he soon alienated the people, who demanded Ptolemy VI's return.

Although he had the upper hand, Ptolemy VI generously partitioned the empire and made his brother king of Cyrenaica, where he ruled as Ptolemy VIII Euergetes II, although he also became known as Physcon, or 'Fatso.' Ptolemy VI did not rule alone in Egypt but with his wife-sister, for documents of the time refer to them as the "pharaohs Ptolemy and Cleopatra, his sister."

Well-intentioned and conscientious, Ptolemy VI was one of the most attractive members of the dynasty. It was said that he never pronounced a death sentence on anyone, though he might have done well for himself and the empire, what was left of it, had he executed his murderous younger brother. He took his royal duties seriously, making himself accessible to the people and receiving their petitions. He foiled his brother's persistent troublemaking and went far toward rectifying many of the problems that beset the Ptolemaic state. Internal rebellion was suppressed. Ptolemaic control was reasserted far into Nubia. Taking advantage of disorder within the Seleucid dominions, Ptolemy VI over-ran Syria and could have gone farther but had no wish to arouse the opposition of Rome, which was more powerful—and threatening—than ever. In his moment of triumph, however, Ptolemy VI was killed by a fall from his horse in 145 BC. The Ptolemaic army returned to Egypt; Syria remained in the hands of the Seleucids.

Ptolemy VI's unexpected death cleared the way for Ptolemy VIII to return to Egypt and claim a place on the throne alongside his sister Cleopatra II, whom he married soon after arriving in Alexandria. His murderous ways were unmended. While the marriage was being cele-brated, political opponents were slaughtered. Ptolemy VIII had the son of Ptolemy VI and Cleopatra II killed in his mother's arms. Yet the royal couple had a son, popularly known as Memphites (whom Ptolemy VIII later killed), the following year. Shortly after Memphites' birth, Ptolemy VIII took the policy of Ptolemaic consan-guinity to new heights, or depths, by beginning a sexual relationship with Cleopatra II's daughter, Cleopatra III, whom he married in 141/140 BC, though he remained married to Cleopatra II, thereby becoming husband to a mother and daughter who were also his full sister and niece. Cleopatra II and III, who were referred to as the 'sister' and 'wife' to distinguish them, became bitter enemies, with disastrous consequences for Egypt.

As Ptolemaic dynastic politics became ever more base and convoluted, several themes emerged. One was the increasing power of Ptolemaic women, culminating in the rule of Cleopatra VII. Some of the women were much more able than their male relatives, but their appearance as major political players meant more centers of power, therefore increasing instability. Another trend was the rise of native Egyptians to high positions in government and at court. Like their Greek counterparts, these new men were much more interested in personal advancement than the welfare of Egypt. Meanwhile, life grew steadily harder for the great masses of the people as civil order collapsed through neglect and dynastic infighting, leaving them prey to brigands—and to rapacious tax collectors, who in turn were impelled by a central government desperate for revenue. Uprisings continued, and parts of the country even went to war with each other. By the end of the second century, the phenomenon of anachoresis (abandonment of land) was becoming widespread as individuals and even entire villages fled their fields.

The most important factor was the increasing assertion of Roman power, which reached the point that the later Ptolemaic Period is an episode in Roman as well as Egyptian history. Throughout the second century BC, Rome had meddled extensively with Egypt through diplomatic means; during the first century BC, Roman interest in Egypt manifested itself in distressingly direct ways, as was soon demonstrated in the case of Cyrenaica, the Ptolemies' oldest foreign possession. When its latest ruler, Ptolemy Apion, died in 96 BC, he willed it to Rome, bringing the expansionist superpower of the ancient world right next door to Egypt. Then, during the 80s BC, Ptolemy X Alexander I pledged Egypt to Rome in return for much-needed financial support in a fight for the throne. Rome did not take full advantage of that, but it placed Egypt's fate squarely in the hands of the Roman Senate, where it was routinely debated thereafter. No one could hope to rule in Egypt without Roman approval.

Obviously, the support of influential Roman politicians was essential, but in the turbulent political context of the late Roman Republic, it was often hard to tell exactly which politicians should be cultivated, for to make a powerful friend was to risk making an even more powerful enemy. This was especially true in the case of Sulla, who crushed his adversaries in Rome and then came east with a powerful army to deal with Mithridates, Rome's enemy in Asia Minor. But in his absence, his enemies regained control in Rome, initiating a deadly power struggle. It was far from clear who would win. A Ptolemaic prince, the future Ptolemy XI Alexander II, chose rightly and attached himself to Sulla, becoming his client, an act with profound diplomatic and political as well as personal implications. When Sulla emerged supreme again, he saw great political advantage in having his loyal client rule in Egypt alongside Berenike III, who had recently ascended to the throne. Yet Sulla, himself a man of notoriously violent temper, did not understand Ptolemaic cruelty. Within a few days of his arrival in Alexandria in 81 BC, Ptolemy XI murdered Berenike III—whereupon a mob of Alexandrians who adored her dragged him from the palace and killed him in the gymnasium.

The Alexandrians had to move quickly to install a new ruler, otherwise Rome might make the choice for them or take Egypt for itself according to Ptolemy X's pledge. Their choice fell on the two sons of Ptolemy IX. One became king of Egypt as Ptolemy XII. The other was made king of Cyprus, the first time that Cyprus was designated as a separate kingdom. The official epithet of the new ruler of Egypt was Neos Dionysus, 'the New Dionysus,' but he was also known as Auletes, or 'flute player,' because he often participated in musical performances at the palace. Neither epithet augured well for the kind of dynamic character that was desperately needed to give Egypt a chance for independent survival. There was probably not much that Ptolemy XII could have done, but he played right into Rome's hands. His main concern was Roman recognition of his status as king, which he secured through massive bribes to Roman politicians. He was particularly generous to Gnaeus Pompey, who was in the east, busily organizing new Roman provinces, including Syria where the obliteration of the remainder of the Ptolemaic dynasty's once-formidable rival kingdom must have been a chilling reminder of what could easily happen to Egypt. In addition to cash outlays, Ptolemy XII sent Pompey a golden crown and subsidized the cost of expensive Roman military operations. To pay for this, Ptolemy XII had to divert funds from essential government expenditures and raise taxes, which were collected ruthlessly and even brutally, pressing the already impoverished masses even further. When those sources ran out, he turned to Roman moneylenders who charged usurious rates, plunging him hopelessly in debt, though he ruled what should have been one of the richest kingdoms in the world. When the First Triumvirate, consisting of Pompey, Julius Caesar, and Marcus Licinius Crassus, was formed in Rome in 60 BC, Ptolemy XII promised Caesar and Pompey six thousand talents of silver, a sum equal to a year's revenue for the entire kingdom. But it turned the trick. The following year Caesar had the Senate confirm Ptolemy XII as king.

If Ptolemy XII thought he could relax on his dearly bought throne, he was quickly disillusioned, for in 58 BC the tribune P. Clodius Pulcher, one of Caesar's close associates, passed a law in the Roman Popular Assembly that made the Kingdom of Cyprus a Roman province on the flimsy pretext that Cyprus had become a haven for pirates. Ptolemy XII certainly should have objected to this, and perhaps something could have been accomplished through diplomacy, but he did nothing, fearing a confrontation with Rome. His brother took poison rather than submit, and Cyprus was annexed by Rome and attached to the province of Cilicia on the southern coast of Anatolia. The Alexandrians had long resented the vast sums that Ptolemy XII was taking from Egypt and handing over to Romans; now the royal court was disgusted with its king. Together they drove Ptolemy XII from Egypt and tried to construct a new monarchy based on his eldest daughter Berenike IV and her mother Cleopatra VI.

Ptolemy XII went to Rome for help. A strong faction in the Roman oligarchy favored outright annexation of Egypt, but another worried that it could provide an ambitious provincial governor with too strong a power base. The Senate debated the matter at length. Meanwhile, Romans saw firsthand just how murderous Ptolemaic dynastic politics could be when the government in Alexandria sent a delegation of a hundred prominent citizens to plead its case. Ptolemy XII dispatched a band of assassins who killed half of them soon after they arrived at the Roman port of Ostia, and many of the others were murdered when they reached Rome. The survivors were silenced by threats and bribery. The Senate resolved to investigate this outrage, but it was swept under the carpet by Ptolemy XII's influential Roman creditors, who could not afford to have the truth come out. In the end, Ptolemy XII's bribes and the support of Pompey won the debate. Ptolemy XII was restored to power by a Roman army. Marcus Antonius commanded its cavalry.

Ptolemy XII's first act was to kill his daughter Berenike IV and her supporters, but his most pressing concern was to satisfy his Roman creditors. One of the principal ones had accompanied the army to Egypt and was appointed chief financial officer of the kingdom. There can be little doubt that this man recovered his investment, and much more, through ruthless taxation without regard to the well-being of the kingdom. The Egyptian people paid a heavy price for the dynastic instability of the late Ptolemaic Period. When Ptolemy XII died in 51 BC, Egypt could be described as autonomous rather than independent.

According to Ptolemy XII's will, two of his children, Ptolemy XIII and Cleopatra VII, became joint rulers. Cleopatra promptly excluded her brother from power and ruled alone for a few months before he in turn drove her from the throne. She was attempting to regain power by force when Egypt was swept into the tides of Roman power politics. The First Triumvirate had become unstable when Crassus was defeated and killed in his Parthian War in 53 BC, and civil war soon erupted between Pompey and Caesar. After Pompey's disastrous defeat at Pharsalus in 48 BC, he fled to Egypt, expecting to be welcomed by Ptolemy XIII, whose father had owed him so much. Instead, he was treacherously murdered. When Caesar arrived in hot pursuit two days later, he was presented with his rival's head.

Caesar settled into Alexandria, enjoying the sights and engaging in philosophical discussions at the Museum. He announced that he would arbitrate the dynastic dispute between Cleopatra and her brother. Cleopatra came to him one night to present her case, and the adventurous Roman politician—"every man's woman and every woman's man," it was said of him—was instantly won by the twenty-one-year old Egyptian queen. He reestablished her as joint ruler with Ptolemy XIII.

Cleopatra's liaisons with Caesar and Marcus Antonius have become the subjects of literature and legend. Caesar was indeed taken with the young woman, but he also thought she and Egypt could serve his purposes, and even Antonius, though doubtless more in love with her, at least initially acted on fairly sound political and diplomatic consider-ations. As for Cleopatra, the romance card was the only one she had to play, and she played it well. Her objective was preservation of Egyptian independence. It was a dangerous game, as she well knew, and she ultimately failed; but her romantic policy accomplished much more, and far more cheaply, that her father's bribes.

Apart from romantic motives, Caesar's primary reason for lingering in Egypt was to establish a secure base for himself in the continuing struggle for power in the Roman world. When it became clear he did not intend to leave Egypt soon, he was confronted by a hostile Alexandrian population and a large Egyptian military force, for Ptolemy XIII enjoyed wide support while Cleopatra had virtually none. Caesar could rely on just one Roman legion, and it would take some time before reinforcements could reach him. Once, when his ship was overwhelmed by an Alexandrian mob and his people fled, Caesar had to dive into the wintry water of the harbor and swim for his life. To prevent the Egyptian ships from being used against him, he had them set on fire. The conflagration spread to the docks, and to the nearby Great Library, which was burned to the ground. Some four hundred thousand books were destroyed, leaving the lesser collection at the Serapeum as Alexandria's main research library. Marcus Antonius later made up some of the loss by transferring the library of Pergamum to Alexandria, but many works were lost forever that night in 48 BC.

Reinforcements finally arrived, and Caesar took the offensive. Ptolemy XIII was killed in a decisive battle in 47 BC. Caesar made Cleopatra queen, though he respected the succession by installing her prepubescent brother, Ptolemy XIV, alongside her in a nominal capacity. He also returned Cyprus to Egypt, a big step toward realizing Cleopatra's ambition of restoring the Ptolemaic Empire. She was, however, still so unpopular that Caesar permanently stationed three legions in Egypt. When he departed in spring 47 BC to new conquests and ultimate victory in the civil war, Cleopatra was pregnant. The boy born the following June was Ptolemy XV Caesar, popularly known as Caesarion, or 'Son of Caesar.'

When Caesar returned to Rome in 45 BC after vanquishing his last enemy, he was undisputed master of the Roman world and received the unprecedented office of dictator for life. After celebrating a triumph in which Cleopatra VII's younger sister Arsinoe IV (later murdered by Antonius at Cleopatra's bidding) was featured as a captive, he set about ordering things in Rome according to his satisfaction. Although he refused the title of king when a crown was offered to him by Antonius, his Eastern experiences, particularly in Egypt, may have turned his head. He accepted some of the trappings of oriental monarchy, such as a purple robe and a temple to his mercy, complete with a priest (Antonius), and had himself depicted on coins, the first living Roman to be so honored. This was widely but impotently resented, as was the presence of Cleopatra, who came to Rome with Ptolemy XIV and lived in one of Caesar's villas. They were accorded the status of "allies and friends of the Roman people."

One of Caesar's legislative initiatives during this period that still directly affects us today was assuredly based on Egyptian influences. This was his reform of the Roman calendar, which was based on the lunar cycle and had become increasingly out of synchronization with the seasons, but which no previous Roman politician had been able to replace. Drawing on the work of the Alexandrian astronomer Sosigenes, whose annual cycle was mentioned in the Canopus Decree as the proper way of reckoning time, Caesar instituted a solar calendar of 365 1/4 days. Hence the Julian Calendar.

Caesar intended to return east to wage war against the Parthians to avenge the defeat of Crassus, but he was forestalled by assassins on the Ides of March 44 BC. Cleopatra returned to Alexandria where she had her brother Ptolemy XIV killed and made Caesarion her co-ruler. Internal conditions were even more wretched than ever. Famine and plague were widespread in the wake of a series of low inundations during the 40s BC. Cleopatra kept the people of Alexandria quiet by distributing grain from the royal stores to them, though to no one else, leaving the Delta and Upper Egypt to fend for themselves. Her attention was fixed on the international scene.

When civil war broke out between the Caesarian party and Caesar's assassins, Cleopatra naturally sided with the former, led by the triumvirate of Marcus Antonius, M. Aemilius Lepidus, and Octavian, whose claim to power initially rested on being named as Caesar's heir but who built his position through political astuteness and patience, qualities the impetuous Antonius did not always display. The forces that Cleopatra contributed to the war promptly went over to the other side, and her personal attempt to intervene at sea was thwarted by storms and illness, but Antonius crushed the assassins at Philippi in 42 BC. When he summoned her to meet him at Tarsus, she went willingly and, as with Caesar, won him over in just one night.

When the triumvirs divided the Roman world, Antonius was given responsibility for the East, which he assumed with energy, reorganizing Roman provinces and establishing client states. Caesar already had returned Cyprus to Egypt; Antonius added the Roman province of Cilicia on the coast of Asia Minor as well as extensive territories in Syria, thereby reviving Ptolemaic Coele Syria. He also restored Cyrenaica to Egypt. For a moment, the Ptolemaic Empire was reconstituted to the extent it had enjoyed in its days of glory, though it was an edifice that rested on the shifting sands of late Roman republican politics. Antonius's enemies portrayed these grants as the acts of a besotted lover who was giving away what should have been Rome's, but they were also motivated by his awareness of the support a revitalized Egypt could give him.

Fraying relations between Antonius and Octavian were patched up when Antonius married Octavian's sister Octavia and the triumvirate was renewed in 37 BC, although Antonius left Octavia in the west and resumed his relationship with Cleopatra, with whom he had two children. His major objective the following year was the conquest of Parthia, but the campaign ended in disaster when he was deserted by his ally, the king of Armenia. During a horrific winter retreat Antonius lost the equivalent of five legions of infantry and another of cavalry. The disaster was compounded by the fact that Octavian took advantage of Antonius's preoccupation with Parthia to eliminate the third triumvir Lepidus in 36 BC. That made it one-on-one between Antonius and Octavian, with no third party to preserve the balance of power.

The last buffer between the two rivals was removed when Antonius rebuffed and divorced Octavia, having already married Cleopatra. Increasingly he took on the role of an eastern monarch. After taking revenge on the king of Armenia, Antonius celebrated a lavish triumph in Alexandria in which he appeared dressed as the god Dionysus. Cleopatra, as Isis, received him on a golden throne. They played the roles of gods to the full. All of this was grist to Octavian's increasingly active propaganda mill, which worked relentlessly to portray Antonius as a debauched drunkard who had fallen under the sway of a "ruinous monster," in the words of the poet Horace. Romans came to believe that Cleopatra had bewitched Antonius, and that if he ever prevailed over Octavian he would transfer the capital from Rome to Alexandria. When public opinion was inflamed, Octavian declared war on Cleopatra, an astute move that compelled Antonius to go to war against him and Rome.

Many factors favored Antonius at first. An experienced general, he commanded substantial land forces supplemented by those of his numerous client kings and allies. The Egyptian fleet was with him, and he still had supporters in the West. His best course of action might have been to strike quickly at Octavian's western power base; instead, perhaps influenced by Cleopatra, he went on the defensive, allowing Octavian's forces to deal several damaging blows. Antonius's large army was blockaded on the Adriatic coast at Actium, which forced him to attempt a break-through at sea. The resulting battle in 31 BC was a disaster for Antonius. Most of Cleopatra's ships escaped, but Antonius's army was compelled to surrender. His position rapidly collapsed throughout the East. Nearly deserted as he prepared a last stand against Octavian outside Alexandria, Antonius received a false report of Cleopatra's death and inflicted a mortal wound on himself. When he learned she was still alive, he was carried to her and died in her arms. Unable to sway Octavian, and determined not to adorn his triumph in Rome, Cleopatra committed suicide on 10 August 30 BC, perhaps by the bite of a cobra.* Seventeen-year-old Caesarion, who had been sent south to safety, was later apprehended and murdered at Octavian's orders, though Cleopatra's children by Antonius were brought to Rome and raised by Octavia. The Ptolemaic dynasty that had ruled Egypt for three centuries had come to an end.

---

* Certainly not by an asp, as is popularly said, for the classical term 'aspis' refers to a snake that can puff its neck into a shield.

8 Egypt in the Roman Empire

In his political testament, the Emperor Augustus, as Octavian was known after 27 BC, stated, "I added Egypt to the empire of the Roman people." Yet Egypt occupied a unique position within the Roman Empire. Following Augustus's settlement in the aftermath of the victory over Antonius and Cleopatra that made him sole ruler of the Roman world, provinces fell into two categories, senatorial and imperial. The former were ruled directly by the Senate, while the emperor governed the latter through legates by a grant of proconsular power that was periodically renewed by the Senate. For the most part, the imperial provinces were those of greater strategic importance where regular legions were stationed, while the senatorial provinces were quieter places with relatively little military presence. In either case, the provincial governor was usually a senator. This arrangement disguised the essentially monarchical character of the Roman Empire and provided reasonably good government for more than two centuries. Egypt, however, did not fit into the system, for the Senate was entirely excluded from its administration, even in theory. Its governor, a prefect appointed by the emperor and responsible only to him, was not of senatorial but of lesser equestrian rank; indeed, it was forbidden for a senator even to visit Egypt without the emperor's express permission. So unique was Egypt's status within the Roman Empire that it has been referred to as the emperor's personal estate—an exaggeration, but one that makes an important point.

The emperor ruled Egypt as a divine king. He was addressed and depicted as a pharaoh, and his name was written in hieroglyphs enclosed in cartouches, as the Ptolemies' had been. The prefect of Egypt lived and governed with his extensive staff from the old Ptolemaic palace complex. Beneath him were four *epistrategoi*, or regional governors, and further down some thirty *strategoi* who governed the individual nomes, which were altered little from Ptolemaic times. Within and alongside this administrative pyramid was an extensive imperial bureaucracy whose duties, according to the Alexandrian philosopher Philo, were "intricate and diversified, hardly grasped even by those who have made a business of studying them from their earliest years." At the very bottom were the towns and villages, which had local responsibilities: seeing to public works, delivery of the harvest to state magazines, collection of monetary taxes, and gathering of manpower for the corvée. There were no town senates or town councils in Roman Egypt until the beginning of the third century AD, but magistrates and lesser officials known as liturgists were appointed, elected, or co-opted into service. These men, whether Egyptian or Greek, were men who had the leisure and financial means to serve—and, ominously, to make good any shortfall in what the state demanded. No significant self-government was involved.

The Roman garrison of Egypt initially consisted of three legions. One was stationed at Alexandria. A second had its fortified headquarters at Babylon,* in present-day Cairo, where a remnant of the ramparts can still be seen, incorporated into the Coptic Museum's entrance. The third legion was posted at Thebes. Later the garrison of Egypt was reduced to two legions, and both of these were moved to Alexandria where they were quartered in Nicopolis. From there they sent detachments throughout Egypt as needed. In addition to the regular legionary garrison, the Roman geographer Strabo reported the presence of several

---

* Several explanations exist for this name, including Strabo's of a settlement of Babylonians, but Egyptian Babylon must not be confused with Mesopotamian Babylon.

cohorts of infantry and cavalry, and there may have been various auxiliary units as well.

The frontiers of the province were established early on and changed little thereafter. The parts of the old Ptolemaic Empire that had been restored to Cleopatra by Caesar and Antonius were again detached. Cyrenaica was combined with Crete to form a senatorial province. Cyprus likewise became a senatorial province, though of lesser importance. Egyptian possessions in Syria went to the imperial of Syria or to various client kings. The Eastern Desert and Red Sea continued to be important, and indeed gained in significance, as will be seen, while imperial presence in the Western Desert is attested by a number of fine temples, especially at Dakhla Oasis. The southern frontier of Egypt was secured by the first two prefects of Egypt, Cornelius Gallus and Petronius. Their campaigns ranged as far south as the Meroitic kingdom, and a garrison was briefly maintained at Qasr Ibrim, but the border was soon established at Hiera Sikaminos, about eighty kilometers south of the First Cataract. The Emperor Nero sent an exploratory expedition far up the Nile, but it confirmed earlier opinions that the area could not justify farther Roman expansion.

The administrative center of Egypt continued to be Alexandria, just as splendid and opulent as before, and still the premier city of the eastern Mediterranean until it was displaced from that position by Constantinople in the fourth century. The Roman presence was evident in the prefectoral headquarters in the Ptolemaic palace complex, in the legionary station of Nicopolis, virtually a suburb of the city, and in the imperial fleet stationed in the harbors, as well as in the droves of Roman officials, businessmen, and travelers who were to be seen around town. Another Roman touch, albeit one taken from pharaonic Egypt, was the two obelisks that Augustus had brought from Heliopolis to stand in front of the temple of the deified Julius Caesar, known as the Caesarium, beside the Eastern Harbor. Long after Alexandria lapsed into insignificance they remained there and became known as Cleopatra's Needles. During the late nineteenth century, they wandered yet farther afield, one to the Victoria Embankment in London, the other to New York's Central Park.

The magnificent Ptolemaic and Roman city of Alexandria has almost vanished. During medieval times, the city was nearly abandoned and fell into shapeless masses of ruins that were pillaged for building materials or anything of value; then, during the late nineteenth and twentieth centuries, almost everything was obliterated by the resurgent modern city. Valuable bits of cultural flotsam and jetsam are preserved in Alexandria's Greco-Roman Museum. The most notable standing monument that remains is the solitary column popularly but incorrectly known as Pompey's Pillar. Otherwise one must look underground to the catacombs or to another subterranean marvel, the ancient cisterns, many of which are still intact, some so spacious and splendid that they must literally be seen to be believed.

True to their policy of tight political control over Egypt, the Romans allowed Alexandria no municipal government during the first two centuries of Roman rule. The city's mob ceased to be a factor because of the immediate presence of the legions, although nasty gang violence persisted. Nevertheless, Alexandria enjoyed a vibrant civic life. Processions and festivals continued to delight the crowds, though they did not match the dreamy splendor of their Ptolemaic predecessors. Public establishments were heavily patronized. The hippodrome was thronged with fans of one charioteer or another, wearing the distinctive partisan colors blue and green, though their rivalry often extended beyond the races. Also highly popular was the theater, one of the few parts of the ancient city still to be seen, having been preserved under the mound of Kom al-Dik that later rose above it. Recent excavations have revealed the theater in an astonishingly good state of preservation, along with some of the immediately surrounding public buildings such as the baths and lecture halls. The graffiti of long-vanished Alexandrians are scratched into the walls.

As during Ptolemaic times, the Greeks continued to dominate Alexandria socially and civically. Special rights and privileges set them apart. These included a lower rate of taxation and a higher degree of protection in the courts. Such distinctions were jealously guarded and regularly affirmed by the early emperors who wanted to maintain stability in the city and ensure smooth operation of grain shipments to Rome. Imperial favor could not be taken for granted, however. When the Emperor Caracalla came to Alexandria in AD 215, he was so infuriated by allegations that he was implicated in the death of his brother Geta—perhaps all the more so since they were true—that he issued orders for the indiscriminate slaughter of the city's youth.

The large Jewish population also continued to play a major role in Alexandria's economic, social, and intellectual life. The prefect of Egypt under Nero and Vespasian was Tiberius Julius Alexander, a member of a wealthy Alexandrian Jewish family and a nephew of the philosopher Philo, although he had renounced the Jewish religion. While less extensive than those of the Greeks, the privileges of the Alexandrian Jews were confirmed by Augustus and renewed by Claudius, although the latter commanded them not to demand more, and not to take undue advantage of the ones they already had.

Yet antagonism between Greeks and Jews in Alexandria grew stronger than ever. This appears to have been based in part on resentment of the Jews' growing numbers and their attempts to have greater access to civic facilities such as the theater and the hippodrome, but it also expressed simple ethnic intolerance, as is clear in the language of a Greek Alexandrian who complained to the Emperor Claudius that the city's Jews "are not of the same nature as the Alexandrians, but live rather after the fashion of the Egyptians." Numerous violent clashes occurred during early imperial times in which houses were burned and Jews murdered. Even so, Alexandria's Jews did not rise as a group in support of the revolt in Judea in AD 66, although sporadic riots required suppression by the legionary garrison. Their loyalty was commended by the Emperor Trajan soon after his accession in AD 98, and the emperor assured them of his intention to provide "for your undisturbed tranquility and your food supply and your communal and individual rights." But the situation was different in the great Jewish Revolt of AD 115–17. This actually began in Egypt, after a Jewish messiah was proclaimed in neighboring Cyrenaica, and spread to Cyprus. Fighting in Egypt was severe, with guerrilla warfare extending into the countryside, causing much loss of life and property. By the time the revolt was suppressed, Alexandria's Jewish community had been devastated, never to recover the numbers or importance it once had.

The commercial importance of Alexandria became greater than ever during the Roman Period, with its harbors open to a sea made safe by the Pax Romana. It was also connected to the Nile by a canal that gave it access to the abundance of the Delta and Upper Egypt—and via the Nile to the overland connections with the Red Sea ports where trade with Arabia and India reached its peak during Roman times. As Dio of Prusa observed during the first century, "Alexandria is situated, as it were, at the crossroads of the whole world, of even its most remote nations, as if it were a market serving a single city, bringing together all men into one place, displaying them to one another and, as far as possible, making them of the same race."[14]

Alexandria also remained at the forefront of intellectual life in the Mediterranean world during the Roman Empire. Although the library never fully recovered from the fire of 48 BC, it was still by far the best in the Roman world, and the Emperor Claudius enlarged the Museum, which continued to be home and training ground for many renowned scholars, and for many more unremembered ones who nevertheless lived the life of the mind and were a vital component of Alexandria's intellectual enterprise. The astronomical work of the second-century Claudius Ptolemaeus, known by its Latinized Arabic name of *Almagest*, is a masterpiece of exposition, observation, and analysis. Although his geocentric theories might seem retrograde from the heliocentric insights of Eratosthenes, Ptolemaeus's work prevailed because of its wealth of data and superior explanatory model. It dominated astronomical theory for over a thousand years until supplanted by Nicolaus Copernicus in the sixteenth century. Almost as influential in its own way was Ptolemaeus's astrological compendium, the *Tetrabiblos*, in which he attempted to provide a scientific basis for the pseudoscience. Ptolemaeus was also a geographer of great ability and influence, and his *Geographia*, like *Almagest*, remained a standard reference work for more than a millennium, although his observational basis was too limited to be of much real use beyond Europe, and his estimate of the earth's circumference was less accurate than Eratosthenes'.

Philosophy flourished in Alexandria, the dominant strain being Platonism. Philo, the preeminent Alexandrian philosopher of early Roman times, also became leader of Alexandria's Jewish community. His work was important for the later development of both Neoplatonism and Christian theology. Neoplatonism, a synthesis of elements from Platonic, Aristotelian, Pythagorean, and Stoic philosophies, carried Plato's passion for ideas into the realm of mysticism. Alexandria was so important in this development that Neoplatonism was often referred to as 'the school of Alexandria.' It was most effectively advanced by the third-century teacher, Ammonius Saccas, who was sometimes called the Socrates of Neoplatonism because of his influence and because, like Socrates, he was a renowned teacher but never wrote. Ammonius Saccas instructed students as diverse as the great Neoplatonist philosopher Plotinus, Origen the Pagan, Origen the Christian, and Longinus. The Aristotelians, however, were never extinguished, and whether Platonic or Aristotelian, most notable philosophers of late antiquity studied at Alexandria.

Alexandrian excellence in medicine continued to be unchallenged. The greatest physician of antiquity, Galen of Pergamum, studied at Alexandria. His influence on later medical thinking, which persisted into modern times, has been compared to that of Aristotle. Some of his ideas, especially about the spread of disease, were still alive during the mid-nineteenth century. Even during the late fourth century, after the Museum had suffered many vicissitudes and other areas of study were in decline, medicine remained strong at Alexandria. As the Roman historian Ammianus Marcellinus observed: "When a physician wants to establish his place in the profession, all he needs to do is say he was trained at Alexandria."

A more arcane though enormously influential intellectual and literary development in Roman Alexandria was Hermeticism. The texts that became known as the *Corpus Hermeticum* were composed in the second and third centuries AD by Greeks in Egypt who wrote under the collective name Hermes Trismegistus. They identified the Greek god Hermes with the Egyptian Thoth and assigned him a place as the essential intelligence of the universe. The texts of the *Corpus Hermeticum*, though claiming to be of remotest antiquity, were in fact a mixture of Platonism, Stoicism, popular philosophy, and probably some Jewish and Near Eastern elements as well. Their subject matter ranged from religion and philosophy to magic and alchemy. Whether any genuine ancient Egyptian elements found their way into the *Corpus Hermeticum* is debated among scholars. The Hermetic writings were, however, given a powerful stamp of authenticity by the Church Fathers, who believed that Hermes Trismegistus was a real person who had lived around the time of Moses. Lactantius identified him as one of the most important of the gentile writers who foresaw the coming of Christianity. St. Augustine was equally impressed and wrote in his *City of God*, "This Hermes says much of God according to the truth."

Hermeticism created a sensation when it was rediscovered during the Italian Renaissance and the *Corpus Hermeticum* was translated from

Greek to Latin by Marsilio Ficino in 1460. It went through numerous editions in many different languages and exerted an influence both profound and persistent. Even after Isaac Casaubon conclusively proved in 1614 that it had been written not in remotest antiquity but in the early Christian era, scholars continued to regard it as authentic. The Jesuit scholar Athanasius Kircher, one of the most learned men of his time, wrote in 1652:

> Hermes Trismegistus, the Egyptian, who first instituted the hieroglyphs, thus becoming the prince and parent of all Egyptian theology and philosophy, was the first and most ancient among the Egyptians and first rightly thought of divine things; and engraved his opinion for all eternity on lasting stones and huge rocks. Thence Orpheus, Musaeus, Linus, Pythagoras, Plato, Eudoxus, Parmenides, Melissus, Homer, Euripides, and others learned rightly of God and of divine things.[15]

The *Corpus Hermeticum* remained influential at least into the nineteenth century and still occasionally serves as a point of departure for speculation and revision, as in Martin Bernal's controversial book *Black Athena*.

Religious life in Roman Egypt continued to display the vitality, diversity, and creativity of Ptolemaic times. The traditional religion—or one might better say, given its complexity, religions—went on smoothly, at least until the troubled third century, though the temples were less affluent than before, and the emperors placed them under stricter bureaucratic control. The elaborate royal cults of the previous regime were discontinued, but Roman emperors were still portrayed as gods in pharaonic fashion and got the reverence they deserved, though less so as time went by. The Emperor Commodus (AD 180–92) was the last to be widely depicted as a pharaoh in Egypt, and Decius (AD 249–51) the last whose name was carved in hieroglyphs.

The early Roman emperors were notable temple builders, and in peripheral areas as well as in Alexandria and the valley of the Nile. The Nubian temple of Kalabsha, dedicated to the Kushite sun god Mandulis, was largely constructed during the reign of Augustus. It has been relocated on a site just above the Aswan High Dam. In Dakhla Oasis one can visit an impressive temple of Amun, Khonsu, and Thoth, begun during the reign of Nero, one of dozens of temples from all periods in that rich archaeological area. The emperors also made notable additions to existing temples, such as the elegant Kiosk of Trajan at Philae. Serapis and Isis flourished, and there were plenty of other deities, some local, some imported, and some composite, presenting the Egyptian worshiper with a wide range of choice. The well-documented town of Oxyrhynchus, which numbered perhaps forty thousand inhabitants and was located near the present-day town of Behnesa, contained three temples of Zeus-Amun, Hera-Isis, and Arargaris-Bethynnis, a large Serapeum, two temples of Isis, one of Osiris, four of Thoeris, and other temples and cult centers for Demeter, Kore, the Dioscuroi, Dionysos, Hermes, Apollo, Agathos, Daimon, Neotera, Tyche, Jupiter Capitolinus, and Mars. The religious spectrum in Alexandria—with its half million people, cosmopolitan population, and more than two thousand temples—must have been mind-boggling. Egypt provided fertile soil for religion. Old ones faded; new ones took root. "They are religious to excess, beyond any other nation in the world," Herodotus had written of the Egyptians in the fifth century BC. Had he visited Egypt in many other periods of its history, he would not have altered his opinion.

Though Greeks and Romans in Egypt brought their own ideas about religion, and about life and death, these notions inevitably took on Egyptian trappings over time. This is evident in the persistence of mummification, which was adopted by the Greeks and maintained in Roman Egypt. In some respects, the practice had deteriorated from the lofty standards of pharaonic days. Basic preparation was less meticulous; internal organs were left in place, and while canopic jars were still provided to contain them, they were dummies. Some body parts might be lacking or additional ones inserted—or the body might be missing altogether—but the external bandaging was done in a geometric manner so distinctive that even a non-expert can often identify a Greco-Roman mummy. Everything was enclosed in a mummy case anyway, so appearances were satisfied, and the family of the deceased was content.

Another distinctive feature of early Roman mummification, and by far the most remarkable, was mummy portraiture. Instead of the traditional three-dimensional funeral masks with their highly stylized representations, sometime during the first century AD it became a common practice to insert a flat, painted portrait bearing a likeness of the deceased. Because so many of these were discovered at Hawara at the entrance to the Fayyum, they have become known as Fayyum Portraits, although they also come from other parts of Egypt. Working in the lifelike tradition of ancient Greek portraiture (of which the Fayyum Portraits provide most of the surviving examples), the best of the painters achieved a high degree of technical mastery that was unequaled in many respects until well into the Renaissance. Usually working in a medium known as encaustic, in which pigment is mixed with beeswax, they used a palette of bright primary colors that were blended to provide a wide range of subtle hues; touches such as highlights in eyes and reflections on jewels convey powerful illusions of reality. To view a Fayyum Portrait is to experience an uncanny sense of direct contact with the distant past as its subject seems to return the gaze, sharing the moment in time. The Fayyum mummies did not represent the only mode of Greco-Roman burial in Egypt, as the second century AD catacombs at Alexandria demonstrate, but a mixture of Greek, Roman, and Egyptian elements is to be found there as well.

Although ordinary folk generally have a disproportionately small part in the historical record of antiquity, we know much more about daily life in Egypt than any other province of the Roman Empire. Information comes from a number of sources, but especially from bits of papyri, preserved through the millennia by Egypt's dry air and sand. The major find was at Oxyrhynchus in the late nineteenth century. Although little of the ancient town remained beyond some ruined, shapeless mounds, the rubbish dumps of Oxyrhynchus contained vast accumulations of papyri, primarily of Roman and Byzantine date. These revealed new dimensions of ancient life through private letters, wills, household and estate accounts, contracts, erotica, legal proceedings, tax receipts, fragments of lost works of great and not-so-great classical writers, and much more.

As in Ptolemaic times, Greeks often occupied a privileged position in Egypt. Native Egyptians were not permitted into the administration, and the Roman army in Egypt was recruited exclusively from the Hellenic population during the early Roman Period. The language of administration in Roman Egypt, like most other provinces in the eastern part of the empire, was Greek. The major centers of Greek population were four towns—Naukratis, Ptolemais, Antinoopolis, and of course Alexandria—which preserved special rights and exemptions well into the third century AD, when such distinctions began to even out; Greeks were also to be found in disproportionate numbers in the nome capitals. While Greek culture continued to exert a strong influence within Egypt, the impact of western Latin culture and society was much more superficial, perhaps because settlement by people from Italy and the empire's highly Romanized western provinces was light. It is significant that during Byzantine times, an Egyptian might boast of Greek or Macedonian descent, but never of Roman.

The Ptolemaic policy of state ownership of land was progressively relaxed during the Roman Period with an increase in private ownership, but a large proportion of land remained as imperial estates and public property from which the state drew produce, rents, and profits from various commercial activities. It was said that the favorite wine of the Emperor Augustus came from his vineyard in the Fayyum. The properties of the temples, virtually sacrosanct under the Ptolemies, were resources too great for the Roman government to leave untouched. The wealth—and consequently the power—of the priesthood was greatly diminished.

It has become almost a truism to say that most native Egyptians, who continued to work the land as their ancestors had done since time out of mind, were little affected by changing regimes, whether pharaonic, Ptolemaic, or Roman, but such a generality should be qualified. The peasants were always intimately connected to the land, and their lives were regulated by the seasons: the inundation with its enforced idleness as they hoped and prayed for a good level, neither too high nor too low; the arduous time of sowing and cultivation; and harvest with its meager margin of survival after the tax collectors, temple landlords, or whatever exploitative agencies had taken their tolls. But unlike the pharaonic periods, very few peasant families in Greco-Roman times were isolated economic entities, growing or producing everything that they needed; instead, they were part of a complex system of market exchange that provided a medium for trading a surplus in one thing in order to supply a deficiency in another. This was partly a matter of barter, but it also involved a significant amount of money, because a large amount of coin circulated in Roman as in Ptolemaic Egypt; some of this filtered down to the masses and was used in their market transactions. Larger estates were centers of complex agricultural activity with vineyards, orchards, wineries, olive presses, breweries, livestock, and many kinds of workshops for processing what they produced. Even some of the smaller villages offered a wide range of goods and services.

As to the overall quality of life of the average Egyptian peasant under Roman rule, the increased order and security provided by the establishment of the Roman Empire in Egypt must have provided at least marginal improvement over the chaotic situation that often prevailed in the countryside during the late Ptolemaic Period. Internal revolts were less frequent during the early Roman Period, the great Jewish Revolt in AD 115–17 being an exceptional case, and a high degree of domestic security prevailed; no significant foreign invasion occurred before the mid-third century. By the same token, however, the empire-wide crisis during the third century imposed great difficulties on Egypt, and it is now understood that there were systemic problems within the empire even during the second century that manifested themselves with exceptional severity in Egypt. Well before the middle of that century, droves of minor officials were fleeing their posts in the recurring desperate Egyptian act of anachoresis, abandoning their land to confiscation, because they could not meet their obligations to the state. Surprisingly large tracts fell into disuse, leaving heavier tax burdens on those people who remained. Anachoresis was already so serious by AD 154 that an edict was issued against it. How could the government drive people to such desperate measures?

The answer lies in Rome's attitude toward Egypt as its breadbasket, a source for exploitation, not an object for development. "Bread and circuses" was more than merely a Roman slogan; it was a basic feature of the system that kept the emperors in power. The Roman people no longer participated in regular democratic processes, but they had to be kept content. Emperors, fearing the consequences if the subsidized grain distributions in Rome failed, did not hesitate to sacrifice the long-term interests of Egypt to ensure their political survival in Rome. Not that exploitation in Egypt was anything new: the Ptolemies had raised it to an exact science, but at least they, foreign dynasty though they were, had functioned as Egyptian monarchs with Egypt as the vital center of their realm. Most of what they took from Egypt was spent or wasted in Egypt, providing a rough balance, at least in good times. Now the seemingly unlimited abundance of the Nile was channeled abroad with relatively little coming in return. The heaviest but by no means the only burden was the *anona*, a tax in kind, which primarily consisted of enormous shipments of grain to Rome. It is estimated that under Augustus well over one million tons of Egyptian grain may have arrived in Rome each year, an amount that probably represented 10 percent, and perhaps much more, of Egypt's entire harvest.

The grain was conveyed in large, specially designed ships. When bad weather forced one of them to take shelter in Athens, a crowd gathered to gape at the enormous vessel with the goddess Isis on its prow. "What a size the ship was!" a witness reported. "Fifty-five meters in length, the ship's carpenter told me, the beam more than a quarter of that, and thirteen meters from the deck to the bottom, the deepest point in the bilge. . . . The crew must have been as big as an army. They told me she carried so much grain that it would be enough to feed every mouth in Athens for a year." With the short sailing season that was observed in antiquity, lasting only from April to October, such a vessel could hope to make two round trip journeys at most. The trip from Alexandria to Rome was the most difficult: because of contrary prevailing winds it could easily take two months, and sometimes three; but the return voyage, propelled by the northwest wind, went much more quickly. When Herod Agrippa was about to leave Rome for the East, the Emperor Caligula told him, "Take a direct sailing to Alexandria. The ships are crack sailing craft and their skippers the most experienced there are; they drive the vessels like racehorses on an unswerving course that goes straight as a die."[16] Caligula may have been insane, but he realized the importance of the grain shipments well enough to know how the ships worked. Secure receipt of Egyptian grain was the primary reason the Emperor Claudius constructed a new harbor at Ostia to which the Emperor Trajan made subsequent improvements. And the grain shipment was only part of what was taken from Egypt. The combination of additional taxes—some in money, others in products and services—probably provided even more revenue than the *anona*.

Although agriculture remained by far the most important economic aspect of Roman Egypt and the primary concern of the vast majority of its population, Egypt entered an unprecedented era of commercial activity under the Roman Empire. Not only were vast quantities of agricultural produce exported, but also an extensive variety of manu-factured goods, many made by highly organized guilds of craftsmen. Egyptian glass was one such product. The exquisite Portland Vase, now in the British Museum, may have been made in an Egyptian workshop. Egyptian trade with Arabia, India, and Ceylon, primarily conducted through the ports on the southeastern coast, increased greatly under the empire, as is documented in the first-century work *Voyage around the Red Sea* by an Alexandrian merchant. The Emperor Trajan reopened the canal between the Nile and the Red Sea. The mineral wealth of Egypt was mined and exported: gold, silver, and turquoise. Yet, despite the cosmopolitan nature of its trading network, Egypt still stood apart in many ways, including its exclusive system of coinage, instituted by the Ptolemies and retained by the Romans until AD 296.

Quarrying had been a major activity in Egypt since Predynastic times, and so it remained under the Romans. Red granite continued to be quarried at Aswan, as was sandstone at Gebel al-Silsileh. But the great Roman quarries in Egypt were in the Eastern Desert at Mons Porphyrites, or Gebel Dokhan, and Mons Claudianus, both instituted during the early Roman Period and abandoned when the imperial system faltered. The product from Mons Porphyrites was imperial porphyry, found only at that site. The color purple, long associated with nobility and later with the Roman imperial family, was especially prized and used for columns, inlays, paneling, and for fine statues, the most famous example being that of the Emperor Diocletian and his colleagues, now at St. Mark's Cathedral in Venice. South of Mons Porphyrites was Mons Claudianus, source of the tonalite gneiss that went into some of Rome's greatest monuments, including the Pantheon and Trajan's Forum. (Italian stonecutters call it "granito del foro," or "granite of the forum.") The size and complexity of these operations is a source of amazement for all who visit them, espe-cially Mons Claudianus where the *castellum*, or settlement, was so well preserved as to give nineteenth- and early twentieth-century travelers the impression that the Romans had just departed a short time before, an impression that is being dulled now that the sites have become more accessible by four-wheel-drive vehicles. The methods by which the por-phyry and granite of Mons Porphyrites and Mons Claudianus were extracted and worked have never been fully explained. The largest columns from Mons Claudianus weighed two hundred tons and were nearly twenty meters long. Such colossal objects had to be conveyed more than a hundred kilometers overland to the Nile, where they were loaded onto barges for the trip to Alexandria; there they were transferred to special vessels to be taken to Italy or elsewhere in the Mediterranean.

Egypt was often in the thoughts and deeds of the early Roman emperors. It supplied the grain for Rome that was important for their political survival; income from its imperial estates was a welcome addition to a budget that was often stretched to the limit; and its stone adorned many of their magnificent buildings that were important expressions of imperial power. Also, no less than three first-century emperors—Caligula, Claudius, and Nero—were directly descended from Marcus Antonius (though through Octavia, not Cleopatra), and proud of it, so the Egyptian associations of their great ancestor came readily into their minds. Another third-century ruler, Vespasian, was first proclaimed as emperor after the fall of Nero by the prefect of Egypt, Tiberius Julius Alexander. This support, backed by the legions in Egypt and control of the grain supply, helped sway other eastern provinces to follow suit. When Vespasian came to Alexandria in AD 69 while waiting for events in the west to be resolved, he was acclaimed in the hippodrome as the son of Amun and the incarnation of Serapis. Augustus had intended to exclude Egypt from imperial political life, but such an important province could not remain irrelevant to the broader concerns of the Roman world.

Rome's most peculiar province also made a strong impression on Roman culture. One manifestation was Roman tourism to Egypt, as Romans were drawn to sights along the Nile—the Pyramids of Giza, the Labyrinth at Hawara, and the temples of Thebes. The two so-called Colossi of Memnon were a great favorite. These giant statues of Amenhotep III were identified in the classical imagination with the Homeric demigod Memnon, son of Eos, the goddess of dawn. On some mornings the northernmost statue would utter a musical sound, described like that of a breaking harp string, as if Memnon was greeting his mother. Various explanations have been offered for this phenomenon, including priestly chicanery, but the most plausible is that it was naturally produced as the sonorous stone was warmed by the sun. Classical tourists arose early to hear it, and they covered the lower part of the colossus with inscriptions and graffiti to commemorate their experiences. A typical one reads, "I came at night to listen to the voice of the very divine Memnon, and I heard it, I, Catulus, chief of the Thebaïd." But when the Emperor Septimius Severus came to hear the statue at the beginning of the third century, it was silent. In an act of propitiation, Severus had the colossus restored, a process that somehow disrupted its acoustic mechanism so that Memnon never again spoke to his mother at daybreak.

Egypt influenced the Roman Empire in many other ways, including religion. As has already been noted, the worship of Serapis spread throughout the empire, and Isis became one of the leading goddesses of the Mediterranean world, portrayed in an idealized, Hellenized manner, but always with an Egyptianizing background. The Senate, seeing her as an assault on traditional Roman virtues (there was a big scandal associated with her cult in 19 BC), repeatedly ordered her temples destroyed, but they were always rebuilt. A vast Isiac temple once stood on the Campus Martius in Rome, and a particularly well preserved one can still be seen at Pompeii.

Romans had a persistent fascination with Egyptian obelisks, beginning with Augustus. Caligula had a special ship constructed to transport one that weighed almost five hundred tons and now stands in St. Peter's Square. Over three hundred years later, the Emperor Constantius had another brought to Rome and erected in the Circus Maximus. It was subsequently moved to its present location at the church of San Giovanni in Laterano. Several other obelisks were transplanted from the banks of the Nile to the imperial city, or were custom-made in Italy, so that Rome has more Egyptian obelisks than Egypt does. Long after knowledge of ancient Egyptian civilization had largely vanished from Europe, these monuments, stately and enigmatic, pointed the way back to the ancient land, maintaining its mystique in popular imagination. Egyptian fashion in Roman decorative arts can be seen in surviving examples at Hadrian's Villa at Tivoli, in the Palestrina mosaic in the Temple of Fortuna Primigenia (who was closely associated with Isis) at Praeneste, and on murals in houses at Pompeii or in private monuments such as the pyramid of Caius Cestius.

Egypt's influence can be readily detected in Roman literature. Plutarch (late first–early second century AD) supplied the most comprehensive and detailed account of Egyptian religion in his *On Isis and*

Osiris. It is particularly important to Egyptology for preserving the story of Osiris-Seth-Isis-Horus, the essential myth for understanding the divine kingship of the pharaohs. In Apuleius's delightful second-century novel *The Golden Ass*, the hero Lucius finds himself turned into a donkey after recklessly dabbling in black magic but is restored through initiation into the mysteries of Isis. The popularity of the goddess Isis is obvious in both works.

The most sensational individual imperial encounter with Egypt was Hadrian's tour. This cultured emperor visited every province of the empire at least once, so it is not surprising that he should pay Egypt particular attention, spending eight to ten months there in AD 130–31. As always, Hadrian was conscientious about his duties, reviewing soldiers and inspecting administration, evaluating and setting standards. He also played the role of Roman tourist *par excellence*. An accomplished amateur philosopher, he disputed with the learned in the Museum, as Julius Caesar had done; he went lion hunting in the desert; and of course he sailed up the Nile. Like many before him, he arose before dawn to stand in the Theban plain to listen for Memnon's musical sound. When the statue was silent, he patiently returned the following morning, and it spoke not once but three times as if to make up for ignoring him the day before. Hadrian and his entourage made a splendid display of imperial might and presence, but a fragment of papyrus from Oxyrhynchus testifies to the harsh financial reality of supporting such a tour. That town had to provide a prodigious amount of supplies, including two hundred *artab*s of barley, three thousand bales of hay, 372 suckling pigs, and two hundred sheep. Other areas in Egypt had to make similar contributions. Tragedy struck near al-Sheikh Ibada when the emperor's favorite, a handsome young man named Antinous, was drowned in the Nile. The grief-stricken emperor had Antinous deified and founded a town, Antinoopolis, on the spot where he died, with a temple for his worship. Its remains were still visible until the early nineteenth century. Hadrian also commanded the construction of a long Roman road, the Via Hadriana, that ran in a long curve through the Eastern Desert from Antinoopolis to the port of Berenike on the Red Sea. Numerous statues of Antinous were made, often depicting him scantily clad in pharaonic costume. Despite sad associations, Egypt made a powerful impression on Hadrian, and he reproduced many of its scenes in his villa at Tivoli.

The reign of Hadrian (AD 117–38) was a relatively orderly time in the history of the Roman Empire, as was that of his successor Antoninus Pius (AD 138–61) who is well attested in Egyptian inscriptions because his reign coincided with the completion of a Sothic cycle, a major event in the ancient Egyptian calendar that occurred only every 1460 years. But the empire was beset by plagues, barbarian incursions, and financial dislocations well before the end of the second century AD, and in the third century it entered a period of prolonged crisis. When Septimius Severus became emperor in AD 193 after a bloody succession struggle, he abandoned the constitutional forms that had concealed the essentially monarchical nature of the empire in favor of undisguised military might. His method, which he advised his sons to follow, was to enrich the soldiers and despise the rest of the world, a policy that cost the empire heavily, with Egypt probably paying more than its share. During a tour of Egypt (when he inadvertently silenced the vocal statue at Thebes), Severus established local councils for the country's towns, but this measure, something the Egyptian municipalities had been requesting for centuries, was motivated not by benevolence but to secure revenues at a time when local magistrates and peasants alike were fleeing their posts and lands to escape tax burdens: the town councils provided a readily identifiable group of men who could be held personally responsible for tax payments, and who had to pay for many of the functions of local government as well. By the same token, when Severus's son and successor Caracalla (AD 211–17) granted Roman citizenship to all communities within the empire, a privilege once highly prized, it was to increase revenue from the inheritance tax that citizens had to pay.

Beset by murder, madness, intrigue, and uprisings—all four of Severus's family members who succeeded him died violent deaths—the Severan dynasty ended in AD 235 with the murder of Alexander Severus. Any shred of legitimate succession was lost, and army commanders fought among themselves to become emperors. No sooner was one established than another rose against him; often several simultaneously competed to wear the imperial purple. Frontiers were neglected and internal security disregarded as would-be emperors diverted all available resources into the struggle for power. Throughout the third century Egyptians were harried with increasing demands for money and goods from the army in addition to regular taxes.

The Nile Valley, which the Pax Romana had hitherto kept secure, was subjected to repeated attacks by nomadic tribes from the Western Desert. The southern frontier was overrun by a people called the Blemmyes. If the classical sources are to be taken seriously, the Emperor Decius (AD 249–51) used some unorthodox tactics against these invaders. According to one writer, Decius "brought from dry Libya poisonous snakes and dreadful hermaphrodites and released them at the Egyptian frontier." The Blemmyes were able to withstand Decius's snakes and hermaphrodites, however, and continued to cause serious trouble; one of their incursions reached as far north as the town of Ptolemais, near present-day Sohag, during the reign of the Emperor Probus (AD 276–82).

Even Alexandria was not safe. With the eastern frontier in disarray, the wealthy buffer state of Palmyra, based on its oasis trading center east of Syria, invaded and overran northern Egypt, capturing Alexandria in AD 270. The Emperor Aurelian (AD 270–75) recaptured Alexandria, regained control of Egypt, and defeated and captured the Palmyran queen Zenobia, but Alexandria suffered heavily from the occupation. The palace complex that had continued to serve as Egypt's administrative center was destroyed, and the Museum probably suffered extensive damage. Alexandria had not recovered before an Alexandrian usurper, Lucius Domitius Domitianus, was proclaimed emperor in AD 297, prompting the Emperor Diocletian (AD 284–305) to subject the city to a siege of eight months. According to one story, Diocletian became so frustrated as the siege wore on that he swore to slaughter the city's inhabitants until their blood reached the level of his horse's knee, but when he finally entered the city victoriously, his horse stumbled, falling to its knees and reducing the vowed level to nothing. In gratitude the city had an equestrian statue made of him that may have once sat atop the column, misnamed Pompey's Pillar, that was actually erected in honor of Diocletian. Significantly, the pillar's Arabic name is al-'Amud al-Sawari, which means the Column of the Horseman.

Meanwhile, the rest of Egypt continued to be ravaged. When a revolt broke out in Upper Egypt in AD 293–94, Diocletian's imperial colleague Galerius personally directed the destruction of the town of Coptos. The effect of the continued turmoil and destruction on Egypt was devastating. The economic and political basis of town life along the Nile, always a fragile institution, was seriously damaged. In the countryside, the situation was probably worse. Even during the peaceful second century, as has been seen, widespread hardship was causing significant numbers of people, both peasants and the relatively well-placed, to flee their lands. During the third century, confronted by invasion, raids, brigandage, tax collectors, economic failure, and sheer despair, anachoresis accelerated rapidly; entire villages were abandoned as their inhabitants fled, seeking refuge in the desert, the mountains, the wadis, and the abundant ancient tombs, leaving some of the most fertile land in the world uncultivated. In the city or in the countryside, whether people fled or remained, their world view was shattered. The imperial system and its local manifestations, which once had provided some degree of security, failed them, disappearing when most needed, returning only intermittently, and then more often to add to their problems, not provide relief. In such circumstances, it is not surprising that many individuals turned to other solutions, spiritual as well as material.

Some semblance of stability returned to the Roman Empire at the end of the third century AD. The Emperor Diocletian, having vanquished all competitors, attempted to shore up the crumbling imperial structure through extensive reorganization. From the top down, he divided and subdivided administrative units, so that supervision could be maintained more closely at all levels. Egypt was eventually split into six separate provinces. The nomes, some of which had existed since Predynastic times, finally lost their significance. To provide frontier security, Diocletian doubled the size of the Roman army and established new fortified systems such as the one that ran along the Red Sea coast. Luxor Temple was turned into a fortified garrison encampment and administrative center. During his tour of Egypt after suppressing the rebellion in Alexandria, Diocletian established the island of Philae as the southernmost frontier post, withdrawing from Hiera Sykaminos in Nubia.

These reforms came at a heavy financial price to the people of Egypt, who were also adversely affected by other economic changes. State ownership of vast amounts of Egyptian land had continued well into the third century, but these were now mostly sold to private individuals, some of whom acquired extensive estates. Small landholders, though comprising a large proportion of the population, were increasingly hardpressed. Many became little better than serfs and slaves on the estates of the privileged, who assumed powers that previously had belonged to the state, giving them even greater control over the peasantry.

Under Constantine (AD 306–37), the political center of gravity of the Roman Empire shifted from the west to the east, where he established a new capital on the site of the old Greek town of Byzantium at the juncture of Europe and Asia in AD 330. Originally called New Rome, the city was soon renamed Constantinople. It grew quickly, surpassing Alexandria to become the greatest city in the eastern Mediterranean. A large portion of the grain shipments from Egypt that had gone to Rome was diverted to Constantinople for distributions to the new city's population.

With the foundation of Constantinople begins what came to be known as the Byzantine Period in history. The Byzantine Empire, the empire of the Greek east with its capital at Constantinople, lasted for another thousand years after the collapse of Roman imperial power in the Latin west at the end of the fifth century AD. Egypt was a part of that empire at first—an uneasy part, and the difficulty was largely because of Christianity. The new religion that should have provided a binding force ironically became a source of irreconcilable differences.

9 Coptic Egypt

The importance of Egypt to the development of Christianity is almost always underestimated or ignored by Christians in general. Egypt was one of the first and most fruitful fields for Christian conversion and the establishment of Christian institutions. Much of the orthodoxy of Christianity was hammered out in Egypt in the first catechetical schools, which were established in Alexandria, and in the bitter theological disputes such as that between St. Athanasius and Arius over the nature of Christ or between Cyril I and Nestorius over the nature of Mary. The Nicene Creed ("I believe in one God, the Father Almighty, Maker of all things both visible and invisible, and in one Lord Jesus Christ, the Word of God . . .") was formulated by Egyptian churchmen. The New Testament in its canonical form was first compiled in Egypt. Far from being an exotic, isolated offshoot, Egypt was first a nursery and then a pillar of the early Christian Church. Although Egypt later became a predominantly Muslim land, a strong Christian minority exists to this day and is an integral part of Egyptian life. The Coptic experience is one of the bases of Egyptian national consciousness. The words 'Copt' and 'Egypt' both derive from the ancient Egyptian *Hikaptah* (House of the Spirit of Ptah) through the

Greek *Aigyptos*. During the early centuries of Islam, the Arabs referred to Egypt as Dar al-Qibt, the Abode of the Copts.

According to a tradition dear to Egyptian Christians—though doubted by historians—Christianity was brought to Egypt during the reign of the Emperor Nero by St. Mark, who was martyred in Alexandria. In fact, little is known about the development of Christianity in Egypt during the first three centuries of the Christian era, but the Christian message obviously fell on fertile soil in the valley of the Nile, probably first establishing itself in the cities through their Jewish communities then diffusing into the countryside. By the time it emerged into historical daylight at the end of the third century, Christianity was a dynamic, growing force in Egypt, once again lending credence, and not for the last time, to Herodotus's assertion that the Egyptians were the most religious of all people.

Conditions in later Roman Egypt were ripe for the spread of a new religion like Christianity. The turmoil of the third century was extremely distressful to a people who prized order as much as the Egyptians did. Just as the government failed to meet people's material needs, so too did many of the existing religious systems fail to satisfy their spiritual needs. Where was one to turn in a world that had become inexplicable, perhaps unbearable?

The elite could find solace in the mystery religions that proliferated during late antiquity—of Isis, Mithra, and others that were to be found in Egypt and throughout the Roman Empire. The mystery religions' appeal was their claim to reveal the hidden meaning that lay behind the shifting appearances of life. The educated also had Neoplatonism, which flourished in Alexandria, with its mix of philosophy, mysticism, and even magic. Through magic one could gain an illusion of being in control that was expressed by one Neoplatonist philosopher who proclaimed, "I do not come to the Gods. The Gods come to me."

Another new religious phenomenon, Gnosticism, offered direct experience of God through knowledge (gnosis) of him. According to the Gnostics, the human self was a spark from the spiritual world caught in a material body that could be transcended. The discovery of a fourth-century Gnostic library at Nag Hammadi in 1945, a find on the order of the famous Dead Sea Scrolls in Palestine, has provided major new insights into not just Gnosticism but also early Christianity.

Manichaeism, a religion emanating from the Persian Empire, arrived in Egypt before the end of the third century and found many followers, mostly in Middle and Upper Egypt. The Manichaeans perceived an underlying duality with a constant struggle between opposing forces of good and evil, a view of the universe that made sense in the troubled times of the later Roman Empire. Hermeticism reassured some with its eternal truths purportedly coming from remote antiquity. Horoscopes, previously rare in Egypt, became popular during the early centuries of the Christian era as anxious people peered into an uncertain future.

All those forces left their mark on Egypt, but the religious choice that took root and covered the land for several centuries was Christianity. It too offered comfort during crisis. To the suffering, it provided reassurance of God's love and a promise of eventual justice and reward in the eternal life that had always been so important to Egyptians. But Christianity's benefits were practical as well as spiritual—a sense of fellowship in a group with a strong sense of identity, a support network in times of distress, and comrades who could be trusted to put on a proper funeral when the time came. As the demands of taxation, civic duties, and conscription became ever more oppressive, increasing numbers of Egyptians fled their homes and villages to seek refuge in the countless tombs and caves that honeycombed the cliffs above the river valley. In fleeing the vicissitudes of this world, it was only a step to move toward contemplation of the next. This was the genesis of the anchorite movement, one of the many contributions Egypt made to the development of Christianity.

Yet another reason for Egypt's receptiveness to Christianity was the way so many of its elements resonated with the ancient religion that had dominated the imaginations of the inhabitants of the Valley of the Nile for thousands of years. The most fundamental ancient Egyptian myth of all, that of Osiris, Isis, and Horus, could be taken as an allegory of the Holy family. Isis easily equated to Mary, and the similarities between Isis caring for the infant Horus and the Christian motif of Mother and Child were obvious. Early Christian artists portraying the Virgin Mary suckling the infant Jesus were copied directly from pagan portrayals of Isis and Horus. The pharaoh as the incarnate son of God prefigured Christ in that same role; likewise, Christian visions of the Last Judgment and entry into a heavenly Paradise or a subterranean Hell were hardly new concepts to Egyptians. Even the doctrine of the Holy Trinity, an alien concept to many non-Christian cultures, was comprehensible to the Egyptians because of their ancient practice of grouping deities into triads. Many other parallels, such as the striking resemblance between the Christian cross and the ancient Egyptian *ankh*, facilitated Egyptian acceptance of Christianity. Yet, while the ancient religion provided a receptive background for Christianity, it subtly imparted distinctly Egyptian qualities to it through the process of syncretism by which one religion incorporates elements from others, even those it supplants.

Although it left few traces in the historical record, Christianity had made great advances in Egypt by the end of the third century, when evidence becomes much more abundant. Churches stood in every part of the country, including the Western Oases, and a hierarchy had been established with bishops in most of the nomes and subordinate to the bishop of Alexandria. Insufficient data exists to estimate numbers of Egyptian Christians at this stage, and they were certainly still a small minority, but they were a particularly dynamic minority, and conversion was increasing steadily, even though it was not easy to become a Christian. A preliminary period of instruction was required before baptism and admission to full communion. The would-be Christian had to stand behind and apart from the rest of the congregation during services. Christianity in Egypt was a serious commitment.

Egyptian Christianity was also acquiring its own language, script, and liturgy, a development that would eventually do much to make the Egyptian church a national one. Three languages were widely used in Roman Egypt: Egyptian, Greek, and Latin. Of these three, Latin had the most superficial impact, reserved chiefly for specialized governmental purposes. There was never a large group of Latin-speaking people in Egypt. Greek permeated deeper into Egyptian society, partly because of the centuries of Ptolemaic rule, and partly because Greek was the language of administration, culture, and commerce in the eastern part of the Roman Empire. Most native Egyptians, of course, continued to speak Egyptian. As has been noted, the script for writing the Egyptian language had undergone several phases, beginning with the hieroglyphs, then hieratic, and finally demotic. Although there were still a few masons in early Roman times who could carve hieroglyphic inscriptions on monuments, almost all Egyptian texts were written in demotic by then, but because the number of people literate in it were few, because it was so difficult to read, and because so much official and business documentation had to be done in Greek, demotic also went into a severe decline. Apart from some graffiti at Philae on the southern border of Egypt, there is no datable demotic text after the middle of the third century. During the early Roman period, therefore, Egyptian continued as a spoken language, but one that was no longer written, a situation that persisted for two centuries. A solution was found in the development of the Coptic language—or to be more precise, in the invention of the Coptic script.

Most Egyptians never learned Greek, but that language affected almost every aspect of their lives, so it was natural for them, lacking a script for their own language, to attempt to write Egyptian words with Greek letters. It was Egyptian churchmen, literate in Greek, who took the initiative for formulating a systematic way of using the Greek alphabet to represent Egyptian sounds, with the addition of seven new letters to represent those sounds for which there were no Greek letters. The Egyptian language written in this script, and with a large accretion of Greek vocabulary, is what became known as Coptic. Although Egyptian had continued to change over the millennia, the Coptic language is directly descended from the language of the pharaohs. When one listens to a Coptic liturgy, one hears an echo of the ancient Egyptian language. Also, many personal names still popular among Coptic families in Egypt are ancient ones. Soon the Bible was being translated into Coptic and new religious works composed in it. Church services were conducted in Coptic. The Gospel could be preached to Egyptians in their own language.

The rapid spread of the church through Egypt and throughout the Roman Empire attracted government notice. Although the Romans were famously tolerant of religions, and usually ready to welcome a new one into civic life, Christianity had some disturbing features. For one thing, it was largely a secret society, something that always made the Romans politically nervous; more worrisome, however, was the refusal of Christians to recognize the state religion, observance of which was equated with loyalty to the emperor and to the state itself. Lurid rumors circulated about Christians, that they indulged in sexual orgies, that they practiced cannibalism, and so forth. The Roman response was persecution, sporadic and often localized, and interspersed with long periods of neglect, but devastating when it was applied. Persecuted Christians were given a chance to save themselves by denying their religion, or by just making a *pro forma* public sacrifice to the gods; those who refused were tortured and put to death, becoming martyrs, or witnesses to the faith.

Egypt was affected by the wave of Christian persecution that swept the empire during the short reign of Decius. Many suffered martyrdom while others, like Origen, head of the Catechetical School in Alexandria, were tortured but later released. After Decius was killed fighting the Goths on the Danube frontier in 251, his successor Valerian continued the persecution, but the next emperor, Gallienus, issued an edict of toleration terminating it. Much worse was the Great Persecution conducted by the Emperor Diocletian, an event of such fundamental importance for Egyptian Christianity that the Coptic calendar, the "Era of Martyrs," begins not with the birth of Christ but in AD 284, the first year of Diocletian's reign.

Diocletian, who had campaigned in Egypt, unleashed his empire-wide persecution in 303. The prefect of Egypt, Sossianus Hierocles, was an especially energetic persecutor. The death toll mounted quickly. Eusebius, author of an influential *History of the Church*, was an eyewitness.

> We were there and observed many executions, some by beheading, others by burning, so many that the execution axe became blunt, worn out, and broke into pieces; the executioners became so exhausted that they had to work in shifts. Yet we always observed a most wonderful zeal, and a truly divine power and eagerness in those who believed in the Christ of God. As soon as the first group was sentenced, others rushed to the tribunal and proclaimed themselves Christians, heedless of the horror and various kinds of torture, speaking boldly and with composure about their religion and the God of the universe. They received their death sentences with joy, laughter, and gladness, singing hymns of thanksgiving to the God of the universe until their last breath.[17]

The list of Egyptian martyrs, many of whom became saints, is extensive, and their stories are carefully preserved in Coptic hagiography. One of the most revered by Coptic Christians is St. Dimiana. Ordered to renounce her faith, she and her companions steadfastly refused, and all were killed. The martyrdom of St. Dimiana and the Forty Virgins is still celebrated annually in the village of Zafaran, and Dimiana's relics are kept in various churches in Cairo. She is a patron saint of women's health and fertility. St. Catherine, a learned young woman, so impressed her persecutor with her knowledge that he sent fifty wise men to persuade her to abandon her faith. When she converted them instead, he had her beheaded. Her incorruptible body was mystically transported to Mt. Sinai, where it was discovered by monks in the ninth century and her famous monastery was established. A modern church marks the site of St. Catherine's martyrdom in Alexandria. How many Christians were tortured, maimed, and executed in Egypt during the Great Persecution is unknown. Coptic estimates, which can run into the hundreds of thousands, are undoubtedly exaggerated, but there can be no doubt that the suffering and loss of life was horrifyingly extensive. Yet, far from eradicating Christianity in Egypt, Diocletian burned it forever into the body of Egyptian life.

Diocletian's persecution was by far the largest, but it was also the last, as the fortunes of Christianity within the Roman Empire abruptly improved. The Great Persecution was terminated by one of Diocletian's successors, Galerius, on his deathbed in 311. A few years later, the Emperor Constantine, contesting for rule of the empire, experienced a vision of Christian favor on the eve of a decisive battle and subsequently issued the Edict of Milan in 313, granting Christians freedom of worship, restoring church property, and permitting Christians to hold public office. This was followed by many more manifestations of imperial support. With the exception of the Emperor Julian (361–63), who attempted to revive paganism during his brief reign, all subsequent emperors were Christians. The way was now clear for Christianity to grow within the empire, and it especially flourished in Egypt. Estimates of the number of Egyptian Christians by the end of the fourth century reach as high as 90 percent, although a more plausible guess is about half the population. Whatever figures are taken, the increase was both rapid and substantial, making Christianity the predominant religion in Egypt.

One of Egypt's most important contributions to Christianity was the institution of monasticism. Although it is historically inaccurate to present St. Antony (251–356) as the founder of monasticism in Egypt, for he had predecessors, he nevertheless became the exemplar, largely through the literary influence of the biography written by his friend St. Athanasius, a work of hagiography in every sense of the word. A more human portrayal of Antony may be found in the *Sayings of the Fathers*. As a well-to-do young man, Antony responded to the call from the Gospel of Matthew: "If thou wilt be perfect, go and sell that thou hast, and give to the poor, and thou shalt have treasure in heaven: and come and follow me." Giving away his inheritance, Antony pursued ascetic lifestyles in ever more remote locations. He was living in an ancient tomb in the desert when he experienced his epochal temptation. The devil tormented him with boredom and laziness, and by apparitions of sensuous, beautiful women, his for the taking, but Antony held fast through the power of prayer. Failing in those approaches, the devil sent troops of demons to abuse him and drive him from his chosen path, but to no avail.

Antony emerged from his trials spiritually and physically rejuvenated, and became an ascetic celebrity. People flocked to hear his teachings. According to the *Sayings of the Fathers*, he told them:

> Always have the fear of God before your eyes. Remember Him who gives death and life. Hate the world and all that is in it. Hate all peace that comes from the flesh. Renounce this life, so that you may be alive to God. Remember what you have promised God, for it will be required of you on the day of judgment. Suffer hunger, thirst, nakedness, be watchful and sorrowful; weep and groan in your heart; test yourselves, to see if you are worthy of God; despise the flesh, so that you may preserve your souls.[18]

As Antony's fame spread, and his following increased, the tombs became too busy to suit him, and he withdrew still farther, eventually retiring to a grotto in the Eastern Desert high above the location where the famous monastery bearing his name was later founded. From this remote retreat, his influence only increased, and many imitated his example, fitting into the long tradition of withdrawing into the desert in times of distress. This did not necessarily mean disrupting all contact with family and friends or support networks, for the wilderness was never more than a few kilometers distant from the Valley of the Nile, and often just a few steps away. Numerous ancient tombs show signs of habitation by religious hermits. But one did not necessarily have to withdraw. Many remained in the towns and villages but adopted strictly ascetic lifestyles while continuing to function within the community. Antony's ideal was one of hermits withdrawing into individual cells near a central place of worship, a mode that came to be known as anchoritic monasticism, but another form of Egyptian monasticism, called cenobitic, became the institutional norm and exerted the greatest influence on Western Christianity. Here too the historical role of the alleged founder St. Pachomius (290–346) has been somewhat oversold, for others were moving in the same direction, but as with St. Antony, St. Pachomius's subsequent fame exerted a profound influence of its own. Instead of seeking solitude, Pachomian monks withdrew into organized convents with shared facilities. Governed by a common Rule, the monks cultivated their lands, practiced handicrafts, and made themselves as self-sufficient as possible, while reaching out to the surrounding communities with services such as giving alms to the poor, caring for widows and orphans, visiting and ministering to the sick, and participating in funeral rites. As they multiplied in number and accumulated resources, the monasteries became a formidable force in Egypt.

Pachomius founded his first monastery at Tabennesi around 320 and proceeded to establish nine more. The first of the several monasteries in Wadi Natrun was founded by Macarius in 330. St. Shenute's administration of the White Monastery near Sohag in the late fourth century was the beginning of another major thrust in Egyptian monasticism. Still more, and diverse, strands of monasticism developed. Communities for women were established. The exact numbers of monasteries and their inhabitants are speculative, but one source claims that ten thousand monks were at Oxyrhynchus at the end of the fourth century; another mentions 2,200 monks and 1,800 nuns at the White Monastery. Even allowing for exaggeration, such numbers, common for other places in Egypt as well, indicate an enormous monastic population. Within a few decades, monasteries were to be found almost everywhere in and near the inhabited portions of Egypt, and some, notably St. Antony's and St. Paul's, in remote locations as well. Many of these became substantial complexes, as surviving examples attest. When the great ancient temples fell into disuse, they made ideal monasteries, with their walls, living quarters, storehouses, and ample spaces for worship. This is still evident in the names of two major monuments at Luxor, where the mortuary temple of Ramesses III is known as Deir al-Medina, or Monastery of the Town, and Hatshepsut's elegant temple is called Deir al-Bahari, the Northern Monastery. Ancient temples became so closely associated with monasteries that the term *deir* was applied to some that never served monastic purposes.

Egypt also provided a theological matrix for the formation of the New Testament, a process that developed during the two centuries or so after the death of Christ. The earliest Christians relied on the Psalms and other elements of the Old Testament in their services, but in addition to these, a wide variety of Christian texts were circulating by the end of the first century—gospels, collections of sayings of Jesus and the Apostles, letters, etc. Some were later incorporated into the canonical New Testament, but there were many others, some with astonishing content and indicating a great diversity in early Christianity, as the Nag Hammadi discovery showed. Growing pressure for conformity required a body of approved texts. The Egyptian Christian establishment played an active role in deciding what to include (the controversial Revelation of St. John only just got in) and what to exclude, or indeed suppress (such as the Gospel of Thomas). The first list of the books of the New Testament as we know it comes from Egypt.

Much of Christian doctrine was forged in Egypt. The influence of the philosophical tradition of the Museum, especially the teachings of Philo, is evident in early Christian thought. In the second half of the first century, the Christians established a Catechetical School at Alexandria. One of its early directors, and one of its greatest scholars, was Clement of Alexandria (c. 150–216). A convert to Christianity, Clement was well versed in Greek literature. Although his writings stressed the superiority of Christian philosophy to Greek, his strong classical background made him appreciate the need for continuity with the past. Eventually Clement came to be perceived as too tinged with classicism. His successor was Origen, a father of the church and a prolific theologian. Origen was the first to clarify such dogmatic principles as the nature of God and Christ, the soul, and salvation. The ideas formulated at the Catechetical School spread throughout the Roman Empire and beyond.

With the church's growth in numbers and organization, it developed an insistence on orthodoxy, literally 'right belief,' the conviction that there was just one true faith, whose principles could be established, and that there was no salvation outside the church that was based on that true faith. Those principles were held to be universal. Anyone who challenged the established orthodoxy was a heretic and was to be expelled from the church. Disputes over dogma could assume titanic proportions, especially after the ingredient of imperial interference was stirred into an already volatile mix. When ethnicity and a sense of nationalism were added, the result could be explosive.

The first major heresy to shake the church was entirely Egyptian in origin. To some degree, it was a personal feud between two Alexandrian churchmen, a presbyter of the Church of St. Mark named Arius and his ambitious adversary Athanasius, who eventually became bishop of Alexandria and a saint. Arius held that since Jesus was begotten of God his nature was similar to God's, but not the same, and it was unequal to God's. Athanasius maintained that God and Jesus were of one indivisible substance. The Arian Heresy, as it came to be, was divisive in Egypt because the Greek Christian community tended to cluster around Arius, while native Egyptian Christians found their champion in Athanasius. But the conflict spread throughout the Roman Empire, and for a time the cause of Arius prevailed. Heated arguments, fighting, riots, and bloodshed ensued, as neither side was willing to give way or tolerate the other. In an attempt to resolve the controversy, the Emperor Constantine convened the first great Ecumenical Council at Nicaea in 325. Arius was condemned and exiled, but his heresy continued to flourish and cause problems until the Emperor Theodosius came down firmly on the side of Nicene orthodoxy in 380.

Early on, Egypt developed an intimate association with the Holy Family. This was based on the passage in the Gospel of Matthew where the angel of the Lord appeared to Joseph in a dream and commanded him to "take the young child and his mother, and flee into Egypt, and be thou there until I bring thee word: for Herod will seek the young child to destroy him." Although the Bible says little more about the Holy Family's sojourn in Egypt, a rich tradition grew up in Egypt about it, and numerous sites were identified with their presence and became objects of pilgrimages. Among them, and still to be seen, are the Tree of the Virgin in Heliopolis and the Church of the Holy Virgin at Musturd in Cairo; in Upper Egypt are the Church of the Holy Virgin at Gebel al-Teir and the Monastery of the Holy Virgin at al-Qusiya.

Pilgrims were also drawn to many other places in Egypt, especially to the great monasteries such as St. Antony's and to local shrines like the one for St. Menas in the town of Abu Mena, southwest of Alexandria. According to one version of the story, the body of this Diocletianic martyr was being conveyed on a camel when the animal refused to continue another step. Although such behavior is not unusual for camels, the inability to move a body farther is traditionally taken in Egypt as a sign that the holy person wishes to be buried on that spot. So it was done; a spring appeared; miracles began to occur. Abu Mena became Egypt's leading pilgrimage site. These shrines attracted pilgrims not only from within Egypt but also from the wider world. A nun, Lady Etheria from Gaul, visited Egypt sometime between 379 and 388. Like so many pilgrims who were to come after her, she looked for sites with biblical associations. She was told that the Colossi at Thebes were Moses and Aaron. Her manuscript, discovered in the late nineteenth century, could be taken as the first of many travelogues about Egypt written by European women.

The Coptic experience profoundly affected Egyptian art and architecture. Churches and monasteries, while drawing on many established designs, had to meet new functional needs. As elsewhere in the Christian world, the walls were decorated with murals; some, including those at the Monasteries of St. Antony and St. Paul, have recently been restored, allowing the visitor to view them in something approaching their original state. Distinctly Egyptian motifs and techniques become readily apparent to the viewer. Tracing the late history of the Fayyum Portraits, one can see pagan portraiture transposing into Christian iconography. Examples of Coptic manuscripts, handicrafts, and precious objects may be seen at the Coptic Museum in Old Cairo.

The Christian Church in Egypt became wealthy, powerful, and influential. A wave of church construction swept the land, lasting for two centuries. From perhaps half of the population in at the beginning of the fifth century, Christian numbers had so increased as to make non-Christians a small minority by the century's end. Churches and monasteries were firmly established everywhere in Egypt, and a clearly defined hierarchy had developed that ran from the bishop of Alexandria, who was the patriarch of Egypt, down to the village priests. The patriarch's authority extended to Cyrenaica, and he and other senior Egyptian churchmen exerted great influence in the councils of the church throughout the Roman Empire. Missionaries went forth. The conversion of Ethiopia was an early accomplishment, and the Ethiopian Christian Church remained a daughter foundation of the Coptic Orthodox Church until 1948. The growth of the church in wealth and property had been immense, with imperial gifts such as that of the Emperor Constantius, who donated the Caesarium in Alexandria to the church in 350, and many individuals made donations and left property to the church and monasteries.

While the Christian establishment was flourishing, paganism in Egypt was suffering a steady decline. The temples had been in trouble as early as the second century when imperial inscriptions become rare, indicating diminishing government support. Deprived of their endowments by the Roman organization of Egypt, they were vulnerable to the unsettled times of the third century and the painful period of readjustment that followed. Pagan numbers shrank conversely as those of the Christians grew. Evidence shows that sacrifice was declining, and some pagan festivals were falling into abeyance. In 341, Constantius, decreeing an end to superstition, ordered that sacrifice be discontinued entirely. The Emperor Julian's quixotic attempt to restore the worship of the old gods had little lasting impact in Egypt.

Toward the end of the fourth century, a period of Christian persecution of paganism began in Egypt with the support of the imperial government. Violent confrontations became frequent in Alexandria between Christians and pagans. But the pagans were few in number, and the Christians received ready, organized support from numerous monasteries nearby that could supply militant gangs of monks on short notice. The Emperor Theodosius initiated a strongly anti-pagan policy that paid particular attention to Egypt: traditional forms of worship were outlawed, temples ordered closed, pagan writings sought and destroyed, the use of demotic, which was still preserved by a few priests, prohibited, and those pagan holidays that had not been appropriated by the church were turned into working days. In 391, Theodosius decreed "no one is to go to the sanctuaries, walk through the temples, or raise his eyes to statues created by the labor of man." The bishop of Alexandria, Theophilus, took this as his cue and obtained legal authority to seize abandoned temples and turn them into churches. In these new churches, he displayed the statues of the gods in a mocking manner, a deliberate provocation to the pagans, who rioted in response.

That was precisely what Theophilus wanted, because it provided a pretext for summoning his monks and mobs. Realizing the precariousness of their situation, the pagans retreated to the great Alexandrian temple complex, the Serapeum, and fortified it for a last stand. The attack soon came. Encouraged by the emperor, the Christian mob smashed through the pagan barricades. They destroyed the colossal statue of Serapis and burned the entire temple complex. Most of what remained of the Great Library of Alexandria was lost in the devastation. Similar attacks on other remaining pagan centers in Egypt ensued. A prophecy attributed to Hermes Trismegistus, still read by some Christians as well as pagans, foretold that:

> The gods on leaving the earth, will return to heaven; they will abandon Egypt. That holy earth, land of sanctuaries and temples, will be completely covered with coffins and corpses. O Egypt, Egypt! Nothing will remain of your religion but fables, and later, your children will not even believe them! The people abandoned, will all die, and then with neither gods nor men, Egypt will be nothing but a desert.[19]

The Christian offensive against paganism in Egypt continued for several decades. Cyril, who became patriarch in 412, had spent years in the monasteries and was well placed to draw on their support. In 415 he directed the monks and incited the mobs against the Jews of Alexandria, destroying their property and driving them from the city. When the Roman prefect attempted to prevent this atrocity, Cyril had his mobs kill him. Then Cyril turned on the philosophical schools, homes of Egypt's remaining intellectual elite, whose members were notoriously pagan and included the distinguished scholar Theon and his gifted daughter Hypatia. The conduct of this independent woman, an accomplished philosopher and astronomer whose lectures attracted a wide following even among Christians, outraged the misogynistic Cyril, who incited the crowds against her. Shortly after the assassination of the prefect, Hypatia was riding through Alexandria in her chariot when a Christian mob set upon her, dragged her into a nearby church, and hacked her to pieces. They paraded through the streets with her remains and burned them in a celebratory bonfire.

Despite Theodosius's decrees and Christian violence, some pagans held firm to their faiths for several generations more, and a few temples in outlying areas continued to function, but by the late sixth century, most people in the countryside had probably converted to Christianity, and the remaining pagans in the cities could no longer practice their religion openly. The last working temple, that of the goddess Isis at Philae, was closed by order of the Emperor Justinian and ceased to function around 535. It is at Philae that we find the last datable hieroglyphic inscription. The ability to read the hieroglyphs probably disappeared at this time, not to be recovered for over a thousand years. The triumph of Christianity in Egypt was complete.

Even as the Christians triumphed in Egypt, however, they found the positions of the Egyptian church and the See of Alexandria threatened by imperial politics and the upstart city of Constantinople. The Emperor Constantine's foundation in 324 of a new capital city on the Bosporus, linking Europe and Asia, fundamentally shifted the political balance within the empire, displacing Alexandria in power, size, wealth, and even prestige. This was galling to civic-minded Alexandrians whose city had been the greatest in the East for centuries before Constantinople even existed. It also had religious implications that were closely intertwined with political considerations, because the church hierarchy in Constantinople soon began to assert a claim to supremacy within the church (with a nominal nod to Rome) commensurate with their city's status in government, a claim that received imperial support. The Second Ecumenical Council at Constantinople in 381 explicitly declared that the patriarch of Constantinople was second only to the bishop of Rome. For the See of Alexandria, with its long tradition in the church to which it had made so many contributions, this was deeply offensive.

The rivalry between Constantinople and Alexandria also found expression in the Monophysite Controversy. The theological debate was over the nature of Christ, a continuing source of controversies since the Arian heresy. The Monophysites believed in the union of Christ's human and divine natures, while the other party, which came to be known as the Melchites or Chalcedonians, held that Christ was of two separate natures, human and divine. As doctrinal differences went, this issue was serious enough, but it was supercharged by the political polarity resulting from the Chalcedonians' identification with the imperial government in Constantinople, while the Monophysite persuasion prevailed in Egypt. The struggle therefore became a political, indeed a national one as Egypt resisted what it considered foreign oppression. It was a prolonged conflict that rocked the church, undermined the unity of the Byzantine Empire, and defined the Coptic Orthodox Church.

The Monophysite Controversy was high on the agenda at the Second Council of Ephesus in 449, which was attended by large numbers of Egyptians, whose rowdy behavior caused the council to be popularly called the Robber Council. Dioscurus, the patriarch of Alexandria and the council's presiding officer, refused to allow the other side to present its case, and with the support of his boisterous followers he rammed through decisions favorable to the Monophysite cause. The Egyptians were, however, unable to defeat a motion to give the See of Constantinople precedence over those of Antioch and Alexandria. Dioscurus was so enraged that he threw the bishop of Constantinople to the ground and stalked out of the meeting.

The churchmen of Constantinople did not accept the decision in favor of Monophysitism at Ephesus and persuaded a new, sympathetic emperor, Marcian (450–57), to summon another council to reopen the question. The Egyptian delegation did not have its way at the Council of Chalcedon, which met in 451 within sight of the imperial capital across the straits. After many complaints were made about the way Dioscurus had conducted the previous council, he was deprived of his seat among the bishops, then deposed from his bishopric. Turning to the pressing doctrinal issue, the council declared as orthodoxy that Christ was of two natures, inseparably united. The Egyptian refusal to accept that decision has been described by one scholar of the early Coptic Church as "a nationalistic statement of cultural independence from foreign occupation." This may be taken as the effective beginning of the Coptic Orthodox Church. It should be noted, however, that Coptic Christians strongly dislike being called Monophysites.

During the decades following the Council of Chalcedon, the imperial government in Constantinople employed a carrot-and-stick approach to try to impose its definition of orthodoxy on Egypt, an effort deter-minedly resisted by the Pachomian monasteries. When frustrated officials in Constantinople intensified their efforts to force religious conformity on Egypt, monastic resistance grew proportionately. An increasingly Egyptian Christianity was forged through that resistance. In 570, Egyptian Christians took the decisive step of appointing their own patriarch.

All the while, Egypt's position within the Byzantine Empire deteriorated, although Egypt's grain and revenue remained extremely important to Constantinople. Another, and more thorough, reorganization of the administration in Egypt by the Emperor Justinian around 537 appears to have been designed to secure the grain supply. The population of Egypt probably declined, perhaps to as low as three million by 600, partly because of steady attrition from ongoing hardship and more precipitously because of a catastrophic outbreak of plague in 542. Brigandage became so bad during the reign of Maurice (582–602) that grain shipments to Constantinople were disrupted. The rebellion against the brutal imperial usurper Phocas, 608–10, caused widespread bloodletting in all the provinces of the Byzantine Empire and left them in a state of disorder, but none suffered as much from the fighting as Egypt. The Byzantine yoke became so odious to Egyptians, both politically and religiously—closely related concepts—that they were not averse to the change of rule that came in the seventh century.

The town of al-Qasr in Dakhla Oasis in the Western Desert *(Jarosław Dobrowolski)*.

Eastern Desert mountains at Mons Porphyrites *(Michael Jones)*.

Standing stones at the prehistoric site of Nabta Playa *(Maciej Jórdeczka)*.

Egypt from space *(Nasa Visible Earth)*.

The Nile at Luxor, the site of ancient Thebes
(R. Neil Hewison).

The annual flooding of the Nile
Delta (John Feeney).

The Step Pyramid at Saqqara with the pyramid of Userkaf on the left (from Frith,
Lower Egypt, Thebes, and the Pyramids).

The Narmer Palette
(Araldo De Luca
© White Star).

Prince Rohotpe (below) and Princess Nofret, from a Fourth Dynasty *mastaba* at Meidum *(author)*.

The Fourth Dynasty king Menkaura with the goddesses Hathor and Bat *(author)*.

The Pyramids of Giza *(author)*.

Nubian pyramid field in northern Sudan from Lepsius, *Denkmäler (Abth. I, 135).*

Hieroglyphs, including cartouches with two of the names of Thutmose III, and hieratic graffiti, in the Hathoric Chapel at Deir al-Bahari *(Araldo De Luca © White Star).*

The obelisk of the Middle Kingdom monarch Senwosret I at Heliopolis *(author).*

Amenemhet III in priest's clothing *(Araldo De Luca © White Star)*.

The pyramid of Amenemhet III at Dahshur *(author)*.

A troop of
Egyptian soldiers from
the tomb of a Middle Kingdom
prince *(Araldo De Luca © White Star)*.

Cattle inspection, in a Middle Kingdom model *(Araldo De Luca © White Star)*.

The first pylon of Luxor Temple *(author)*.

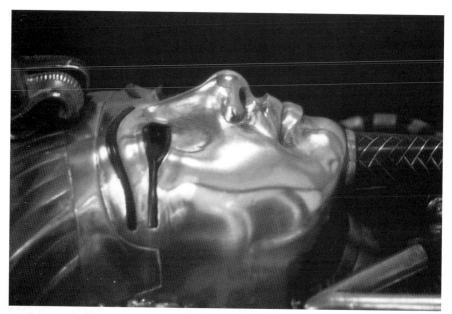

Golden mask of the coffin of the boy-king Tutankhamun *(author)*.

Prone colossal statue of Ramesses II at Memphis *(author)*.

The Colossi of Memnon (actually Amenhotep III) at Thebes as depicted in the French *Description de l'Égypte (A. II, 20)*.

Seti I and the goddess Hathor *(author)*.

The mortuary temple of Hatshepsut at Deir al-Bahari, Thebes *(author)*.

The hypostyle hall of the Hibis Temple, Kharga Oasis, built during the Persian Period *(author)*.

Coin depicting Alexander the Great with attributes of the Egyptian god Amun (from Bevan, *A History of Egypt*).

Ptolemy I Soter *(author)*.

Silver coin from 32 BC featuring the faces of Cleopatra and Mark Antony (© *The Trustees of the British Museum*).

The Ptolemaic temple of Isis at Philae as depicted by the nineteenth-century Scottish artist David Roberts (from Roberts, *Egypt and Nubia*).

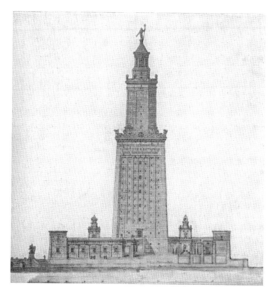

The Lighthouse at Alexandria as it might have appeared (from Bevan, *A History of Egypt*).

A Fayyum portrait. Mid-second century AD *(author)*.

Abandoned columns in the Roman quarry of Mons Claudianus in the Eastern Desert *(Robert K. Vincent, Jr. © ARCE-EAP)*.

The recently uncovered Roman theater at Alexandria *(author)*.

The second-century Tegran Tomb at Alexandria *(author)*.

The Roman kiosk at Qertassi, re-sited on higher ground after the construction of the Aswan High Dam. Lake Nasser is in the background *(author)*.

The emperor Hadrian, the most celebrated of many Roman tourists to Egypt *(R. Neil Hewison)*.

The Greco-Roman god Serapis *(author)*.

The emperor Diocletian (left), embracing his colleague Maximianus, on St. Mark's Basilica in Venice *(Michael Jones)*.

The column popularly known as Pompey's Pillar in Alexandria at the site of the ancient Serapeum *(author)*.

St. Menas, traditionally shown between two camels, was martyred during the Great Persecution under the emperor Diocletian *(author)*.

Coptic script, on a page from a Coptic psalter found at Oxyrhynchus *(Boulos Isaac)*.

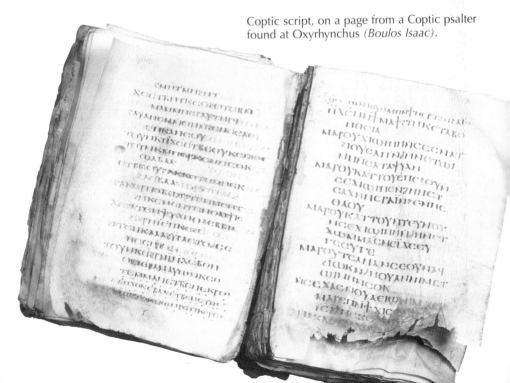

St. Antony, credited with being the founder of Egyptian monasticism *(Boulos Isaac)*.

The Mosque of Amr, aerial view *(Rajan Patel © ARCE-EAP)*.

The Roman fort at Babylon as depicted by Robert Hay in the nineteenth century (from Hay, *Illustrations of Cairo*).

The minaret of the Mosque of Ibn Tulun, by Robert Hay (from Hay, *Illustrations of Cairo*).

A Fatimid gold dinar, minted soon after the foundation of Cairo, bearing the names and titles of the caliph al-Muizz (from Nicol, *Sylloge Vol. 6;* catalogue number 264).

The entrance to al-Azhar, the oldest university in the Middle East, as drawn by Edward William Lane in the early nineteenth century (from Lane, *Modern Egyptians*).

The Fatimid gate Bab al-Futuh in the northern wall of al-Qahira. The distinctive minaret of the Mosque of al-Hakim is behind it *(author)*.

Salah al-Din in a modern statue in Damascus *(R. Neil Hewison)*.

Late Mamluk architecture. Dome and minaret of the madrasa and tomb of
Sultan Qaitbey, from the author's window *(author)*.

Sultan Hasan Mosque, Cairo, built between 1356 and 1361, as it appeared in the early nineteenth century (from Coste, *Architecture Arabe*).

Fort Qaitbey at Alexandria, built in 1479 on the site of the ancient Lighthouse, and probably with some of its stones, in a vain effort to deter the Ottomans *(author)*.

A Mamluk manual of arms and horsemanship.

Opposite: A recitation in a Cairo coffee house (from Lane, *Modern Egyptians*).

General Bonaparte in Egypt, by Jean-Léon Gérôme *(Dahesh Museum)*.

Murad Bey, from the French
Description de l'Égypte (E.M. II, G).

Ibrahim Pasha (from Hassan, *House
of Muhammad Ali*).

The Muhammad Ali Mosque at the Citadel, as it appears on modern paper currency.

مُحمّد علي

Muhammad Ali (from Hassan, *House of Muhammad Ali*).

Khedive Ismail (from Hassan, *House of Muhammad Ali*).

Ahmed Urabi (from Guerville, *New Egypt*).

Qasr Ibrim on the Nubian Nile by the nineteenth-century photographer Francis Frith (from Frith, *Lower Egypt, Thebes, and the Pyramids*).

The opening of the Suez Canal in 1869, in a period print *(A. Siliotti © Geodia Edizioni)*.

Khedive Tewfiq (from Colvin, *The Making of Modern Egypt*).

The Earl of Cromer (from Colvin, *The Making of Modern Egypt*).

Abbas Hilmy II (from Penfield, *Present-Day Egypt*).

King Fuad and his son, the future King Farouk (from Hassan, *House of Muhammad Ali*).

Saad Zaghlul *(Lesley Lababidi)*.

Hoda Sharawi with members of the Egyptian Feminist Union (from Wassef and Wassef, *Daughters of the Nile*).

The Free Officers. Seated on the couch are Gamal Abd al-Nasser, Muhammad Naguib, and Abd al-Hakim Amer. Anwar al-Sadat is on the far right *(Egypt Historical Archive)*.

The Aswan High Dam *(author)*.

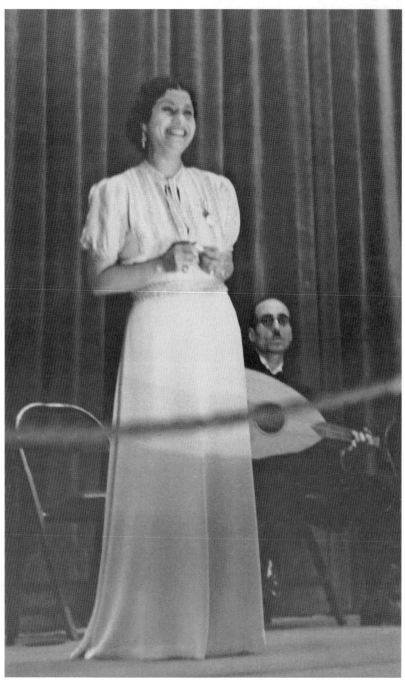

Umm Kulthum in performance *(Courtesy of the Rare Books and Special Collections Library, The American University in Cairo)*.

Naguib Mahfouz.

Anwar al-Sadat, Jimmy Carter, and Menachem Begin at the signing of the peace treaty between Egypt and Israel, 1979 *(Library of Congress Prints and Photographs Division)*.

The October War of 1973, as depicted in a large mural at the Cairo Citadel (detail) *(Anna Ziajka)*.

President Mubarak in a cabinet meeting, 2008 *(Ahmed Fouad © al-Ahram).*

A Cairo traffic jam, a common sight by the late twentieth century *(Jarosław Dobrowolski).*

The once-lonely stretches of Egypt's Mediterranean coast west of Alexandria are rapidly being filled with concrete structures *(Jarosław Dobrowolski).*

10 The Advent of Islam

In 603 the Byzantine and Persian Empires, adversaries for centuries, began an especially vicious struggle that brought first one then the other to the brink of destruction, and left both exhausted at its conclusion. At first the fortunes of war favored the Persians. After years of steady advances, they captured Damascus in 613, and Jerusalem the following year. While the Byzantines fell back to defend their Anatolian heartland, the Persians turned south to Egypt. The fortress of Babylon fell in 617, and Alexandria in 619. The Persians occupied all of Egypt, dealing a heavy blow to the Byzantines by depriving Constantinople of its grain supply.

Within Egypt, the Persians initially inflicted little physical destruction, although there were massacres of Christians. This latest Persian occupation was certainly politically disruptive, however, and the institutions of Roman–Byzantine rule quickly deteriorated. As during previous periods of Persian domination, the Egyptians did not care for these particular foreign masters, but there is no evidence of Egyptian attempts to expel them. When the Persians departed, it was because of events elsewhere, not in Egypt.

Chosroes II, the Persian King of Kings, rejected generous peace offers and prepared the total conquest of the Byzantine Empire. By 622

Constantinople itself was in danger. The city held fast within its formidable walls, but it appeared that the Byzantine Empire had entered its final agonies. In a last, desperate throw of the dice, the Emperor Heraclius set sail from Constantinople with his field army, landing at the eastern end of the Black Sea and marching south into Mesopotamia, striking for the very heart of the Persian Empire. The gamble paid off. Heraclius decisively defeated the Persians near the ancient city of Nineveh, leaving the central provinces of their empire exposed. Chosroes' regime collapsed; he was deposed and killed; the Persian Empire slipped into anarchy. The next Persian king made peace, returning all conquests to the Byzantines, including the province of Egypt, which the Persians evacuated in 629.

When the Byzantines resumed control in Egypt, therefore, it was after a hiatus of more than a decade, and they did little to make their return welcome. Reestablishment of Byzantine rule meant high taxes, which were predictably unpopular, as were other measures; but the worst was Heraclius's appointment in 631 of Cyrus as prefect of Egypt and patriarch of Alexandria. After an inept attempt at reconciling the Coptic and Chalcedonian points of view, Cyrus conducted a zealous anti-Coptic persecution, expelling unorthodox bishops and monks; at one point he even attempted to kill the Coptic patriarch. The lesson that many Egyptians learned was that loyalty to both the Byzantine Empire and the Coptic Christian Church was impossible. Egypt's Jews were also punished because they had supported the Persians.

Heraclius returned to Constantinople and a glorious ovation, but his victory had come at heavy cost. What the Byzantine Empire needed after its triumph was time for recovery; instead, it had to confront an unexpected challenge from deep within the Arabian desert. Around the year 610, Muhammad, a merchant of the commercial city of Mecca in west central Arabia, received the first of a series of divine revelations and began to share them with his fellows. The message, delivered in powerful, memorable words, was one of an almighty but compassionate god who would hold people responsible for their actions on a Day of Judgment. Furthermore, this god, the same god as that of the Jews and the Christians—whose revelations had been distorted—was the only god. All others were false. This was the message of the Qur'an, the foundation of Islam.

Converts were few at first, and Muhammad's monotheistic preaching in polytheistic Mecca made many enemies. Forced to flee in 622, he found refuge in the city of Medina to the north and made it his headquarters. As converts swelled their numbers, the Muslims became powerful. They defeated the Meccans, and the new religion spread quickly across the Arabian Peninsula. Arabia's tribes, previously weak and prone to fighting among themselves, were galvanized into a united force, motivated by deep religious commitment. Muhammad told the people on his final pilgrimage to Mecca, "Listen to my words and take them to heart! Understand that every Muslim is a brother to every other Muslim, and that you are now one family. It is not legitimate for any one of you, therefore, to take anything that belongs to his brother unless it is willingly given to him." Among other things, that meant the raiding that formed a basic part of the Arabian economy had to be directed externally. A new force was unleashed as Muslim warriors swarmed out of Arabia to begin an epic series of conquests that eventually reached as far west as Morocco and Spain and to India in the East.

The year after the Prophet's death in 632, Muslim armies of conquest invaded Syria and Mesopotamia. The Battle of the Yarmuk in 636 made them masters of Syria as the remnants of the Byzantine forces reeled northward in defeat, while the Muslim army in Mesopotamia, profiting from the devastation and anarchy in the aftermath of Heraclius's campaign, crushed the Persians. Egypt's overland connection with Constantinople and the center of the Byzantine Empire was severed. It was toward Egypt that a small Muslim army of four thousand men under the command of Amr ibn al-As marched south from Syria in late 639.

Given the overall strategic situation, and considering the prowess of the Arab armies during the early stages of their conquests, a successful defense of Egypt against the Muslims probably stood little chance, yet the defense could have been conducted much better than it was. But the central government in Constantinople kept its best regular soldiers to hold Anatolia and guard the approaches to the imperial capital, for there was no way to tell which way the Muslims would strike, and the Byzantine regime would not risk another battlefield disaster. Still, the provincial and local forces on hand in Egypt were certainly much larger than the Muslim army of invasion, even after it was reinforced to perhaps fifteen thousand. Unfortunately, their quality was poor, and instead of effective leadership, only dissention emerged, with the prefect/patriarch Cyrus playing a particularly disruptive role.

The Arabs met some resistance when they reached Egypt in December 639, but Pelusium fell in July 640, enabling them to race through the Delta and win a major victory at Heliopolis later that month. Before year's end, the Muslims had taken the town of Babylon and besieged the adjacent fortress. Local forces were disinclined to fight the Muslims with no prospect of provincial or imperial support; besides, the Coptic population, whose hatred of the Byzantines had been intensified by the religious persecutions immediately preceding the Arab invasion, witnessed Byzantine failure with satisfaction. The Bishop of Nikiu wrote, "Everyone knows that the defeat of the Greeks and the conquest of Egypt by the Muslims was in punishment for the tyranny of Emperor Heraclius and the wrongs he inflicted on [Egyptians] through the patriarch Cyrus." Yet there was no significant fifth column of disaffected Coptic Christians at work within Egypt.

The likelihood of imperial aid became even more remote when the Emperor Heraclius died on 11 February 641, and internal strife paralyzed the central government. The fortress of Babylon fell in April. In September the Muslims entered Alexandria. The Byzantine Empire formally surrendered Egypt on 28 November 641; the last Byzantine troops evacuated the country within a year. When the imperial government finally resolved to fight in Egypt and sent a large force under Manuel the Augustulis in 644/5, it was too late to retrieve the situation. Another Byzantine effort in 654 was likewise defeated. Egypt was permanently lost to the Byzantine Empire.

It is said that Amr ibn al-As had visited Alexandria when he was a child, but the rest of the Arab soldiers, fresh from central Arabia, must have been astounded at the city's splendid palaces, sumptuous private homes, imposing public buildings, and complex port and commercial facilities. A story developed that Ibn al-As was uncertain what to do about the large library at the former Serapeum, so he wrote to Caliph Umar for instructions. The caliph replied, "As to the books which you have mentioned, if they contain what is agreeable with the book of God, [then] the book of God is sufficient without them; and if they contain what is contrary to the book of God, there is no need of them: so give orders for their destruction." The contents of the library were then taken and used to heat the baths. Within six months all had been burned. Like some of the other pithy anecdotes associated with the second caliph, this one should be treated with skepticism because it is most unlikely that many books remained after the repeated devastations of the Great Library's collections by Julius Caesar, the Christians, and others.

But the Arabs chose not to rule Egypt from Alexandria. Instead, in a momentous point of departure for Egyptian history, they created an entirely new capital, Fustat, near the fortress of Babylon. The Mosque of Amr ibn al-As, the first mosque in the continent of Africa, was established there in 641–42 and still exists, although it has been completely rebuilt over the centuries. At first Fustat was probably very much the large military encampment that its name literally means in Arabic, but it soon developed into a flourishing city. Though overshadowed in historical memory by Cairo, which was not founded until three centuries later, Fustat was one of the principal cities of the Islamic world during its heyday, second only to Baghdad, and long remained important even after Cairo surpassed it in size. According to the traveling geographer Ibn Hawkal in the tenth century, it contained fine markets and extensive gardens, with mud-brick houses as tall as six stories. A bridge of boats connected Fustat with the island of Roda, and another ran from Roda to Giza on the opposite shore. Alexandria, after being Egypt's capital for nine hundred years, began a long process of decline, although it too continued to be a significant city for some time.

Egypt therefore became a province in the growing Arab Empire, ruled first by the caliphs from Medina and then from Damascus after the Ummayad Caliphate was established there in 661. The chief administrative official in Egypt was the governor. Beneath him were other important officers such as the *qadi*, the chief judicial officer, for the Arabs also brought a new legal system to Egypt. The governor's authority ultimately depended on the Arab garrison, which could be most unruly if not paid regularly. A small but growing—and extremely quarrelsome—community of Arab settlers also played a major role in the government and society of early Muslim Egypt.

The first governor was Amr ibn al-As, but he was soon recalled by Caliph Uthman, who resented the semi-independence that Ibn al-As enjoyed, and wanted to centralize the caliphal administration. His successor, Abdallah ibn Saad ibn Abi Sarh, was an able person, however, who repelled the belated Byzantine attack on Alexandria in 646 and initiated the development of a Muslim navy that inflicted a severe defeat on the Byzantines off the coast of Asia Minor in 654. Ibn Abi Sarh also invaded Nubia, then solidly Christian, in 651–52 but was unable to conquer it, though the resulting treaty, known as the *baqt* (from the Latin *pactus*), required Nubia to pay an annual tribute of slaves to Egypt, an arrangement that continued for centuries. Egypt's southern border was fixed at Aswan.

The Egyptian population was quiet at first. There were no local rebellions. Within the Muslim system, the Christians and Jews were *dhimmi*s ('protected ones'), which in practical terms meant that they would largely be left alone as long as they paid their taxes, a most welcome change for the Egyptian Christians after putting up with centuries of stubborn Byzantine insistence on religious orthodoxy. The Arabs cared nothing about points of Christian theology, therefore they showed little preference for one sect over another. Nor did the Arabs take the Christians' homes and land. The Christians were taxed, of course, but that was nothing new, and although the taxes were substantial, they were not initially extortionate. A tradition of the Prophet was often quoted: "Be full of consideration with regard to Egypt, do not crop her as you would a field of grass." Only later, when taxes became much more oppressive, did revolts begin to break out, but there is little evidence of a desire for a return to Byzantine rule at any time. Even five centuries after the Arab conquest of Egypt, a Christian writer could still assert with strong feeling that, "It was no small advantage to us to be freed from the cruelty of the Romans [Byzantines], their malice, their anger, their cruel zeal toward us, and to be left in peace."

Toleration did not mean equality. Christians were debarred from military service and the highest offices of the state; on the other hand, Arabized Christians were essential during the early decades of Arab rule in Egypt, especially in the area of financial administration. All officials in the countryside were Christians during the century following the conquest. Over time various sumptuary laws were enacted against Christians that required distinctive dress or prohibited certain activities like riding horses, but these were not strictly and consistently enforced. Egypt's Jews, now much diminished in numbers, also had reason to be optimistic about the change of rulers, and they were at least initially justified in their expectation that they would be treated with a tolerance often denied them during late Roman and Byzantine times.

The pace and processes by which Egypt was transformed from a predominantly Coptic-speaking Christian land to an Arabic-speaking Muslim one are difficult to document. The Muslim conquerors did not attempt a mass conversion from Christianity to Islam, if only because that would have reduced the taxes non-Muslims were compelled to pay, but a number of other factors were at work. Arab men could marry Christian women and their children would become Muslim. Large-scale Arab immigration into Egypt began during the eighth century. Personal ambition could be a reason to convert, because although Christians were long retained in important government positions, they were increasingly targets of harassment and violence, and conversion opened opportunities for advancement. The extension of taxation in 705 to churches and monasteries, originally exempt, pushed the monasteries into decline, withering one of the church's most vital institutions in Egypt. When Christians began to revolt under Arab taxation and discrimination, the brutal repressions that followed brought waves of converts seeking to escape the violence, as was especially notable after the Bashmuric revolt of 832. And there was the powerful message of Islam itself, made ever more accessible to the Egyptians as more of them learned Arabic.

The spread of Arabic in Egypt can be traced more precisely than conversion. The language of administration in Egypt continued to be Greek until 706, when a caliphal decree replaced it with Arabic so that Greek almost entirely disappeared from official documents. Egyptian scribes, and others who relied on literacy for their living, had to learn Arabic to keep working. Most Egyptians, of course, spoke not Greek but Coptic during the early centuries of Muslim rule. The displacement of Coptic by Arabic as the popular tongue occurred over a long period of time, but the process was inexorable and thorough. By the fourteenth century, Coptic had virtually disappeared in the countryside and had become almost entirely a liturgical language, like Latin in the Roman Catholic Church.

After the murder of the third caliph Uthman in Medina in 656, the Prophet's son-in-law Ali assumed the caliphate under bitterly contested circumstances. The most formidable challengers were the Ummayads, a wealthy and influential Meccan family with a strong power base in Syria. Egypt became a major battleground in the ensuing war between

Ali and the Ummayads led by Muawiyah. Fighting broke out in 657, with the Ummayads quickly getting the upper hand. Ali responded by appointing Muhammad ibn Abu Bakr, son of the second caliph, as governor of Egypt in 658 to restore control, but Ibn Abu Bakr's stern measures only drove more people into Muawiyah's camp and provided Muawiyah with an opportunity for a counterstroke by sending Amr ibn al-As, who yearned to return to the land he had conquered and governed, to Egypt in command of an Ummayad army. The opposing forces met in a bloody battle between Fustat and Ain Shams in late summer 658 from which Ibn al-As emerged victorious. Egypt was firmly attached to the cause of Muawiyah, who became the first Ummayad caliph in 661. Grateful for his support, Muawiyah permitted Ibn al-As to rule Egypt as he pleased until his death in 664.

When Caliph Marwan I went to Egypt in 684 to establish his authority, he appointed his son Abd al-Aziz governor, initiating a period of peaceful rule in the country that lasted twenty years. During that time Egypt served as the base for—and received the booty from—the completion of the Muslim conquest of North Africa. One of al-Aziz's nominees later commanded the Muslim invasion of Spain. After al-Aziz, the government of Egypt was progressively tightened; taxes were collected much more thoroughly, a tendency that culminated in Ubayd Allah ibn al-Habhab's appointment as the head of taxation in Egypt in 724. Selected to increase the province's revenues, Ubayd Allah made a comprehensive, detailed survey of the country and required every man to wear a numbered badge. Taxes were raised by more than 10 percent and collected ruthlessly, even cruelly. It was then that Egypt's Coptic population, which had patiently accepted Muslim taxation since the Arab conquest, exploded into a series of rebellions. These uncoordinated, unprogrammatic, and leaderless risings had little chance of success, but they placed a heavy strain on the Muslim military establishment, which crushed them with great loss of life.

The later years of the Ummayads were a period of decline. Administrative and military establishments deteriorated. Scandalous stories circulated about their immorality. Meanwhile, centers of opposition developed. One was led by the Abbasid family, so called because they traced their lineage to Abbas, one of Muhammad's uncles, thereby asserting a claim of closer relationship to the Prophet than the Ummayads. In 747 the Abbasids revolted, drawing strength from many disaffected elements. The caliph, Marwan II, was overwhelmed by them in 750 at the Battle of the Zab, after which the Abbasids slaughtered every member of the Ummayad family they could catch. Marwan II escaped to Egypt, but before he could consolidate his position he was killed by closely pursuing Abbasid forces at Busir in Middle Egypt on 1 August 750.

The Abbasid Caliphate, which moved the capital of the empire from Damascus to Baghdad, maintained a strong central government for nearly a century under powerful caliphs such as Harun al-Rashid (786–809). Determined not to rule Egypt from the Ummayad foundation of Fustat, the Abbasids established a new town, al-Askar, a short distance to the north, for the government and soldiers. This did nothing to diminish Fustat, which profited from the proximity of the new administrative center. The Abbasid caliph Mamun, Harun al-Rashid's son, visited Egypt in 832 in the wake of a serious rebellion by both Copts and Arabs. According to legend preserved in the *Arabian Nights*, it was Mamun who caused the breach (now the tourists' entrance) to be made in the north face of the Great Pyramid in search of treasure.

Egypt remained fairly secure during the second half of the ninth century apart from the occasional rebellion, but the Abbasid Empire, like its Ummayad predecessor, also entered a period of decline. The caliph's position became more one of prestige than power, while the provinces of the empire became less subordinate to central authority. Provincial governors began to regard themselves as legitimate rulers in their own right and attempted to establish their families in power. That is precisely what happened in Egypt with the two gubernatorial dynasties known as the Tulunids, 868–905, and the Ikhshidids, 935–69.

Ahmed ibn Tulun, the son of a Turkish slave-soldier sent to the caliph in tribute from Central Asia, arrived to govern Egypt in 868. He built yet another new town a short distance to the north called al-Qatai (the Concessions or the Plots). The mosque that Ibn Tulun erected in his new city is now Cairo's largest, and it is the oldest that retains its original fabric. Ibn Tulun restored economic stability within Egypt by restoring the waterworks and reforming taxation; abroad, he won control of Syria as far as the Byzantine frontier. So successful was he that he became independent of Baghdad to an extent that the caliph eventually found unbearable. At one point Ibn Tulun was even able to intervene in a struggle between two contenders for the caliphate.

When Ibn Tulun died in 884, he was popular and left a full treasury. He was succeeded by his son Khumarawayh, the first time such a large province of the Arab empire was claimed by hereditary right without the permission of the caliph. Khumarawayh began as a strong ruler. He dictated terms to the caliph and extended Tulunid possessions in Syria, but he was careless with expenditures and could not manage when the economy precipitously declined. Khumarawayh was murdered by his palace eunuchs, who were engaged in sexual liaisons with the women of his harem in 896, and his dynasty dissipated into drunkenness, intrigue, and murder. Baghdad saw the opportunity to restore control and sent an expedition to Egypt in 905 that razed al-Qatai to the ground except for Ibn Tulun's mosque and the aqueduct.

For the next thirty years Egypt was directly controlled by Baghdad through a series of military commanders. The system did not work well, however: administrative quality was poor, taxes were kept at much too high a level, and disorder was continuous. When external threats to the empire required the central government's full attention, Caliph al-Radi appointed Muhammad ibn Tughj as governor of Egypt in 935 with the expectation that he could handle things there on his own.

Ibn Tughj was awarded the title Ikhshid, a Persian word meaning 'Leader,' which attached to the short-lived dynasty that he established. Like the Tulunids, the Ikhshidids made themselves effectively independent but astutely kept on good terms with the Abbasids. Maintaining a large standing army, Ibn Tughj repelled an invasion by the Fatimids from Tunisia and retained much of Syria. He was succeeded by his two sons, but they were minors, so power was exercised by their tutor, a former Nubian slave named Kafur. An extremely able man, Kafur had to deal with stupendous problems: rebellions, invasions, naval disasters, an earthquake, famines, and a series of low Niles from 963–68, one of them the lowest ever recorded. When Kafur died in 968, the new governor was unable to cope, and guidance came not from the East in Baghdad, but from the West, the Maghreb, where the Fatimid caliph al-Muizz in Tunisia was planning a new invasion of Egypt and directing a steady stream of propaganda at it. With things in such a bad state in Egypt, and with no aid coming from a distant, increasingly impotent Abbasid dynasty, many Egyptians reasonably concluded that Fatimid rule might be a change for the better.

11   The Fatimids and Ayyubids

The origins of the Fatimids lay in the fundamental differences, and eventually deep schisms, that stemmed from the divisive question of who should be the caliph ('deputy' or 'successor') of the Prophet. The main thrust of Islam, which became known as Sunni, accepted the succession of the Four Rightly Guided Caliphs—Abu Bakr, Umar, Uthman, and Ali—but others held differing views. Among the dissidents were the Shia, the 'Partisans' of the Prophet's cousin and son-in-law Ali, who believed that the succession had gone wrong from the very beginning, that Ali was the rightful successor to Muhammad, and that the Ummayad and Abbasid caliphates were illegitimate.

Itself the product of schism, Shiism was a prolific begetter of schisms. The Fatimids belonged to the Ismaili branch of Shiite Islam, which was unusually well organized and adept at communicating its message. Unable to exert power in the East, a group of Ismailis emigrated from Syria in 909 and settled in present-day Tunisia, where they established a dynastic state ruled by Fatimid caliphs. This, however, they regarded merely as a base from which to wrest control of the Islamic world from the Abbasids. Egypt was the first step on the way to Baghdad.

The Fatimids' initial attempts to conquer Egypt failed, but they continued to prepare the way through missionaries and a sophisticated propaganda campaign that undermined the Ikhshidids' right to rule. After Kafur's death in 968, the new governor was a cultured but ineffective man named Ibn al-Furat. When a struggle over the succession broke out between the followers of Kafur and the Ikhshidid claimants, Ibn al-Furat could not handle the situation and listened to Fatimid emissaries who persuaded him to open Egypt to their troops and put it under their protection. The Fatimid caliph, al-Muizz, dispatched his general Jawhar, who entered Fustat with little opposition in July 969.

Jawhar immediately set about building still another city, again to the north of the preceding ones, in obedience to al-Muizz's instructions to found a capital that would be suitable for the world dominion the Fatimids intended to exercise one day. Several stories circulated about the origins of the new city. According to one, Jawhar marked out the places for everything with stakes and string, with bells attached. At the time the astrologers had calculated most favorable, he intended to ring the bells by shaking the strings, the signal for construction to begin. But before the heavenly bodies moved into proper alignment, a crow alighted on one of the strings, jangling the bells. The workmen obediently set to work. The astrologers were aghast. Mars was in the ascendant at that moment. The city would fall to the Turks one day, they direly predicted. However inauspicious its beginning, construction was far advanced when al-Muizz arrived from Tunisia in June 972. The new city was called al-Qahirah ('the Victorious'), which eventually became westernized into the name Cairo.

Unlike its nearby predecessors Fustat, al-Askar, and al-Qatai, all open cities, Cairo was enclosed within heavy, gated walls of mud brick, later replaced in stone by the vizier Badr al-Jamali. The great historian of medieval Egypt, Taqi al-Din al-Maqrizi (1364–1442), saw some remains of the first wall several centuries later and wrote, "I witnessed the greatness of the bricks, which in our times excites wonder, for each brick was a cubit [well over half a meter] in length and two-thirds of a cubit in breadth. The width of the wall was several cubits, enough for two horsemen to ride upon it abreast." Inside the walls lay a profusion of opulent palaces, pavilions, residences, offices, baths, gardens, fountains, pools, and kiosks, in addition to such workaday establishments as the mint, arsenal, and stables. On the eastern side of the new city was the great palace, sprawling across 13,475 square meters. Besides being the caliph's primary residence, the eastern palace housed the ministerial offices. Caliph al-Aziz built another, smaller palace on the west amid immense gardens reserved for the women of the royal harem. A tunnel large enough for the caliph to ride through on horseback connected the two palaces. Above ground was a spacious parade ground large enough for ten thousand soldiers known as the Bayn al-Qasrayn ('Between the Two Palaces'), a name that survives although the palaces, along with most of Fatimid Cairo, have vanished. Within their splendid surroundings, the caliphs maintained lifestyles of ostentatious luxury as a deliberate policy to proclaim their political power and religious mystique.

Fatimid Cairo was a forbidden city, reserved for the caliph, his entourage, the government, and the army, various attachments of which were assigned portions of the town for their residences. One of the military units, composed of a Berber tribe called the Zuweila, gave its name to the city's principal southern gate. Egyptians from Fustat and the surrounding area worked in Cairo and provided it with goods and services, but when they finished their duties, they were expected to leave by Bab Zuweila, which served as a sort of servants' entrance. That meant that Fustat, far from being diminished by Cairo's appearance, was further stimulated by the proximity of such a vast courtly and administrative city. Fustat's greatest days, in fact, were those after the foundation of Cairo, when it supplied Cairo's enormous elite establishment and served as its commercial link with the outside world, while enjoying enhanced economic reach because of the Fatimids' international power.

Fatimid patronage of learning found ample expression in Cairo. Jawhar laid the foundations of the great mosque al-Azhar in 970. It became a teaching institution under Caliph al-Aziz in 989 and continues to flourish as a university more than a thousand years later. Cairo also boasted a large caliphal library. Among the many other Fatimid institutions of learning, the most notable was Dar al-Hikma ('House of Wisdom'), founded by Caliph al-Hakim in 1005 and staffed with learned men representing many disciplines. The House of Wisdom contained a library and reading room open to scholars and interested general readers, who were supplied with paper, pens, and ink. For a time there was an astronomical observatory, but it was dismantled after the vizier who patronized it fell from favor. The Fatimids also stimulated music and literature, as many surviving works from their time attest.

Based in Egypt, the Fatimid Empire encompassed Syria and the Hijaz on the east, and the northern coast of Africa, plus the island of Sicily to the west. At the apex of the Fatimid political, social, and religious systems stood the caliph, who governed through a highly organized bureaucracy headed by the caliph's chief officer, the vizier. During the later years of the Fatimid dynasty, the caliph became a gaudy figurehead, but the first three Fatimid caliphs to rule in Egypt—al-Muizz, al-Aziz, and al-Hakim—were absolute monarchs in full control of the government. Their viziers were strictly executive officers who did their bidding and were dismissed by them at will. The caliphs commanded a strong army and navy. The soldiers were mostly slaves: Berbers from the Fatimids' Maghrebi dominions, Sudanese, and Turks. Eventually the Turkish element became dominant, much to the annoyance of the Berbers, who had brought the Fatimids to power in Egypt. At sea, a strong naval force protected Fatimid interests in the Mediterranean and turned the Red Sea into a Fatimid lake.

Another basis of Fatimid power was a strong economy. Exploiting their position astride the Mediterranean and the Red Sea, the Fatimids controlled the trade between the Mediterranean—including Christian states like Byzantium, Venice, and Genoa—and India and the Far East. Fatimid Egypt also exported high-quality handicrafts such as fine textiles, exquisite glassware, and ceramics of a standard never before attained. The Nile Valley was well exploited, producing surpluses to add to the Fatimids' favorable balance of trade. The waterworks were carefully maintained and burdensome taxes reduced, making the dynasty popular in the countryside and increasing the land's productivity. Ample supplies of gold enabled the Fatimids to mint a plentiful money supply. Fatimid gold coins maintained their level of purity almost until the end of the dynasty.

With the exception of the eccentric caliph al-Hakim, the Fatimids' policy toward the *dhimmi*s, the Christians and the Jews, was highly tolerant and sometimes even supportive. Many Christians held good positions in Fatimid government and society, although it was in the early Fatimid period that the Christians ceased to be the majority in Egypt. The Jews of Egypt probably enjoyed their best times ever under the Fatimids. A

Jewish community, the largest in Egypt since the demise of Alexandria's, developed in Fustat, where the Ben Ezra Synagogue had been founded in Tulunid times. "The Jews who live there are very rich," wrote the visitor Benjamin of Tudela in 1170. Fustat became a Jewish center of power for Palestine and Syria as well as Egypt.

Because of Fustat's Jewish community, we have an exceptional source for daily life in medieval Egypt that is especially rich for Fatimid times but also important for other periods. At the Ben Ezra Synagogue was a *genizah*, a word that might be loosely translated as 'cache,' where worn-out Hebrew bibles and other religious works were deposited because it was unlawful to destroy a document with the name of God on it. Over the centuries, therefore, scrolls and codices (bound books) were discarded in the *genizah*. The criteria for what should be deposited became ever looser so that a wide range of documents accumulated in the Fustat *genizah* that dealt not only with religion but also with everyday matters like marriage, divorce, business, magic, medicine, and education, with relevance to all of society, not just the Jewish minority. Often the documents speak with strong personal voices. "God knows, prices are so unpredictable these days," a businessman frets, while a frustrated wife complains that her husband has not had sex with her for nine months: "I am a thirsty woman; the man is useless. Let him separate; let's annul the marriage."

During the reign of al-Muizz's successor, Caliph al-Aziz (975–96), the Fatimid Empire attained its greatest strength. True to the Fatimids' policy of ostentatious caliphal lifestyles, al-Aziz spent heavily on luxuries—once he had cherries flown to him from Lebanon on the legs of carrier pigeons—but he was also a conscientious administrator. Egypt flourished under his rule. Outside Egypt, al-Aziz was most active in Syria where his military operations had mixed results. Al-Aziz was preparing to lead his army in person against the Byzantines in northern Syria at the time of his death. That would have been the preparatory move to turning toward Baghdad and realizing the Fatimids' long-standing dream of destroying the Sunni caliphate.

Al-Aziz was succeeded by his eleven-year-old son al-Hakim (996–1020). During his first years as caliph, al-Hakim was dominated by his counselor, a eunuch named Barjawan, but when he was fifteen he suddenly ordered Barjawan killed and exercised a powerful personal rule for the remaining two decades of his reign. Truth is hard to separate from legend with al-Hakim. Some of the stories of his excesses could be exaggerated while others may have a plausible basis, but at the least he was very eccentric. It was said that he could lavish gifts on favorites one moment and have them executed the next. He even had all his concubines killed in their bath one day. Strongly Shiite, al-Hakim pursued anti-Sunni policies—though he appointed a Sunni as *qadi* because he was the best-qualified man for the job—but unlike the other Fatimid caliphs he was especially harsh on Christians, forcing them to wear marks of religious identity and prohibiting them from riding horses or purchasing slaves. Many were forcibly converted to Islam, and several church officials suffered execution, including two of al-Hakim's uncles (al-Hakim's mother was a Christian). He ordered the Church of the Holy Sepulcher in Jerusalem demolished, along with numerous churches in Egypt. Al-Hakim also treated Jews poorly, destroying many of their synagogues. His ordinances against women—who were forbidden to wear jewelry and eventually even to go out of doors—were especially severe, as were his punishments if they were ignored. He hated dogs and twice commanded that all of them in Cairo be killed.

All the other Fatimid caliphs were remote rulers, appearing in public only on major occasions amid great pomp, but al-Hakim's personal conduct was astonishingly unaffected. He maintained a simple lifestyle, dressing in plain woolen garments and rarely wearing the diamond-studded turban of the caliphs, and forbade his subjects to prostrate themselves before him or address him as "Lord." He rode freely around town on a donkey without guards, mixing easily with the people as if he were one of them. A few years after his death, one writer remembered al-Hakim as "a pleasant man with a sense of humor. He often exchanged jokes with the people he spoke to in the streets." Al-Hakim liked to go walking or riding alone in the Muqattam hills behind Cairo. But near the end of his reign it was rumored that he had come to believe that he was a manifestation of Allah and would soon proclaim his divinity. When that caused rioting in Fustat, he turned his soldiers loose on the city and withdrew to the hills to watch as they rampaged through the town with appalling carnage.

One night al-Hakim went on one of his solitary Muqattam rides and never returned, vanishing without a trace apart from a bloodstained cloak found a few days later. He was almost certainly murdered, but some of his followers believed that he did not die but merely retreated from the world to reappear someday as the Mahdi, or Savior. These became the Druzes, who established themselves in Lebanon and still revere al-Hakim. Al-Hakim's imposing mosque, completed in 1003, stands just inside Bab al-Futuh behind the northern wall of Cairo.

Al-Hakim was succeeded by another minor, his nephew al-Zahir, but the power behind the throne was the new caliph's aunt, al-Hakim's sister Sitt al-Mulk, who may have been complicitous in her brother's murder. Just before his disappearance, al-Hakim and Sitt al-Mulk had a bitter quarrel after he accused her of adultery. Sitt al-Mulk was also worried about al-Hakim's plans for the succession. The reign of al-Zahir (1020–35) was marred by serious problems both at home and abroad, relations with the Byzantines being particularly vexatious. Sitt al-Mulk was still a formidable force in 1035 when al-Mustansir became caliph. After her death al-Mustansir finally achieved a measure of independence, only to lose it during the last part of his exceptionally long reign of fifty-eight years.

Things had been slipping out of control as early as al-Zahir's reign. Part of the problem was extensive recruitment of slave soldiers. Because they were drawn from different ethnic sources, they were prone to factional fighting and became increasingly insubordinate. In 1060, in conjunction with a series of low inundations that created widespread shortages, devastated commerce, and bankrupted the government, Egypt entered a period of anarchy that lasted thirteen years. Unpaid soldiers went on an extended rampage, taking what they could; factional fighting turned into outright warfare. The Sudanese soldiers seized much of Upper Egypt, while the Berbers held the Delta. The Turks, who occupied Cairo, ransacked al-Mustansir's library and forced him to sell his treasures for their benefit. Security disappeared in the countryside. The Lawata Berbers attacked and sacked the Wadi Natrun monasteries, taking Patriarch Christodoulos hostage. During this "Great Crisis," as it came to be known, the situation was so dire that people resorted to cannibalism, sometimes eating their victims while they were still alive, if the accounts can be believed.

In desperation, al-Mustansir appointed the governor of Acre, a former Armenian slave named Badr al-Jamali, vizier in 1074. Bringing with him a reliable personal army of Armenian soldiers, Badr al-Jamali soon crushed opposition and restored order. A three-year suspension of taxes gave the country time to recover. In Cairo, Badr al-Jamali replaced the city's mud-brick ramparts with stone walls interspersed with imposing gates, three of which remain: Bab Zuweila on the south, and Bab al-Nasr and Bab al-Futuh in the northern wall. But these services came at a price. Previously the viziers had usually been civilians obedient to the caliph; henceforth they were military men who exercised effective control of the state. Badr al-Jamali went on to rule Egypt for twenty years, and he was succeeded as vizier by his son al-Afdal Shahanshah. But Badr al-Jamali could not restore the overall situation of the Fatimid Empire. Sicily had been lost in 1071; now much of Syria fell away as well with a reassertion of tribal rule and the establishment of minor dynasties, reducing the Fatimids' Syrian possessions to the coastal strip running south from Tyre, although al-Afdal recaptured Jerusalem in 1098 (just in time to lose it to the Crusaders the following year).

When al-Mustansir died in 1094, al-Afdal placed the late caliph's younger son al-Mustali on the throne. The elder son, Nizar, revolted and was killed, but some of his supporters refused to accept the result and in a further Ismaili schism joined the Assassins' sect in Syria. With the accession of al-Mustali, Fatimid court factionalism and intrigue became nearly continuous. Although the viziers had seized power from the caliphs, contention for the vizierate was so intense that the institution could never develop sufficient stability to govern effectively. It was a dangerous time for political weakness, especially with the appearance of another formidable military force that threatened the Fatimids' remaining Syrian possessions, and even Egypt itself.

The Seljuk Turks were part of the great Turkish nomadic migration from Central Asia. From his base in Khurasan, Tughril, the true founder of the Seljuk dynasty, expanded into Iran and then turned west. When Tughril entered Baghdad in 1055, the Abbasid caliph recognized him as sultan ('he with power'). Sultan was henceforth the preferred title of Turkish rulers. In 1071, Tughril's successor, Alparslan, dealt a devastating defeat to the Byzantines at the Battle of Manzikert, smashing the Byzantine field army, capturing the emperor, and opening the Anatolian heartland to the Turks. Alparslan's son, Malikshah, thrust south through Syria to take Damascus, Jerusalem, and even part of Arabia.

Egypt was the obvious next conquest for the Seljuks. Fortunately for the Fatimids, however, Nizam al-Mulk, the brilliant vizier who had guided Alparslan and Malikshah through many of their successes, was killed by the Assassins in 1092, the same year Malikshah died. A vicious power struggle ensued in which central control over the Seljuks' wide dominions, including Syria, was lost. The Fatimids were thereby spared a military confrontation that might well have been their undoing. But Egypt had not heard the last of the Turks by any means.

The situation in the East, then, at the end of the eleventh century was one of weakness and division, leaving a power vacuum in Syria and Palestine. The Byzantine Empire was undergoing a prolonged recovery from a disastrous defeat. The Fatimid Empire was in deep decline, unable to maintain much more than a token presence in Palestine. The Seljuks were rendered impotent by their internal problems. Although both the Fatimids and the Seljuks claimed that Syrian domination belonged to them, neither was able or willing to protect the area which had splintered into competing principalities. Into that fragmented political landscape, yet another force unexpectedly intruded: the Western Crusades, with which Egypt was to be deeply involved from their beginning until their end several centuries later.

The Crusades originated in 1095 at the Council of Clermont, where Pope Urban II issued a call to free the oppressed Christians in the Holy Land and remove the stigma of having the holy places occupied by Muslims. (In fact, the Christians in Palestine were reasonably well treated, and Jerusalem and other sites were open to Christian pilgrims.) France was overcrowded, Urban continued, whereas Palestine was a land of milk and honey. He urged the nobles to stop fighting each other and turn their swords against the infidels. "Let robbers become knights!" he cried, and the nobles enthusiastically answered, "God wills it!" Crusading zeal swept Europe. The moment was right, for it was an age of great pilgrimages and crusades. The struggle of the Normans against the Saracens in Sicily was recognized as a crusade, as was the Reconquista, the recovery of Spain from the Muslims. Even Duke William of Normandy received the pope's crusading banner in his speculative invasion of England in 1066. Christendom was undergoing great political, economic, social, and religious changes, creating energies that could be diverted outward.

The first effort was the People's Crusade in 1096, but that lawless, disorganized band of peasants led by Peter the Hermit and Walter the Penniless was annihilated in October before reaching the Holy Land. The following month, however, a much more formidable force began to assemble at Constantinople with contingents and small armies mostly drawn from French, Flemish, and Norman areas. After testing its military ability against the Turks in Anatolia, the Crusader army reached Syria in the fall of 1097 and captured Antioch after an eight-month siege. In January 1099 they opened their offensive against Jerusalem, unhindered by serious resistance, reaching its walls in June. The feeble Fatimid garrison held the city for more than a month, but the Crusaders took it on 15 July 1099. The governor and his entourage were allowed to leave, but the rest of Jerusalem's population, including the Christians whom the Crusaders had ostensibly come to aid, was massacred. Al-Afdal's relief army from Egypt started too late and was defeated at Ascalon, although that town remained in Egyptian hands when the Crusader leaders turned to disputing among themselves, and it continued to be an outpost against the Crusaders for another half century. An important act of cultural preservation occurred at Ascalon when the Fatimid garrison ransomed a collection of valuable manuscripts that the Crusaders had looted from Jerusalem.

The leaders of the various crusading forces had pledged to restore lands formerly held by the Byzantines, but instead they carved out four Crusader states for themselves: the County of Edessa, the Principality of Antioch, the County of Tripoli, and the Latin kingdom of Jerusalem. The last of these was the largest and enjoyed the prestige of controlling the Christian holy places. The Latin kingdom was also the one that directly confronted Fatimid Egypt. The initial period of conquest was necessarily followed by one of consolidation as the Crusaders, few in number, imposed their rule on a large, diverse population that was alien to them in language, culture, and religion. Increasingly short of both manpower and money, the Crusader states were also threatened with resurgent Muslim forces in Syria. It was fortunate for Egypt that the Second Crusade (1147–49) was primarily directed into a futile effort to capture Damascus, causing a projected offensive against Egypt to be abandoned.

Meanwhile, conditions within Egypt continued to deteriorate. Contention for control of the government became ever more ruthless with repeated usurpations of the vizierate, murder of the caliph, and massacre of all the royal princes save one, who was preserved as a shadow caliph. From the outside, the Latin kingdom exerted increasing pressure. Egypt was compelled to pay tribute to the Crusaders. Ascalon fell to them in 1143, removing the remaining Fatimid bridgehead into Palestine and opening the way into Egypt. Two decades later, after the Latin kingdom had recovered from the fiasco of the Second Crusade, its new, energetic king Amalric thought Egypt was ripe for the taking. He invaded in 1163 and reached Bilbays in September, but the defenders cut the dikes, releasing the impounded waters of the recent inundation, flooding the fields and forcing the Franks (as all Europeans were called) to withdraw, though soon to return.

The Crusaders were not the only ones interested in Egypt. Out of the confusion following the deaths of the Seljuk sultan and vizier in 1092, Zangi, the son of their governor of Aleppo, established an autonomous regime in northern Syria. His capture of Edessa in 1144, the first recovery of a Crusader capital by the Muslims, made him a champion of the faith. When Zangi divided his dominions among his sons before being murdered by a Frankish slave in 1146, the second son, Nur al-Din, received northern Syria. Nur al-Din continued his father's holy war against the Crusaders, recapturing more territory from them, and realized Zangi's ambition of taking Damascus in 1154, uniting Muslim Syria under a single ruler. One of Nur al-Din's powerful vassals was his military commander Shirkuh, whose brother Ayyub (hence the name of the subsequent dynasty) was often accompanied on campaigns by his son Salah al-Din, generally known in the West as Saladin. The Ayyubids, it might be noted, were neither Turkish nor Arab: they were Kurdish.

When Amalric invaded Egypt again in 1164, Nur al-Din responded to appeals from the Fatimid vizier by allowing Shirkuh to lead an army to Egypt. Over the next three years fighting ranged from the Delta as far south as al-Babayn in Middle Egypt. At Alexandria, Salah al-Din withstood a Crusader siege. Unable to achieve a decisive result, both sides evacuated Egypt in August 1167, but Amalric had won some advantages: Egyptian tribute to the Latin kingdom was increased, a Frankish resident was established in Cairo, and a Frankish garrison was posted at the gates of the city.

Amalric should have been content, but he attempted a complete conquest of Egypt the following year. This time he captured Bilbays, the city that had thwarted him earlier, and massacred its population. The Crusader chronicler William of Tyre recorded, "Our men entered the city with swords drawn and started to massacre all whom they found, men and women, old and young, sparing no one. . . . When they found maidens or old people hidden in rooms, they ran them through with their swords, sparing only those who might provide a substantial ransom. The destruction was horrifying, and the pillage no less so."[20]

The approaches to Cairo lay open. The vizier ordered Fustat to be set on fire so it could not serve as a base for the invaders. The town burned for nearly two months, a disaster from which it never recovered. The caliph personally appealed to Nur al-Din and Shirkuh for aid. Shirkuh's rapid approach compelled Amalric to withdraw, losing all he had gained. Shirkuh's motive for coming to Egypt had probably been personal ambition all along, for in January 1169, he had the Fatimid vizier killed and took the post for himself. When he died a few weeks later, Salah al-Din, a young man of thirty, succeeded him.

Salah al-Din's position was uneasy at first. A Sunni vizier to a Shiite Fatamid caliph, he controlled only a small part of the military establishment while rivals contended for power in a disordered country. Yet by systematic, ruthless elimination of opponents, he consolidated his power. When the Fatimid caliph al-Adid died in September 1171, Salah al-Din proclaimed himself sultan. The name of the Abbasid caliph al-Mustadi was pronounced in the mosques at Friday prayers. Egypt returned to the Sunni fold. Sunni *qadis* of the Shafii legal school were appointed to office. The caliph in Baghdad formally recognized Salah al-Din's position. In form, therefore, Salah al-Din ruled Egypt as the deputy of his overlord Nur al-Din under the overall sovereignty of the Abbasid caliph; in fact, he had acquired such a strong power base that relations between him and Nur al-Din became strained. A clash would have occurred had not Nur al-Din been removed by death in May 1174, making Salah al-Din even more secure in Egypt and allowing him a freer hand in Syria.

In Cairo, Salah al-Din established the dominating Citadel and built immense new walls. He ejected the remaining members of the Fatimid family from the city and opened it to the general population. With its proximity to power and the decline of Fustat, Cairo grew quickly as people of all classes moved there. Prosperity returned to the countryside. But although Egypt was without doubt the most important part of his empire, Salah al-Din largely viewed it as the means for securing and extending his possessions in Syria, where he spent most of his time. He never organized his various dominions into an institutional whole, instead entrusting their governance to individuals, often members of the Ayyubid extended family, who effectively became autonomous princes whose precise relationship to the sultan in Cairo was never clearly established.

Salah al-Din's expansionist activities during the first part of his reign were principally directed toward winning the old Zangid realms. Damascus fell to him almost without resistance in 1174. Aleppo and Mosul proved more obdurate, but he eventually gained recognition as overlord from them as well. He was also recognized as sultan in the Hijaz and Yemen. Relations with the Latin kingdom were mostly pacific during this period because Amalric died in 1174 and was followed by the minority rule of the leprous king Baldwin IV. The weakened Latin kingdom needed coexistence, not conflict. Salah al-Din conducted a raid up the coast of the kingdom in 1177 but neglected to secure the towns of Ascalon and Gaza in his rear and was lucky to escape when he suffered a severe defeat near al-Ramla in November. He returned to win some victories in 1179 and made a four-year truce with the Latin kingdom in 1185.

But when Baldwin IV died the following year, he was succeeded by Guy of Lusignan, who adopted a more bellicose policy, hoping to break out of the kingdom's spiraling decline. He was strongly supported by his noblemen, one of whom infuriated Salah al-Din by attacking a caravan bound from Egypt to Syria, seizing its cargo, and slaughtering its people. When Salah al-Din retaliated, Guy of Lusignan marched to meet him with a great host comprising almost all the military might of his kingdom. The decisive battle came at Hattin, near the town of Tiberius, on 4 July 1187. Though superior in numbers, the Crusaders allowed themselves to be surrounded. Cut off from water, and scorched by fires started by their adversaries to make their thirst unbearable, many were slain where they stood; the rest, including King Guy, surrendered.

Hattin left the Crusader state nearly defenseless. Acre fell without a fight. Salah al-Din then advanced on Jerusalem, which surrendered on terms on 2 October 1187. In marked contrast to the savage behavior of the Crusaders eighty-eight years earlier, Salah al-Din permitted the population to go free. The urge to recapture Jerusalem must have been irresistible, but Salah al-Din would have done better to have moved first against Tyre, the last port remaining in Crusader hands. Immediately after Hattin, it was weak, ready for the taking. Its capture would have severed the Crusader's communications with Europe, removing hope from their remaining pockets of resistance in Syria and Palestine. Jerusalem could then have been captured at leisure. By the time Salah al-Din reached Tyre, it had been reinforced; his siege had to be abandoned when his eastern allies withdrew at the end of the year's campaigning season. The door remained open for Crusader reinforcements, which were not long in coming.

News of Jerusalem's fall caused consternation in the Christian west. Pope Urban III collapsed and died when he heard about it. A new wave of Crusading zeal erupted. Christendom's three most powerful monarchs, Emperor Frederick Barbarossa of the German Holy Roman Empire, Philip Augustus of France, and Richard the Lion-Heart of England answered the call, each at the head of a strong army. Most of the Germans turned back after the emperor was drowned on the way, but Philip Augustus and Richard arrived in Palestine at the end of spring 1191. Their first objective was Acre. Its surrender on 12 July was followed by the execution of three thousand of its defenders. Although the contest between Richard and Salah al-Din became synonymous with chivalric behavior in Western legend, true chivalry was usually—though not invariably—to be found with Salah al-Din.

Richard and Philip Augustus quarreled so bitterly over the division of spoils in the aftermath of their victory at Acre that Philip Augustus and his army returned to France, leaving Richard to face Salah al-Din in a series of coastal engagements over the next year in which the fortunes of war went back and forth—Jaffa changed hands more than once—but Richard was never able to mount an assault on his primary objective, Jerusalem. When they reached a stand-off, Richard and Salah al-Din concluded a three-years truce in September 1192 that acknowledged Muslim control of Jerusalem but allowed unarmed Christian pilgrims to visit the city. Richard departed for Europe the following month.

After Salah al-Din died in 1193, his Ayyubid family continued to rule for more than a century. Because of the conglomerate nature of his dominions, never forged into a closely united monarchy, it was usually a matter of one powerful Ayyubid prince maintaining an uneasy ascendancy over the others. The first of these was Salah al-Din's brother, al-Adil Sayf al-Din, who adroitly maneuvered Salah al-Din's sons out of power and took the sultanate for himself in 1198, distributing important principalities to his own sons. Content with his brother's hard-won conquests, al-Adil kept the peace with the Latin kingdom. A new Crusade had materialized in 1197, but its limited force was directed toward the north, where the capture of Sidon and Beirut provided the Crusaders with more breathing space. The wretched Fourth Crusade in 1204, which originally had Egypt as its primary objective, never came near Egypt because the Venetians who were transporting the Crusaders to the East diverted them against Venice's commercial rival Constantinople, an act of greedy folly that devastated the Byzantine Empire and weakened Europe's southeastern bulwark against Muslim conquest. The Ayyubids, however, were delighted to be spared attack and rewarded the Venetians with commercial privileges in Alexandria.

The Fifth Crusade in 1218 was an altogether different matter. Again Egypt was the primary target, and this time the Crusaders carried through, intending to strike directly at the base of Ayyubid power, loosening its grip on Palestine and Syria, and of course gaining immensely rich possessions in the land of Egypt. They invaded Egypt through the eastern Delta and laid siege to Damietta. At that critical moment al-Adil died, leaving his son al-Kamil, whom he had appointed as his deputy in Egypt, to confront the Crusaders. Al-Kamil offered extravagant terms, including the return of all territories once held by the Latin kingdom west of the Jordan, but the Crusaders, confident of total victory, haughtily refused them.

The Crusaders' arrogance seemed justified when Damietta fell to them in November 1219. "All the rest of Egypt and Syria was on the point of collapse," the Arab historian Ibn al-Athir wrote, "and everyone was terrified of the invaders and went in anticipation of disaster night and day. The population of Egypt was even ready to evacuate the country for fear of the enemy." But the Crusaders had overplayed their hand. After wasting time with internal dissension, they found themselves cut off by the rising Nile the following summer and were forced to evacuate Egypt. When Emperor Frederick II arrived on his reluctant crusade in 1229, al-Kamil responded with such effective diplomacy that this latest adversary sailed away without an armed encounter.

Al-Kamil's death in 1238 set off the third and last round of Ayyubid family fighting that ended with his son al-Salih Ayyub becoming sultan in Egypt and establishing his supremacy in Syria. Al-Salih Ayyub had long been recruiting slave-soldiers known as Mamluks ('owned men'), primarily Kipchak Turks. They came to be known as Bahri, or River Mamluks because their barracks was located on Roda Island in the Nile. They quickly proved themselves to be his most reliable soldiers by far. Al-Salih Ayyub was taking steps toward institutional integration of his disparate possessions when he fell seriously ill. At that moment of vulnerability, the Crusaders invaded Egypt again.

The Seventh Crusade was a well-financed, well-manned initiative by the king of France, Louis IX. Like his predecessors, Louis saw Egypt as the key to the Holy Land, a rich base from which to conduct operations—and a rich prize in itself. Damietta could have been defended this time, but its garrison and inhabitants panicked and fled. The Arab historian Ibn Wasil called it "a disaster without precedent." The unprecedented disaster was compounded by the death of Sultan al-Salih Ayyub in camp at Mansura in November 1249. The conquest of Egypt by the Crusaders appeared imminent.

12 The Mamluks

hen al-Salih Ayyub died, his widow, a resolute Turkish woman named Shajar al-Durr, took control of the situation. Working with a powerful Mamluk named Fakhr al-Din, she concealed the news of her husband's death and forged his signature to decrees. The army, government, and people were compelled to swear loyalty to al-Salih Ayyub and his heir al-Muazzan Turan-Shah. That bought time for Turan-Shah to come from his remote principality in upper Mesopotamia. Meanwhile, she appointed Fakhr al-Din commander-in-chief and entrusted him with administrative control of the country. According to the historian Ibn Wasil, "The Sultan's decrees were to be issued at her command and in her name, and marked with her royal stamp." Ibn Wasil is explicit about Shajar al-Durr's status: "From that time she became titular head of the whole state; a royal stamp was issued in her name . . . and the *khutba** was pronounced in her name as Sultana of Cairo and all Egypt. This was an event without precedent throughout the Muslim world."[21]

---

* In which the name of the ruling sultan was mentioned during Friday prayers in the mosques.

The Franks attacked Mansura in February 1250. The fighting was intense; Fakhr al-Din was killed, but his Mamluk soldiers performed valiantly, and the Crusader assault failed. The new sultan Turan-Shah arrived, and the Crusaders' position before Mansura became untenable. Their retreat to Damietta deteriorated into disaster; Louis IX was taken prisoner. His queen had to negotiate the surrender of Damietta and the release of her husband for an enormous sum, literally a king's ransom. The Crusaders evacuated Egypt in May 1250, but Turan-Shah had no opportunity to enjoy the triumph, for he was murdered by a conspiracy within the Bahri Mamluks who were offended by promotion of his Mamluks over them. They also resented his ill treatment of Shajar al-Durr, who was a fellow Turk and who was probably part of the conspiracy to kill him. His murder marked the end of the Ayyubid dynasty and the beginning of centuries of Mamluk rule in Egypt.

Because she was a woman, Shajar al-Durr could not take personal command of the army, and some outlying dominions refused to acknowledge her rule, so she married a Bahri Mamluk named Aybeg al-Turkumani. But the power continued to lie with Shajar al-Durr, who controlled Aybeg. When Aybeg attempted to consolidate his position by promoting his Mamluks and making a significant marriage alliance by taking another wife, Shajar al-Durr had him killed in his bath in April 1257. A faction formed around his young son, however, and Shajar al-Durr was herself killed a few days later.

Using Aybeg's son as a shadow sultan, leading Mamluks maneuvered for power in a pattern that would be repeated throughout the Mamluk Period. For a time the ascendancy was with Kutuz, one of Aybeg's favored Mamluks, who already held key state positions. Another threat from outside immediately appeared. Since their unification under Ghengis Khan, the Mongols had swept out of their homeland, overrunning China, Central Asia, Russia, and much of Central Europe, driven by dreams of world conquest, dreams that often seemed horrifyingly possible. In 1255, under command of the Great Khan's brother Hülegü, they invaded Syria and Mesopotamia, capturing Baghdad in 1258, devastating the city and killing the caliph. Aleppo and Damascus fell the following year, with the Crusaders of Tripoli and Antioch lending aid to the Mongols. The conquest of Egypt was the Mongols' next objective. Hülegü dispatched envoys to Cairo with a terrifying ultimatum:

Be warned by the fate of others and hand over your power to us before the veil is torn and you are sorry and your errors rebound upon you. For we do not pity those who weep, nor are we tender to those who complain. You have heard that we have conquered the lands and cleansed the earth of corruption and killed most of the people. . . . You have no deliverance from our swords, no escape from the terror of our arms. Our horses are swift in pursuit, our arrows piercing, our swords like thunderbolts, our hearts like rocks, our numbers like sand. Fortresses cannot withstand us; armies are of no avail in fighting us. . . . If you resist you will be destroyed.[22]

Nor were these empty words, as many had learned. No one had been able to withstand the Mongol onslaught.

But Kutuz, strongly supported by the Bahri Mamluk faction in Syria and its prominent member Baybars, chose to resist. He answered Hülegü's letter by cutting the envoys in two and putting their heads on display at Bab Zuweila. Not waiting to be attacked, Kutuz led his army north to Palestine, spurning an offer of support from the Latin kingdom, and found the Mongols at Ain Jalut near Mount Gilboa. The desperate battle, which came on 3 September 1260, resulted in complete victory for the Mamluks. Though coming close to defeat more than once, Kutuz rallied the Mamluks, who smashed the Mongol army, killing many. A Mamluk pursuing force under Baybars chased the survivors out of Syria. The Mongols, it might be noted, were weakened by the departure of their leader Hülegü after the death of his brother the Great Khan, and they were operating at extreme distance from their bases. Even so, the Mamluk victory was a great feat of arms; it was also decisive, winning northern Syria for the Mamluks and freeing Egypt from the threat of Mongol invasion.

When he distributed Syrian principalities to the Mamluk amirs, Kutuz passed over Baybars, who had distinguished himself at Ain Jalut, just as he had against the Crusaders at Damietta, even though he had been promised Aleppo. This reignited factional sensibilities among the Bahri Mamluks, who resented Kutuz and his rival faction. Kutuz was returning to Egypt when Baybars and some accomplices killed him on a hunting trip. Baybars thereupon claimed the sultanate. His reign is one of the outstanding chapters in Mamluk history and legend, for the *Life of Baybars* became immensely popular and was performed by professional reciters for centuries.

Before turning to the political history of the Mamluk Period, something should be said about the extraordinary organization of this military elite that dominated Egypt for the next several hundred years. Inductees were purchased as young boys in slave markets, often on the Black Sea, beyond the realm of Islam. Agents transported them to Egypt where they were repurchased by heads of the various Mamluk houses, or perhaps by the sultan, who was often a Mamluk himself and who headed the largest Mamluk house of all. The youth became part of a Mamluk household and was instructed in Islam and trained in the arts of war, especially horsemanship. At the conclusion of his education, when he attained manhood, he received his freedom and usually continued to serve in his former master's personal train of knights; later he might start a household of his own and become an amir, or commander, the measure of his power being how many Mamluks he could afford to buy.

Members of Mamluk households, whose heraldic emblems were proudly displayed and worn, developed strong loyalties to their own households and rivalries with others. The restored house of the amir Taz, near the Mosque of Ibn Tulun, provides a good example of a great Mamluk household. Taz was purchased as a boy by Sultan al-Nasir Muhammad. After gaining the favor of the sultan, who made him his *saki*, or cupbearer, Taz was given his freedom and rose rapidly, first becoming an amir of ten Mamluks and finally of a thousand, establishing himself as one of the six most important amirs in the land. Powerful Mamluks like Taz dominated the highest offices of state through this remarkable system that could enable a boy to rise from slavery to a level where he could make or break sultans, or even become the sultan. The expensive Mamluk lifestyle was supported by extensive grants called *iltizam*s. These were essentially a process of tax farming that gave the people who were awarded them, called *multazim*s, virtual control of the land and its produce. This of course imposed a heavy burden on the peasantry, whose position became ever more wretched as increasing exactions were imposed on them. Most of the revenue from the land in Egypt went to the Mamluks.

A crucial aspect of this unique system is that it was not hereditary. Almost all its members were first generation. The sons of Mamluks might someday be given good government posts, but they were not Mamluks and could never be accepted into the Mamluk oligarchy. The only way to become a Mamluk was by being purchased as a slave and rising through one of the Mamluk military households. When a Mamluk died or otherwise vanished from the political scene, his estate was reassigned to other Mamluks.

At its apogee, the Mamluk Empire was a formidable power. Much more coherent than the Ayyubid Empire, its outlying provinces were ruled by governors answerable to the sultan, not by autonomous princes with unclear loyalties and power relationships. Internal affairs were eased by a reformed legal system. A sophisticated diplomatic service maintained relations as far east as the Golden Horde and with the maritime kingdom and city states of Aragon, Genoa, and Venice in the west. Byzantium received careful diplomatic attention, and relations with the Crusader kingdoms required constant activity, since truces had to be renegotiated constantly. Through their control of important trade routes, the Mamluks grew wealthy from commerce. Expeditions into Nubia reestablished Egyptian control there and maintained the *baqt*, the annual levy of slaves that the Nubians were required to send north.

The Mamluks also enhanced their prestige through shrewd religious policy. In addition to restoring the caliphate, they asserted a special relationship with the holy cities Mecca and Medina. The Cairo Caravan was already one of the major components of the annual hajj; now the Mamluks obtained the coveted privilege of making and sending to Mecca the *kiswa*, the curtain that covered the Kaaba, the focus of the pilgrimage. The Mamluk sultans were awarded the title "Servitor of the Two August Sanctuaries." The Mamluk sultans also encouraged Sufism, the mystical dimension of Islam, and endowed many Sufi convents throughout their realms. Mamluk policies toward Christians and Jews, however, were harsher than those of the preceding regimes.

The rise of Sultan Baybars (1260–77) was a classic Mamluk success story, from his purchase as a boy slave through his training in a military household and his ascent to the pinnacles of social and political power. After defeating the Mongols at Ain Jalut and murdering Kutuz, he assumed the throne in Cairo on 25 November 1260. Relying on his firm base among the Bahri Mamluks, he maintained good relations with key Mamluk magnates who assumed posts of high administrative importance. In 1261 he restored the Abbasid caliphate in Cairo, installing an Abbasid prince who had fled the sack of Baghdad. The office no longer had significant political authority but retained considerable prestige, and it was useful for ratifying and processing legal matters. The caliph's presence bestowed additional legitimacy on the regime. Baybars' large mosque, built in 1266–67, is a prominent monument in northern Cairo.

Baybars was especially concerned with Syria, where the last of the Abbasid principalities, wrecked by the Mongols, had fallen into Mamluk control. Those areas had to be organized. The menace of the Mongols also remained just over the horizon, so he had to be prepared to meet them, but Baybars' major efforts were directed against the Crusader states. These were not nearly as strong as they had been, lacking capable leaders and divided by numerous jurisdictions; besides their governments, important crusading organizations like the Knights Templar jealously guarded their prerogatives. Above all, the Crusader states lacked a steady supply of fighting men from Europe, where support for the Crusades was intermittent. Displaying generalship that can be favorably compared to Salah al-Din's, Baybars campaigned against the Crusaders almost every season, achieving a stunning stream of successes. His raids reached the walls of Acre. In 1268 he captured Antioch; in 1271 he took Krak des Chevaliers, the strongest of all the Crusader castles.

During his final years Baybars devoted much of his energy to making the sultanate hereditary, but his careful plans for the succession lasted only a short time before his sons were shunted aside by an old Mamluk colleague, another Kipchak Turk named Qalawun, who took the title as well as the power of the sultanate for himself. Once he had consolidated his position—no easy task—Qalawun pursued a policy similar to that of Baybars. He was heavily involved in Syria, where he too had to keep a watchful eye out for a resurgent Mongol threat. After removing that danger by defeating a second Mongol invasion of Syria at Hims in October 1281, he likewise turned to the remaining Crusader possessions, which were weaker than ever, riven by a disputed claim to the crown of the Latin kingdom and by other fissures that ran throughout the collapsing Crusader system. When Qalawun captured Tripoli in April 1289, the only major city remaining to the Crusaders was Acre. He had gathered his forces for an assault on that city when he died in November 1290.

Like Baybars, Qalawun wanted to establish the succession in his family, and he was somewhat more effective in doing so. His son al-Ashraf Khalil succeeded peacefully to the throne and completed his father's military initiatives by conquering Acre and mopping up the remaining Crusader coastal enclaves, expelling the Crusaders entirely from the mainland, but he fell victim to court animosity and Mamluk rivalry. His father had begun a practice, one that al-Ashraf Khalil expanded, of importing Circassian Mamluks. These became known as Burgi ('Tower') Mamluks because Qalawun quartered them in the towers of the Citadel. The Bahri Mamluks, primarily of Turkish origin, resented the Burgis' presence and the favors shown to them. When al-Ashraf Khalil was killed by a disgruntled Bahri magnate in December 1293, a violent confrontation ensued between the Bahris and Burgis that was resolved by installing the late sultan's child half-brother on the throne.

The ensuing reign of al-Malik al-Nasir Muhammad covered nearly half a century and was interrupted by two usurpations and restorations. During its first phase he was a shadow sultan; during the second, a genuine autocrat. The uncertainty surrounding his early years was demonstrated by his deposition in December 1294 after a rule of just one year and replacement by a Bahri Mamluk amir who was overthrown two years later in the ongoing struggles between the Mamluk factions. After that latest ruler was murdered at prayers in January 1299, the fourteen-year-old al-Nasir Muhammad was brought forth from the Citadel, where he had been carefully kept in reserve, and reinstalled as a stopgap sultan. The force behind the throne was an uneasy coalition of two Mamluk amirs, Salar and Baybars al-Jashnikir, one representing the Bahris, the other the Burgis.

Yet the state could still function effectively, as was shown by the defeat of the last great Mongol threat in 1303. The Mongols were approaching Damascus when the Mamluk army, headed by Salar, Baybars al-Jashnikir, and al-Nasir Muhammad met and destroyed them. Frustrated that his attempts to gain actual power were repeatedly thwarted by Salar and Baybars al-Jashnikir, al-Nasir Muhammad abdicated in 1309 and withdrew to a stronghold to work for an effective restoration. Baybars al-Jashnikir replaced him as sultan, but support for the amirs was crumbling amid continuing factionalism and general hardship caused by a series of low Niles and epidemic disease, enabling al-Nasir Muhammad, now aged twenty-five, to return as sultan for the second time in March 1310. Baybars al-Jashnikir was strangled in his presence the following month. Salar attempted to come to terms with the resurgent al-Nasir Muhammad, but he was arrested and executed in August. In a purge of the Mamluk establishment, al-Nasir Muhammad arrested twenty-two amirs and raised thirty-two of his own Mamluks to the amirate; two years later he promoted forty-six more.

Al-Nasir Muhammad's reign from his second restoration in 1310 until its end in 1341 was extraordinarily free of foreign problems, enabling him to devote much of his time and energy to internal matters, particularly fiscal reform. His restored rule was marred, however, by a serious wave of anti-Christian riots that swept Cairo in 1321. Many Christians were massacred and their churches looted and destroyed; Copts were expelled from government offices, and sumptuary laws such as prohibitions against Christians riding horses and requirements to wear distinctive clothing were enforced. Many Copts converted to Islam in the aftermath of the persecution.

As he had wished, al-Nasir Muhammad was succeeded by his descendents, preserving the Qalawunid line for several decades, but none of these sultans had any real power. The first reigned merely a few weeks before being deposed in favor of a younger brother, who was replaced by yet another brother, also deposed. Thus in little more than a year, three of al-Nasir Muhammad's sons were moved in and out of the sultanate (and eventually were all killed), and later yet more followed, but none lasted long. More than a score of sultans reigned in the century following Qalawun's death, and nearly as many in the next century. The power almost always lay with the Mamluk magnates, who sometimes assumed the sultanate, but often ruled through shadow sultans.

One of al-Nasir Muhammad's successors who displayed some of his energy and objective was his son al-Nasir Hasan, who became sultan in 1347 at the age of eleven when his predecessor, his half-brother al-Muzaffar Hajji, was killed in an unsuccessful confrontation with Mamluk amirs. When Sultan Hasan attempted to assert himself in August 1351, he was deposed, to be restored three years later after making a compact with the amirs. This time, however, Sultan Hasan was determined to exercise real power. Using his household Mamluks to good effect, he battled dissident forces; he suppressed the mighty Mamluk who was the power behind the throne; and he appointed descendents of Mamluks to the highest military and administrative posts, an unprecedented move that he defended: "These people are reliable and under my flag. They go where I tell them, and when I want to remove them from office, I can do so easily. Also they treat my subjects kindly, and understand the regulations." Sultan Hasan anticipated the inevitable backlash from the Mamluk magnates; even so, his supporters were defeated in a fight, and he was killed in March 1361 by a Mamluk named Yalbogha who had been brought up in his household, ending an innovative experiment of adjustment and development of the Mamluk regime.

Sultan Hasan's first period of rule coincided with the cataclysmic Black Death that struck Egypt in fall of 1347. Al-Maqrizi recounted its appearance: "A ship arrived in Alexandria. Aboard it were thirty-two merchants and a total of three hundred people—among them traders and slaves. Nearly all of then had died. There was no one alive on the ship, save four of the traders, one slave, and about forty sailors. These survivors died in Alexandria."

This was the bubonic plague, a highly contagious, fast-killing disease from Central Asia, spread by a symbiosis of fleas and rodents. Within a year it had run throughout Egypt with appalling mortality. In Cairo, a thousand people a day were dying. The city was described as "an empty desert" through which one could walk from one end to the other without seeing another person. By the time the Black Death abated in Egypt in 1349, a third of the country's population had died of it. Visitations of bubonic plague became a recurring feature in Egypt, abruptly diminishing the population. In the fifteenth century alone there were no less than nine severe outbreaks. The last great epidemic of plague in Egypt, deadly as ever, occurred in 1834–35.

The devastation of the disease had the paradoxical effect of enabling Sultan Hasan to construct one of the most remarkable buildings in the Islamic world, his enormous madrasa at the foot of the Citadel. Partly made of stone from the Pyramids of Giza, it is inlaid with other fine stone, all rendered with exquisite workmanship, although the decoration was never finished. It was built with astonishing speed considering the conditions of the time between 1356 and 1361—too quickly, perhaps, because an intended fourth minaret over the entrance toppled in 1361, killing several hundred people. One of the remaining three collapsed in

1659, and the dome fell in a year later. According to al-Maqrizi, the expense of the madrasa was colossal, but money was flooding into the treasury at an unprecedented rate from death duties and confiscation of estates without heirs.

Having disposed of Sultan Hasan, Yalbogha ruled behind shadow sultans. It was during the nominal reign of the second of these, a grandson of al-Nasir Muhammad named al-Ashraf Shaban (whose father, remarkably, was never sultan), that Egypt suffered its last blow from the Crusades in the form of an attack on Alexandria by Peter I of Lusignan, the Crusader king of Cyprus and titular king of Jerusalem, in October 1365. The death and destruction dealt by the Crusaders as they captured the city was vividly described by al-Maqrizi:

> The Franks took the people with the sword. They plundered everything they found, taking many prisoners and captives, and burning many places. The number of those who perished in the crush at the Rosetta Gate was beyond counting. . . . So they continued, killing, taking prisoners and captives, plundering and burning from the forenoon of Friday to the early morning of Sunday.[23]

But the objectives of this Crusade of Alexandria remain unclear, for after only eight days the Franks loaded their loot and a thousand captives into their ships and sailed away before the relieving force from Cairo under Yalbogha arrived. Yalbogha was killed in yet another round of factional fighting in December of the following year.

The dynasty of Qalawun came to an end in November 1382, when the Circassian Mamluk amir Barquq deposed its last representative, al-Salih Hajji, and took the sultanate, initiating the era of Burgi Mamluk rule. His position was precarious at first as he was surrounded by powerful amirs, and in June 1389 he was deposed by some of them in favor of al-Salih Hajji. But their coalition soon dissolved, and Barquq returned as sultan at the beginning of the following year, permitting al-Salih Hajji to enjoy a comfortable retirement in the Citadel. This time Barquq took care to install amirs favorable to him and was able to die peacefully in 1399.

Like other Mamluk sultans, Barquq had also hoped to found a dynasty, but he and other like-minded Burgi sultans did not enjoy even the nominal successes in this regard that their Bahri predecessors had achieved. Despite solemn oaths that Barquq extracted from the principal amirs and the great officers of state to support his son, the boy sultan al-Nasir Faraj quickly became a pawn in the ongoing contest between Mamluk factions. When he was old enough to show signs of independence, al-Nasir Faraj was deposed in favor of his infant brother, who ruled under the title al-Malik al-Mansur. Al-Nasir Faraj later reclaimed the throne but could never control his unruly Mamluk magnates in Syria and eventually lost his life trying to bring them into line. His successor was another nonentity who was in turn replaced by the power behind the throne who decided to put himself on it. This latest usurper, a Mamluk called Sheykh, attempted attempted to establish a dynastic succession, but fourteen months after his death in January 1421, Barsbay al-Zahiri, one of Barquq's Mamluks, took the sultanate.

Barsbay's reign has been called "the Indian summer of the Mamluk sultanate." Fortunately Egypt had been spared the hideous depredations that the Mongolian Turks led by Tamerlane inflicted as they ravaged much of Western Asia, leaving destruction and mountains of human heads in their wake for a quarter of a century between 1380 and 1405. The great cities of Central Asia, northern India, Persia, and Mesopotamia fell to Tamerlane's armies and were destroyed. During al-Nasir Faraj's reign he captured Aleppo and Damascus, but instead of turning south toward Egypt he went west against the Ottomans and devastated the Turkish heartland before marching across Asia to attack China. Northern Syria suffered dreadfully from Tamerlane's incursion, but Mamluk administration was soon restored there.

Consequently, the Mamluks were little threatened from abroad during Barsbay's reign, and the country was relatively free of internal rebellion. Mamluk Egypt was still strong at sea, and the lucrative Red Sea–Indian Ocean trade was expanding, furthered by Barsbay's aggressive policies in the Red Sea, which also reinforced the Mamluks' prestigious traditional role as protectors of the Holy Cities. Barsbay dispatched several successful expeditions against the remaining Crusader outpost in Cyprus, from which pirates continued to menace Mamluk commerce. The Crusader king of Cyprus, Janus, was brought captive to Cairo, and the new Cypriot king swore fealty to Barsbay. Like other Burgi sultans, Barsbay attempted to found a dynasty, and like them he failed. After

Barsbay's death on 7 June 1438, his son Yusuf lasted only three months on the throne before another Barquq veteran, Chakmak al-Zahiri, usurped it and reigned as al-Malik al-Zahir.

The Mamluk Period is one of the most glorious times in the history of Egyptian art. The most obvious manifestation of the Mamluks' artistic impulse is in architecture, for the Mamluk sultans constructed notable buildings from the beginning almost to the end of their era. Sultan Baybars was the greatest builder of medieval times in the Middle East; al-Nasir Muhammad was almost as prolific; and many great Mamluk amirs also used their substantial incomes to build testaments to their power and wealth, always vying to outdo each other. A splendid result of that competition is the Tomb and Khanqah of Qurqumas, a Mamluk amir who rose high under Sultan al-Ghuri, in Cairo's Eastern Cemetery. To walk along the axis of the Eastern Cemetery or down the old north–south main street of Cairo between Bab al-Futuh and Bab Zuweila is to see the monuments of the leading Mamluks, one after another. The Mamluk minaret became a standard Egyptian architectural feature, as did many other Mamluk innovations in building. The Mamluk Period is also notable for less imposing but equally brilliant accomplishments in other media such as miniature painting, metalwork, glassware, ceramics, and textiles.

The Mamluks were strong patrons of scholarship. Medieval Islam's greatest historian, Ibn Khaldun (1332–1406), was a native of Tunisia, but he spent his later years in Cairo where Sultan Barquq made him a grand *qadi*. "What one can imagine always surpasses what one sees," Ibn Khaldun once wrote, "because of the scope of the imagination, except Cairo because it surpasses anything one can imagine." Ibn Khaldun had seen too much of the world to be easily impressed, but Cairo clearly took his breath away:

> Cairo, metropolis of the world, garden of the universe, meeting place of nations, human anthill, heart of Islam, seat of power. Here are palaces without number, and everywhere flourishing madrasas and khanqahs, while its scholars shine like dazzling stars. The city stretches over the banks of the Nile, river of paradise and receptacle of the rains of heaven, whose waters quench men's thirst and bring them abundance and wealth. I

have walked its streets: they are thronged with crowds, and the markets are overflowing with every kind of merchandise.[24]

Living in the troubled fourteenth century, and having traveled as far west as Reconquista Spain and east to the court of Tamerlane, whom he met before the fall of Damascus, Ibn Khaldun was fascinated by the forces he saw at work and sought to explain them: "When the universe is being turned upside-down, we must ask ourselves whether it is changing its nature, whether there is to be a new creation and a new order in the world. Therefore to-day we need a historian who can declare the state of the world, of its countries and peoples, and show the changes that have taken place in customs and beliefs."[25]

Ibn Khaldun's cyclical view of history, combined with his wide perspective, influenced many subsequent historians, particularly in the West. In his greatest work, the *Muqaddima*, he explained how the people of the desert are imbued with *assabiya*, a sense of group strength that empowers them to conquer and rule over more civilized people who have grown effete in their urban lifestyles. But the process is ongoing: once the conquerors establish themselves, they in turn succumb to civilization and lose their *assabiya*, rendering them in turn vulnerable to conquest by a new, hardier people. The process is unstoppable and endless.

Although the flow of travelers to Egypt diminished during medieval times, some intrepid wanderers came and recorded curious impressions of their visits. Occasionally pilgrims stopped on their way to the Holy Land, as did Bernard the Wise and his two companions in 870. They were thrown into jail in Cairo and had to buy their way out. Even so, Bernard managed to look around, concluding that the Pyramids of Giza were the granaries that Joseph built during his time in Egypt. Benjamin of Tudela, who sojourned in Egypt from 1165 to 1177, fared much better, even serving as vizier for a time. Because he arrived from the south through Abyssinia, he was the first to describe how the annual inundation was caused by seasonal rains in the Ethiopian highlands. In his opinion, the Pyramids of Giza were built by witchcraft.

Abd al-Latif, an Arab physician from Baghdad and later a teacher of philosophy and medicine in Cairo, wrote an account around 1200 that is remarkable for its lack of biblical preconceptions. By then, the pillaging of Giza was far advanced; many of the small pyramids had been robbed of their stones to construct walls in Cairo; but the Great Pyramid had not yet lost its casing stones and was covered, Abd al-Latif noticed, with writings "of an ancient character" that he could not read. The Sphinx was still largely intact when Abd al-Latif saw it, and still showed the red paint that had covered it in antiquity. The destruction of its nose, often but wrongly blamed on Napoleon's soldiers, was probably committed soon after Abd al-Latif's visit.

Egypt was also part of the itinerary of the greatest of all Middle Eastern travelers, Ibn Battuta from Morocco, who came to Egypt in 1326. Ibn Battuta wrote, "I arrived at length at Cairo, mother of cities and seat of Pharaoh the tyrant, mistress of broad regions and fruitful lands, boundless in multitude of buildings, peerless in beauty and splendour, the meeting-place of comer and goer, the halting-place of feeble and mighty, whose throngs surge as the waves of the sea, and can scarce be contained in her for all her size and capacity."[26]

The medieval traveler whose work received the most renown in the West, however, may have been entirely a fictional creation by a four-teenth-century French author who traveled no farther than his library. The book was *The Voiage and Travaile of Sir John Maundevile, K^t.*, to give it in its English translation, for it was widely read and translated into many languages. The pseudonymous Sir John held to the biblical view of the function of the Pyramids. "And thei ben made of Ston, fulle wel made of Masonnes craft; of the whiche two ben merveylouse grete and hye; and the tother ne ben not so grete. And every [one] hathe a Gate, for to entre with inne . . . And with inne thei ben alle full of Serpentes. And aboven. . . . with outen, ben many scriptures of dyverse Langages. And sum Men seyn, that thei ben Sepultures of grete Lordes, that weren sometyme, but that is not trewe, for alle the commoun rymour and speche is of alle the peple there, bothe fer and nere, that thei ben the Garneres of Joseph."[27]

After the reign of Barsbay, signs of decline in the Mamluk Empire became obvious. One of the most ominous was a breakdown in the Mamluk system itself. Young Mamluks had once been strictly trained in all the arts of war, especially the equestrian ones, and were not promoted until they had mastered them. These exercises fell into disuse, and the Mamluks' quality as soldiers correspondingly declined. Yet, even as they neglected their traditional strengths, they refused to recognize how much technology was altering the nature of warfare. Slow to adopt the use of cannon, they despised handguns as weapons for common foot soldiers, not elite mounted warriors. Furthermore, their discipline was breaking down, making them unreliable as soldiers and dangerous to social and economic order. Riots by Mamluks troopers became common occurrences; shops and bazaars were pillaged; public safety declined.

The economy that supported the Mamluk system had been in a state of increasing crisis since the Black Death. Recurring epidemics of bubonic plague prevented the population from recovering. The irrigation systems decayed. Revenues dropped precipitously. In 1215, land tax receipts for Egypt had been more than nine million dinars; by the end of the Mamluk era in 1517, they had shrunk to less than two million. Besides damaging the economic base of the Mamluk regime, the plague also took an unusually heavy toll among Mamluks. For whatever reasons, there were probably fewer than half as many Mamluks on the eve of the Ottoman conquest at the beginning of the sixteenth century than there had been during the great days of the Mamluk Empire.

Another serious blow to the Mamluk economy came at the end of the fifteenth century, when the Portuguese found the ocean route around Africa, providing Europe with a direct connection to India, the Far East, and the east coast of Africa, disrupting the Mamluk's lucrative Red Sea trade and diminishing the importance of Egypt as a commercial connection between the Mediterranean and the Red Sea. Within a few years the Portuguese were threatening the Mamluk maritime position within the Red Sea itself, and only with timely aid from the Ottoman Empire were the Mamluks able to thwart the European interlopers.

The most interesting of the later Mamluk sultans was Qaitbay (1468–96), in part because of his exquisite architectural statements but primarily because, unlike most of his immediate predecessors, he was not ephemeral, ruling across nearly three decades. These were not trouble-free years, however, for the behavior of the Mamluks grew progressively worse, and Qaitbay could never fully control them. The countryside fell into increasing disorder as Bedouin tribes attacked settled areas, destroying their productivity, and even raided downtown Cairo on one occasion. When large-scale tribal rebellions broke out in Upper Egypt, the government's military responses were more like punitive expeditions than reassertions of law and order, and they only caused the situation to deteriorate further. The bright spot in Qaitbay's reign is his building program. Its masterpiece, and one of the jewels of Islamic architecture, is his madrasa and mausoleum, built 1472–74, in Cairo's Eastern Cemetery. But such expensive buildings may have placed a further burden on an already overstrained economy, and the apparent stability of Qaitbay's long reign turned out to be illusory, for five sultans followed it in the space of as many years.

At the time of Qaitbay's death in 1496, the three great powers in the Middle East were the Mamluk Empire, the Ottoman Empire, and the Persian Safavid Empire. Of these, the Mamluk Empire was by far the weakest and at best could hold the balance between the other two. The Ottoman Empire, on the other hand, was in an especially dynamic phase, growing stronger in precisely the areas where the Mamluk Empire was declining. Recovering from the ruin that Tamerlane inflicted on it, the Ottomans prospered and expanded under the rule of four able sultans, Murad II, Mehmed II, Beyezid II, and Selim I. In 1453 they captured Constantinople, and as Istanbul it became the greatest city in Europe and the Middle East, and grew wealthy from expanding trade. The Ottomans extended their dominions in every direction. A thorough overhaul of the empire's financial system gave the Ottoman sultan direct control of most of the empire's tax revenues. A powerful navy was built, and a large standing army established, trained in new techniques of drill and skilled in the use of artillery and muskets.

Given the Ottoman Empire's expansionism, a clash between it and the Mamluk Empire was probably inevitable, but relatively little hostility preceded the Ottoman invasion. There had indeed been a desultory war beginning in 1484, but it concerned peripheral issues. Qaitbay won a number of victories over the Ottomans but lacked the resources to defeat them decisively. Peace was arranged in 1491. As late as 1511, the Ottoman sultan Beyezid II sent aid to the Mamluks in their confrontation with the Portuguese in the Red Sea.

When the Ottomans turned on the Mamluk Empire in 1516, it was almost as an afterthought, resulting from a dispute between the Ottoman and Safavid Empires. Troubled by revolts in his eastern dominions fostered by the Safavids, Selim I struck hard against the Persians, carrying his campaigns deep into their territory. This tilted the balance strongly in favor of the Ottomans, therefore the Mamluk sultan al-Ghuri responded to a Safavid plea for help by sending forces into northern Syria. Selim I, who was at that moment preparing another campaign against the Safavids, decided not to leave his right flank exposed to this threat and attacked the Mamluks instead. The Mamluks were no match for the Ottomans, who were superior in organization, discipline, numbers, and equipment. Betrayed from within their ranks, the Mamluks were routed at Marj Dabiq, north of Aleppo, on 24 August 1516. Damascus and Jerusalem surrendered without a fight.

Al-Ghuri suffered a fatal attack of apoplexy during the Battle of Marj Dabiq. Only with difficulty did the Mamluk magnates in Cairo persuade his nephew Tumanbey to assume the sultanate. There was not much the reluctant new sultan could do except hope that Selim I would be content with his Syrian conquests and proceed against the Safavids, but with the encouragement of many disaffected Mamluks, Selim continued south and entered Egypt unopposed. Tumanbey made a stand outside of Cairo but was defeated. He escaped, only to be defeated again at Giza and betrayed into Ottoman hands. He was hanged at Bab Zuweila on 14 April 1517. The rope broke twice. Not until the third try was the execution completed, ending the era of the Mamluk sultans in Egypt.

13 Egypt in the Ottoman Empire

In one form or another, Egypt was a province of the Ottoman Empire for four hundred years. Describing the first part of the Ottoman experience in Egypt presents some difficulties because Egypt's history became inextricably involved with Ottoman history, with the unfortunate result that Egypt's history often often seemed less important as the center of attention shifted from Cairo to Istanbul. Also, historiography suddenly fell into abeyance in Egypt for more than a century and a half after the Ottoman conquest. Whereas Egyptian historians, chroniclers, and biographers had abounded during the Fatimid, Ayyubid, and Mamluk times, almost none were to be found until the great Abd al-Rahman al-Jabarti emerged at the end of the eighteenth century. Some illumination can be derived from the Ottoman archives in Istanbul, but this cannot replace the detail and immediacy of local history. Furthermore, and until fairly recently, early Ottoman Egyptian history has received less than its share of attention from modern historians.

Yet it is clear that Egypt preserved its distinctiveness, even after 1517. It was ruled in ways unique within the Ottoman Empire, an institution with a remarkable ability to adjust its yoke to different peoples, for the Ottomans realized early on that Egypt required special treatment.

Although the Ottoman sultan Selim I remained in Egypt several months after taking possession of it, he made few administrative changes in his new province. He had not planned its conquest, and he had prepared no program to govern it. In contrast to Syria, which he detached from Egypt and on which he imposed a structured provincial government, Egypt received no such reorganization. To an astonishing degree, Selim left things as they were by entrusting Egypt's government to the powerful Mamluk amir Khair Bey, one of those who had betrayed their fellows at the Battle of Marj Dabiq. Khair Bey, who maintained great state in the Citadel, ruled Egypt not as a regular Ottoman governor but as Selim's vassal and viceroy. Once it was safe, many other Mamluks came out of hiding, were well received by Khair Bey, and began to serve official functions. In 1522 the new sultan, Suleiman I, employed Mamluk troops in his expedition against Rhodes and pronounced himself highly impressed with them.

One of the remarkable things about the Ottoman conquest of Egypt, in fact, is that although it meant the end of the Mamluk sultanate, it by no means meant the end of the Mamluks. On the contrary, the Mamluks flourished anew to such an extent that one can speak of a neo-Mamluk system that prevailed within Ottoman Egypt. The Mamluk magnates who had fought the Ottomans were proscribed, but many others had stayed out of the fray, and still others had actively collaborated with the invaders and were handsomely rewarded. Young Mamluks continued to be imported, primarily from Circassia, although second-generation Mamluks also became common, and many Mamluks continued to maintain great military households. Neo-Mamluks retained and increased their control of most of the state revenue through *iltizam*s (thereby ensuring that much of the land's wealth would continue to be wasted on factional fighting), and they came to hold many of the highest government offices in Egypt. On the one hand, the neo-Mamluks fitted well into the Ottoman system and served its purposes while serving their own, but on the other they helped preserve Egypt's distinctiveness within the empire. They quickly reinserted themselves into Egypt's overall military establishment and again became the most powerful force in the land.

Selim's confidence in Khair Bey appears to have been justified by the fact that Egypt remained quiescent while he was in control. Within two years of his death in 1522, however, two revolts broke out, indicating that some adjustments in institutional control might be necessary. The first was an insurrection by two Mamluk amirs against the new viceroy of Egypt, Mustafa Pasha, the sultan's brother-in-law, but the rest of the Mamluks did not rally to the rebels so that Mustafa Pasha was able to defeat them with the Ottoman garrison that had been left in Egypt after the conquest. The second revolt was instigated not by malcontent Mamluks but by the new Ottoman viceroy, Ahmed Pasha, who had hoped to be named grand vizier in Constantinople. Dissatisfied with his appointment to Egypt, Ahmed Pasha rebelled in 1524, proclaiming himself sultan and adopting the trappings of royalty. His revolt was much more difficult to suppress.

Clearly something needed to be done about the troublesome new province, so the grand vizier, Ibrahim Pasha, an unusually able man who had the complete confidence of Sultan Suleiman, came to Egypt in 1525 and imposed an administrative code. At the apex of the new organization was the viceroy. His residence was established in the Citadel, and strict guidelines were laid down to preserve the dignity of the office. Beneath the viceroy was a council of state, or *divan*, with which he was required to meet regularly. Further down, there was a remarkable amount of accommodation of longstanding regional and local arrangements, and many features from the Mamluk sultanate were incorporated.

In the accompanying economic reorganization, the Ottomans basically kept the commanding heights under their supervision, but left many administrative tasks to institutions such as guilds and religious endowments, or *waqfs*. The economic power of the *waqfs* grew steadily until about 20 percent of the land was religiously held by the end of the eighteenth century. The Mamluks, in their capacities as *multazims*, continued to control much of the rest.

A modicum of order was maintained by the viceroy's Turkish garrison, which was mostly composed of soldiers from the older provinces. Egypt resumed its role as breadbasket to a foreign power, and the portion of the land tax that was forwarded to Istanbul was a welcome addition to the imperial coffers. Egypt also provided a valuable base for Ottoman operations in the Red Sea, where the Portuguese constituted an ongoing threat, and for the protection of the holy cities Mecca and Medina in Arabia, the responsibility and prestige of which now fell to the Ottoman sultan.

Following Ibrahim Pasha's visit, Egypt was quiet for several decades as the Ottoman Empire went from strength to strength. The empire extended from Mesopotamia through Syria and Anatolia, deep into southeastern Europe, almost to the gates of Vienna, and across northern Africa as far west as Algeria, besides running well down both coasts of the Arabian Peninsula. Under the extraordinarily talented leadership of Suleiman I, who reigned for forty-six years, there were new conquests, increasing military power, and growing governmental organization. Suleiman's revenues were far greater than those of any other monarch in Europe or the Middle East. Brilliant military and political achievements were equaled by glorious cultural accomplishments.

Because Egypt was just a province in such a vast empire, many of its resources were drained into the imperial treasury, and it could no longer manage foreign affairs to its own advantage. Instead of being the exploiter, it was often exploited. Far from stagnating, however, Egypt did fairly well overall under Ottoman rule, as is evident from the growth of its population from perhaps three million to four and a half million in 1798, a watershed year in the Ottoman Period. There was some decline during the eighteenth century, but even that had a positive side because fewer people meant higher wages. Integration into a large Mediterranean empire brought more commercial opportunities than limitations. Textiles were a major Egyptian export. Even during the politically troubled eighteenth century, the decades between 1700 and 1760 were a time of economic prosperity in Egypt.

Yet, progress was slow, with plenty of setbacks, and it was not uniformly spread throughout the land. Alexandria continued its long decline until it was little more than the fishing village it had been when Alexander visited it more than two thousand years earlier. No longer was it a great center of trade, and it had never recovered from the damage inflicted by the Crusade of Alexandria in 1356. Its population was also devastated by the bubonic plague, but unlike Cairo, it did not rebound to pre-plague levels. Cairo, on the other hand, remained one of the great cities of the East, despite its provincial status. Umm al-Dunya, it was called, the Mother of the World. From probably less than one hundred thousand at the beginning of the Ottoman period, its population had doubled by the time of the French invasion at the end of the eighteenth century.

Ottoman influences in Egypt were subtle, but they had a long time to work and left a lasting imprint. Their numbers were never large—as late as the end of the eighteenth century there were only about ten thousand Ottoman Turks in Egypt, a sliver of the total population—but the Turks exerted a strong social influence in manners, dress, and general lifestyle. Many Turkish words entered the spoken language of Egypt, and Turkish was to be the language of much of Egypt's ruling elite into the early twentieth century. And although they could be haughty, often insisting on status and deference, the Turks were not regarded as a foreign occupying force but accepted as a functional component of Egyptian society. There had, after all, been a Turkish presence in Egypt long before the Ottoman conquest, for many Mamluks had been Turkish in origin, language, and culture. Even today it is not uncommon to hear an Egyptian speak proudly of Turkish ancestry.

The impact of Ottoman influences on the urban fabric of Cairo was almost imperceptible at first, but over time they became an integral part of the visual presentation of the city. The age of the great Mamluk builders ended with Qaitbay and al-Ghuri; most of the Turkish viceroys did not have sufficient longevity and resources to continue it, nor did they have the interest: they were Ottoman gentlemen who wanted to make their mark in Istanbul, not Cairo, which was just a stop on their road to advancement and reward. Cairo's first major monument to be built entirely in the Istanbul tradition was the Mosque of Sinan Pasha; but it was not constructed until 1571, and although it occupied a prominent location in Bulaq, where it was one of the first things anyone saw when they came to Cairo, it had little influence on Cairene architecture.* Gradually, however, more Turkish-style mosques with their distinctive pencil minarets were built, and Turkish *sabil-kuttab*s, a combination of public drinking fountains and schools, began to appear so that during the nearly three centuries of Ottoman rule before 1798, the Ottomans constructed seventy-seven mosques and forty-one *sabil*s in Cairo. But neo-Mamluk elements persisted and often dominated in these monuments as the Mamluk tradition continued, in architecture as in society.

---

* A much less conspicuous but notable Ottoman monument of earlier date is the Mosque of Suleiman Pasha, constructed in 1528 in the Citadel.

The most famous Ottoman mosque in Cairo was constructed during the nineteenth century: the Mosque of Muhammad Ali in the Citadel, which has become so emblematic of the city that it is depicted on Egyptian currency. Less dramatically, though more intimately, Turkish domestic architecture insinuated itself into the city, transforming ideas about design and use of interior space.

It was also at the beginning of the Ottoman Period in Egypt that coffee was introduced into the country. Though viewed with deep suspicion by religious and political authorities, the new drink quickly took hold in Egypt, and coffee shops sprang up everywhere in Cairo. These became important social centers where men beguiled the hours in conversation and games. The shops had platforms for musical performances, of which the Egyptians were intensely fond, and professional reciters held audiences in thrall by recounting well-established favorites such as the *Life of Baybars* and the *Romance of Abu Zeid*. Cairo became a major entrepôt between Yemen and Europe for the coffee trade, with a large proportion of the city's *wekala*s, or caravanserais, devoted to the storage and transshipment of the bean.

Although the Ottoman Empire reached its zenith during the sixteenth century, before the end of that century it entered an extended period of painful readjustment, and Egypt shared in the difficulties. Once at the forefront of technological and administrative innovation, the empire began to suffer from excessive conservatism, even anti-intellectualism, that had a number of negative practical effects. As the army and government grew larger, it became harder to control, while the central government also found it increasingly difficult to mobilize the empire's resources effectively. Commerce declined significantly as world trade shifted from the Mediterranean to the Atlantic. At the same time, price inflation swept through Europe and the Middle East, caused by an influx of silver from Spain's American colonies. Yet, while prices rose steeply, salaries stayed the same. Corruption and insubordination became widespread in the government. It is probably no coincidence that at about this time the Ottoman viceroys in Egypt, after enjoying several decades of fairly tranquil and effective governance, encountered problems within their own establishment that undermined their authority and eventually tilted the balance of power in the direction of the neo-Mamluk magnates.

The viceroys rarely had much time to consolidate their authority in Egypt. During the 281 years between the establishment of Ottoman rule in 1517 and the coming of the French in 1798, Egypt had 110 viceroys. Just two, both in the sixteenth century, governed for long stretches of time. For them to govern effectively, especially with the Mamluks resurgent, the loyalty of the Ottoman garrison was essential, but that loyalty was shown to be seriously eroded in 1586 when the soldiers revolted, suspended the viceroy from office, and arrested him. The next viceroy fared even worse when he faced a similar rebellion in 1589. Several members of his retinue lost their lives, and his private quarters were plundered. No one was able to control the turbulent soldiers, who revolted twice more in 1598 and 1601. The viceroy who arrived in 1604, Ibrahim Pasha, was determined to restore order and took a hard line from the beginning, refusing the soldiers' demand for the donation that was customary from new viceroys. They promptly rioted and took the money. Nevertheless, Ibrahim Pasha persevered in his firmness until the soldiers decided to get rid of him entirely. They broke into his retreat at Shubra and killed him in September 1605.

This was going too far, and with strong imperial support the next viceroy exacted some measure of justice by arresting the ringleaders of the murder and executing them. A further viceregal measure prohibited collection of the *tulba*, an illegal tax that some of the soldiers extorted from the peasantry. When those soldiers rose in rebellion in 1609, the viceroy, Muhammad Pasha, allied himself with a powerful neo-Mamluk magnate and suppressed them with an overwhelming show of force followed by harsh punishments. When Muhammad Pasha departed Egypt in 1611, he thought viceregal authority had been restored; in fact, the situation was precisely the opposite, for he had prevailed only with Mamluk support. Unable to rely on their own loyal base of military support, the viceroys were compelled to turn to the neo-Mamluk magnates, called beys, who collectively became known as the beylicate.

Although the members of the beylicate had no specific administrative functions, they came to control many of the highest offices in Egypt, and through them to exercise both fiscal and administrative control of the country. Each of these beys had a large train of household soldiers; combined, the beys were by far the strongest military force in Egypt. In practice, however, they were often disunited, belonging to different factions whose rivalry routinely erupted into open combat. Over time the beylicate grew increasingly formalized, with investiture by the caliph, distinctive regalia, and a set membership of twenty-four. By the middle of the seventeenth century the viceroys were mere figureheads. The beys ran the country. Yet the beys usually cooperated with the viceroys, and the taxes were forwarded to the imperial coffers; indeed, one of the senior beys was specifically entrusted with the responsibility of conveying the revenue to Istanbul.

Any viceroy who got too far out of line, however, got a hard lesson about the power of the beylicate. One was administered in 1631 during the viceroyalty of Musa Pasha, who feared a powerful bey named Qeytas and had him killed when he came to the Citadel on a ceremonial occasion. Furious at this murder of one of their own, the beys demanded an accounting for it. When Musa Pasha refused, they deposed him and appointed a *qaimaqam*, a lesser officer, to govern in his place until a new viceroy arrived. By acquiescing in this *fait accompli*, the Ottomans allowed it to become a standard procedure that the beys used more than once to remove troublesome viceroys.

The greatest of the seventeenth-century beys was Ridwan Bey al-Faqairi, leader of one of the most powerful factions. Well connected and immensely popular in Cairo, he may have flirted with royal notions but never openly challenged the sultan. Even so, the Ottoman viceroys tried every means, foul and fair, to maneuver him out of power, only to be thwarted every time. The last one to try found that it was he not Ridwan who was deposed. Ridwan still held power when he died in 1656, but after his demise factional fighting resumed and became more extreme than ever.

So divisive became the enmity between the factions that the viceroy Mustafa Pasha was able to exploit it from 1660–62 by playing one against the other, providing the opportunity to execute some of the odious beys and exile others while generally weakening their factional power. These manipulative tactics enabled the viceroys to govern with some degree of genuine authority for the next thirty years. Beys held high offices and commanded military expeditions as before, but they did not challenge the authority of the viceroys again until the beginning of the eighteenth century, when they experienced a major resurgence of their political power.

As before, the problems began within the viceroy's own military establishment. Rivalries between the seven corps that composed the

Ottoman garrison had been building up for years when they burst into a violent confrontation in March 1711 that left the viceroy helpless. The beys were drawn into the fighting along with their Mamluk households as the latent rivalry between Mamluk factions exploded again. When the Great Insurrection of 1711 was over, the beys once again ruled Egypt, and in grand style with their palaces, lands, Mamluk soldiers, and numerous other retainers. The household of a bey might contain hundreds of Mamluks, dozens of female slaves and concubines, and scores of other personnel. Although their power ultimately rested on their military might, the great beys and amirs also exerted influence through extensive patronage networks that reached into almost every sector of society. Between themselves, the beys contended for the *riasa* ('headship'), the real power in Egypt as opposed to the formal power of the viceroy and other Ottoman officers.

The revival of the beylicate came at a time when the Ottoman Empire could do little about it. Throughout most of the seventeenth century the empire had maintained its reputation for military strength. The fact that it could lay siege to Vienna as late as 1683, and nearly capture the city, clearly demonstrated that it could still threaten Europe. But by the end of the century, European perceptions of the empire had begun to change. Outside observers commented on its internal decay, noting its weaknesses, that it was in recession, and that many of its prize territories were ripe for the taking.

The difficulties afflicting the Ottoman Empire at this stage were strikingly similar to those that had hindered later Mamluk Egypt. Sources of income had declined precipitously; the once-feared Ottoman soldiers had become indolent and undisciplined, falling behind in tactics and technology, yet stubbornly resisting change. Added to that, the sultans had withdrawn from state affairs, yet the grand vizierate never achieved sufficient autonomy to make policy free of harem politics and the machinations of court favorites. On the Empire's northern frontiers, the aggressive Hapsburg and Russian Empires were determined to expand at the expense of the Ottomans, diverting Istanbul's attention from Egypt.

The restored beylicate was a time of political instability that was sometimes moderated by spells of personal ascendancy such as that established by the duumvirate of Ibrahim Kahya and Ridwan Kahya between 1748 and 1754. Ibrahim Kahya saw to practical matters while

Ridwan Kahya lent his support to the regime but devoted his energies to patronizing poets, building palaces, and living luxuriously. Ridwan's thoughts were never on politics, and Ibrahim's death was soon followed by Ridwan's assassination.

Six years later, a much more formidable ascendancy was established by the greatest of the eighteenth-century beys, Ali Bey al-Kebir, who held the *riasa* from 1760 to 1772. Resolutely asserting his authority, Ali Bey accumulated soldiers, repressed rival beys, and promoted his followers. He took significant steps toward establishing a centralized administration. Inevitably, his actions aroused opposition, and his enemies actually drove him from Cairo in March 1766, but the rival coalition lacked staying power, and Ali Bey returned in the fall of the following year.

After taking thorough revenge on his opponents, Ali Bey deposed the viceroy; when the replacement arrived, he deposed that one too. He flirted with trappings of royalty and even had his name minted on coins instead of the sultan's as he dreamed of restoring the Mamluk sultanate. Already known as 'al-Kebir,' or 'the Great,' he now displayed such shocking despotism and ambition that he also came to be called 'Bulut Kapan,' or 'the Cloud-Catcher' as well. When the Hashemite ruler of Mecca was driven out of that city and appealed to the sultan for aid, Ali Bey was authorized to mount an expedition to restore him. Ali Bey did so, but he also replaced the Ottoman governor of Jeddah with a Mamluk appointee of his own, thereby gaining the prestige of protector of the holy places. He sent two expeditionary forces into Syria, overrunning Palestine and taking Damascus in the summer of 1771.

In some ways, Ali Bey's program with its tripartite base of Egypt, the Hijaz, and Syria, combined with a willingness to challenge the sultan, seems both reminiscent of the empire of the Mamluks and prescient of Muhammad Ali's future one, but he lacked the power base to maintain it. His commanders suddenly evacuated Syria and returned to Cairo before the end of 1771. The reasons for their actions are unclear but probably included his generals' reluctance to antagonize the Ottoman Empire and the eruption of yet another factional struggle, one that included members of his own household whose ambitions had diverged from his own. The ground crumbled beneath Ali Bey's feet. Despite a tenacious fight, he was defeated in April 1772 and fled to Palestine. When he attempted to return to power at the head of a pathetically small force in May 1773, he was defeated and taken to Cairo where he died after a week's imprisonment.

After Ali Bey's fall, the struggle for supremacy among the beys resumed, with dire consequences for Egypt. Despite the ongoing political turmoil, the first half of the eighteenth century had been prosperous, but from 1760 the factional strife seriously disrupted the Egyptian economy. The resulting hardships were compounded by a series of overly abundant inundations, while recurring epidemics of plague ravaged the population, so that conditions only worsened during the last two decades of the century.

The political history of the beylicate is extraordinarily complex with factions shifting almost too fast to follow. Fortunately a contemporary Egyptian historian of great narrative skill appeared, Abd al-Rahman al-Jabarti (1753–1825 or 1826), author of an outstanding account of the events from 1688 through the establishment of Muhammad Ali's rule in the early nineteenth century. To compose his comprehensive *'Aja'ib al-athar fi-l-tarajim wa-l-akhbar*, al-Jabarti drew on a variety of original sources, including Mamluk documents; for the later years, and especially the events surrounding the French invasion and occupation, he could also rely on his experiences as a participant/observer. Unfortunately al-Jabarti fell into disfavor with the government so that his work was suppressed and received little general attention until the twentieth century.

Also, a small but steadily increasing number of Western travelers continued to make their way to Egypt and recorded their impressions. Three particularly notable accounts appeared in English by James Bruce, Richard Pococke, and Frederick Lewis Norden. Like so many that came after them, they were heavily inclined toward antiquities, and in the case of Bruce, motivated by desire for further discovery, for he was among the first to set off on the quest to find the sources of the Nile. But these books had little impact on the popular imagination at the time because no sensational event had directed attention to Egypt and the English general readership was not yet large enough to sustain interest in the country, a situation that was to change sensationally at the beginning of the nineteenth century. The two best eighteenth-century French accounts of Egypt were by Claude Étienne Savary and Constantin Volney. In contrast to the British publications, the French books were carefully studied, at least by a small but influential readership. The French interest, however, was not entirely one of pure scholarship, for running through the works of Savary and Volney is a frank appraisal of the Egypt's potential value as a French colony.

The political confusion following the fall of Ali Bey al-Kebir diminished in 1784 when two Mamluk contenders, Ibrahim Bey and Murad Bey, made up their differences and united to obtain the *riasa* jointly. Once in power, they were secure from domestic opposition but had to face a determined attempt by the Ottoman government to restore its authority. Appalled at the unacceptable state of affairs in Egypt, from which Ibrahim and Murad had ceased sending revenues, the Ottomans sent a fleet to Alexandria in July 1786. Its admiral, Hasan Pasha, issued proclamations against the beys and announced that taxes would be reduced; henceforth, the administration of Egypt was to conform to the arrangement made by Ibrahim Pasha in 1525. The Mamluk grandees were having none of that. Murad Bey, more warlike than his colleague, led a force against the Ottomans but was defeated in the Delta at al-Rahmaniya. Hasan Pasha entered Cairo without further resistance on 8 August 1786 and appointed a compliant Mamluk, Ismail Bey, to govern Egypt.

Hasan Pasha and his supporters were masters only of Lower Egypt, however; Murad and Ibrahim remained in the field in the south. Neither side could defeat the other decisively. At one point Murad and Ibrahim advanced to the Pyramids of Giza, only to be driven back into Upper Egypt, but when the Ottomans pursued them to Aswan, they fled out of reach into Nubia. Attempts to negotiate a settlement failed. Meanwhile, time was running out for Hasan Pasha because of a looming crisis between the Russian and Ottoman Empires. He and his fleet were urgently needed. After making what arrangements he could to shore up the reformed administration in Cairo, Hasan Pasha sailed away in September 1787. His work was soon undone. By the time Ismail Bey died in 1791, Murad and Ibrahim had restored their authority, and they maintained it until the arrival of the French in 1798.

14 The Birth of Modern Egypt

he expedition that Napoleon Bonaparte led to Egypt in 1798 was
the product of the French Revolution and the ensuing conflict
between France and Britain. Frustrated by its inability to invade
Britain or defeat it on the high seas, the Directory, as the government in
France was called at that moment, decided to strike an indirect blow by
seizing Egypt. That would cut Britain's overland communications with its
most prized colonial possession, India, from which the British had ousted
the French a few decades earlier. Besides, ideas had been circulating for
years in France about making Egypt a colony. This was the opportunity.
And an expedition to Egypt also provided an opportunity to get the
ambitious Napoleon Bonaparte out of France, and perhaps get rid of
him entirely. Accordingly, the Directory entrusted the young general
with command of a force of more than fifty thousand soldiers, conveyed
by a fleet of nearly four hundred vessels.

When the French landed at Alexandria on 1 July 1798, Napoleon
issued a proclamation that he and his army came as true Muslims to
rescue Egypt from the rapacious rule of the Mamluks and restore rightful Ottoman authority. This was a blatant propaganda ploy designed to
weaken the Mamluks and establish a pretext for the French to take

control of Egypt. Of course they firmly intended to keep the country for themselves, but the French were serious about eliminating the Mamluks, and they rationalized that the benefits of their enlightened domination would greatly improve the lives of the Egyptian people.

The French moved quickly against Cairo. Murad Bey met them on 21 July in a decisive battle at the village of Imbaba that became known as the Battle of the Pyramids (although the Pyramids of Giza were ten miles distant). The Mamluks were not lacking in courage, as their repeated cavalry charges proved, but they were outnumbered, and their bravado could not overcome the disciplined French soldiers for whom it was merely a matter of technique to repulse such impetuous attacks. The contemporary historian al-Jabarti noticed the superiority of French military drill:

> They follow the orders of their commander and faithfully obey their leader. Their only shade is the hat on their head and their only mount their own two feet. Their food and drink is but a morsel and a sip, hanging under their arms. Their baggage and change of clothing hang on their backs like a pillow and when they sleep they lie on it as is usual. They have signs and signals among themselves which they all obey to the letter.[28]

The Mamluk horsemen were slaughtered as they threw themselves against the French formations; more were drowned in the Nile when the French advanced and overwhelmed their fallback positions. According to official reports, between 1,200 and 2,000 Mamluks perished in the Battle of the Pyramids, in sharp contrast to the French loss of only twenty-nine men. Murad Bey and his surviving Mamluks fled into Upper Egypt; his colleague Ibrahim Bey, who was guarding the right bank of the river, slipped away to Syria with the Ottoman viceroy. The French army entered Cairo on 25 July.

One week after the Battle of the Pyramids, however, the British fleet under the command of Lord Nelson, who had just missed intercepting Napoleon at sea, caught up with the French fleet and destroyed it as it lay at anchor at Abu Qir, east of Alexandria. In Cairo, Napoleon found that people were not convinced of the worthiness of

French intentions; some, like al-Jabarti, ridiculed his proclamation and the Arabic it was written in. Then, on 11 September, Sultan Selim III declared war on France, thoroughly discrediting Napoleon's claims to be protecting Ottoman interests in Egypt.

Even so, Napoleon was master on the ground for the moment. He set about reorganizing Cairo, destroying gates and houses to make it more amenable to military control, assiduously courting the influential men of the city, and creating new civic institutions. To pursue Murad Bey and the Mamluks he dispatched his energetic general Desaix south on a victorious rampage that reached as far as Aswan, although the Mamluks, practiced in this line of retreat, ultimately managed to stay out of his reach. Meanwhile, Cairo grew restive under the French yoke. Strict security measures such as public executions alienated the people, who found French rule just as burdensome as that of the Mamluks—and indeed worse, for to pay for the occupation the French did not just collect the old Mamluk taxes but collected them much more ruthlessly and imposed new ones. Popular resentment exploded into rebellion on 21 October. The French suppressed it with a two-day artillery bombardment of the city from the Citadel.

Cut off from France by sea and facing imminent Ottoman attack, Napoleon was in precarious possession of a distant land. Rather than wait on events, he sought to widen the playing field by invading Syria. Al-Arish fell, as did Jaffa where the French slaughtered the garrison, but the key to the situation was Acre, to which Napoleon laid siege on 19 March 1799. Sustained by the Ottoman fleet and a small British naval force, the city held out while Napoleon's army was decimated by bubonic plague. In May he had to give up and return to Egypt. He promptly crushed an Ottoman army that landed at Abu Qir, but it was clear that Egypt offered no further prospects for his growing ambition, and would soon be lost in any event, so on 22 August he slipped away to try his fortunes in Paris, leaving General Jean-Baptiste Kléber in command in Egypt.

Kléber's situation was so bleak that his only concern at first was to evacuate himself and his army from Egypt. He negotiated an agreement with the Ottomans to that effect, but the British, whose navy would have to carry the French army back to Europe, vetoed it, insisting on surrender. That stiffened Kléber's will, and he inflicted a sharp defeat on an

Ottoman army when it appeared at Ain Shams outside of Cairo on 20 March 1800, though his depleted army was outnumbered by as much as six to one. Another popular insurrection, this one of protracted duration, broke out in Cairo, and was only suppressed after more than a month of disorder. A Syrian assassin's knife ended Kléber's life in June 1800.

Command devolved on General Abdullah Jacques Menou, a convert to Islam, but the combined British and Ottoman forces were closing in. Among the Ottomans was a strong detachment of Albanian soldiers, including the young officer Muhammad Ali. The French were defeated outside Alexandria on 21 March 1801, although the British commander, Sir Ralph Abercromby, was killed in the action. Another army approached Cairo. The game was up. Menou surrendered Cairo on 18 June; Alexandria surrendered on 3 September. In the end the French were evacuated according to the terms they had negotiated with the Ottomans.

The British had no intention of remaining in Egypt on this occasion. As they prepared to depart, they would have preferred to see a restoration of the Mamluks because that would have weakened the Ottoman government and provided opportunities for Britain in Egypt, but they were operating in cooperation with an Ottoman army, the Mamluks were biding their time at a safe distance in Upper Egypt, and the Ottoman government was determined to regain control and rule Egypt through the new viceroy Khusraw Pasha. In March 1803 the British withdrew from Egypt according to the terms of the Treaty of Amiens, which brought a brief lull to the contest between Britain and France.

The immediate effects of the French occupation, lasting less than three years, were superficial. None of the French objectives were achieved. Often heralded as the event that precipitated modern Egypt, the French interlude was more of a disturbance than a creative force. It was, however, a disturbance that opened the way for new developments, especially by stirring the mix of political forces that operated within Egypt. And although neither France nor Britain lingered this time, the occupation brought Egypt squarely into the diplomatic sights of both Paris and London, and it remained there for the next century and a half.

Though the French expedition's military accomplishments were transitory, it made a contribution to scholarship that was both lasting and of monumental proportions. A large group of learned men, the Commission on the Sciences and Arts, accompanied the army to Egypt.

Their purpose was to inventory the entire country—its geography, cities, hydrology, manufactures, agriculture, natural history, its glorious and still very mysterious past—all the things that would be of interest in the prospective colony, but it was also an endeavor very much within the ideals of the European Enlightenment. By an order of 22 August 1798, Napoleon created the Institute of Egypt as headquarters for his scholars and outlined its objectives: "(1) the progress and propagation of the sciences in Egypt; (2) research, study, and publication of natural, industrial, and historical data on Egypt; (3) advising on various questions concerning which the government shall consult it."

The opportunity for the French scholars was unprecedented, and they made the most of it. Protected by the army, they could move wherever the army went and work under its protection. This took them to most of the major archaeological sites then known in the Egyptian Valley of the Nile (the army stopped at Aswan on the threshold of Nubia). The savants studied the various subjects assigned to them, but antiquities exerted the most powerful attraction, so much so that the hydraulic engineers often neglected their important work to sketch ancient monuments instead. The scholars also made a good collection of ancient Egyptian antiquities. When the French evacuated Egypt, the British took their antiquities and sent them to London, where they became the basis for the British Museum's superb Egyptological collection. Among the items was the famous Rosetta Stone that recorded Ptolemy V's decree, discovered by a French soldier working on fortifications near Rashid, or Rosetta as the French called the town. With its trilingual inscription in hieroglyphs, demotic, and Greek, it promised to be the key to deciphering the hieroglyphs and reading the ancient Egyptian language, knowledge of which had been lost in antiquity. The French kept their papers, threatening to burn them rather than surrender them, and labored for the next two and a half decades to produce the *Description de l'Égypte*, one of the most magnificent of all works of Egyptian scholarship and the foundation of systematic Western study of Egypt, ancient and modern. Divided into sections on antiquities, the modern state, and natural history, its monumental folio volumes contain some of the most striking images of Egypt ever produced.

The Egyptian political scene was fundamentally altered by the French interlude. Murad Bey had died, but the Mamluks reasserted themselves under new leadership from their base in Upper Egypt. They were still a force to be reckoned with now that the French were gone, but their numbers had been severely depleted and their economic and political bases damaged. Further weakening the Mamluks was their never-ending factionalism, which made it possible for other outsiders to play one group against another. More importantly, there were other forces in Egypt now; no longer did the Mamluks have the field to themselves. A determined Ottoman viceroy, Khusraw Pasha, had soldiers to back him up, and there was a third factor in the Albanian detachment that had originally come to fight the French but never departed. Often unruly, the Albanians rioted over arrears in pay in May 1803, forcing Khusraw to flee to Damietta. This complex, unbalanced political equation caused two years of turmoil and complicated maneuvering from which Muhammad Ali emerged as the ruler of Egypt and remained so for more than four decades, founding a dynasty that lasted for a century and a half.

Muhammad Ali was born in the Macedonian town of Kavalla in 1769. After gaining early experience fighting bandits and pirates, he became an officer in the Ottoman army and was second-in-command of the Albanian detachment that was sent against the French. When his commanding officer was killed soon after, Muhammad Ali assumed command of the Albanians. Over the next two years, he skillfully played the political field, using one Mamluk faction against another and then turning against both, courting and breaking with the Turkish governor, and gaining the support of Cairo's *ulama*, the learned, highly respected religious leaders whose opinions carried great weight in government and society, until he was in a position to demand that the Ottomans make him viceroy, or pasha, of Egypt. This the Ottomans were reluctant to do—previous pashas had been regular career men working their way through the regular system, not upstarts like Muhammad Ali—but the Ottomans also had a practical way of adjusting to reality. In July 1805 Muhammad Ali received the *firman* from Istanbul that appointed him pasha of Egypt.

Muhammad Ali's early years as pasha were extremely difficult. His power base among the turbulent Albanians was shaky at best. Several times they took pot shots at him while he rode through the streets when he fell behind in their pay, as he often did in those initial years. The Ottoman government was not reconciled to his presence in Egypt and caused problems for him whenever it could. The Mamluks threatened from their base in Upper Egypt, where they denied him control of that part of the country. Then, in 1807, he had to deal with a British invasion. Hostilities had resumed between Britain and France. British relations with the Ottomans had deteriorated, and Britain had become highly reliant on Egyptian grain shipments. To the British, who had never been happy with the settlement in Egypt, it appeared an opportune moment to establish a base there, safeguarding the grain supply and the overland route to India, while denying it to the French. An expeditionary force accordingly landed at Alexandria and seized it without difficulty in March 1807, but when the British sought to extend their control to Rashid on the western branch of the Nile Delta, the result was fiasco. The advance guard was cut off. Many British soldiers were killed; others, taken prisoner, were later compelled to carry the severed heads of their slain comrades in a procession in Cairo. The remaining British forces, closely confined in Alexandria, were evacuated from Egypt only after Britain had negotiated their release with Muhammad Ali in September 1807. From that point on, things steadily improved for the pasha. A change of sultans in 1807 distracted Istanbul's attention from Egypt for nearly twenty years, making it easier for Muhammad Ali to consolidate his position. Fortuitously, the principal Mamluk leaders died. Muhammad Ali recaptured their Upper Egyptian cities in 1810 and compelled the Mamluk amirs to come to Cairo and take up their residences there, where he could keep an eye on them.

Muhammad Ali was far from finished with the Mamluks, however. These remnants of the military elite that had dominated Egypt before the French invasion were still armed, greedy, and dangerous. They were easier to manage in Cairo, but they maintained their military households and armed retainers, supported by their lands and revenues. There was no reason to doubt they would try to destroy Muhammad Ali whenever it suited them; meanwhile, they were unalterably opposed to the new military system he wanted to introduce into Egypt, just as the Janissaries in Istanbul had violently opposed Sultan Selim III's similar reforms and deposed him in 1807. When Muhammad Ali held a celebration in the Citadel on 1 March 1811 for the appointment of his son Tusun to command the expedition against the Wahhabis in Arabia, he invited all the principal people of Cairo, including nearly five hundred

Mamluk amirs. Afterward, as the Mamluks were leaving through the Citadel's descending Interior Road, which may still be seen, they found the exit locked. Albanian sharpshooters appeared on the walls above and shot them dead. Another thousand were hunted down and killed in Cairo over the next few days. The surviving Mamluks once again fled far up the Nile, first to Upper Egypt, where another of Muhammad Ali's sons, Ibrahim, pursued them the following year and killed yet another thousand, sending the survivors fleeing still farther into Nubia and beyond. Muhammad Ali was now truly master of Egypt. He could move ahead with his ambitious programs at home and abroad.

Muhammad Ali's rule was marked by a number of military operations outside of Egypt that brought far-flung areas under his control. The first came at the request of the Sultan in Istanbul, who was troubled by the rise of the zealous Wahhabis who had established a state in central Arabia, captured Mecca and Medina, and banned the Ottoman pilgrimage caravans from entering them. This was embarrassing to the sultan, who was responsible for protecting the holy cities. The Wahhabi state encroached on his domains, yet he could do nothing. Appeals to his governors in Syria and Iraq fell on deaf ears. It was Muhammad Ali who, after massacring the Mamluks, sent an expedition to Arabia under the command of Tusun Pasha. Problems of supply were stupendous, enemy numbers almost overwhelming, promised help from the sultan unforthcoming. At one point Muhammad Ali had to appear in person to direct operations. But in 1814 he decisively defeated the Wahhabis and killed their amir, Faisal ibn Saud. The following year, Tusun concluded a truce with the new amir, Abdallah ibn Saud, and returned to Cairo to a hero's welcome and an unexpected death from bubonic plague a short time afterward. Muhammad Ali built a sumptuous *sabil-kuttab* in the best Turkish fashion on the main street in memory of his son. It has recently been restored.

Soon after Tusun's departure from Arabia, Abdallah ibn Saud Wahhabi broke the truce and resumed offensive operations from the security of his inland power bases. Muhammad Ali responded quickly, entrusting his son Ibrahim with the command of a new expedition. Ibrahim proved to be a gifted commander. A contemporary observer described him as "always dignified and just; his word is law; he is firm and resolute, valiant and though a strict disciplinarian, kind and indulgent; and he never expects the meanest man in his army to do that which he would not do himself. No man is more rigorously obeyed, for he is able to punish; nevertheless, he is in full possession of the hearts of his soldiers."[29]

Ibrahim made steady progress, capturing the Wahhabi capital in September 1818. Amir Abdallah was taken prisoner and sent to Istanbul, where he was beheaded. From his foothold in the Hijaz, Muhammad Ali took the opportunity to expand south into Yemen, sending forces there as early as 1813; by 1819 he was virtually in control of the Red Sea. He became master of the entire western Arabian coast from Aqaba in the north to Mocha in the south, thereby arousing the suspicions of the British, who were also extending their influence in that area.

Muhammad Ali's next act of expansion was directed southward against Nubia and northern Sudan. In 1820, a force under the command of his third son, Ismail, departed from Aswan. By June of the following year, Ismail had reached Sennar, where he received the submission of the local leaders. Meanwhile, another force under the command of Muhammad Ali's son-in-law Muhammad Bey Khusraw conquered Kordofan. But Ismail behaved willfully and foolishly, disregarding his father's instruction to listen carefully to the advice of his senior officers. Ismail's arrogance and brutality, against which Muhammad Ali had also cautioned, made him hated by the newly conquered people. In the fall of 1822 a chief whom he had insulted burned him alive in his hut; the people rose in rebellion. Muhammad Bey Khusraw came from Kordofan and put down the uprising with great cruelty. Egyptian rule was established throughout Nubia and in the north of Sudan, or what became known as Egyptian Sudan.

But Muhammad Ali's attention was primarily fixed on Egypt. He wanted to transform it into a modern industrial society and major military power by selectively taking European models, techniques, and expertise, and applying them within an Egyptian context. To that end, he hired many Europeans for purposes such as factory management, civil engineering, military training, and medicine. His talent scouts scoured the Mediterranean, recruiting likely individuals to come to Egypt and assume responsible positions. Whenever European travelers arrived in Egypt, they were likely to be taken to Muhammad Ali for a personal interview as he sought to draw as much information from them as possible. But he intended that Egyptians should eventually occupy the important posts in government, industry, the military, and education. Some were to be educated at home in newly established schools; others were sent abroad to study and bring back much-needed skills. One of the traveling students, Rifaa al-Tahtawi, who later became an influential writer and educator, left a memoir of his student impressions of French society.

Muhammad Ali needed money to finance his ambitious programs, yet he had won control of a country whose wealth had been mismanaged for centuries. But Egypt's agricultural potential remained, and within a few years he achieved nearly total control of it. The vast estates of the Mamluks were confiscated, as were the endowments of the *waqfs*, which owned fully one-fifth of all Egypt's agricultural land. Rigorous title searches brought in more. The tax structure was revised so that almost all of Egypt's land came under state ownership. Muhammad Ali could decree what to plant, then purchase the produce at a low price set by the state and export it for cash. During the Napoleonic Wars, which ended in 1815, grain was a lucrative export. In 1821, Muhammad Ali introduced long-staple cotton, which became Egypt's major export crop. Egyptian cotton is of high quality, and prized to this day by discerning buyers for fine cotton articles. There was a shift from subsistence crops to cash crops that earned foreign exchange. Muhammad Ali obtained a large, dependable income to finance his projects in what may have been the most efficient exploitation of the resources of Egypt since Roman times.

In order to expand agricultural production and move goods to markets, Muhammad Ali conducted an extensive program of public works. One well-placed contemporary observer credited him with thirty-two canals, ten dikes, and forty-one dams and barrages. Some of these projects were enormous. One of the canals, the Mahmudiya, ran for seventy-two kilometers between Alexandria and the western branch of the Nile. It was constructed between 1817 and 1820 with corvée labor of as many as 300,000 conscripted workers (of whom between twelve and one hundred thousand are said to have died, according to widely varying accounts). Thousands of feddans of agricultural land were reclaimed from the desert along the way. A new barrage located just north of Cairo was only partially successful but nevertheless raised the productivity of the Delta. And this was just new construction: many existing canals had to be deepened; all had to be maintained. Altogether Muhammad Ali brought over a million feddans (one feddan equals slightly more than one acre and about two-fifths of a hectare) of new agricultural land into cultivation. Productivity was further increased by the introduction of perennial irrigation so that two or even three crops per year could be grown instead of just one. His ability to assemble large numbers of corvée workers showed how completely he commanded the resources of Egypt.

Muhammad Ali was not merely interested in increasing Egypt's agricultural output. He intended to use the money earned from agricultural exports to modernize and industrialize the country. A careful student of British affairs, the lessons of the Industrial Revolution and its contributions to British power were not lost on him. Factories of all kinds appeared—textile, sugar, munitions—and numerous increasingly specialized ones to meet the country's growing needs. Muhammad Ali wanted to be as self-sufficient as possible. His new industries were strictly protected from the threat of foreign competition through a system of monopolies that excluded unwanted imports. For example, cheap British cotton cloth was not permitted to compete with Egyptian cloth, which sold widely through Egypt and beyond. Steadily growing orders from the military and government provided plenty for the factories to do. Egypt became the leading industrial nation in the eastern Mediterranean.

The rebirth of Alexandria began during Muhammad Ali's rule. By 1805 the population of the once glorious queen of the Eastern Mediterranean had shrunk to perhaps fifteen thousand people, and the town occupied but a tiny fraction of the ancient city, which lay all around in shapeless heaps of rubble. The new Mahmudiya Canal brought a reliable supply of drinking water and more direct communication with the Nile. Muhammad Ali's strong emphasis on foreign trade made the city's two harbors busy again. With the establishment of the Arsenal in 1829, Alexandria became a major shipbuilding center and the base of Muhammad Ali's large, modern navy. When Muhammad Ali died in 1849, Alexandria's population had risen to 100,000, putting it well on the way to recovering its long-lost status as a major city. Cairo and Alexandria were linked by a semaphore telegraph. Messages could pass between those two points in as little as half an hour.

To serve his rapidly growing governmental needs, Muhammad Ali thoroughly reorganized Egypt's administration. For advice, he instituted deliberative councils. Although these were consultative, not legislative, many of their suggestions became policy. A centralized bureaucracy was established with responsibility divided between major departments. By 1837, there were seven: the departments of the interior, the treasury, war, the navy, education and public works, foreign affairs and commerce, and industry. Each department was subdivided into bureaus and workshops. Meanwhile, district and local organization within Egypt was regularized and rationalized, with clear lines of authority running from the pasha through various layers of the hierarchy down to each village headman. Although Muhammad Ali listened carefully to his advisors and delegated much authority to his officials, the ultimate power of decision always lay with him alone. Much of his work was later undone, but Muhammad Ali's administrative reforms outlived him and became part of the modern Egyptian state.

With the Mamluks out of the way, Muhammad Ali moved ahead to build an entirely new military establishment rather than rely on the remaining Ottoman forces in Egypt. After an unsuccessful attempt to recruit an army of slaves from Sudan, he took the novel step of conscripting Egyptian peasants into the ranks. His new army was called the Nizam Jedid. At first its officers were Europeans, but Egyptians were commissioned as graduates appeared from the new military training schools. The Egyptians hated conscription, fleeing to avoid it, and even resorting to self-mutilation to make themselves unfit for service. But to no avail. When young men, in desperation, began having one of their eyes put out, the pasha merely formed a regiment composed of one-eyed men. Yet, once in the ranks, however reluctantly, the Egyptians made very good soldiers. Muhammad Ali's Nizam Jedid proved itself repeatedly in many different places and situations, especially in the war against the Wahhabis, the Greek War of Independence, and the Syrian campaigns. It was also reliable at home. When a major uprising occurred in Upper Egypt in 1824, Nizam Jedid regiments suppressed it decisively. At its largest, Muhammad Ali's military force numbered nearly a quarter of a million men. Egypt became the major military power in the eastern Mediterranean, making Muhammad Ali much stronger than his nominal master, the sultan in Istanbul. Although Muhammad Ali was compelled by treaty to reduce the size of his army in 1840, it remained a permanent Egyptian institution. He also built a large navy, of which he was intensely proud. There was nothing else like it in the Islamic world, he boasted.

To meet the growing needs of his military and government, Muhammad Ali embarked on extensive development of higher education. Beginning with a school of surveying in 1816, a number of technical schools were established. A staff college to train officers for the Nizam Jedid began in 1825. The first school of medicine opened in 1827. A foreign language institute, founded in 1836 under the direction of Rifaa al-Tahtawi, provided increased access to publications in European languages. Closely related to his educational innovations was Muhammad Ali's foundation of a government press at Bulaq around 1822. At first it mostly printed technical manuals for military and government officials, but later published many works of different kinds, including an influential Arabic edition of the *Arabian Nights*. Newspapers appeared in both Arabic and French. Print media became a regular part of Egyptian life.

Disease ravaged Egypt during the first half of the nineteenth century, threatening to deplete the ranks of the Nizam Jedid and limiting the overall manpower pool. Every year smallpox killed over fifty thousand children; great epidemics, such as the outbreak of bubonic plague in 1834–35, carried away as much as a third of Cairo's population; other diseases, like cholera, added heavily to the toll. As early as 1819, Muhammad Ali ordered a program of vaccination against smallpox. Strict quarantine measures restricted the spread of epidemics. His French medical expert, Clot Bey, established the Abu Zabal Hospital (later the Qasr al-Aini Hospital) in 1827 to care for the Nizam Jedid. Medical officers were assigned to the regiments; field hospitals were prepared. But the pasha's concern was not confined to the military, for in 1832 a school for midwives opened in Cairo to train women to provide a wide variety of important medical services. Then, in 1837, a new hospital, exclusively for civilian use, went into operation in Cairo. It had a ward for women and a pediatric ward where thousands of children received smallpox vaccinations every month. Of all Muhammad Ali's programs, his medical reforms may have achieved the greatest success in the long run.

Muhammad Ali's accomplishments came at a heavy price to the Egyptian people. The degree of control that the pasha exerted in Egypt was probably unprecedented since ancient times, and he used it to extract everything he could from the country to support his schemes. No source of revenue was neglected. Every productive strip of land, every palm tree, every donkey, everything that could represent value was assessed and taxed at the maximum it could bear. He imposed the corvée repeatedly for works such as the Mahmudiya Canal and countless smaller irrigation projects throughout Egypt. Many foreign observers were aghast at the human cost, yet some speculated that it might be worth it if his projects succeeded.

The people complained incessantly, but they obeyed, for the pasha's authority was absolute. A simple horizontal motion of his hand meant execution. Yet he was not capriciously or willfully cruel. Severity served specific purposes. Nor did he use his position for excessive self-aggrandizement. His residences were comfortable but not particularly opulent. He went around town on a simply caparisoned horse with just one or two attendants. Uninformed observers never knew an important person had passed. His subjects addressed him plainly as 'Muhammad Basha.' According to a well-informed contemporary description, "The personal appearance of this extraordinary man but little corresponds with his character. He is rather short, somewhat corpulent, and has an animated countenance, expressive of benignity rather than severity. His beard is now grey. The Turkish and Albanian languages he naturally speaks with fluency; but of Arabic, the language of Egypt, he knows very little. In his later years, he has learned to read & write."[30]

In 1821, many parts of Greece, which was also part of the Ottoman Empire, rose in violent rebellion against their Turkish masters. After three years of fighting, suffering defeat after defeat, the sultan again turned to Muhammad Ali. The pasha responded quickly and effectively. Within five months he sent a strong naval force and several regiments of the Nizam Jedid to Greece under the command of his son Ibrahim. The Greek rebels were no match for the well-led, tightly disciplined Egyptian soldiers. Ibrahim won an impressive string of victories, capturing Athens in June 1827. But while Muhammad Ali was master of the military situation, the sultan controlled foreign policy. He disregarded Muhammad Ali's concerns about conflict with the Western powers, resulting in the unplanned Battle of Navarino, 20 October 1827, in which the combined Turkish and Egyptian fleets were destroyed by the British navy, assuring Greek independence.

Muhammad Ali was furious over the outcome of the Greek adventure, which he had never welcomed anyway, and which had cost him his prized navy in a most unwanted confrontation with the Western powers.

He had expected to be awarded Syria for his labors, which had achieved much more than anything the sultan had managed to do. When he was fobbed off with Crete instead, he resolved to take Syria by force. Withdrawing his army from Greece, he filled its ranks by increased conscription. The new Arsenal in Alexandria quickly built new ships to replace the ones that went down at Navarino. In November 1831, he ordered Ibrahim to invade Syria at the head of a force of sixteen warships, seventeen transports, and thirty thousand soldiers and sailors. Most of Palestine and Lebanon submitted quickly. Ibrahim captured Acre, the city that had successfully defied Napoleon, after a siege of six months. During the second half of 1832, he fought three major battles against numerically superior Ottoman forces, winning decisively every time. After the last, near Konia in December 1832, the road to Istanbul lay open. The Sultan had to make peace. Muhammad Ali was master of Syria.

Neither Sultan Mahmud II nor Pasha Muhammad Ali was satisfied. The sultan resented having to acknowledge the pasha's control of Syria, while the pasha became impatient with recognizing the sultan as his master. In 1838, Muhammad Ali decided to move for independence. The sultan struck first, invading Syria in April 1839 and declaring Muhammad Ali a traitor. The Egyptian response was quick and decisive. On 24 June 1839, Ibrahim crushed the Ottomans in the Battle of Nezib, the last of his great victories. The Ottoman position appeared hopeless. Sultan Mahmud II died on 1 July to be succeeded by a mere youth. The Ottoman fleet sailed to Alexandria and surrendered. It seemed as if Muhammad Ali had achieved all his goals.

He had succeeded too well. The Ottoman Empire teetered on the verge of collapse, something the Western powers were determined to prevent. All of them intervened diplomatically. A British force confronted Ibrahim and forced him to withdraw to Egypt; a British naval force anchored at Alexandria. Muhammad Ali had to admit defeat. The ensuing settlement ended many of his dreams by reducing the size of the army and navy, and compelling him to withdraw from Crete, Syria, Arabia, and Yemen. His system of monopolies was abolished, allowing European merchants access to Egyptian markets.

Muhammad Ali's last years are often described in terms of decline and senility. Many of his programs had fallen far short of his hopes. But he left Egypt with a better administrative system than it had had in centuries; the army, though reduced, was still the best in the region; few nations of that day could match his accomplishments in public health. He was even capable of new initiatives, including a national census of high quality in 1848. The resources of Egypt, over which the government retained strong control, were still sufficient to meet basic governmental needs and more. Everything had been done without incurring foreign debt. And he had achieved one of his most prized objectives, for in a *firman* of 1841 the sultan bestowed the hereditary rule of Egypt on Muhammad Ali and his family. Muhammad Ali died on 2 August 1849 and is buried in his great mosque in the Citadel overlooking Cairo.

15 Mid-Nineteenth-Century Egypt

According to the *firman* of 1841, which confirmed the succession on the eldest prince of the house of Muhammad Ali, the next pasha was Abbas Hilmy I, the son of Muhammad Ali's beloved son Tusun, who had died of the plague in 1815. The possibilities that lay before Abbas were enormous. Although Muhammad Ali had lost much of his empire, the Egyptian portion of it was intact and granted to his descendents, and he retained his Sudanese possessions. The army and navy had indeed been reduced, but what remained was more than enough to meet Egypt's needs; many of his institutional reforms persisted. And he had left the country in good economic condition. Many tools were at hand to realize Egypt's vast potential, but Muhammad Ali's successors did not make the most of their inheritance.

Far different in temperament and policy from his grandfather, whom he heartily disliked, Abbas showed his contempt for Muhammad Ali by the meanness of the funeral he accorded the late pasha. Unlike Muhammad Ali, Abbas was anti-Western and discouraged European influences. Many of the reforms initiated by Muhammad Ali were cancelled or neglected. Factories fell into disuse and were sold. Schools were closed and educators discouraged by undesirable transfers such as that of the director of the language school, Rifaa al-Tahtawi, who was sent to Khartoum. These actions have given Abbas a reactionary reputation, perhaps partially deserved, but some of the shutdown began during the last days of Muhammad Ali.

There was more to Abbas than unreflective conservatism. He initially resisted the introduction of railroads into Egypt, but soon realized that he needed to give in. The contract for a railway linking Alexandria and Cairo was signed in 1851, and it was completed in 1856. Soon another railway ran between Cairo and Suez, all with great benefit for Egypt, whose pace of railroad construction compared well with that of the most advanced nations of Europe. Abbas strongly opposed the far-reaching reforms emanating from Istanbul during the Tanzimat era not because he was reactionary but because they threatened his autonomy. Nevertheless, history has not been kind to Abbas, usually painting him in somber tones— brooding, superstitious, and difficult, as he may have been. He certainly made plenty of enemies in his own time. When Abbas was murdered by two of his slaves in July 1854, he was not sorely missed.

Abbas was succeeded by Muhammad Ali's fourth son, Muhammad Said. Once again cultural orientation shifted because Said was much more Western-oriented than his predecessor. Railroad construction continued. The pace of public works picked up with new irrigation projects, bridges, and roads. The electric telegraph was introduced to Egypt. Continuing the viceregal policy of keeping religious authorities weak, Said suppressed religiosity within the army. To save money, he steadily cut the army's size from its level of about 80,000 under Abbas, until it had declined to 25,000 by 1860; though any saving was more than offset by the expense of Egypt's participation in the Crimean War, 1853–56, when Said sent an army of twenty thousand to support the Ottomans, borrowing heavily from European bankers to pay the bills.

Debt became a snare that increasingly entangled the first three of Muhammad Ali's successors. Despite cutting programs, Abbas was never quite able to make ends meet. Said, who swore never to follow Abbas into deficit spending, nevertheless died owing £7 million sterling. Then his successor Ismail accelerated the borrowing to such an extent that it destroyed his regime and delivered Egypt into the hands of the Europeans.

Said's most momentous act, however, was his decision to support construction of the Suez Canal. Ideas about digging a canal across the

Isthmus of Suez, thereby linking the Red Sea and the Mediterranean and greatly shortening the maritime distance between Europe and the East, had circulated since antiquity. In more recent times, the French expedition had toyed with the notion, and later it was picked up and advocated by a group of French visionaries called the Saint-Simonians, who saw canals as a means to unite a socially and techno-logically transformed world. More idealistic than practical, the Saint-Simonians were nevertheless effective in popularizing the concept of a canal at Suez.

The technical challenge was straightforward: digging a large ditch across 170 kilometers of mostly flat desert land between two bodies of water of the same level, with four lake beds along the route to save much of the digging, although a fifth lake, Manzala, was both marshy and shallow, requiring construction of a banked channel through it. Three significant stony ridges stood in the way. Those obstacles could all be overcome, given sufficient resources in money, manpower, and basic machinery. The much more formidable difficulty, posed by the unfavorable winds that had always inhibited sail navigation of the Red Sea and Indian Ocean for much of every year, was rapidly being removed by the introduction of maritime steam technology that enabled ships to go against contrary winds and currents.

The canal became a reality because of a childhood friendship between Said and Ferdinand de Lesseps, who was French consul in Egypt. Because young Said was so overweight, Muhammad Ali put him on a strict diet, but the boy would slip away to de Lesseps, who allowed him to gorge on macaroni, his favorite food. For years after leaving Egypt, de Lesseps nurtured a vision of building the canal at Suez. When he heard that Said had come to power, de Lesseps promptly traveled to Egypt, where his old friend received him warmly and readily agreed to his proposal for the canal. According to the original understanding, Said was to receive personal ownership of 15 percent of the shares of the Suez Canal Company, with another 15 percent going to Egypt. In return, Said would grant the concession for the canal and supply a large, continuous work force. Through purchase of additional shares, Said's stake in the company eventually rose to 44 percent. The total cost of the canal was estimated at £6 million, the money to be raised through an international sale of shares in the new company.

After seemingly endless problems and delays, digging began in 1859. Despite de Lesseps's rosy projections, subscriptions for the Suez Canal Company's shares fell short of expectations, while expenses far exceeded the original budget. Said made up much of the difference. As promised, he furnished the labor to dig the canal through the ages-old institution of the corvée as some twenty thousand peasants were conscripted every month, herded to the canal zone, and put to work. That meant that every month, twenty thousand conscript laborers were on their way to the canal zone, twenty thousand were actually at work there, and another twenty thousand were returning to their homes, so that during the course of a year, more than half a million laborers were involved with the canal in one way or another, and this process continued for ten years. Working conditions were often horrific; sometimes the men had to dig with their bare hands, paid only a pitiful allowance, with barely enough food to sustain them. Dredging machines (paid for by Egypt) were not used extensively until the final phase of work on the canal. The number of lives lost from neglect, overwork, malnutrition, or accident has been estimated at the same number as the basic quota of workers: twenty thousand. Such a large, continuing drain on Egyptian manpower at a time when the total population of the country was perhaps five million created general economic difficulties. It was in large measure because of Egyptian money, labor, and lives that work on the canal was well advanced when Said died after a prolonged illness in 1863.

Said's successor was Ismail, the son of Ibrahim, the brilliant general and son of Muhammad Ali. In his early thirties, the new pasha made a good first impression. He was a hard worker, putting in long hours, sometimes far into the night. Nothing escaped his attention. He also had an ambitious program for reform and development on a scale not seen since Muhammad Ali's great days. And for a time it appeared that he had ample means to accomplish his goals, for the commencement of his reign coincided with the peak of cotton prices caused by the American Civil War, which deprived Europe of its supply from the southern United States. By 1865, the value of Egyptian cotton exports had risen to a level more than ten times higher than at the beginning of the decade.

Ismail also had an exalted notion of the state that the ruler of Egypt should keep, and he expressed it in his lavish lifestyle. One of his many palaces, Abdin, was begun during the first years of his reign. To make room for its more than five hundred rooms and lobbies, hundreds of houses were demolished. He was also eager to upgrade his status from that of mere pasha, and willing to pay for it through increased tribute to Istanbul. In 1866 the sultan conferred on him the title of khedive, derived from a Persian word for king, that set him on a level above other Ottoman governors. Then, in 1873, he obtained from the sultan a *firman* that settled the succession on the khedive's eldest son. The sultan also granted Ismail authority to make internal laws and regulations, and to enter into treaties and commercial relationships with foreign powers. He was permitted to increase the size of his army and navy. These are elements of sovereignty. Ismail must have thought he was equaling and even excelling the accomplishments of his grandfather Muhammad Ali.

Construction programs were continued and new ones begun as more roads, bridges, railways, and waterworks were built. A high-quality postal service was established in which steamboats carried the mail up and down the Nile. Ismail was especially active in education. He created a ministry of education, one of whose directors was the noted Egyptian intellectual Ali Mubarak. Numerous schools were opened, including one for girls in 1873. The school of languages, closed by Abbas, was reopened under the direction of Rifaa al-Tahtawi, recalled from his exile in Khartoum. Literacy in Egypt by the end of Ismail's reign may have risen to about 5 percent. Reversing his predecessor's policy, Ismail increased the size of the army to a high of 120,000.

Foreign conquest beckoned. Ismail sent expeditions south, enlarging Egypt's Sudanese possessions and establishing outposts beyond. Two campaigns against Abyssinia failed disastrously in 1875 and 1876, but another force entered through Somalia and captured the town of Harar. Most of the western coast of the Red Sea was brought under Egyptian control. The Sudanese slave trade was also suppressed for a time, but this severely disrupted the area's economy while the administrators that Ismail appointed, often Europeans who spoke no Arabic, could not cope with the new dominions. A British traveler, returning to Sudan after it was conquered by the Egyptians, was dismayed at the changes he saw:

> The rich soil on the banks of the river, which had a few years since been highly cultivated, had been abandoned. Now and then a tuft of neglected date-palms might be seen, but the

river's banks, formerly verdant with heavy crops, had become a wilderness. Villages once crowded had entirely disappeared; the population was gone. Irrigation had ceased. The night, formerly discordant with the creaking of countless water wheels, was now silent as death. There was not a dog to howl for a lost master. Industry had vanished; oppression had driven the inhabitants from the soil.[31]

By the end of Ismail's reign the situation in Sudan was approaching anarchy, ripe for the revolt of the Mahdi that came soon after.

Within Egypt, major social changes were occurring, though slowly, and sometimes unnoticed. The population grew steadily from about 4.5 million in 1800 to 5.5 million at mid-century. By 1882 it had reached 7.8 million. Several reasons can account for the increase. The productivity of the land had been improved; no great outbreak of bubonic plague occurred after 1834–35, although other epidemic diseases continued to take their toll; and perhaps Muhammad Ali's public health program had beneficial effects. This did not mean better lives for most peasants, of course, who had to compete for limited resources, and who were so squeezed by government exactions of taxes, military conscription, and corvée labor that they often resorted to the ages-old measure of fleeing their lands to escape.

Patterns of land ownership also changed. Muhammad Ali had expropriated the land of the Mamluks and the *waqfs*; over time he and his successors granted much of it to various Ottoman courtiers, creating a new Turkish-speaking aristocracy that owned vast estates. Village headmen were also well placed to exploit the privatization, so that a native Egyptian landed elite emerged. This new, privileged class of landowners would become a powerful conservative force in early-twentieth-century Egyptian politics. Landowning rights of peasants increased, so that many had acquired full ownership of their small holdings by 1871, but their lands were heavily taxed while those of the aristocracy were assessed at much lower levels. A peasant's lot was still a hard one.

Another significant social development was the formation of an urban middle class, composed of government workers, teachers, and people in business and the professions. Their numbers were tiny at first, but they were educated and occupied positions from which they could follow political and social issues. They were also articulate, able to express their concerns, so that they too would eventually make their political voice heard. Their growing influence diminished that of traditional authorities such as the *ulama*, who formerly controlled much of the country's educational and judicial functions.

But to an astonishing degree, Khedive Ismail's attention was not fixed on his own society. Much more pro-Western than any of his predecessors, he was fond of saying, "My country is no longer in Africa; we are now a part of Europe." After a visit to France in 1867, he returned to Egypt dazzled by the transformation that Napoleon III's engineer Haussmann had imposed on Paris with its great public buildings, expansive gardens, and wide boulevards. He resolved to turn Cairo into a Paris along the Nile. Dissatisfied with medieval Cairo's intricate maze of streets, he sent his crews crashing through old neighborhoods, destroying many architectural treasures along the way, so Cairo could have boulevards of its own. New gardens were laid out. A big opera house was built at Ezbekiah. It opened with a performance of Verdi's *Rigoletto* in November 1869 and premiered that composer's *Aida* on Christmas Eve 1871. The Opera was a notable Cairo landmark until it burned down in 1971. A new Opera complex was then built in Zamalek.

Egypt was also much more welcoming to Western visitors during the nineteenth century than ever before, and unprecedented numbers of travelers took advantage of that openness. Many were drawn by the temples, the tombs, and the pyramids, by the mystique of ancient Egypt that had captured the popular imagination in the aftermath of Napoleon's Egyptian expedition. Others came because of the climate: physicians sometimes prescribed a sojourn in Egypt for a variety of ailments. Some were attracted by the exotic settings of contemporary Egypt. Not a few came because of the Bible, for many travelers found the scenes in Egypt somehow much more convincingly biblical than the ones they saw in Palestine, even in Jerusalem. Once the French had departed and Muhammad Ali imposed order and security on the land, a steadily growing stream of Western travelers was to be seen on the Nile.

Most came, saw, and departed, but some sought a closer acquaintance with Egypt. John Gardner Wilkinson (1797–1875), the founder of Egyptology in Britain, spent twelve years in Egypt during the 1820s and 1830s, traveling, studying, and recording monuments, then communicating his unequaled vision of ancient Egyptian society to a wide reading public. Wilkinson's friend Edward William Lane (1801–76) immersed himself in Turkish and Egyptian society and wrote his classic *An Account of the Manners and Customs of the Modern Egyptians* (1836) that is still used as a basic text by scholars of Egypt, and indeed of the entire Middle East. Many other nineteenth-century Western travelers and sojourners—mostly amateurs in the strict sense of the word but deeply committed to their subjects—made significant studies of Egypt, both ancient and modern.

But even travelers without a scholarly bent were moved to write about their experiences and impressions in Egypt. Probably no other country has been the subject of so many travelogues. Two Egyptian travel memoirs stand out above the others. Amelia Edwards's *A Thousand Miles up the Nile* (1877) is an account of a winter voyage from Alexandria to the Second Cataract by a professional writer who evokes the scenes along the way with a high degree of literary skill. Edwards developed a lifelong interest in Egypt and became one of the co-founders of the Egypt Exploration Society in Britain. Lucie Duff Gordon's *Letters from Egypt* (1865) was the product of another accomplished writer who came to Egypt hoping to find relief from her tuberculosis and found the love and sense of family that she had lacked in England. Because she was a sojourner in Egypt, not a mere tourist, Duff Gordon's letters show unusually deep insight. And there are many other worthy nineteenth-century travelogues about Egypt, including Florence Nightingale's book, also entitled *Letters from Egypt*, but helpfully subtitled "A Journey on the Nile, 1849–1850." Nightingale was scathingly critical of many things in Egypt, but she recognized the transforming quality of a personal encounter with the land: "One wonders that people come back from Egypt and live lives as they did before."[32]

Egypt was also a magnet for nineteenth-century artists. In the first decades of this artistic encounter, which might be called the draftsman phase, artists strove to record the phenomenally profuse subject matter that Egypt offered, whether the intricacies of Islamic architecture or the ancient monuments. Finished work was often presented as an itinerary in which the monuments along the Nile appeared in topographical order. This is evident in the first great draftsman work of the nineteenth century, the French *Description de l'Égypte* (1809–24), and reaches its culmination

in the striking chromolithographic images of David Roberts's *Egypt &*
Nubia (1846–48) that have become virtually ubiquitous. Robert Hay's
Illustrations of Cairo (1840) was almost ignored when it appeared, but
many of its plates were so widely reprinted during the twentieth century
as to become some of the best-known images of Islamic architecture in
the city.

The second part of the nineteenth-century artistic encounter could
be termed the orientalist phase. Documentation became less important
than communicating the textures and sensations of the East. Not that
accuracy became unimportant; on the contrary, orientalist artists, with
their fastidious academic training, were often able to render their subjects
in meticulous detail, but even then the objective was to overwhelm the
viewer with that detail and invite him/her to experience its sensuousness.
The English writer William Makepeace Thackeray (another author of a
travelogue) noticed the possibilities. "There is a fortune to be made for
painters in Cairo," Thackeray wrote, "and materials for a whole Academy
of them. I never saw such a variety of architecture, of life, of picturesque-
ness, of brilliant colour, and light and shade. There is a picture in every
street, and at every bazaar stall."³³ John Frederick Lewis spent more than
a decade in Egypt, accumulating materials for the works that made him
Britain's greatest orientalist artist. In France, the major artistic force for
imparting Egyptian images to the viewing public was the prolific painter
Jean-Léon Gérôme, whose images were widely reproduced in a variety
of media. Remarkable for their technique and power, the orientalist
artists provided irresistible impressions of Egypt and the East as places
of danger and decadence, as well as seductive beauty.

Another contribution that Egypt made to Western visual arts was its
important role in the history of photography. Egypt's bright, clear light
combined with its inexhaustible supply of dramatic subject material
guaranteed that it would become a favorite resort of photographers. The
pathfinder was Francis Frith, who published his *Cairo, Sinai, Jerusalem,
and the Pyramids of Egypt* in 1860. Another major early photographic
study of Egypt is that of Maxime du Camp, who traveled with the French
writer Gustave Flaubert (author of yet another memoir of a journey along
the Nile). Frith's and du Camp's photographic descendants proliferated
into the hordes of tourists who are to be found almost everywhere in
Egypt with their cameras today.

By mid-century the stream of travelers swelled into an inundation. The age of mass tourism had arrived. Thomas Cook became an important name in arranging package tours. The first two European-style hotels, the Hôtel d'Orient and Shepheard's English Hotel, appeared in Cairo. They were "as large and comfortable as most of the best Inns of the South of France," according to Thackeray. No longer were travelers on their own, left largely to improvise as best they could. John Murray's *Handbook for Travellers in Egypt* (written by Wilkinson) appeared in 1847, followed by several more editions. The first of many Baedeker guide books for Egypt was published in 1878.

But most Europeans in Egypt were present not primarily for travel, writing, painting, or photography. Increasingly they were there to make their living, in some cases their fortunes, and they looked at Egypt from a practical perspective. Their numbers too were growing rapidly. It is estimated that by the end of Ismail's reign as many as 100,000 Europeans lived in Egypt. This large expatriate community became a permanent feature of Egyptian life. Pro-Western though he was, it presented many difficulties for Ismail and his government.

The biggest problem was the Capitulations. These had existed in the Ottoman Empire since the sixteenth century, when the sultan granted Europeans certain privileges such as exemption from taxation and the right to be tried under their own laws—expedient measures that permitted European merchants to trade in the East, secure in person, money, and property. The Capitulations had not been a significant factor under Muhammad Ali because Europeans in Egypt had been few, and he was too strong for them to abuse their privileges. But as the numbers and power of the Europeans kept growing, the situation got out of hand. European consuls compelled Muhammad Ali's successors to extend the Capitulations and became more aggressive in demanding rights for their nationals. It reached the point where consuls had full jurisdiction in civil and legal matters concerning citizens of their countries, who could even bring claims against the Egyptian government in the consular courts. The people being protected were not just honest businessmen and harmless travelers; there was also a *demi-monde* of undesirable characters who were always flirting with trouble, including drifters from diverse places who successfully claimed citizenship in one European country or another, thereby obtaining consular protection.

There were seventeen different consular jurisdictions in Egypt, each following a different code of law. If an Egyptian had a claim against a foreigner, it had to be pursued in a consular court. The system was an enormous assertion of privilege by the Europeans in regard to the Egyptians, and it placed a large segment of the society and economy beyond the reach of the Egyptian government.

Meanwhile work continued on the Suez Canal. The magnitude of the undertaking had been colossal. Not only did an immense amount of earth and rock have to be removed: the Sweet Water Canal had to be built from the eastern Delta to the canal route to provide drinking water, a channel had to be formed in the quagmire of Lake Manzala in the north, harbors had to be constructed; two entirely new towns, Ismailia and Port Said were built. The diplomacy was especially tricky, involving a complicated interchange between Cairo, Istanbul, London, and Paris. The sultan was jealous of his rights to approve such a major work; Britain was adamantly opposed to the canal at first—a position that would change after it opened—seeing it as harmful to its connection with India. And even France, though ultimately the staunchest of European supporters for the canal, often proved difficult.

Egypt's share of the burden of making the canal repeatedly grew heavier than anticipated. According to the original agreement, Ismail continued to supply the large teams of workers to do the digging. As far as Egypt was concerned, this was just another application of the corvée in which labor had been conscripted for public works projects for millennia. Muhammad Ali had used it extensively on projects like the Mahmudiya Canal; Said had called on the corvée for railroad construction; occasionally foreign travelers had sadly noted the heavy human cost, but no one in Europe had paid much attention. Now, however, the Suez Canal was being built under close European scrutiny. Opinion was shocked when horrific corvée conditions were publicized. Antislavery societies and British politicians strongly objected to what could be considered slave labor, although much of the British response was motivated less from humanitarian concerns than a desire to impede work on the canal. Under intense diplomatic pressure, the sultan in Istanbul ordered Ismail to withdraw the workers. Construction came to a halt in the spring of 1864.

This impasse was partly the work of Ismail, who had fanned the flames of the corvée controversy, not from qualms about the institution itself (which he intended to keep for other purposes), but to use the issue to wrest control of the canal from de Lesseps because he believed Said had gone too far in his concessions. He made a grave error, therefore, in allowing the dispute to be arbitrated by the French emperor Napoleon III, who was related to de Lesseps by marriage and had every reason to be biased toward the French interests that were heavily invested in the company. The decision in favor of de Lesseps should not have been a surprise, but the size of the award was staggering. Since the Egyptian government would not be supplying labor, and in consideration of other revisions that Ismail wanted to make in the agreement, the judgment required him to pay more than four million pounds sterling in compensation. It was a windfall for de Lesseps, for not only did the Egyptian laborers (whose pay was still wretchedly small) return, but he could also purchase steam dredging machines to speed the work along. Even so, there was just enough money to complete the construction of the canal. Without Egyptian contributions, it would not have been done. Ismail's gambit could hardly have failed more dismally. The British urged him to contest the decision, but he accepted it: cotton prices were still high, and he negotiated a loan with European bankers to cover the unexpected cost.

The Suez Canal was opened on 17 November 1869 amid great fanfare. For Ismail, it was a chance to display to Europe just how much he had accomplished in Egypt. More than a thousand European guests were invited to the opening, all expenses paid, and treated to a dazzling round of ceremonies, feasts, and tours that cost Ismail another £1 million. Although the number of transits through the canal was disappointing during the first years following its opening, pushing the Suez Canal Company to the brink of insolvency, traffic increased so that the Company was making consistent profits after 1875. But Egypt derived little benefit from that. Altogether, Said and Ismail spent about £11.5 million sterling on the canal, and the indirect costs to Egypt were incalculable. Also, the canal greatly increased the strategic importance of Egypt to Europe at a moment when Egypt was losing control of its own destiny.

The problem was money. By the late 1860s, cotton exports were bringing in less than half of what they had in 1865, but Ismail's spending commitments were greater than ever. As cotton income declined, so too did internal tax receipts. Disastrous ripples went through the entire economy, with a rash of bankruptcies and foreclosures in the countryside, yet the land tax was repeatedly raised to crushing levels. The perceptive British sojourner in Egypt, Lucie Duff Gordon, wrote from Upper Egypt in 1867:

> I cannot describe to you the misery here now, indeed it is wearisome even to think of: every day some new tax. Now every beast; camel, cow, sheep, donkey, horse, is made to pay. The fellaheen can no longer eat bread, they are living on barley meal, mixed with water and new green stuff, vetches etc., which to people used to good food is terrible, and I see all my acquaintances growing seedy and ragged and anxious. . . . The taxation makes life almost impossible—100 piastres per feddan, a tax on every crop, on every annual fruit, and again when it is sold in the market; on every man, on charcoal, on butter, on salt, on the dancing girls.[34]

When nothing more could be squeezed from the peasants, Ismail resorted to the sale of future tax revenues in 1871. Any landholder who paid an amount equal to six times the annual land tax in advance would be relieved of half of future tax liabilities and receive full ownership of the land. This brought only slight, temporary relief and forfeited future revenues. That left foreign loans, in which Ismail indulged to a degree that dwarfed the indebtedness of his two predecessors. The terms of these loans were extremely onerous. Not only were interest rates high, as much as 12 percent, but large commissions, origination fees, and steep risk discounts were also deducted from the principal so that Ismail received far less than a loan's face value. On one loan of £32 million in 1873, he actually received just £18 million, yet he still had to pay high interest rates on the larger amount. And this was but one of several major loans.

Although Ismail was sliding ever deeper into debt, he was unmindful of its fatal danger and continued to be active in all areas of government, including institutional reform. He and his influential minister Nubar Pasha were especially interested in limiting the damaging effects of foreign jurisdiction under the Capitulations. Their solution was the Mixed Courts, established in 1875. This judicial innovation was given jurisdiction in civil and commercial cases between foreigners and

Egyptians, in criminal cases involving foreigners, and even in cases between Europeans and the Egyptian government, which sometimes obligated the government to enforce decisions against itself. The judges of the Mixed Courts were to be European and Egyptian, the latter appointed by the khedive, hence the name Mixed Courts. Ostensibly equally balanced, the Mixed Courts fell under the domination of European judges, who were paid by the Egyptian government but nominated by the European powers. Also, the Mixed Courts affected not the entire Capitulation system but merely portions of it. The Capitulations remained on the books until they were finally abolished in 1937.

By the mid-1870s, Ismail was desperate. One-third of Egypt's revenue was going to service the debt. In 1875 he sold his shares in the Suez Canal Company to Britain for £4 million, about a quarter of what they had cost (and much less than they would soon be worth), but that exhausted his assets, and his credit had reached its limit. The following year, Egypt stopped making payments on its loans. The country was bankrupt. Ismail's total debt stood at about £100 million. It is hard to make that number meaningful today, but the amount could fairly be described as astronomical, far beyond anything that he or his country could be expected to manage. The entire annual Egyptian budget was less than £10 million.

Foreign bondholders had been circling for some time. Considering the interest rates and fees that they had charged, their loans should have been considered high-risk ventures where the lenders bore any loss, but Britain and France, where most of the debt was owed, were consistently supportive of their bankers and business people abroad. Confronted with pressure from both countries, Ismail had to agree to the formation of a European commission to manage the debt, with representatives from Britain, France, Italy, and Austria. The Caisse de la Dette Publique was established on 2 May 1876. Originally intended to receive some revenues and process debt payments, the Caisse quickly became a powerful institution. When payments were less than expected, the Caisse promptly brought an action in the Mixed Courts that compelled the government to hand over the moneys to the Caisse. And far from being a mere processing body, the Caisse came to exercise extensive influence over government financial policy and over Egypt's economy.

The Dual Control was established in 1878, giving France and Britain supervision not only over revenues but also government administration and operations. Two Controllers, one British and one French, oversaw collection of revenues to make debt payments and supervised the accounts of government departments. They instituted an austerity program of cuts in pay and expenditures that caused widespread hardships during a year of low inundation and created bitter resentment at foreign interference. Ismail's treasury had slipped out of his hands, and he was fast losing control of the rest of his government. As one historian noted succinctly, the Western nations and creditors used the Egyptian debt to establish a state within the state that eventually took over entirely.

At that point, when it was already too late, Ismail tried to change course. Army officers whose pay had been severely cut rioted, probably at the instigation of Ismail, who made a dramatic personal appearance to quell them. He dismissed the Dual Control and installed a new ministry more to his liking with nationalist inclinations. Pay cuts were rescinded. A new constitution was drafted, giving control of finance to the Assembly of Delegates, a rubber-stamp body that Ismail had created in 1866 to provide political cover. This measure courted popular support and would have been a significant constitutional point of departure. The Assembly accepted the constitution. But these initiatives merely convinced France and Britain that Ismail had to go, and they secured his exit from the scene with surprising ease.

Ismail was at one of his palaces in Alexandria on 25 June 1879 when two telegrams arrived from Istanbul. One was addressed to "Ismail, ex-Khedive of Egypt"; the other to "His Highness Khedive Tewfiq." Thus Ismail learned that he had been deposed and replaced by his twenty-seven-year-old son. It had been a fairly simple matter for Britain and France to pressure the sultan to act in the interests of those countries' bondholders. The sultan and his ministers had wanted to clip Ismail's wings for some time. This was an opportunity they had been waiting for. There was nothing Ismail could do. His country was already deep in the pockets of the European bankers and the governments that supported them. He sailed away from Egypt on the khedival yacht, *al-Mahrussa*, into a long exile, first in Italy and finally in Istanbul when after, repeated requests, the sultan granted him permission to live there. The deposition of Ismail marked the end of the interesting experiment in autonomy that Muhammad Ali had begun. Henceforth, Egypt, though still a province of the Ottoman Empire, was under European control.

The new khedive Tewfiq understood that perfectly. He would have preferred to go in his own direction, but caught between the Charybdis of Egyptian nationalism and the Scylla of Western control, he steered toward the West, despite his early nationalist associations. The Assembly of Delegates was dissolved, and the Dual Control reestablished. One of the Controllers was the young Evelyn Baring, later to become Lord Cromer. An International Commission of Liquidation, consisting of members from Britain, France, Austria, and Italy, was appointed. It recommended that about half of Egypt's revenue go to government expenditures and the other half to the Caisse de la Dette for paying the interest on the debt and retiring its principal, further strengthening the role of the Caisse in Egypt. Once again stringent austerity measures, including cutting the size of the army to twelve thousand, were imposed, again inflicting great hardships.

Perhaps it was financial difficulties that motivated a group of disaffected army officers to form a secret society whose members wanted to see Egypt act in its interest, not the West's. Its members included Colonel Ahmed Urabi. By the end of Ismail's reign, the officers had been joined by religious elements, and they had attracted support among students and peasants, who were hard hit by a severe economic contraction in 1877–79 that was widely blamed on European interference. It was a nationalist movement, explicit in its slogan: "Egypt for the Egyptians."

When it became obvious that Tewfiq was ineffectual against the Europeans, anger within the nationalist movement grew, but the various groups within it were busy maneuvering for dominance, so nothing was done until the army officers emerged supreme. In a dramatic scene at the Abdin Palace on 9 September 1881, Urabi presented the khedive with three demands: change of ministry, convocation of the Assembly of Delegates, and increase in the size of the army. With the army strongly supporting Urabi—even the palace guards went over to him—Tewfiq had to agree. The Assembly of Delegates met in December and immediately attempted to assert control over finance, something totally unacceptable to the Caisse. Urabi joined the government as minister of war with strong popular support.

These developments, which threatened the security of the Suez Canal and the collection of the debt, alarmed Britain and France. First they tried threats, issuing a stern Joint Note that affirmed their support for the khedive. That, of course, had precisely the opposite effect in Egypt, cementing support between nationalist elements in the Assembly of Delegates and the army. Neither Britain nor France was eager for military action, so they resolved to raise the stakes with a show of force, sending a combined naval force to Alexandria where it anchored offshore on 19 May. This move, intended to strengthen the khedive vis-à-vis his adversaries, again had the contrary effect of reinforcing Urabi's political position, and it inflamed popular resentment which exploded in Alexandria on 11 June in anti-European riots that killed over two thousand Egyptians and fifty Europeans. The Egyptian cabinet declared war on Britain.

Joint British–French intervention in Egypt was the inevitable next step, but at that moment an ironic event occurred. All along it had been the French who had taken the lead in this confrontation, prodding the British into action, but suddenly the French government was paralyzed by a parliamentary crisis in Paris. Unable to act, the French fleet sailed away, leaving the British alone. Things had gone too far for the British to stop, even had they wanted to, but they were still reluctant to commit themselves to an invasion of Egypt. Perhaps a naval bombardment of Alexandria would topple Urabi, they thought. That was done on 11 July 1882 with what should have been predictable results: it made Urabi even more of a national hero and put him firmly in control of events. Tewfiq fled to the British.

The British had played all their lesser cards. Nothing was left but full-scale military action, a decision made easier by growing interventionist sentiment in Britain during the course of the crisis. The British invaded the canal zone in August. Urabi's forces made a stand on 13 September 1882 at Tell al-Kebir, just east of the Delta on the road to Ismailia, but were decisively defeated by the British army under the command of General Garnet Joseph Wolseley, who was raised to the peerage as Viscount Wolseley of Cairo and Wolseley for his services. Urabi was tried for treason and condemned to death, but the sentence was commuted to exile in Ceylon. The British had no desire to make a martyr of him. Tewfiq was restored, but the British had occupied Egypt.

16 The British Occupation of Egypt

hen the British occupied Egypt in 1882, their objective was simple and limited: restore khedival authority and withdraw. That was the firm intention of the prime minister, W.E. Gladstone, explicitly stated in a speech at the Guildhall in 1883. But this objective contained a dilemma: if the British left, the political situation in Egypt would quickly become unacceptable again, at least from Britain's point of view. A nationalist government might reassert itself and repudiate the debt, then things would be as before, or even worse. And if the British left precipitously, they could lose control of the Suez Canal, having just gained it. A rival European nation might snatch up Egypt, a very real concern in the predatory world of nineteenth-century imperial diplomacy. It soon became apparent that a short occupation would be necessary. It lasted seven decades.

Since it was necessary to tarry, someone needed to be in charge and take responsibility for the many governmental responsibilities that had fallen into abeyance or had been largely taken over by Europeans. After a preliminary survey of the situation in Egypt by Lord Dufferin, the British ambassador in Istanbul, and implementation of some urgently needed stopgap measures, Gladstone's choice fell on Evelyn

Baring, later Lord Cromer, whom Gladstone appointed consul general on 11 September 1883. Cromer's credentials made him ideal for the job. Originally a military officer, he had served for years as the private secretary to the viceroy of India, then in 1877 had been appointed to the Caisse de la Dette Publique, giving him experience in administration and an intimate knowledge of the Egyptian government and economy. As far as Gladstone was concerned, however, what made Cromer perfect for the job was the fact that he shared the prime minister's belief in early withdrawal from Egypt.

But within a year, Cromer decided that early withdrawal was impossible; eventually he would move away from the idea of withdrawal altogether. Egypt was in chaos. The county's infrastructure was a mess; the irrigation system had been neglected, threatening even worse agricultural times. Administrative reorganization was a high priority. The size of the army was reduced, schools closed, and the bureaucracy slashed to try to balance an almost impossible budget in which half the country's revenues had to go to service the debt. How could anyone think of leaving when there was so much to be done?

Cromer also came to believe that the Egyptians were incapable of governing themselves and needed an extended period of preparation under British tutelage. His attitude toward Tewfiq was condescending at best, and he was never satisfied with the khedive's ministers, complaining of their "want of energy" and that "any impulse which is given soon dies out unless constant efforts are made to keep them up to the mark." Even after many years in Egypt he asserted that "Egypt hasn't produced a man yet" who was a fully capable administrator. This view was all the more influential because it was widely shared in the British community and eloquently expressed in Lord Edward Cecil's blasé memoirs, *The Leisure of an English Official*. Funny at first, Cecil's book quickly turns tiresome with its relentless portrayal of the Egyptians as incompetent, bumbling children who never got anything right and were incapable of distinguishing between important matters and trivia. Yet, while Cromer's administrative knowledge of Egypt was comprehensive, he had relatively little insight into Egyptian society, and he learned virtually no Arabic during his three decades in Egypt. He did, however, enjoy the services of his most trusted adviser, the Oriental secretary Sir Harry Boyle, a man with a prodigious capacity for languages. Boyle used to go about in

Cairo disguised as a Turk, talking to the people, learning their true sentiments, serving as Cromer's eyes and ears.

Cromer's official position in Egypt was the modest one of British consul general, yet he wielded power that many kings and sultans might have envied. His authority rested on no formal basis. Legally, Egypt was still a province in the Ottoman Empire, so the senior British diplomatic officer in Egypt was the consul general, the full ambassador being in Istanbul. The khedive still governed nominally through his ministers, who exercised control over their ministries. In fact, the khedive could be controlled; he knew he owed his throne to the British; and alongside each of the government ministers was a British 'adviser' whose advice carried the force of command. Cromer referred to the arrangement as the "dummy-Minister-plus-English-adviser" system of government. One of his senior officials described it as the "veiled protectorate," a term that stuck. Ministers soon learned that they would lose their posts if they paid no heed to their advisers. The long-serving prime minister during Cromer's rule, Mustafa Fahmi, was noted for his subservience to the British. Cromer's position was further strengthened by the presence of a British military garrison nearly ten thousand strong, while the Royal Navy could appear at Alexandria or Suez at any time, and the police forces in the cities were under European command. Cromer might perhaps be best described as a modern proconsul.

Wide though they were, Cromer's powers were by no means unlimited. The French, highly annoyed at being deprived of what they considered their share of Egypt, still had a strong presence in many areas of Egyptian life. They often used their key position on the Caisse to make budgetary problems for the British and generally did what they could to obstruct the occupation. The internationalism of Egypt was a problem for British rule, just as it had been for Ismail, because the Capitulations and consular jurisdiction placed much of the large European population of Egypt beyond government oversight, some-times allowing them to do much as they pleased, while Cromer was helpless to intervene.

Another factor preventing early withdrawal was a big mess in Sudan, where Ismail's adventures had created confusion. In June 1881, a Sudanese man named Muhammad Ahmed had declared himself the Mahdi, the messiah who according to Muslim belief was to appear in the last days of the world. Preaching a kind of revolutionary Islam that invoked the early days at Mecca and Medina, the Mahdi quickly gained support. The rotten Egyptian regime in Sudan crumbled before his army of dervishes in their patched gowns. An Egyptian expeditionary force commanded by William Hicks Pasha was annihilated two months after Cromer assumed the consul generalship, leaving the Mahdi in control of most of Sudan.

Neither Cromer nor the British government had any intention of being drawn into Sudan, an adventure that Egypt could not afford in any case, but the Egyptian and European communities needed to be evacuated from Khartoum, and the southern border of Egypt strengthened. General Charles George Gordon, an officer with long experience in Egypt and Sudan, was sent to Sudan in 1894 with orders to conduct the withdrawal. When he reached Khartoum, however, Gordon threw his instructions "to the winds," as Cromer put it, and decided to hold the town, even though it was poorly prepared to withstand a siege by the Mahdi's forces. His stubborn resistance captured the imagination and sympathy of the British public. The British government was furious with Gordon for his disobedience but feared the popular reaction if he were abandoned. Accordingly, a relief expedition was dispatched under Lord Wolseley, but it was long in preparation and did not reach Khartoum until 28 January 1885, two days after the city fell and Gordon and his forces were massacred. The outcry in Britain was overwhelming. Gladstone had previously been known as the 'G.O.M.' (Grand Old Man); now he was called the 'M.O.G.' (Murderer of Gordon). People demanded revenge. Wisely Gladstone made no move to recover Sudan, but the prospect of British withdrawal from Egypt was now more remote than ever. Egypt clearly required close attention for some time to come.

As the British settled into their prolonged occupation of Egypt, they could soon claim a number of successes despite the stringent financial constraints under which Cromer and his officials labored. Taxes were collected efficiently, and even reduced to lessen the crushing burden on the peasantry. The Caisse was expanded in 1885 to include Germany and Russia, which at least diluted France's ability to obstruct British interests through that powerful body. The economy showed signs of recovery. By 1889 there was a regular and growing budget surplus.

Far from encouraging Cromer and the British to leave, however, these budgetary accomplishments merely convinced them that their presence was more indispensable than ever.

The British record in public works in Egypt was impressive. The central concern, of course, was the waterworks, first putting them in working order—clearing the canals, maintaining the sluices, doing all of the laborious but highly organized tasks necessary for their functioning—after they had fallen into disrepair during the turmoil of the recent years. This was accomplished quickly and efficiently. The next step was programmatic improvement of the hydraulic infrastructure, because even a cursory survey of the land showed that much of Egypt's agricultural capacity went unused because of lack of water, yet most of the Nile's waters flowed unexploited into the sea. Through improved water management, productivity could be substantially increased. The first such project, undertaken in 1884, was refitting Muhammad Ali's Nile barrages below Cairo, which had been intended to deliver a more reliable flow to the Delta over the course of the year but were built on unsound foundations. A modest investment of £25,000 resulted in an immediate increase of £1,050,000 in Egypt's cotton revenues.

The most ambitious hydraulic project was the Aswan Dam (not to be confused with the Aswan High Dam of several decades later), a finely dressed granite structure sited across the rocks of the First Cataract a short distance below Philae Temple. It retained a portion of the inundation for the following months, extending perennial irrigation to many more parts of Egypt, although it also had the unfortunate effect of submerging Philae Temple and forever dimming the brightly colored paintings on the walls that had still seemed almost fresh after more than two thousand years. In addition to these large projects was a profusion of lesser yet still considerable ones, like the Asyut barrage in Upper Egypt, and the Zifta barrage on the Damietta branch of the Nile. Although Cromer was notoriously miserly in most budgetary matters, he strongly backed these hydraulic improvements. He was even willing to borrow in order to fund them: he expected them to pay, and they did. The resulting jump in agricultural productivity was a big factor in Egypt's speedy return to solvency.

Agricultural successes reinforced the British attitude that Egypt was primarily an agricultural country, consequently there was no need to industrialize it, and no effort was made in that direction. On the contrary, Egyptian manufacture was discouraged. Some commercial development occurred, notably in insurance and service areas, but those businesses were mostly under foreign control. Technical development continued within the country, however. Railroad mileage was extended. The telephone was introduced during the 1880s. In some areas much was accomplished; in others, Egypt was deliberately allowed to fall behind.

In the area of government administration, the British could point to marked improvements. Corruption was almost eliminated and a much higher level of efficiency attained. But the British did not move quickly or energetically enough to undertake a thorough reform of the legal system, where French and other foreign interests were determined to keep their extraterritorial privileges, creating what Cromer described as "the judicial labyrinth which time and international rivalry have built up in Egypt." Even so, the court system worked better under the British, at least until 1906, than it had previously. Justice could be strict, but it was generally perceived as impartial and fair. Here too, corruption and inefficiency were sharply reduced. Cases could be resolved much more quickly, therefore more cheaply, than before. Judges were chosen with greater care and their work subjected to closer scrutiny. British officers reconstructed the Egyptian army, instructing it in drill and equipping it with up-to-date weaponry, including machine guns. But Cromer did little to create institutions for Egyptian self-government, for his belief that the Egyptians were not ready to handle their own affairs became ever more firmly fixed with time. After his retirement, when he published his memoirs in 1908, he asserted, "It may be that at some future period the Egyptians may be rendered capable of governing themselves without the presence of a foreign army in their midst, and without foreign guidance in civil and military affairs; but that period is far distant. One or more generations must, in my opinion, pass away before the question can be even usefully discussed."[35]

The British record in education was atrocious in Egypt. Literacy, which had risen slightly under Ismail, hardly changed under the British, who allowed education to stagnate, and even discouraged it. There might have been a weak excuse for reduced government support immediately after 1882 when budgets were tight; but by 1889 there were annual surpluses, yet Cromer was unwilling to divert them to education.

To limit graduates to a level that government employment could absorb, he imposed tuition fees; when the number of applicants rose anyway, he raised the fees. Cromer was boasting when he wrote, "In the early days of the British occupation, nearly all the pupils who attended the Government schools were taught gratuitously. Before many years had passed, by far the greater proportion paid for their instruction." The British never spent more than 3 percent of the budget on education. They ignored demands for a national university, fearing it would become a center of nationalism and believing that Egypt was not sufficiently advanced for such an institution. When one was finally founded in 1908, it was entirely because of Egyptian initiative.

As ever-increasing numbers of British officials arrived in Egypt, they crystallized into a separate community. Many among the earlier generations of British travelers and sojourners had at least superficially delved into Egyptian society, made Egyptian acquaintances, learned some Arabic, and even adopted Eastern clothing and lifestyles. No longer. The new British administrators had almost no contact with Egyptians apart from the men they worked with at the ministries and the servants who cared for them in their homes. They were encouraged to maintain detachment from the Egyptian community; their wives did not network into Egyptian women's society. The segregation extended all the way down. Houses of prostitution in Cairo and Alexandria contained women from many European countries, but Cromer forbade British women to practice the trade in Egypt.

The British adviser to the ministry of public instruction, Douglas Dunlop, went so far as to discourage Englishmen who entered his department from learning Arabic because "it only gave them romantic ideas about the natives, and they would waste their time explaining what they taught to the natives in Arabic instead of making them learn English." And most new officials came through his ministry, because teaching was the task usually assigned to novice English administrators. When Dunlop went to interview applicants, he refused to consider any from Cambridge who were graduates of that university's Arabic examinations. Fortunately, Dunlop's view did not prevail absolutely, for Cromer's administration gave grants of £100 to officials who learned Arabic, but any resulting facility with the language served only the most basic of functions, not to interact with Egyptian society.

Segregation was reinforced by numerous institutions in Cairo. The Gazira Sporting Club, established in 1882 on a plot of land behind the Gazira Palace, was very English in appearance and had an eighteen-hole golf course, a race track, and a polo field. People thought of it as Cairo's country club. It had some continental European members, but the Turf Club, centrally located downtown on present-day Adli Street beside the Jewish Synagogue, was almost exclusively British. One visitor noted, "almost every Englishman in decent Society belongs to it." Sir Ronald Storrs, who worked his way up to the heights of the civil service—and was exceptional in his fluent Arabic and intimate knowledge of the Middle East—described the Turf as "the social and national fortress of the higher British community" and explained the role it played in his colleagues' lives:

> The British official in Cairo and Alexandria . . . was a hard and honourable worker, punctual and punctilious in his Department or Ministry from early morning until well after noon. He would then drive or bicycle to the Turf Club or his flat for luncheon, play tennis or golf until dark at the Sporting Club, return to the Turf Club to discuss the affairs of the day and dine there or at his flat. All, therefore, that the Egyptian official, high or low, saw of the average British official was a daily face gazing at him across an office desk from 8 a.m. to 1 p.m., Fridays excepted. The unofficial Egyptian saw not even that.[36]

It was at these clubs that much of the actual business of governing Egypt was conducted, and new arrivals from Britain inducted into the social system. The clubs also buttressed the separation between Europeans and Egyptians, for neither the Gazira Sporting Club nor the Turf Club allowed more than a few token Egyptian members. According to Storrs, "It was difficult for foreigners to be elected and not easy for Egyptians even to make use of either club; as I discovered by the glances cast in my direction when I came in with one of the few Egyptian members to play tennis." And that Egyptian was a future prime minister. Other institutions like the great hotels such as Shepheard's and the new Semiramis, awash with tourists during 'the season' that ran from November through March, also served European social and business purposes, and helped to make European society a world apart in Egypt. Encounters with Egyptians were unavoidable at some official functions, but even those were kept to the minimum. Eldon Gorst, Cromer's successor, was heavily criticized by his British subordinates for inviting so many Egyptians to his daily lunches and weekly dinners.

Tewfiq died in 1892 and was succeeded by his seventeen-year-old son Abbas Hilmy II, who was studying in Austria. Tewfiq had been easy to work with. "I pulled the strings," Cromer wrote to the British foreign secretary. Cromer thought the new khedive would also be easy to control but soon learned otherwise, for Abbas was far less malleable than his father. The first clash came within a year, when Abbas wanted to appoint his own prime minister after the pliable Mustafa Fahmi fell ill. Cromer objected strenuously and secured London's backing in successfully demanding that the appointment be withdrawn; furthermore, Abbas had to promise that he would always "most willingly accept British advice."

The following year Abbas was on a military tour of inspection and said uncomplimentary things about some troops and their British officer, whose performance he considered substandard. Cromer, who had been waiting for the chance to take the khedive down another notch, took deep offence and demanded a public statement of support for the army from Abbas. Since the demand was backed up by London and a threat to put the Egyptian army under formal as well as actual British control, Abbas had no choice but to comply. A British journalist wrote admiringly how "this opportunity was made full use of by our Consul general to explain to the young Khedive the exact relation in which it would henceforth be necessary for England and Egypt to stand towards one another."

Cromer was winning the matches, but he was earning lasting resentment from Abbas, whose position was distinctly uncomfortable with Cromer as an adversary and with the Egyptian government and army answerable not to him but to Cromer. Years later Abbas recalled, "I ruled therefore without any backing, constantly worrying about having to guard myself against ambushes whose purpose was obvious to me. Surrounded by men without energy—who were accustomed to bowing before the demands of a foreign power calling itself protector and friend, but whose designs on Egypt have been long known—I had only my constant vigilance to help avoid any blunder that could destroy my dreams."[37]

Abbas's distrust and dislike of the British impelled him to turn to nationalism, which was reemerging as a force in Egypt—indeed Abbas was one of its early instigators, personally leading a secret nationalist society in which the young Mustafa Kamil was involved. The movement appealed to the more Westernized and affluent middle class, but a number of religious thinkers also supported it. Its ideas circulated through a growing and astonishingly outspoken Egyptian press that Cromer made little effort to control. Perhaps he had ideas about freedom of the press; more likely, he thought it would have negligible impact since such a small minority of Egyptians was literate. In any event, he underestimated its force. By the time the British attempted to rein in the Egyptian press in 1909, it had become difficult to control.

The nationalists also received encouragement from the Ottomans and the French, though this proceeded more from desire to stir up trouble for the British than genuine sympathy for the nationalist cause. Many fundamental differences existed between Abbas and this second wave of nationalists, and eventually they would part ways. Abbas was a genuine Egyptian patriot, more so than many of the nationalists who also dabbled in pan-Ottomanism and pan-Islamism, and his primary objective as a true descendant of Muhammad Ali was to restore the authority of the khedive within Egypt, whereas many of the nationalists were more concerned with public opinion and the establishment of parliamentary democracy. But for the moment, the alliance with the nationalists was the only one open to Abbas, and it served the immediate purposes of both parties.

By 1890, the British attitude toward Sudan had changed. In place of the reluctant imperialism of Gladstone was the unabashed imperialism of the new prime minister Salisbury, who had no intention of evacuating Egypt and indeed had decided to use it as a base for the reconquest of Sudan. In this he was backed by his Conservative Party and by growing imperialist sentiment among the general public, which still wanted to avenge the murder of Gordon and was fed propaganda about horrific conditions in Sudan and the bloodthirsty tyranny of the Khalifa, who had assumed power when the Mahdi died shortly after the fall of Khartoum. Sudan was actually part of a much larger strategy, determinedly pursued, of gaining complete control of the Nile from its headwaters to the sea, an ambition that was ultimately achieved. Cromer, always mindful of the nature of the hydraulic civilization he ruled in Egypt, supported his government's Nilotic ambitions, once he was sure the Egyptian government could afford them. "When, eventually, the waters of the Nile, from the Lakes to the sea, are brought fully under control," he said, "it will be possible to boast that Man—in this case, the Englishman—has turned the gifts of Nature to the best possible advantage."

Once the decision was made, several years elapsed before Sudan was invaded. That was because the Egyptian government had to pay for the campaign, and only after the series of budget surpluses in the early 1890s could it do so. Not until March 1896 did Salisbury order Sir Herbert Kitchener, commander of the Anglo-Egyptian Army in Egypt, to advance up the Nile. About one-third of the expeditionary force was British; the rest was Egyptian. Progress was slow, hindered by low water and an outbreak of cholera that killed more soldiers than the fighting; also, the Egyptian government ran out of money, and the Caisse refused to authorize an advance, forcing Kitchener to stop until the government could raise more. Railways had to be built in Nubia to support the invasion, causing further delays.

The first major encounter between the Anglo-Egyptian army and the Khalifa's forces was a sharp, bloody battle at the confluence of the Atbara and Nile Rivers on 8 April 1898. Losses on both sides were heavy, though the Sudanese suffered disproportionately, with three thousand dead and four thousand wounded against total British casualties of 551. The decisive battle occurred at Omdurman, across the Nile from Khartoum, on 2 September. Some sixty thousand of the Khalifa's dervish soldiers, armed with spears and muskets, came out to fight a well-drilled Anglo-Egyptian army of less than half that size but equipped with modern rifles, artillery pieces, and machine guns. For five hours the courageous dervishes attacked repeatedly, only to be mown down by devastating fire. One British participant remembered, "They were not driven back; they were all killed in coming on." When it was over, Omdurman had cost the Sudanese at least eleven thousand dead and sixteen thousand wounded (many of whom were subsequently killed), against a total British loss of forty-nine dead and 382 wounded.

As the Khalifa retreated to Kordofan with the remnants of his army, the Anglo-British army entered Khartoum, looting the city. The Mahdi's tomb—"the centre of pilgrimage and fanatical feeling," according to

Kitchener—was destroyed at Kitchener's orders and the Mahdi's body thrown into the Nile. Kitchener kept the skull, much to the horror of Queen Victoria when she heard about it. Although Omdurman broke the power of the Mahdist state, resistance continued until the Khalifa was caught and defeated at Umm Diwaykarat on 24 November 1899. After the battle he was found dead on his prayer rug.

The reconquest of Sudan posed an immediate problem of what to do with it. There was no question in British minds of restoring it to Egyptian rule as before and risk having things go awry again. Besides, all recent problems in Sudan were blamed on the Egyptians, and it was against Egyptian rule that the Sudanese had revolted in the first place. Annexation of Sudan to the British Empire would have appealed to many British statesmen at the end of the nineteenth century, but that would have violated Egyptian claims, and Egypt had contributed most of the money and manpower to the war. Cromer's solution was the Anglo-Egyptian Condominium. According to this device, confirmed in 1899, sovereignty of Sudan was shared by the khedive and the British crown. British and Egyptian flags flew side by side. Any claims of the Ottoman sultan were disregarded. The government of Sudan was vested in a governor-general appointed by the khedive but nominated by the British government. None of the European privileges such as the Mixed Courts and consular jurisdiction that so vexed the British in Egypt were allowed in the Condominium.

Despite its ostensible equality in British and Egyptian participation, the Condominium was dominated by the British from the beginning. All the governors-general were British, and so were all the senior administrators; Egyptians were relegated to minor posts. Egypt was not permitted to legislate for Sudan. The Condominium soon became a source of continuing resentment for Egyptians, especially after they gained control of their own affairs and vainly sought truly equal participation with the British in Sudanese administration; nevertheless, the Condominium would prevail until 1956.

The first governor-general of Sudan was Kitchener, but he was soon succeeded by Sir Reginald Wingate, whose highly successful term extended from 1899 to 1916. Wingate was ably assisted by his inspector-general Rudolf Slatin, a uniquely qualified person. Slatin had been serving in Sudan as governor of Darfur when he was captured during the outbreak of the Mahdiya. To save his life he converted to Islam and became the Khalifa's slave, gaining insights that were very useful to the British in dealing with Sudan after he escaped. The British generally pursued two policies in that large country. In the north they mostly worked through the prevailing Islamic institutions and conducted business in Arabic. In the south, however, where Christians were more numerous, the English language was encouraged, and Christian missionary activities supported, while Arabic and Islam were discouraged. This bifurcation had lasting consequences for Sudanese internal affairs.

The need to staff the Sudanese administration led to one of Cromer's last major measures, the creation of an Anglo-Egyptian Civil Service. Young British men had of course been recruited for service in Egypt and Sudan for years, but no set standards had been established for their selection or for regulating their subsequent careers. Drawing on his experience with the Indian Civil Service, Cromer established a system where applicants, mostly from Oxford and Cambridge, were carefully vetted according to several criteria, including intelligence, personality, and health. The ideal recruit was described as a young man with "real energy and administrative ability." Once selected, the new official was assigned either to Egypt or Sudan—he had no choice in that—and began as a lowly paid inspector, but could hope to rise to a good position and comfortable salary. The standards of the Anglo-Egyptian Civil Service were high, comparing favorably with those of the Indian Civil Service.

Although it may have seemed like a natural measure of reform, creation of the Anglo-Egyptian Civil Service further institutionalized British rule and made the prospect of British withdrawal more remote than ever. Increasing numbers of British officials meant that Egyptian officials were further marginalized, thereby denied responsibility and experience. As far as the British were concerned, the Egyptians were incompetent anyway, but if that was so, then the new system only further deprived them of the opportunity to learn from their mistakes by handling their administrative affairs. The new British recruits were no help as teachers for the Egyptians and were certainly not their colleagues; instead, they settled comfortably into the European private clubs, hotels, and sporting organizations, while Egyptian and British society became ever more segregated. Egyptian nationalists saw the new civil service as a big step backwards and resented its existence.

Toward the end of his long, uncrowned reign, Cromer grew increasingly autocratic (behind his back, he had long been referred to as "Over-Baring," a play on his original name). He issued instructions directly to government departments, bypassing the Egyptian ministers entirely. Advancing age and deteriorating health made him irritable and short-tempered. Still, as British rule in Egypt neared its quarter century mark, he must have felt proud of what the British had done under his supervision and confident things would continue to run smoothly. The new civil service was functioning well, and relations with France took a sharp turn for the better as Britain and France were driven together by their mutual fear of Germany. In the Entente Cordiale of 1904 the French formally accepted the indefinite British occupation of Egypt. This made Cromer's job much easier by removing not only French obstructionism in official business but also French support for the nationalists. There was no sign of widespread dissatisfaction, let alone any prospect of an uprising or even serious disturbance, apparently justifying Cromer's belief that if the British managed Egypt well, then the masses of people would be grateful and remain quiet, marginalizing the nationalists who in any case were still few in number. That calculation was upset by events in a village in the Delta in 1906.

On 13 June of that year a group of British officers went shooting pigeons near the village of Dinshawi. That in itself was an act of great cultural insensitivity, the equivalent of walking into an English farmer's barnyard and blasting his chickens, for the Egyptians regarded these pigeons as domestic animals and housed them in the cone-shaped cotes that were often part of their houses. It was probably just bad luck that a nearby threshing floor caught fire at that moment. Thinking the British had started it, an angry crowd, armed with the heavy wooden staves carried by Egyptian peasant men, swarmed out of the village to confront the officers and disarm them. A gun went off; a woman fell to the ground, apparently dead; several men were peppered with shot. Infuriated, the crowd set on the officers and beat them. The officers fled to safety, although a captain suffered sunstroke and died, despite an attempt by a villager to help him. When a party of British soldiers arrived on the scene, they assumed the villager had killed the captain, so they beat him to death.

Cromer was about to depart for England on his annual summer leave and did not tarry, leaving the matter in the hands of lesser officials who had no hesitation in taking prompt, cruel action. They established a special tribunal that was bound by no legal code and from which there was no appeal. Nearly all the judges were European. Fifty-six villagers were speedily put on trial on 24 June. After three days, the verdicts were announced. Thirty-one of the accused were acquitted, but the sentences given to the convicted men were shockingly severe. Four were condemned to death by hanging. Others received sentences up to life imprisonment and fifty lashes from the whip. The punishments were executed publicly outside Dinshawi with the villagers forced to watch.

The international reaction to these proceedings was revulsion; in Egypt, outrage. Mustafa Kamil and the nationalists received a rush of public support; the khedive and Kamil, who had broken two years earlier, patched up their differences. Perhaps the British could have salvaged something from the situation had Cromer acted quickly and fairly when he returned to Egypt by reprimanding his officials and issuing an acknowledgment of, if not an apology for, what had happened at Dinshawi, but he decided he had to support the establishment. The Dinshawi Incident was a major turning point, as the Egyptian people came to the inescapable conclusion that true justice could never be expected from the foreigners who ruled their land.

Meanwhile, a new government had come to power in Britain. The strongly imperialist Conservative Party, which had dominated British politics for two decades, suffered an overwhelming defeat in the general election of 1906. Many who were concerned about preserving the Empire feared that the new Liberal government would give it away, but the Liberals had no such intention. Their changes were merely matters of degree, not of fundamental imperial policies. In Egypt, confronted by the unmistakable rise in nationalism, the Liberals' strategy was to attract enough moderate nationalists into a working relationship to leave the more extreme elements isolated and ineffectual. At the same time, they wanted to win over the khedive, thereby not only gaining his support but also splitting his alliance with the nationalists. The long-term objective was to prepare Egypt for more self-government. The new approach failed, in part because of the inept way it was applied, in part because it did not go nearly far enough, and in part because the Liberals underestimated the force of Egyptian nationalism.

Cromer is unlikely to have realized just how thoroughly the basic premise of his approach to governing Egypt had been undermined when he resigned in 1907, but the appointment of Eldon Gorst to succeed Cromer was a clear sign of a change of direction. Unlike Cromer, Gorst spoke fluent Arabic and was prepared to be much more conciliatory. He quickly cultivated friendly relations with Abbas, whom he easily detached from the nationalists by a grant of additional powers, for the khedive's alliance with them had always been more a matter of necessity than preference. But wooing the nationalists was more difficult. Cromer had already taken some reluctant initiatives by encouraging moderate nationalists to form their own political party, and had appointed one of them as minister of education. Gorst followed up by diminishing the British role in administration and giving a greater role to the Legislative Council and the General Assembly, consultative bodies that were established by the British after the Assembly of Delegates ceased to exist at the beginning of the British occupation. This failed to satisfy the nationalists' demands for a constitution with proper legislative institutions, something Gorst was unwilling to concede. The nationalists were also annoyed by Gorst's close relationship with the khedive, whom they welcomed as an ally and a focus for nationalist sentiment, but not as a political player in his own right, and certainly not one with increased power.

Then Gorst infuriated the nationalists, and a good many others besides, by appointing Boutros Ghali (grandfather of the secretary-general of the United Nations) as prime minister in 1908. The appointment of this Christian who had served as a judge of the Dinshawi trials could hardly have been more maladroit, especially at a time when the government was becoming perceived as pro-Christian. The political atmosphere was further soured by a nasty debate over a proposal by the Suez Canal Company to have its concession, due to expire in 1969, extended another forty years. It was intended as a fair proposition that would provide annual payments to the Egyptian government, which would also receive an increased share of profits from the canal, but the nationalists denounced it heatedly in the Legislative Council, accusing Boutros Ghali of a dishonorable sellout. The proposal was eventually rejected, but Ghali was assassinated by a Muslim nationalist in 1910. The resulting backlash of repression against extreme nationalism effectively ended Gorst's policy of gradually transferring responsibility to the Egyptians and undid his minor accomplishments. Having failed with the Egyptians—and with the British, who had come to believe that he was giving away too much and that his relations with the Egyptians were too close—Gorst returned to England a sick man and died in 1911.

The replacement of Gorst by the autocratic Kitchener signaled yet another change of course by the British government, which had had more than enough of Gorst's conciliatory policies. The new approach would be more hardline. Kitchener took stern steps against the nationalists and made no effort to conciliate Abbas Hilmi II, with whom he had repeatedly clashed before. He would have preferred to remove Abbas, but did not think the offense to Egyptian public sentiment would be worth it. Even Kitchener could not turn back the clock, however, and he moved ahead with modest political reform, creating a legislative assembly with more elected members and wider powers than the old Legislative Council. Meanwhile, he paid close attention to administration, especially to irrigation and agriculture, and to relieving the peasantry of debt, measures to which he was genuinely committed.

Although nationalism had grown much stronger after Dinshawi, the movement was not united, ranging from groups that wanted to cooperate with the khedive and the British, through those who favored parliamentary democracy, to extreme wings that advocated terrorism and violent revolution. Mustafa Kamil's death in 1908 removed the uniting force of the National Party, which had the broadest popular following, and no leader of equal stature emerged to replace him. The Ummah Party, formed primarily by landowners and intellectuals, was more moderate and included several people who became prominent in Egyptian political and literary life. One of those was Saad Zaghlul.

The son of a wealthy village headman, Saad Zaghlul had so enthusiastically joined the revolutionary movement in 1882 that he narrowly escaped execution when it was suppressed. Thereafter he followed a more conventional career as a lawyer and judge. Extremely well connected and able, he won approval from the establishment. "He possesses all the qualities necessary to serve his country," Cromer said of Zaghlul. "He is honest; he is capable; he has the courage of his convictions. He should go far." Cromer appointed Zaghlul minister of education in 1906, where he proved his mettle by standing up to his British adviser and insisting on Arabic, not English, as the language of instruction in government elementary schools. In 1910, he was given the more important portfolio of minister of justice. As a moderate, Zaghlul had maintained working relationships with the nationalists, the khedive, and the British; but by 1912 he had become committed to political independence and parliamentary democracy. After a disagreement with the khedive, Zaghlul resigned from the government and won election to the new Legislative Assembly as a member of the Ummah Party.

The Ummah Party dominated the Legislative Assembly, of which Zaghlul was elected vice president. Perhaps the khedive, who had little following in the Assembly, could have salvaged something had he invited Zaghlul to form a cabinet, but he distrusted both Zaghlul and the Ummah, and instead appointed Husein Rushdi, whose family had long served the Muhammad Ali dynasty, as head of the cabinet. Unfortunately, Rushdi had slight standing in the Assembly and turned out to be disloyal in the long run, while Zaghlul became an effective leader of the opposition to the government. The Legislative Assembly did not begin work until January 1914 and met for only a few months, yet in that short time, under Zaghlul's leadership, it made real progress toward gaining control of the cabinet and government administration. It is tempting to speculate what might have resulted from this experiment in limited parliamentary democracy had it not been cut short by events in Europe.

When the First World War began in August 1914, the Ottoman Empire came under heavy pressure to ally with either Germany or the Entente (Britain, France, and Russia), but for several weeks the Ottomans refused to commit one way or another. Khedive Abbas was at that moment in Istanbul on his usual summer vacation, prolonged by injuries received in an attempt on his life. When he was well enough to return to Egypt, the British ordered him to stay away for the duration of the war. The Germans were pushing deep into Belgium and France, stretching British and French forces to the limit, when the Ottoman Empire came down on the side of Germany on 29 October 1914. This threatened Egypt and the vital Suez Canal. On 2 November the British declared martial law in Egypt. They adjourned the Legislative Assembly and imposed censorship; dissidents were placed under house arrest; political activity was suspended.

With the Ottoman Empire as Britain's declared enemy, the fiction that Britain was acting in Ottoman interests by occupying Egypt could no longer be maintained. On 18 December Britain declared a Protectorate over Egypt. The veiled protectorate was unmasked. Another proclamation the following day deposed Abbas Hilmy II for having "definitely thrown in his lot with His Majesty's enemies." Departing from the succession as it had been established in 1866, the British replaced Abbas with his uncle Husein Kamil, an elderly man, easily managed. As a slap at the Ottomans, Husein Kamil was given the title of sultan. Abbas never returned to Egypt, spending the rest of his life in exile until his death in Geneva in 1944.

One of the Ottomans' primary military objectives was the reconquest of Egypt. They were heavily committed against Russia, however, and the assault at Gallipoli by Commonwealth troops, though futile, tied down a large portion of the Ottoman army which in any case was not prepared for an offensive campaign against Egypt. Even so, the Ottomans launched a daring surprise attack in February 1915 that reached the east bank of the Suez Canal, and even penetrated to the western side, but they were too weak to hold their ground and had to withdraw to Palestine. The Ottoman command ordered a massive assault for February 1916, but lack of transport delayed it until the scorching heat of midsummer. The defenses held firm and repelled the Ottomans with heavy losses. Even so, for two years the threat of Ottoman invasion compelled the British to station large forces along the canal zone. During 1917, the British took the offensive in Palestine and, after initial reverses, pushed the Ottomans back, capturing Jerusalem on 11 December, ensuring Egypt's safety from Ottoman attack.

The war's greatest impact on Egypt came not from military operations on Egyptian soil but from the vastly increased British presence and level of control imposed by the Protectorate. Hundreds of thousands of British and Allied soldiers and sailors were stationed in Egypt during the war at one time or another, turning the country into an enormous military base. Droves of additional civilian officials came from Britain to staff the Egyptian Civil Service. The chief British officer in Egypt under the Protectorate was a high commissioner. Kitchener was in England when war broke out and did not return, having been made secretary of state for war, so the first high commissioner was Sir Henry McMahon, followed by Sir Reginald Wingate in 1917. The high commissioners ruled with authority greater than Cromer's, largely unhindered by interference either from the French or from the Egyptians, whose means of expressing opposition had been suppressed. Little trouble could be expected from the new sultan Husein Kamil, a creature of the British with no independent power base. Unfortunately, McMahon was inexperienced, and Wingate lacked the personal skills to rule Egypt in the interests of the Egyptians. British attention focused almost exclusively on the war effort.

Egypt contributed heavily to that effort, often under extreme compulsion. Taxes were high during the war; the cost of living rose sharply. Supplies and buildings were requisitioned. In what amounted to a revival of the corvée, large numbers of men were conscripted into auxiliary forces such as the Camel Corps and the Labour Corps. Beginning in 1916, desperate for soldiers, the British began drafting Egyptians into the army. The British also conscripted people's livestock, taking the donkeys and camels that were often necessary for subsistence, but without giving adequate compensation. These hardships were partially offset by increased prosperity resulting from military expenditures within Egypt. Aware of the importance of the Egyptian cotton crop, for example, the British made sure that vital commodity was purchased, and at a reasonably good price, although this action was also motivated by the need to secure a strategic material for war, and eventually led to higher prices for food because land was diverted into cotton production.

The tightness of the British grip on Egypt became glaringly apparent when Sultan Husein Kamil died in October 1917 and the British again altered the terms of succession so that he was succeeded not by his son, who was viewed as anti-British, but by his half-brother Ahmed Fuad. At first, Fuad served British purposes well enough, but over the long run he proved to be ambitious, autocratic, and devious. Above all, he did not want to be a mere puppet. To gain allies, Fuad began to draw closer to Saad Zaghlul, who was acquiring a powerful popular following; but Fuad was no friend to parliamentary democracy, as subsequent events repeatedly demonstrated.

The First World War ended on 11 November 1918. Despite the widespread resentment of the Protectorate and the manifold hardships that Egypt endured during the war, there had been relatively little protest or dissension. British officials in London and Cairo thought they had the forces of nationalism well under control in Egypt. In fact, nationalism had been made stronger by the wartime experience and was about to enter its most explosive phase yet.

17 The Parliamentary Era

hen the British declared the Protectorate in 1914, they promised that it would be only for the duration of the war, but
when peace came they gave little thought to their promise.
Egypt was not ready for self-government, they believed; and strategic
considerations, especially the Suez Canal, precluded their early withdrawal.
They might be willing to consider adjusting their level of control over
Egypt, but there was no question in British minds of abandoning it.

A growing body of opinion in Egypt thought otherwise. As early as the
fall of 1917, various nationalists including Saad Zaghlul were discussing
sending a delegation *(wafd)* to state their case to Britain. It would also
present Egypt's case to the peace conference that could be expected to
follow the war, and to the world. On 13 November 1918, two days after
the Armistice in Europe, Zaghlul met with the British high commissioner
Sir Reginald Wingate and demanded autonomy for Egypt, offering a
treaty in return. The Egyptians were, Zaghlul told Wingate, "an ancient
and capable race with a glorious past—far more capable of conducting a
well-ordered government than the Arabs, Syrians and Mesopotamians, to
whom self-government had so recently been promised." Zaghlul also
stated his intention to go with a delegation to England to present the

nationalist cause. The Foreign Office would have none of this and brushed off Zaghlul's proposed visit, saying that everyone was too busy preparing for the upcoming Paris conference to talk to the Egyptians.

Zaghlul responded by organizing nationalist committees throughout Egypt. A petition that asserted the right of the Wafd, as the movement came to be known, to speak for the Egyptian people received 100,000 signatures, stimulating anti-British, pro-nationalist sentiment. This was a big move toward a party with organization and following. As the situation deteriorated, the British tried to take a hard line. On 8 March Zaghlul and some associates were arrested and transported to Malta. The Egyptian reaction took the British completely by surprise. Within days insurrection spread throughout the country. Students went on strike, followed by government workers, judges, and lawyers, and then by many others all across society in a dismaying display of national solidarity. Copts and Muslims alike preached unity against the British. The feminist leader Hoda Sharawi lent her voice to the protest. Demonstrations turned violent as shops were looted, telegraph wires cut, railroads blown up, and buildings burned. Six British officers were murdered in a railroad car. By the time the British rushed in troops and restored order later in the month, more than a thousand Egyptians were dead from the violence, as were thirty-six British military personnel and four British civilians.

Zaghlul and his party were released on 7 April 1919 and proceeded directly to Paris, where the peace conference was underway. He had high hopes of the American president Woodrow Wilson, author of the Fourteen Points with their ringing support for the principle of national self-determination. Other former provinces of the Ottoman Empire were slated for independence at the conference; surely Egypt's case was much stronger than theirs. His hopes were dashed. On the very day Zaghlul arrived in Paris, Wilson recognized Britain's protectorate over Egypt. Wilson, whose eyes were fixed on other goals, especially his cherished League of Nations, did not care what happened to Egypt, nor did anyone else at the conference. Despite his failure, however, Zaghlul returned to a hero's reception in Egypt, where new demonstrations broke out across the land. The British found it difficult to persuade anyone to serve as prime minister. It was too dangerous.

It had become obvious that the British were not going to be able to keep the Protectorate, and some efforts were made to negotiate a treaty to terminate it, but Lord Edmund Allenby, the former British commander in Palestine and Syria who had replaced Wingate with the enhanced title of "special high commissioner," was unwilling to deal with Zaghlul, whose power he wanted to break. Yet such was Zaghlul's support in Egypt that no treaty could be effectively concluded without his participation. To break that impasse, Allenby decided that Britain should make a unilateral grant of independence to Egypt and traveled to London to persuade the government to accept his plan. The foreign minister was opposed, and the prime minister, Lloyd George, was reluctant, but the cabinet approved. Accordingly, the British government proclaimed on 28 February 1922 that "The British protectorate over Egypt is terminated, and Egypt is declared to be an independent sovereign State."

But there were qualifications. The proclamation continued: "The following matters are absolutely reserved to the discretion of His Majesty's Government until such time as it may be possible by free discussion and friendly accommodation on both sides to conclude agreements in regard thereto between His Majesty's Government and the Government of Egypt." According to those qualifications, which became known as "the Reserved Points," Britain retained the right to maintain the security of British imperial communications through Egypt (i.e., the Suez Canal); Britain could intervene to protect Egypt against foreign aggression or interference; foreign interests and the rights of minorities in Egypt were to be safeguarded; and Britain alone would decide the status of Sudan. Egypt had therefore been granted a condition that could be better described as national autonomy than true independence, since so many elements of sovereignty were withheld. Also, many Egyptians were affronted that their 'independence' came as an announcement by another nation.

A new constitution was drafted and agreed to on 19 April 1923. It established a constitutional monarchy in which legislative power was vested in a parliament composed of a Senate and a Chamber of Deputies, although the king was granted extensive powers such as appointing ministers, vetoing legislation, and dissolving parliament. He could even issue decrees when parliament was not in session. These powers, combined with the fact that the royal family owned about one-tenth of the arable land in Egypt, should have been enough to make him an effective head of government as well as head of state; even so, Fuad deeply resented the

Constitution of 1923 and worked to subvert it, as did his successor Farouk. Moreover, by making ministers responsible to parliament, yet having them serve at the king's pleasure, the framers of the constitution created an ambiguity that could be an ongoing source of conflict.

What ultimately undid the system, however, was the three-sided nature of the forces involved. Had the contest merely been one of king against parliament, one or another would have prevailed over time, but the British were a third factor in an unstable power relationship that precluded progressive constitutional development. Nor were the British subtle about making their wishes known. More than once Royal Navy warships appeared before the palace windows in Alexandria when the British wanted a controversial decision to go their way. A strong British military presence remained in Egypt, not only in the canal zone but also in Alexandria and in Cairo, where the British army barracks stood in the middle of town on the site now occupied by the Nile Hilton Hotel. A British high commissioner also continued to be stationed in Egypt, and he was quite willing to intervene when he thought it necessary to do so.

Even so, the beginning was promising. Saad Zaghlul returned to Egypt for the parliamentary elections in January 1924. The Wafd, now a formal political party, won 190 out of 214 seats in the Chamber of Deputies, nearly 90 percent of the total. The king appointed Zaghlul as prime minister. With a party that enjoyed the complete confidence of the country in full control of parliament, led by a politician of towering stature, it must have seemed that something could be done to address the problems and embrace the opportunities that confronted Egypt.

There was much to be done. Egypt's population was growing rapidly. From about ten million in 1900, it would double by 1950. Yet most Egyptians were still poor peasants while the number of rich landlords was increasing, widening the gap between rich and poor. According to one count, 75 percent of Egypt's arable land was owned by approximately 150,000 people in large and medium-sized holdings. The remaining 25 percent, mostly in plots too small for subsistence, was held by well over a million people. Fully one-fifth of rural families owned no land at all. When the Great Depression hit Egypt at the beginning of the 1930s, and cotton prices plunged, the plight of the rural poor worsened. There was pressing need for land reform, crop diversification, and increased productivity from the land, which was not keeping pace with population growth. Public health and sanitation were also important issues, especially as people moved away from the countryside in hope of better opportunities, so that the two great cities of Egypt, Cairo and Alexandria, grew even faster than the country's overall population.

Commerce and industry were obvious ways to employ a growing population, but Egypt was starting from far behind in that regard because the British had retarded Egyptian industrialization as a matter of policy. Many of the businesses that did exist in Egypt were owned by foreigners. Economic development went slowly. People who had capital preferred to put it into land or other conservative investments, not industry; also, imports, industry, and commerce had to bear the brunt of the tax burden, while land taxes were kept low. There were some success stories, such as Talaat Harb and his conglomerate, the Misr Group. Bank Misr was founded entirely with Egyptian capital. But these were exceptional cases.

There was no strong governmental effort to address economic or social problems until right at the end of the parliamentary period, when it was too late. Some of the blame lies with the complacency of the Wafd, many of whose parliamentary members were great landowners who tended to be reluctant to see rapid agrarian change, and were indifferent to industrial development. But it was also a function of that unstable three-sided relationship between the king, parliament, and the British, which meant that compelling foreign policy issues and constitutional crises tended to absorb the attention of the country's politicians at the expense of important internal matters.

The record in education was somewhat better. Saad Zaghlul had always been a strong believer in educational improvement, and one of the first acts of his government was to establish compulsory education free of charge. Education rose from 4 percent of the national budget in 1920 to 13 percent in 1951. In higher education, the Egyptian University, which had languished since its founding in 1908, was reestablished as Fuad I University (now Cairo University) on a new campus in Giza, where its dome is a prominent landmark. But growing numbers of students in a greatly improved educational system had to confront the stark reality that a limited number of jobs awaited them after graduation.

For those who could afford to participate in it, early national Egypt offered a stimulating cultural and intellectual life. News media expanded rapidly with the advent of parliamentary government; literary and political reviews proliferated; Cairo became the publishing center of the Arab world. The long literary career of Naguib Mahfouz (1911–2006) was crowned with the Nobel Prize in 1988. The educator and writer Taha Husein (1889–1973) became known as "the Dean of Arab letters." Ahmed Shawqi (1868–1932) was recognized as "the prince of Arab poets"— although his enemies called him "the poet of Arab princes" because of his close ties to the royal court. Shawqi's rival, Hafez Ibrahim (1871–1932), acclaimed as "the poet of the Nile," was much more populist in his orientation. The best known of the visual artists was probably Mahmud Mukhtar (1883–1934), many of whose works such as *Egypt's Awakening* can be seen in prominent locations around Cairo. The great singer Umm Kulthum (1904–75) can only be described as an international superstar.

Egyptian cinema and radio became the most influential in the Arab world. Movie theaters had been popular before the First World War, and Egypt moved to the creation of its own films with the work of Muhammad al-Bayyumi, the first Egyptian director. Several film companies were established during the 1920s. Talaat Harb's Misr Group provided funding and handled distribution. Egyptian state broadcasting began when Radio Cairo was founded in 1932.

Those were also great days in the scholarship of ancient Egypt. The most sensational event in the history of Egyptology came on 4 November 1922 with the discovery of the tomb of Tutankhamun in the Valley of the Kings by Howard Carter. International attention was focused on Egypt. But that was only part, and not even the most important part, of an ongoing institutional process for exploring Egypt's past. The Egyptological establishment was dominated by Western scholars, but a number of native Egyptians like Labib Habachi also began to make their mark in the study of their country's ancient history.

Political developments did not keep pace with cultural ones. Despite his popularity and huge majority in parliament, Saad Zaghlul's eleven months as prime minister were difficult. This was partly because of obstructionism by the king, who loathed the constitution and resented the fact that parliament, which Zaghlul ran so strictly that some members began to resent it, was not under his control. But it was the third point of the triangular power relationship, the British, that brought Zaghlul's ministry to its premature end. Zaghlul was committed to removing the

Reserved Points, and failing to obtain that objective in a visit to London, he supported demonstrations against the British in Egypt and Sudan. A number of secret terrorist societies had been formed during the 1919 revolution; some were still operating. In November 1924, a Muslim member of one of them assassinated Sir Lee Stack, the commander-in-chief of the Egyptian army and governor of Sudan. Some well-placed Wafdists were implicated. Lord Allenby, the British high commissioner, retaliated with a devastating ultimatum, delivered personally to the Chamber of Deputies. Its demands included a large indemnity and a public apology in addition to prosecution of the murderer. Sudan was to be assigned a larger share of the Nile's water. What was worse, the ultimatum clearly implied that the Egyptians were not a civilized people. Perhaps Zaghlul should have stood his ground, but he chose to resign instead, leaving office after less than a year, never to hold power again. Even when the Wafd decisively won the parliamentary elections in May 1926, the British high commissioner refused to let Zaghlul take office as prime minister, calling a gunboat to Alexandria to emphasize his point. Saad Zaghlul died the following year.

The king, who detested Zaghlul and was jealous of his popularity and power, was not sorry to see him go. During the next several years Fuad attempted to assert royal power. With the death of Zaghlul, leadership of the Wafd fell to Mustafa al-Nahhas, who served briefly as prime minister. Fuad maneuvered him out of power, although al-Nahhas would be a recurring factor in Egyptian politics for the next quarter of the century, and dissolved parliament, suspending the constitution for three years. There was another parliamentary election in December 1929, which the Wafd won with the largest majority to date, taking 90 percent of the seats in the Chamber of Deputies, and al-Nahhas returned to office. He was making some progress with the British about the Reserved Points, though he could not get them to budge on Sudan, but was forced out after just six months by Fuad, who replaced him with Ismail Sidqi at the head of a pro-palace government. Parliament was again dissolved and a new constitution written that placed power firmly in the king's hands. Palace governments ruled for the next five years.

The years of palace rule, 1930–35, were not particularly tyrannical, and were even marked by a number of small accomplishments such as adjusting the agreement over the Nile waters. But discontent rose, students rioted, and pressure mounted on the king to restore the Constitution of 1923, pressure to which the British added their weight, concerned about the deteriorating political situation in Europe and wanting to negotiate a treaty with Egypt. They needed a more stable Egyptian government to deal with. Fuad succumbed in 1935. He reinstated the Constitution of 1923 and installed a caretaker government. Negotiations with the British began.

Mutual self-interest made conditions unusually favorable for reaching an agreement. The British, fearing the growing power of Germany and Italy, were anxious to secure their position in the Eastern Mediterranean and control of the Suez Canal in case of war. The Egyptians were apprehensive about the Italians next door in Libya, and after 1935 in Abyssinia (Ethiopia). They also calculated that if war did break out, a treaty could prevent the British from interfering in Egypt to the degree they had done during the First World War. Fuad was removed by death in April 1936, while negotiations were under way. The Wafd won another resounding victory in the parliamentary elections. Al-Nahhas returned as prime minister, unfettered by royal obstructionism. He personally headed the Egyptian delegation; the British were led by Foreign Minister Anthony Eden. The Anglo-Egyptian Treaty of 1936 was concluded on 26 August.

Although Egyptians later came to take a jaundiced view of the treaty, they considered it a substantial step forward at the time. It provided for a twenty-year alliance between Britain and Egypt. British military presence was reduced to ten thousand and confined to bases in the canal zone, which the British were to occupy for twenty years, but at Egyptian expense. The office of high commissioner was abolished. The British promised to do something about the Capitulations, which still largely exempted a quarter of a million foreign residents from Egyptian law, and to promote Egyptian membership in the League of Nations. The issue of Sudan was postponed; in the meantime the status quo was to be maintained. The Anglo-Egyptian Treaty of 1936 indeed fell short of what the nationalists wanted, but at least a definite end to the British occupation and full independence for Egypt was on the horizon.

Another apparent change for the better was the accession of the seventeen-year old Farouk as king. Educated at Britain's Woolwich Military Academy, Farouk was handsome, well spoken, and religious.

He appeared to have the makings of a true statesman. Unlike his predecessors, who spoke Turkish, Farouk spoke fluent Arabic. The Egyptians responded to their new monarch with genuine affection. Yet another improvement came at the Montreux Convention in 1937, which finally abolished the Capitulations and provided for the Mixed Courts to be phased out by 1949. As promised, Britain sponsored Egypt's application to become a member of the League of Nations, which it did later in 1937. Egypt now had full control of its foreign policy. For the first time, it established embassies around the world.

When Farouk attained his majority at age eighteen in 1937, the palace again became politically active. The young king soon displayed the same autocratic tendencies as his father. He did not like the Wafd, and he particularly disliked al-Nahhas. After eighteen months, al-Nahhas resigned, enabling the king and palace insiders to gain full control of the government by constructing a coalition of anti-Wafd ministers. Their work was made easier when the Wafd suffered an electoral defeat in the parliamentary elections of April 1938 because of corruption scandals. Farouk's relations with the British were also bad. He viewed them as a competing source of power, while the attitude of the British ambassador Sir Miles Lampson was patronizing at best. Lampson always referred to Farouk as "The Boy," even when the king was in his twenties. The oscillating power relationship of king–parliament–British thus kept reasserting itself throughout the parliamentary period, never allowing the system to settle into equilibrium for constructive work.

The Second World War badly upset the balance. It began on 1 September 1939 when Hitler attacked Poland, causing Britain and France, which had belatedly awakened to the Nazi menace, to declare war on Germany. Egypt did not become a formal belligerent, but according to the Anglo-Egyptian Treaty of 1936 martial law was declared, port facilities converted to military use, censorship imposed, and the country generally placed on a war footing. But the war itself was far away and of little direct concern to the Egyptians as the Germans overran Poland, then turned West in the spring of 1940. In an amazingly successful series of lightning strikes, Hitler seized Denmark and Norway, and broke into the Low Countries and France. Unprepared for Germany's blitzkrieg tactics, with their emphasis on armor and air power, the French were knocked out of the war. Only by an apparent miracle were the British able to extricate their army over the beach at Dunkirk, losing most of their equipment along the way. Alone against Germany, Britain's very survival was at stake; during the summer of 1940 the German air force relentlessly pounded the island nation with a bombing attack. Invasion was a real possibility. The German air assault was fended off, but German submarines were sinking British ships at a rate that threatened to starve Britain into submission.

Suddenly Egypt became a critical theater of operations. Sensing great spoils for his new Roman Empire, Italy's fascist leader Mussolini entered the war on Germany's side in June 1940. Italy was well established in its province of Libya and had recently conquered Ethiopia. It could threaten Egypt from two directions. But while the Italians had half a million men in those places, supplied with a colossal amount of matériel, the British could muster just 55,000 in Egypt and Sudan. Britain had little to spare in the way of soldiers or supplies, and what it sent had to run a gauntlet through the Mediterranean Sea, which was mostly controlled by the enemy. Many of the soldiers who came to defend Egypt were from the Commonwealth and Empire, especially from Australia, New Zealand, and South Africa, and these did not arrive until early September. When speaking of British forces from now on, it should be understood that they were largely composed of soldiers from the Commonwealth. The Italians delivered their attack from Ethiopia into British Somalia in June 1940, threatening Sudan; in September they invaded Egypt from Libya. The situation confronting Britain in Egypt was daunting, to say the least. Loss of that country, with the concomitant loss of the Suez Canal and the undermining of the entire British position in the Middle East, would have been difficult, perhaps impossible, to redeem, and Egypt would have fallen into the hands of occupiers incomparably worse than the British had ever been.

When the Italians invaded Egypt, the British fell back to Marsa Matruh, about a third of the way to the Delta. Had the Italians pressed on, it is difficult to see how the scant British numbers could have stopped them, but they paused at Sidi Barrani to consolidate their position and prepare a fortified base, complete with luxurious creature comforts, before advancing to the Nile. The Italian commander suffered from excessive caution and was made even more hesitant by a series of audacious British bluffs that concealed Allied weaknesses and prompted him to strengthen his fortifications even more. Meanwhile, through their forward tactics, the British discovered a large gap in the Italian front that allowed them to slip through, roll up the Italian positions from behind, and make an enormous catch of prisoners and matériel. By the end of 1940, the Italians had been thrown out of Egypt. Meanwhile, the British counterattacked from Sudan, crushing the Italians in the south as well and restoring Ethiopian independence.

Continuing their offensive in the north, the British attacked the heavily fortified bases the Italians had established in Cyrenaica, the eastern portion of Libya. Tobruk fell within a few hours on 21 January 1941; advancing to Benghazi, the British occupied all of Cyrenaica; they had taken 130,000 Italian prisoners. For a tantalizing moment, complete victory in North Africa lay within British grasp. Tripoli, the port of entry for Axis forces, was about seven hundred kilometers to the west by the land route from Benghazi, on the other side of the Gulf of Sidra. The distance was long, but the Italians were collapsing, and a determined push probably would have firmly closed the door to Africa against the Axis. But events in the overall theater of war clouded the issue, allowing the moment of opportunity to slip away. A German invasion of Greece was imminent. Although that country had repeatedly refused British urgings to join against the Axis, it now turned to Britain for aid. The only place from which help could be sent quickly was North Africa, so the advance across the rest of Libya had to be postponed while forces were diverted in a futile effort to save Greece from German conquest.

That pause was nearly catastrophic. Unwilling to see his Italian ally defeated, Hitler dispatched a panzer army, the Afrika Korps, to Libya under the command of General Erwin Rommel, who began a surprise German offensive on 1 April 1941. Through daring, innovative tactics, Rommel smashed through an uncoordinated British defense and swept eastward to the Egyptian border at Halfaya Pass. What saved the situation for the British was the epic defense of the Libyan fortress town of Tobruk, which threatened Rommel's line of supply and brought his advance to a halt. A new British commander, Claude Auchinleck, launched Operation Crusader in mid-November 1941, forcing Rommel out of Egypt and back to his starting point southwest of Tobruk.

Operation Crusader brought a reprieve, but the British position in Egypt and worldwide remained precarious. Rommel was still dangerous, and experience had shown that he could strike quickly and effectively. On 7 December 1941, the Japanese attacked the Americans and the British in the Pacific. The long-term results of this were immensely beneficial to Britain, bringing the United States into the war not only against Japan but also against Germany, but in the short run the Japanese won a dismaying series of victories in the Western Pacific and Southeast Asia. Australia and New Zealand were in danger of being cut off and invaded. Their governments began to press for the return of their troops from Egypt to defend their homelands.

To shore up the crumbling strategic situation, the British were determined to have a government in Egypt that would uphold the 1936 treaty. Farouk had been dabbling in anti-British activities for some time; now he wanted to replace his pro-British prime minister. On 4 February 1942 occurred what came to be known as the Great Humiliation. Sir Miles Lampson surrounded the Abdin Palace with tanks. Inside, he ordered "The Boy" to make a choice: appoint al-Nahhas and an all-Wafd cabinet or abdicate. Despite al-Nahhas's irritating anti-British rhetoric, the British knew he could be counted on to back the treaty that he had proudly negotiated, and he was anti-fascist. Farouk could do nothing but agree.

Britain felt justified in using force with its survival at stake, but Egyptians bitterly resented having the monarch of their independent state forced to appoint a government at gunpoint. For Farouk it was a personal turning point onto a long road of moral decline. He became notorious for womanizing—often with shocking flagrancy—and gambling, passing much of his time at night clubs. Possibly because of a glandular disorder, he grew grossly obese. A comparison of the photographs of the bright young king at his accession and the debauched, middle-aged playboy is a study in contrast. The Egyptian monarchy lasted another ten years, but the Great Humiliation mortally wounded it.

Rommel launched a new offensive on 24 May 1942; again he broke through and swept around the British lines. Most unwisely, the British prime minister Churchill ordered that Tobruk be held, although it was in no way prepared to withstand another siege. The city fell to the Germans on 21 June, with thirty thousand prisoners and a big cache of supplies that enabled Rommel to strike into Egypt. As the British reeled eastward in retreat, it seemed that all was lost. Smoke from burning state papers rose from the British embassy in Cairo. Anti-British crowds shouted, "Press on, Rommel." Mussolini had a white horse flown from Italy to Africa for his triumphal entry into Cairo. Last-ditch preparations were made to attack the Germans in the flank as they swept through the Delta to the Suez Canal. But the British made a stand at al-Alamein, little more than one hundred kilometers west of Alexandria, where the Qattara Depression on the south and the Mediterranean on the north limited German scope for maneuver. The fortunes of battle swayed to and fro in July 1942 as each side came close to complete victory and utter defeat. Rommel actually won the race to al-Alamein, but his forces were so overstretched by their rapid advance that he was unable to consolidate his position before the British rallied and launched a counterattack that would have destroyed the Afrika Korps had it not miscarried.

Exhausted, both sides settled into their entrenchments and minefields at al-Alamein to recover for another effort. This time the pause served British purposes much more than German, because the British had but a short distance to their base of supply, into which vast amounts of American matériel were now flowing. Rommel, on the other hand, was at the end of a supply line that ran hundreds of kilometers along the northern coast of Africa far into Libya, and was joined to Europe by a most uncertain sea passage, the Germans having failed to take the island fortress of Malta. Also, Hitler, who never grasped the strategic possibilities of the war in Africa, was throwing all his available resources into a second great offensive against the Soviet Union. He sent little to Rommel. Auchinleck could bide his time while preparing a stroke that had an excellent chance of destroying the Afrika Korps entirely.

The decisive battle would have come sooner had Churchill not lost patience and replaced Auchinleck with Bernard Montgomery, for although Montgomery essentially followed the plan Auchinleck had devised, he developed it with his customary caution. Meanwhile, Rommel, realizing that time worked against him, made a desperate effort to break through the British left wing and dash for Cairo and the Suez Canal. This was the Battle of Alam Halfa, which lasted from 30 August to 6 September 1942. But Rommel's attack, long anticipated by the British, failed against heavy minefields and ample, well-placed reserves. The denouement came at the Second Battle of al-Alamein, 23 October to 3 November, when Montgomery finally unleashed his attack on the Germans. Despite his overwhelming force, Montgomery's tactics were so conservative that Rommel nearly repulsed the assault, and after he was defeated he managed the even more remarkable feat of extricating his army from Egypt. But Egypt was saved from Nazi conquest, and the battles at al-Alamein were a welcome change in Allied fortunes. Taken in conjunction with German failures in Russia and Japanese disaster against the Americans at the Battle of Midway, they marked the irreversible decline of the Axis.

Egypt played a supporting role during the rest of the war, serving as a base for further operations in North Africa and the Mediterranean. The Cairo Conference in November 1943, between Churchill, Franklin D. Roosevelt, and China's Chiang Kai-shek, decided many major issues about postwar Asia and the Pacific. At its peak, the British military presence in Egypt amounted to 250,000 personnel. The hardships on the Egyptian people were less than during the First World War, and were partially offset by the creation of new jobs and stimulation of some manufacturing; the service sector of the economy was especially active. Wages rose, but prices rose even faster, and widespread layoffs occurred after the war. Egypt made a much needed infusion into the British treasury with loans that totaled £400 million sterling over the course of the war, but Egypt was not an official belligerent until February 1945. Most of the fighting was done by British and Commonwealth troops, as the geometrically arranged crosses in the Commonwealth Cemetery at al-Alamein attest. Egyptian attitudes toward the war were mixed. Some, like the young officer Anwar al-Sadat, worked actively with the Germans, not so much because they were Nazi sympathizers but because they saw the Germans as a means to get the British out of Egypt once and for all. But there was never a groundswell of genuine sympathy for the Germans, from whom most Egyptians expected no better than from the British, and perhaps worse.

The Egyptian political scene during the Second World War was often sordid. Al-Nahhas had already been implicated in one serious corruption scandal when he was forced out of office in 1928, and after returning to power he became notorious for nepotism. The Wafd party in general showed itself to be corrupt and inefficient time and time again. Once the party of nationalism, it suffered from coming to power through British guns. Prominent Wafdists quarreled with al-Nahhas and formed splinter parties. Many Egyptians like the young army officer Gamal Abd al-Nasser became disgusted, not just with the Wafd, but with the entire system they took it to represent, and began thinking about fundamental change. Al-Nahhas's relations with the king were venomous. Things became so bad that the British permitted his dismissal. The Wafd boycotted the parliamentary elections of January 1945, enabling the Saadists, one of the breakaway Wafdist parties, to win, and its leader Ahmed Maher became prime minister. Maher was assassinated a month later by an Egyptian fascist while leaving the parliament building after announcing his intention to declare war on Germany so Egypt could become a charter member of the United Nations. He was succeeded by Mahmud Fahmi al-Nuqrashi, who had been implicated in the assassination of Sir Lee Stack, and who in turn fell victim to an assassin three years later.

As people became increasingly disillusioned with the Wafd, entirely new parties emerged of all political hues. The Egyptian Communist Party was formed in 1949, but a much more formidable political force had long been gaining strength at the other end of the political spectrum. This was the Muslim Brotherhood, founded in 1928 by Hasan al-Banna. In some ways it is misleading to describe the Muslim Brotherhood as a political party, because it worked outside the parliamentary system and was opposed to all secular political parties. Its objective was to establish Islam in every aspect of life—political, social, and economic, as well as religious. By the beginning of the Second World War, the Brotherhood may have had a following as large as a million people from all walks of life. Al-Banna formed the terrorist wing of the Muslim Brotherhood early during the war. He was supportive of the Axis and urged people not to help the British. The movement reached its greatest strength immediately after the war as it engaged in extensive disruptive activities ranging from demonstrations to terrorism. Correctly perceiving the Muslim Brotherhood as a revolutionary threat, al-Nuqrashi used his martial law authority to dissolve it in November 1948. When al-Nuqrashi was assassinated a month later by a student attached to the Brotherhood, the government responded by murdering Hasan al-Banna. The Muslim Brotherhood was suppressed, although it would reemerge as a factor in Egyptian politics.

The postwar years should have been a time for the parliamentary regime to let the domestic political process sort itself out and turn to the many pressing internal problems, but foreign affairs kept dominating the agenda. Now that the war was over, pressure to revise Egypt's treaties with Britain grew. By 1946, riots and demonstrations were common occurrences. On 21 February, an organized crowd of workers stormed the British army barracks at Ismailia. Soldiers opened fire with machine guns, killing twenty-three and wounding another 120. The new Labour government in Britain attempted to defuse the situation by withdrawing troops from Cairo and Alexandria and placing them in the canal zone, although that increased the military presence there to several times the level authorized by the Treaty of 1936. Egyptians were also frustrated about the issue of Sudan, on which years of negotiations with the British had accomplished nothing except postponement. As far as Egyptians were concerned, Sudan belonged to Egypt by right of conquest; the British were depriving them of what was rightfully theirs.

In addition to the running problems with the British, a major disaster developed in Palestine. After the First World War, in the division of spoils between France and Britain, France received the areas that later became Syria and Lebanon. Britain's portion was Palestine, Transjordan, and Iraq. Of those, Transjordan (later renamed Jordan) and Iraq soon became sovereign nations, though under a British tutelage that lasted into the 1950s, but Palestine remained a British mandate. Because of Zionism, a movement dedicated to establishing a Jewish nation in Palestine, and then because of the ghastly situation that was developing for Jews in Nazi Germany, increasing numbers of Jews immigrated into Palestine during the 1920s and 1930s, leading to a confrontation with the Palestinians, who saw their presence as a threat to Palestinian rights and aspirations. Violence between Jews and Arabs broke out in Palestine, and Zionist militias were formed, including terrorist groups who conducted operations against the British. Egypt was the scene of one of these in November 1944 when Lord Moyne, the highest-ranking British official in the Middle East, was assassinated in Cairo by the Stern Gang, the group with which Yitzhak Shamir, later prime minister of Israel, was associated. Nor was that the last time Egypt was visited by Zionist terrorism during this phase of the struggle, for the Zionists also staged attacks on Egyptian Jews to frighten them into leaving Egypt for Israel, with unfortunate success.

The situation in Palestine deteriorated rapidly after the Second World War. Determined to extricate themselves, the British referred the Palestinian question to the United Nations, where the General Assembly voted on 27 November 1947 for the partition of Palestine into Jewish and Palestinian states. Britain announced that the mandate would be terminated on 15 May 1948. On the preceding day, David Ben-Gurion and his colleagues announced the creation of the Israeli state. Civil war immediately erupted in Palestine.

In a meeting at Inshas Palace, Farouk had already agreed to join other Arab nations in war to prevent the partition of Palestine and the establishment of a Jewish state. The prime minister, cabinet, and general staff did not think the Egyptian army was ready, but popular support for intervention was strong. The Muslim Brotherhood began sending volunteers to Palestine even before the British had withdrawn. Farouk saw the opportunity to cut a fine figure for the monarchy and play a leading role among Arab nations. Almost everyone underestimated the difficulties that lay ahead.

Two Egyptian forces advanced into Palestine, one along the coast through Gaza toward Tel Aviv, the other through the Negev toward Jerusalem. Other Arab forces of various sizes converged from Jordan, Iraq, Syria, and Lebanon. The Arabs' appearance of unity and strength was deceptive, however, for they were beset by lack of coordination and conflicting goals, while the Israelis, who had carefully planned for the moment, had clear objectives and more fighters with better arms. Soon the Arabs were in retreat almost everywhere.

The naysayers were proved right. Egypt was not ready for the war. Farouk was a troublesome, interfering grand strategist; equipment was inferior or missing, support always inadequate. The Egyptian forces were pushed back to Gaza, and the Israelis, who had invaded Sinai, would have pressed on to the Suez Canal had they not (with an irony that must have been wryly appreciated by a few Egyptians) been stopped by the British, who threatened to invoke pertinent clauses of the Anglo-Egyptian Treaty of 1936. The only bright spot in the fiasco was a heroic stand in the Palestinian village of Falluja, led by General Muhammad Naguib. By the time Egypt signed the armistice in early 1949, the Arabs had been defeated. The Israelis had established their state and precluded the establishment of a Palestinian one. Hundreds of thousands of Palestinian refugees poured into Gaza, where Egypt assumed administrative control. Egyptian losses in the war were two thousand dead and many more wounded and missing. The army was bitterly angry at the government. Ugly rumors circulated that members of the royal court and high-ranking officers had colluded to supply the military with inferior equipment for personal profit.

When parliamentary elections were held in January 1950, the Wafd won most of the seats, but with only 40 percent of the popular vote because of all the scandals and defections that had afflicted the party. Al-Nahhas returned as prime minister. The domestic legislative initiatives that followed were some of the most interesting and innovative to be seen during the parliamentary era—land reform, social security, abolition of school fees, and more—measures that might have made a world of difference had they been put forward earlier, but as it was they came much too late to save the parliamentary monarchy.

Meanwhile al-Nahhas, mired in corruption as usual, was becoming unpopular. To divert attention from his personal problems, he reverted to his customary anti-British rhetoric. In October 1951 he unilaterally abrogated the Anglo-Egyptian Treaty of 1936 and the agreements between Britain and Egypt that had established the Condominium over Sudan in 1899. Although the British refused to recognize any change in treaty status, al-Nahhas's actions implied that the British military occupation of the canal zone was no longer legal, encouraging Egyptian workers at the military bases to go out on strike; local tradesman refused to supply goods and services. The British response was to seize control of communication centers in the canal zone, prompting the Egyptian government to retaliate by dismissing all its British employees. It also encouraged activists, including policemen and government workers, to form fedayeen groups and attack British troops on the canal. The British countered by mounting an assault on the police headquarters at Ismailia, which they had identified as a trouble spot, killing more than fifty Egyptians.

The next day, 26 January 1952, became known as Black Saturday. Demonstrators gathered at Cairo University (then still named King Fuad I University) and marched downtown. Violence broke out. Mobs formed and rampaged through the streets, carrying cans of kerosene and setting fire to buildings. Thus burned to the ground many well-known Cairo landmarks such as the Turf Club and the old Shepheard's Hotel. Some four hundred buildings were destroyed, and thirty people lost their lives. Only after several hours of unhindered rioting and looting did the army restore order.

Farouk dismissed al-Nahhas after the riots. During his last six months as king he appointed four more cabinets. A royal prince remembered, "Yet more and more signs of unrest were clearly visible: violent demonstrations of university students, political assassinations (unfortunately of the most worthy people), a free press maligning surreptitiously, and then more and more openly, all forms of stability, and finally—most important of all—an unstable political situation with a continual change of government. There no longer seemed to be anyone at the helm."[38] The regime was beyond repair. By the summer of 1952, few informed observers would have been surprised by a major challenge to the monarchy, but when change came it was from an unexpected quarter.

The Free Officers' movement was a conspiratorial group of young military officers. Memories varied about how it originated. Anwar al-Sadat claimed he founded it at the beginning of the Second World War, but more likely it coalesced in the aftermath of the Palestinian fiasco, which convinced many in the military that the old regime was so rotten that it had to be overthrown. The army, as Nasser put it, was the "only force capable of action." At the heart of the Free Officers' movement was a central committee of nine members, six from the army and three from the air force. Its chairman was Gamal Abd al-Nasser, although it would be some time before he established full dominance over the other members. The central committee controlled a network of cells that extended widely through the services, involving several hundred officers altogether. Because of their youth and obscurity, they chose as their titular leader General Naguib, a war hero and man of great integrity who was well known and admired throughout the military. Other groups of plotters were at work in Egypt, but the Free Officers excelled them in planning, organization, timing, and luck.

The Free Officers set the date of their coup for 5 August 1952, but the king received word that something was up. Warned that he was going to move against them, the Free Officers decided to act on the evening of 22 July. Things could hardly have gone more smoothly. Key posts in Cairo and Alexandria were occupied almost without resistance. By the morning of 23 July the Free Officers were in control. Most of the seasoned politicians like al-Nahhas who might have made annoying noises were in Europe on their summer vacations. Popular opinion had long since grown tired of the regime and was happy to see it go.

There was a brief debate among the Free Officers about what to do with Farouk. Some favored public trial and execution, but Nasser and the majority decided he should be allowed to abdicate in favor of his infant son and leave Egypt.* On 26 July, Farouk sailed from Alexandria aboard the royal yacht *al-Mahrussa* into an inglorious exile that ended with his death in a Rome nightclub thirteen years later. "Your task will be difficult," he told Naguib as he departed. "It isn't easy, you know, to govern Egypt."

---

* Technically Egypt remained a monarchy with Farouk's son Ahmed Fuad as king until the following year, when the nation was formally declared to be a republic.

18 Nasser

The Revolutionary Command Council (RCC), as the central committee of the Free Officers now called itself, had taken control of the Egyptian state, but it had no coherent agenda or definite objects. Its members differed widely in ideas, and those ideas changed over time. Nasser, for example, began as a strong proponent of democracy, but when he became president he ruled the country autocratically. Also, Nasser had not yet emerged as the recognized leader of the RCC and was little known to the general public. Naguib, who became prime minister and president, was the man out front. Nasser's offices were deputy prime minister and minister of the interior. The initial plan was for the army to retain power for three years, after which some form of constitutional government would be established. But Nasser and the rest of the RCC, having experienced power, rapidly acquired a taste for it.

Naguib threatened that power. What the Free Officers had expected of him or what role he thought he was going to play is a matter of controversy, but he had no intention of being a mere figurehead. Dignified but affable, he quickly became popular throughout the country. He also had a clear vision of how to govern, one that emphasized reform within the context of continuity, a parliamentary system similar to the old one, but without its corrupt, obstructionist elements. To that end, he developed working relations with many existing political leaders. That was anathema to Nasser, who was determined to make a clean break with the past, not reform it.

The conflict between Naguib and Nasser unfolded in two stages, with Naguib emerging triumphant from the first. Objecting to Nasser's harsh measures against traditional political parties—including the proposed arrest of al-Nahhas—and other high-handed actions, Naguib sent his resignation as president in February 1954. The RCC promptly got a jolting lesson about their ostensible leader's popularity. Protests and demonstrations erupted in support of Naguib and parliamentary democracy. Worse, substantial groups within the army took the same position and expressed it loudly. Nasser and his colleagues hurriedly backed down. Naguib returned as president, and an elected parliament was promised for the near future.

But what appeared to be a strategic victory for Naguib was merely a tactical withdrawal by Nasser. With Naguib lulled into a false sense of security, Nasser, the practiced conspirator, worked quietly behind the scenes, removing or marginalizing Naguib's supporters in the army and police, and developing a following in the trade unions. When the moment was right, the purged army demonstrated its support for the RCC, and the unions organized coordinated strikes and demonstrations, catching Naguib and the partisans of parliamentary democracy off guard. In late March the RCC announced it would remain in power and the elections would not be held. Naguib quickly faded from the political picture. He was deprived of the presidency in November 1954 and placed under house arrest, where he remained until after Nasser's death. Nasser became acting president and eventually assumed the presidency.

In October 1954 Nasser survived an assassination attempt by a Muslim Brother when he was giving a speech in Alexandria. That provided the pretext to strike decisively at the Brotherhood, which probably constituted the most dangerous opposition to the RCC. In a nationwide repression of great brutality, perhaps as many as fifty thousand people were arrested and over a thousand put on trial; six Brothers were hanged. Sayid Qutb, who had inherited Hasan al-Banna's mantle as its leading member, spent the next ten years in prison. Within a month, all political parties had been abolished, their leaders imprisoned, and the opposition press closed.

Hitherto a shadowy figure, Nasser emerged into the spotlight. With practice, he blossomed as a politician, developing a gift for communicating with the people, making them identify strongly with him. Although he still had to take into account the RCC, the reins of power were increasingly in his hands—the government ministries, the military, and the security service. Political parties had already been dissolved; now, under one pretext or another, he suppressed remaining ideological opposition, whether on the left or on the right. The initiative lay with him.

Nasser's first notable moves as a statesman were in the realm of foreign affairs, but these initiatives were also closely linked to domestic concerns. The obvious place to begin was with Britain, which still maintained a strong military presence on Egyptian soil. Negotiations for the British Egyptian Treaty, to supersede the 1936 treaty, went well. British troops were to be withdrawn within two years, although the treaty had an unpalatable reactivation clause that allowed the British military to return in the event of war, but this difficulty was eased by an American promise to provide aid to Egypt if the treaty was signed, as it was in October 1954. The last British troops duly departed Egypt in January 1956, ending more than seven decades of occupation. There was, however, to be one more violent military encounter between Britain and Egypt before that year was over.

Negotiations regarding Sudan, where Britain still retained control, did not go nearly as well for Egypt. Sudanese and Egyptian histories had been closely intertwined since pharaonic times, and Egypt considered Sudan to be Egyptian by right of conquest following Muhammad Ali's annexation of northern Sudan in the 1820s. But the divided nature of British administration of Egypt and Sudan with the Condominium had weakened those ties, and the Sudanese harbored some grievances toward Egypt, including the division of the all-important waters of the Nile. They were particularly offended by the treatment of Naguib, who was half Sudanese. Even so, Egypt was optimistic and appeared to win the upper hand by negotiating Sudanese right of self-determination with the reluctant British, thinking the Sudanese would respond to Egyptian overtures, but Britain countered by encouraging Sudanese independence, which was proclaimed on 1 January 1956.

Seeing Egypt (and himself) as the natural leader of the Arab world, Nasser became an ardent proponent of pan-Arabism. His message was broadcast by radio to other Arab countries, winning many Arab supporters outside of Egypt—and making not a few enemies among some Arabs who were offended at the broadcasts' often strident tone, and who feared Nasser would stir up trouble in their countries. This was particularly true among prominent circles in Saudi Arabia and Jordan. Nasser strongly opposed the Baghdad Pact between Britain, Turkey, Iran, and Pakistan, thereby angering Britain and its ally Iraq, because the pact helped preserve British influence in the Middle East. The United States was also disturbed because it saw the Baghdad Pact as a bulwark against the Soviet Union.

When Nasser reached out beyond the Arab world to non-Western nations and the communist bloc, he received a warm welcome. It was a heady experience to be the youngest leader at Sukarno's nonaligned conference in Indonesia in April 1955, mixing with others who sought to avoid being drawn into the gravitational fields of either the Soviet Union or the United States in an increasingly polarized geopolitical environment. Nasser saw the nonaligned movement as a stage where he could be a star. He met the Chinese premier Chou En-lai, who treated him with a respect he never received from Britain or the United States as those countries became increasingly cross with his behavior. Chou also provided a practical solution to one of Nasser's most pressing problems.

For some time Nasser had been attempting to obtain arms from Western sources. A major Israeli raid against Egyptian forces in Gaza in February 1955 painfully demonstrated the need to modernize Egypt's military establishment and replace its outdated equipment. The United Sates had made promises of aid, but with conditions so restrictive, especially in regard to anything that might involve Israel, that nothing was concluded. Chou arranged a deal for Nasser with the Soviet Union, though the weapons were formally provided to Egypt by Czechoslovakia. The West was appalled by what it considered a dangerous extension of Soviet influence into the Middle East, but for Nasser it was just a matter of pragmatic necessity. As he later said, "We would have preferred to deal with the West, but for us it was a matter of life or death."

Gratifying though Nasser's diplomatic achievements were, his success as a politician, and possibly his political survival, depended on what he could accomplish within Egypt. He had raised people's expectations to a high level, and there was much that needed to be done. The RCC moved early on with land reform in September 1952 by limiting the size of a family holding to two or sometimes three hundred feddans. This dealt a blow to Egypt's landowning class, highly influential in the proscribed Wafd Party, which Nasser despised, but the overall impact of the measure on Egypt was limited. According to one estimate, it affected only 10 percent of Egypt's arable land and 200,000 peasants, therefore it benefited just a small portion of the landless rural population.

But what Egypt needed most was industrialization, something that had been systematically denied by the British, then was slow to develop during the parliamentary period. Such private capital as existed within Egypt was not being invested in industry, and Egypt's increasingly controversial policies did not endear it to international financial markets. Nasser had to find some way to finance Egypt's most ambitious public works project: the construction of a high dam at Aswan that would not only greatly increase the agricultural productivity of Egypt but also generate a prodigious amount of electricity for industrial development as well as increasing people's general quality of life.

Nasser negotiated funding for the High Dam from the World Bank, with a substantial contribution coming from the United States and a lesser one from Britain. The United States supported the project at first because it provided a means to counterbalance what was perceived to be growing communist bloc influence in Egypt, but reservations and opposition emerged. The astringent American secretary of state, John Foster Dulles, saw the geopolitical situation as a Manichaean struggle of good against evil, with the United States representing the former and the Soviet Union the latter. Such a view allowed no in-between position. Dulles was still annoyed by Nasser's opposition to the Baghdad Pact, and the man who had so notoriously refused to shake hands with Chou En-lai at the Geneva Conference in 1954 was highly displeased by Nasser's diplomatic recognition of communist China. Meanwhile, the Zionist lobby was exerting negative pressure on the US Senate, where southern members worried that irrigated Egyptian cotton might compete with one of the staple crops of their region. Conditions for support were imposed, so many that Nasser believed they infringed Egyptian economic sovereignty, but he reluctantly agreed to them all, only to be told by Dulles that the United States was withdrawing the deal.

Dulles thought that would be the end of the matter, but Nasser responded quickly and boldly. On 26 July 1956, thereafter celebrated as a national holiday in Egypt, he announced the nationalization of the Suez Canal. Egypt would build the High Dam with profits from operating the canal. The British government was outraged, but having withdrawn its last troops from the canal zone a few months earlier, the only thing it could do was to have the Suez Canal Company's European pilots walk off the job in the expectation that traffic would come to a stop. Instead, the few Egyptian pilots who remained, forty out of a force of more than two hundred, carried on so valiantly that the canal continued to operate. The British prime minister Anthony Eden longed to use force against Egypt, but it took time to move military units into position; besides, there was insufficient justification: the canal was open, the world's commerce was moving through it, and most nations affirmed the right of a state to nationalize institutions within its borders.

In collusion with Israel and France (which was angry with Nasser for his support of Algerian rebels), Eden invented a pretext to invade Egypt and seize control of the canal. According to the scenario, Israel would attack, seize Gaza and Sharm al-Sheikh on the tip of the Sinai Peninsula (desirable because it would open the approach to the southern Israeli port of Eilat), and advance to the Suez Canal. Britain and France would then issue an ultimatum to both sides to withdraw from the canal. Israel, having obtained Gaza and Sharm al-Sheikh, would comply, but Egypt could be counted on to refuse, whereupon Britain and France would attack Egypt, seize the canal, and depose Nasser. That plan was implemented by an Israeli attack on 29 October; the ultimatum was delivered the following day. When Egypt refused it, the British and French assault began. Nasser was taken by surprise, and the Egyptian army driven back. Everything was working as planned.

Then Eden's scheme began to unravel. Though defeated, Egyptian forces fought tenaciously, winning sympathy around the world. The Egyptians also sank ships in the canal, blocking it and cutting oil shipments to Europe. International opinion was overwhelmingly critical of the invasion. The Soviet Union threatened a nuclear attack on London, but more realistically used the commotion in the Middle East to distract attention while it brutally crushed an uprising in its satellite Hungary. The United Nations condemned the British, French, and Israeli action—

as did the United States, for President Eisenhower was furious, having been led to believe that a diplomatic approach was being pursued. He complained, "The US was not consulted in any phase of these actions, which can scarcely be reconciled with the principles and purposes of the United Nations." In Britain, support for the government rapidly eroded in parliament, where Eden was forced to lie about the degree to which the plan had been premeditated. When loss of oil supplies caused a run on the pound sterling, the United States made it clear that it would not intervene in support. The weakness of the British position was exposed, leaving Eden with no choice but to call off the invasion. France and Israel, who might have persevered had they acted without Britain, had to follow suit.

In retaliation for what became known as the War of the Tripartite Aggression in Egypt, the Egyptian government sequestered all French and British property. Citizens of those countries who were resident in Egypt were ordered to pack one suitcase and depart immediately; those abroad, as many were during the summer, were not allowed to return. The Suez Canal did not reopen until March 1957. Its closure probably did more economic harm to Britain than to Egypt. Nasser certainly emerged from the crisis confirmed in power at home—and indeed was energized into his socialist, anti-Western phase—and his reputation was greatly enhanced abroad. Eden, who had intended to topple Nasser, was himself forced to resign, replaced by Harold Macmillan, initially a strong supporter of the invasion but also an adroit politician who knew how to shift his stance effectively.

Despite Nasser's assertions at the beginning of the Suez Crisis, revenues from the Suez Canal were insufficient to pay for the High Dam's construction costs, nor did Egypt possess adequate technical resources to build it. Funding and engineering were provided by the Soviet Union, which thought it could extend its influence in Egypt, a calculation that turned out to be somewhat over-optimistic in the long run. In 1958 the Soviets announced their support for the monumental project. Ninety thousand Egyptian workers provided the labor. Construction began in 1960. Four years later, shortly before he was ousted from power, the Soviet premier Nikita Khrushchev visited to celebrate completion of the first stage of work, and the reservoir began to fill, ending the annual inundations of the Nile in Egypt. The dam was completed in 1970; the reservoir reached capacity in 1976.

The Aswan High Dam far exceeds any other dam in the world in magnitude. With a length of 3,600 meters, 980 meters wide at its base, and 111 meters high, it contains more than forty-four million cubic meters of material, a volume equal to eighteen Great Pyramids—an appropriate comparison for those who thought Nasser had pharaonic tendencies. The reservoir, named Lake Nasser after Nasser's death, contains 169 billion cubic meters of water, equal to two years' flow of the Nile; it extends 550 kilometers to the south, through all of Egyptian Nubia, past the Second Cataract (which it submerged), and well into Sudan. Virtually the entire population of Egyptian Nubia had to be relocated. Concerted international effort led by UNESCO (United Nations Educational, Scientific, and Cultural Organization) rescued a number of major ancient monuments, including Abu Simbel, which was re-sited on higher ground, and conducted extensive emergency salvage archaeology, but the archaeological loss from the obliteration of ancient Nubia is incalculable.

Other negative effects of the High Dam include loss of water through seepage and evaporation. Most of the millions of tons of nutrient-rich silt that the annual inundation used to deposit on fields downstream falls to the bottom of Lake Nasser as sediment. Chemical fertilizer must be used on the fields, which also suffer from increased salinity now that they are no longer washed by the inundation. All along the river valley there have been difficulties caused by a rising water table resulting from a more constant level of the Nile; the shoreline of the Delta has deteriorated, and the fishing industry in the adjacent Mediterranean waters has been devastated. All of this is not the exclusive fault of the High Dam, however, for perennial irrigation had already had a negative impact, as had the lesser dams and barrages constructed earlier on the Nile. Significant increases were feared in waterborne diseases such as schistosomiasis, but for the most part these have not materialized.

Although many writers (this one included) often complain about the High Dam, present-day Egypt is inconceivable without it. The dam has unquestionably caused many problems, but a careful cost-benefit analysis showed that the advantages far outweighed the disadvantages, and that has largely proved true. The High Dam has increased the amount of arable land in Egypt by nearly a million hectares; Upper Egypt now produces three crops a year instead of one; and ten billion kilowatt hours per year have been added to the Egyptian electrical grid. Almost all Egyptian villages have electricity. At the beginning of the twenty-first century, about one-third of Egypt's electricity is provided by the High Dam. The dam proved its worth almost immediately, when the great droughts of the 1970s and 1980s brought famine to many African nations. Egypt was able to draw on the reservoir and maintain a constant supply of water to its fields. Conversely, Egypt was spared the damaging consequences of excessively high floods, including that of 1975, the third highest on record.

The Revolutionary Command Council faded as a political force in the aftermath of the Suez Crisis. Some of its members continued to hold high offices and retained influence—Nasser's old henchman Abd al-Hakim Amer, for example, was particularly important—but it was individual influence, not collective. Power was now firmly consolidated in Nasser's hands. The long-promised new constitution had finally been drafted and approved by the country. It provided for a wide suffrage and a representative assembly, but there was little that was democratic in the new system: the assembly was consultative, not legislative, and political parties were banned. Only the state-controlled National Unity Party was allowed to exist. Nasser was elected as president with 99.9 percent of the vote in a plebiscite in June 1956. He was the only candidate, but there was no question of his popularity, and following Suez he was riding the crest of a wave. Yet, although Nasser was president, his power and position actually transcended that of any institutional office. He was *al-Rais*, the Leader, the Man in Charge. As one prominent Egyptian scholar reflected in later years, "the executive, legislative and judicial, even the fourth power, that of the press, were fused. They became the four arms of the Leader in whom was the will of the State."

Consolidation of power enabled Nasser to embark on major programs that ultimately transformed the Egyptian government and economy. The 1956 Constitution promised social welfare to Egyptians. Nasser made good on that promise by establishing a minimum wage, making health care more widely available, and constructing subsidized housing for low-income families. Education was vastly expanded. Yet in almost every area, problems in financing, staffing, and implementation severely limited the benefits of these initiatives.

The situation in education is illustrative. Under Nasser, enrollments in primary schools tripled, although they still reached only about two-thirds of eligible students. Secondary enrollments increased by a factor of eight, and the number of university students rose to nearly five times what it had been in 1952. Obviously there were some benefits; approximately half of all Egyptians were literate by the time of Nasser's death. But the increase in numbers was not matched by increased funding, construction of new facilities, or new faculty hires. Classrooms were grossly overcrowded. University standards plummeted. Faculty salaries remained dismally low. Many Egyptian professors eventually went abroad in search of better opportunities. And where were the swelling numbers of university graduates, or those of the secondary schools for that matter, to find the jobs for which their education raised their expectations?

Nasser's attempts to address Egypt's economic problems can be divided into two phases. The first, which featured state supervision, began in 1957. The resolution of the Suez Crisis put Egypt well on the way to a mixed economy with the nationalization of the canal and extensive sequestration of numerous British and French properties, including large business holdings such as those of Barclays Bank and Credit Lyonnais. The High Dam project also deepened government involvement in economic development. The Economic Development Organization was established in 1957 to supervise these concerns and create new ones, with authorization to make necessary capital investments. The large Helwan steel works began under its auspices. State ownership of business increased significantly, but there was still room for private commercial activity, as Nasser made clear: "When the state intervenes in industry," he said, "it does not mean at all that it is the only capitalist."

One might have expected a rapprochement between Egypt and the United States following the Suez Crisis, but that did not occur for many reasons. Nasser could be a difficult, headstrong person who was not always easy to work with. His rambunctious diplomacy in the Middle East caused serious concern in the United States and among its Western allies, especially Britain. Increasing enmity between Egypt and Israel hindered better relations between Cairo and Washington because Israel had strong political support in America. But one of the most serious problems was the perception that Egypt was furthering the interests of the Soviet Union and the spread of communism, even slipping into the Soviet sphere of influence. Nasser reinforced that impression by establishing commercial relations with the Russians, trading Egyptian cotton for Soviet arms, and accelerating the pace of his socialist programs within Egypt. And as far as the American secretary of state Dulles was concerned, Nasser's espousal of nonalignment could only further Soviet aims, for in Dulles's polarized view, anyone who was not with the West was against it.

Deeper analysis would have revealed a more complex picture. Nasser, as he had publicly stated, would have preferred to purchase his arms from the West, but they were not forthcoming. Also, his relations with the Soviet Union were not nearly as warm as Washington assumed. Some of his disagreements with Moscow were intensely acrimonious, and he steadfastly refused to allow Russian troops on Egyptian soil. The extent of Soviet influence in the entire Middle East was usually overestimated. Washington strategists did not always realize that nations like Syria, Iraq, and Egypt, all perceived to be in the Russian camp at one time or another, were just playing their communist patrons for all they were worth. As one frustrated Soviet diplomat said of his alleged Syrian clients, "They take everything from us except advice."

As for Egyptian socialism, and Arab socialism in general, it was hardly of the Soviet or Marxist variety. Rejecting ideas of class struggle, the Arab socialists had a non-doctrinaire conviction that there were better ways to produce and distribute resources, and that these could be achieved through state management. As Muslims, Arab socialists were adamantly opposed to the atheism of Soviet communism, which never had much of a chance in the Middle East. Eisenhower and Dulles, however, saw the region as a field ripe for communist advancement. For that reason, the Eisenhower Doctrine was promulgated in January 1957. It promised military aid to any Middle Eastern nation threatened with aggression by a country that was controlled by "international communism." That could easily be construed to apply to the pan-Arabist ambitions of Egypt, as Nasser clearly understood.

Not that he cared. In a speech to the Egyptian people in November 1956, Nasser had asserted, "Whenever Washington speaks, I shall tell them, 'Perish in your fury.' Death is preferable to humiliation." Nasser's position as a pan-Arab leader, already established by the arms purchase from the communist bloc, soared in the wake of Suez. "I do not think of myself as a leader of the Arab world," he disingenuously told a foreign journalist. "But the Arab peoples feel that what we do in Egypt reflects their collective hopes and aspirations." Egypt was indeed a good base from which Nasser could champion the cause of pan-Arabism. The Constitution of 1956 stated that Egypt was an Arab country and part of the Arab nation. (That, it might be noted, officially marked a major point of departure: twenty years earlier, few Egyptians would have considered themselves Arab.) The Arab League was headquartered in Cairo. Egypt's lead in publishing, cinema, and broadcasting provided the means to disseminate Nasser's message, much to the fury of his many Arab enemies and rivals. Not just in Egypt but in many parts of the Arab world there were claques of adulatory fans cheering Nasser on, believing—and making him believe—that he had the solutions, when in fact he was making it up as he went along.

As the outstanding advocate of Arab nationalism, Nasser experienced some exalting moments and abysmal failures. The idea of a union with Syria was actually not his but that of a new Syrian regime that needed political cover and turned to Nasser. This invitation, coming from the nation most notable for pan-Arabism in the Middle East, was difficult to refuse. Nasser accepted, but largely on his terms: full union, and he would be firmly in charge. The United Arab Republic was accordingly proclaimed on 1 February 1958.

Welcomed with great enthusiasm by the Syrian people, the formation of the UAR created a sensation throughout the Middle East. For a moment, it seemed that Nasser, Nasserism, and his brand of pan-Arabism might sweep the region. In Lebanon, which most Syrians considered to be a rightful part of Syria, pro-Nasser demonstrations, incited by Nasser's agents, broke out among Muslims who looked to Nasser against their Maronite Christian opponents. Palestinians saw the UAR as a prelude to the restoration of their homeland. Yemen formally joined the UAR in March, though its participation never went beyond lip service.

But other Arab nations reacted with dismay, and Western attitudes were hostile. King Saud of Saudi Arabia went so far as to bribe a Syrian to assassinate Nasser, one of several stupid acts that eventually cost him his throne. Jordan and Iraq hastily formed a counter-union, an act that was fiercely denounced by Nasser and that was undone on 14 June 1958, when a brutal coup overthrew the pro-Western Iraqi monarchy. There was serious talk of Iraq joining the UAR, but self-interest prevailed when its new leader, Abd al-Karim Qasim, reflected on the immense oil wealth of his country and decided not to share it with Egypt's tens of millions. The Christian president of Lebanon, Camille Chamoun, took refuge in the Eisenhower Doctrine. In response to his request, the United States sent army and marine detachments to Lebanon in July 1958 to shore up the situation. Jordan's King Husein faced down his pro-Nasser officers, though he felt compelled to call in the British army for additional support, a measure that must have been especially humiliating, since he had dismissed his British commander of the Arab Legion, Sir John Glubb Pasha, just two years earlier. But had it not been for US marines and British paratroopers, Lebanon and Jordan might well have found themselves members of Nasser's United Arab Republic.

The union between Egypt and Syria presented numerous difficulties. The countries had widely differing political, economic, and social circumstances. They were separated by nearly a thousand kilometers with a hostile nation, Israel, squarely in between. Neighboring countries were mostly opposed to the union. It would have taken unusual political skill and careful diplomacy to make the United Arab Republic work. As it was, Egypt's handling of the UAR could hardly have been more maladroit.

The Syrians had reasonably expected to play a major if not quite equal role in the UAR. Nasser was the president, Syria's Shukri al-Kuwatli the vice president. A unified national assembly was composed of three hundred Egyptians and a hundred Syrians. But it soon became clear that Egypt was going to rule its 'northern province' in an arbitrary manner. In the government, Egypt kept the major ministerial portfolios of defense and foreign affairs; the Syrians, who had hoped to have at least one of those, were fobbed off with lesser posts. A cumbrous, Egyptian-style bureaucracy was imposed on Syria, heavily staffed by Egyptians. Syrian political parties were abolished, local political figures pushed aside. The Syrian army was frustrated by Egyptian domination of the military. And although Syria was probably a more advanced socialist society than Egypt, it also had a much more highly developed capitalist sector, which was hampered by increasingly stringent Egyptian controls, culminating in the July Laws of 1961. A coincidental spell of droughts and the closing of the border with Lebanon in response to UAR-inspired troubles compounded economic woes. Many Syrians were disappointed that other nations did not join the UAR. Nasser's appointment of his long-time Free Officer friend Abd al-Hakim Amer as special commissioner in Syria was extremely counterproductive.

By 1961, every center of power in Syria—the Baath Party, the business community, the bureaucracy, and the military—had had enough of the UAR. When Nasser finally recognized the problems and attempted to improve Syria's role in the union in August, it was far too late to save the situation. The Syrian army staged a coup on 28 September 1961 and proclaimed the end of the UAR. Nasser, who still enjoyed a high degree of popularity in Syria, briefly considered using military force, but thought better of it. He blamed Syrian capitalist influences for the split, but no one had done more to bring it about than himself, as he may have realized. "It should have been made gradually over a number of years," he said on reflection. When Syria and Iraq, after experiencing further coups, approached him two years later with ideas about reviving and extending the UAR, Nasser committed himself cautiously so that he was not embarrassed when the union failed to materialize.

Just as the union with Syria was coming unstuck, Nasser's economic policy entered its most radical phase. The failure of the UAR may have impelled him to stronger measures, but given Nasser's penchant for controlling things, it was inevitable that he should tighten his grip on Egypt's economy. Intimations of change had been present for some time. The slogan of the UAR was "Freedom, socialism, unity." The Economic Development Program had been steadily extending the state's reach, through stricter licensing of private businesses and creation of new, state-owned enterprises. In 1959, the first five-year plan was announced. Nasser's objective was to double the national income. His experts told him it would take at least twenty years; he said it had to be done in ten. Even so, few can have anticipated the sweeping changes that Nasser had in mind. The Free Officers' seizure of power in 1952 had been a military coup; the revolution began with the July Laws of 1961.

These measures nationalized most of Egypt's factories, banks, insurance companies, transport facilities, import-export companies, large hotels, print and broadcast media, and many other areas of the economy. Those left outside of state ownership were brought under comprehensive regulation. A salary cap of LE 5,000 was imposed. Incomes greater than LE 10,000 were subjected to a confiscatory rate of taxation. The property of the six hundred wealthiest families in Egypt was sequestered. Many were arrested and imprisoned. Henceforth, no individual was permitted to own more than one hundred feddans of land; the rest was to be distributed to landless peasants. All foreign-owned agricultural land was sequestered. Altogether, the state seized some three hundred businesses in 1961. Another round of nationalization in 1963 brought in three hundred more.

After a final series of decrees in 1964, the state's takeover of the economy was complete. The power of the old landowning aristocracy was broken once and for all. But many once-affluent families were subjected to needless humiliation and hardship. The break in continuity was severe—economically, politically, and socially. So much of the previous system, which had not been totally dysfunctional or impervious to reform, was dismantled that it would be impossible to go back. Most of the politically active members of the old regime were sidelined, and many of their institutions dismantled. Nasser was betting heavily that his experiment would work, and in the long run its results would be dismally disappointing.

In the short run, it was possible to point to gains in productivity, employment, and incomes, but over the long haul, the government-owned businesses were a drag on the economy. They never made money and had to be heavily subsidized. The bureaucracy expanded rapidly, then was further bloated when Nasser attempted to meet the expectations of the burgeoning numbers of university graduates by guaranteeing them all jobs, if necessary in the government or in the public sector of the economy. The number of government workers in 1967 was 1.5 million.

A more sinister aspect of government expansion was the proliferation and intrusion of the security and intelligence services, collectively known as the *mukhabarat*. Nasser's first concern was to guard against plotting in the army, but the security services were pervasive throughout society as well, to the point that *bawwab*s, or doormen, were required to report on the activities of people within their buildings. Contact with foreigners was regarded with particular suspicion and could be extremely dangerous. The 1965 trial and conviction of Mustafa Amin, the former publisher of *al-Akhbar*, for being a US spy was not an isolated incident. Although foreign tourists were still encouraged to come to Egypt and spend their urgently needed hard currency, they were strictly prohibited from going beyond areas like Cairo and Luxor, the site of ancient Thebes. Travel abroad was restricted for Egyptians; even applications for purposes such as a course of study in a Western university were likely to be refused. The effect was stifling. People were afraid to speak openly. Nor were their fears groundless. Arbitrary arrests and imprisonments occurred constantly. Torture and even death might be the lot of those who fell into the hands of the *mukhabarat*. No one could hide from watchful eyes. Nasser received reports on even his highest and closest associates. Having risen to power through secrecy, conspiracy, and dissimulation, he maintained those characteristics, indeed strengthened them, even after there was no serious threat to his position. Portraits, busts, and statues of Nasser became ubiquitous, reinforcing a sense of constant observation.

The dissolution of the union with Syria and the sweeping economic changes within Egypt meant that a new constitution had to be prepared. Nasser made a number of liberal gestures: martial law was lifted (though it was reimposed the following day in a different guise), and the Muslim Brothers, who had languished in prison for a decade, were released and permitted to resume their propaganda. But there was little democratic substance to the Constitution of 1964. Virtually all power and initiative remained in the presidency. There was an elected National Assembly, but at most it could censure the government or one of its ministers; the president could dissolve it at will. Nasser's authority was unchallenged. In the ensuing plebiscite, he received the usual 99.9 percent of the vote.

Another post-UAR innovation was the creation of the Arab Socialist Union (ASU) to replace the National Unity Party. The ASU was a monolithic combination of state party and national bureaucracy, whose representation, including elected "farmers and workers," was to provide a bridge between the government and the increasingly nationalized economy while outlining national policy, thereby putting it into an ambiguous relationship with the National Assembly. Its tightly knit pyramidal structure reached directly from the president's office right down to the village level, providing multiple connections throughout the economy and society. Instead of becoming a deliberative, consultative body, however, the ASU primarily served as a medium for the central government to impose its policies. Although he instituted the ASU, Nasser came to regard it as a potentially threatening power base and treated it with suspicion, as did his successor Anwar al-Sadat.

Nasser could make the electorate respond to his will, but he was less successful with the economy. The years 1965–66 were a prolonged economic crisis, in part because of the transformation wrought by the July Laws. The new organization in the countryside was not working well. Many of the state-owned businesses required heavy subsidies, and the establishment of new ones needed investment capital, something Egypt always had difficulty mobilizing. Meanwhile, political considerations demanded that more money be put into services like housing. Prices had to be stabilized, wages bumped up. The ever expanding bureaucracy took a big bite, while military expenditures soaked up a quarter of the budget. Egypt could not meet those expenses through internal taxation; it was necessary to borrow heavily abroad, creating serious balance of payments problems. By 1967, the debt stood at two billion dollars.

The situation was made even worse by a Western economic boycott of Egypt. Relations between the United States and Egypt, which had not been altogether bad under Presidents Eisenhower and Kennedy, soured under Lyndon Johnson, who terminated the shipments of surplus American wheat that had helped make up for Egypt's growing agricultural shortfall, another new and troublesome economic development. The prime minister, Zakariya Muhi al-Din, took the extreme step of easing emigration controls, beginning the mass exodus of Egyptian workers abroad, a situation that continues to the present. This relieved some of unemployment pressure, and remittances from the expatriated workers became a major component of the Egyptian economy, but it also meant a constant drain of valuable skills that might have been put to use at home.

Although it was kept secret from the public, Nasser's health was deteriorating. He may have suffered a mild heart attack in the summer of 1965. Then in August it was suddenly announced that a plot by the Muslim Brotherhood to kill him and several senior ministers had been uncovered. Perhaps there really was a conspiracy—given the conditions in the country, there must have been some clandestine opposition—but Nasser had a way of lashing out when his programs ran into trouble, expressing his personal frustration and diverting public anger over his failures from himself to other targets. More than 220 Muslim Brothers were arrested; seven, including Sayid Qutb, were hanged for treason. But Nasser's rage was not confined to the Muslim Brotherhood. Alleged communists were arrested, as were 'feudalists' in the countryside.

In addition to deteriorating health and mounting economic and political concerns, Nasser was increasingly mired in another foreign misadventure. Egypt's union with Yemen had ended with the United Arab Republic debacle. It was never more than a matter of form anyway, and Yemen's intensely conservative ruler, Imam Ahmed, had been openly critical of Nasser's policies. For some time, this isolated nation on the southwestern corner of the Arabian Peninsula had become increasingly unstable, as progressive elements pressed for modernization. When Imam Ahmed died on 19 September 1962, a group of army officers led by General Abdallah al-Sallal staged a violent coup, quite possibly with Egyptian encouragement. It was thought that the Imam's successor, Crown Prince Muhammad al-Badr, had been killed. The officers con- stituted themselves as a Revolutionary Council. They executed all the royalist leaders they could find and appealed to Nasser for help against what they claimed were just a few diehard reactionary elements.

Nasser was sympathetic. The situation in Yemen, about which he was poorly informed, appeared similar to the one in Egypt when he took power. Also, it was an opportunity to extend his influence in the Arabian Peninsula, an especially inviting prospect since Yemen was located right next to Britain's great base at Aden. With a small invest- ment of soldiers and material support, Nasser thought he could sustain the fledgling regime, enhance his pan-Arab credentials, which had been tarnished by the failure of the UAR, and counter the influence of his favorite Western adversary.

It was a serious miscalculation, as he later admitted. Al-Badr had not been killed; he had fled into the mountainous interior of Yemen, where loyal tribesmen rallied to his cause and continued the fight. The royalist regimes of Saudi Arabia and Jordan, determined to resist the spread of Nasserite republicanism (and long annoyed by the hostile propaganda emanating from "Voice of the Arabs" radio programs from Cairo), lent generous assistance to them. So to some degree did Britain, Israel, and Iran, none of whom were friends to pan-Arabism. By the end of 1963, twenty thousand Egyptian troops were fighting in Yemen; a year later there were seventy thousand, fully one-third of the Egyptian army, and no end was in sight. If Egypt withdrew, al-Sallal's regime would be defeated.

Early on, Nasser began looking for a way out and proposed to withdraw from Yemen if Jordan would do the same, but the Jordanian and Saudi regimes were not about to cooperate: if Nasser withdrew unilaterally, his pan-Arab reputation would be further damaged; if he stayed, he would be that much less likely to cause trouble elsewhere as he expended resources on what was clearly a hopeless struggle. Using guerrilla tactics and operating on home terrain, al-Badr and his men were more than able to hold their own against an inefficient Egyptian army led by Nasser's corrupt, incompetent henchman Abd al-Hakim Amr. The Yemeni war eventually cost Egypt ten thousand men and an immense amount of money it could ill afford before a settlement was finally arranged that enabled Egypt to withdraw from Yemen in 1968.

What extricated Nasser from Yemen was the incomparably worse disaster of the war with Israel in June 1967. Although the struggle against Israel in 1948 was a major factor in Nasser's political radicalization, he was realist enough to accept the *fait accompli* of the establishment of the new nation, and he thought it had some progressive qualities that corrupt Arab regimes would do well to copy. An incipient dialogue developed. But soon a more hawkish government came to power in Israel, while Egypt was drawn into the general Arab opposition to Israel that was intensified by the festering Palestinian problem. Nasser's claim to the mantle of leader of the Arabs meant that he would be involved in any developments, even those that did not directly affect Egypt. As he repeated in 1960, "We can never relinquish the rights of the Palestinian people, because, as I said in the past, the honor of the Palestine people is the honor of the Arab nation." The Suez War in 1956 had hardened the adversarial attitude between Egypt and Israel, but it also greatly diminished the prospect of another full-scale war between the two countries because of the insertion of a United Nations Emergency Force (UNEF) on their shared border. And although Nasser's rhetoric about Israel became increasingly strident over the years as he denounced it as an imperialist outpost and called for the liberation of Palestine, he did not necessarily advocate its absolute destruction. Had Egypt pursued a policy more focused on its own interests, perhaps a more constructive policy toward Israel would have evolved; as it was, Nasser's prominence as an Arab leader severely limited his freedom of action.

Nasser's opposition to Israel was mostly confined to strident statements as he sought to maintain his ascendancy within the Arab world, but in early 1966, a new faction of officers came to power in Syria and began supporting Palestinian raids into Israel from Jordan. This resulted in severe retaliation by Israel against a Jordanian town in November 1966. The Syrians shelled Israeli communities in Galilee from their commanding position on the Golan Heights; in an aerial dogfight over Damascus in April 1967, several Syrian MIGs were downed. Soon afterward, Syria and Egypt established a joint military command, pledging to stand together if there was a war with Israel. Nasser thought the alliance would enable him to restrain Syria; instead, it put him at the mercy of events beyond his control.

In May 1967, the Soviet Union, for reasons that remain unclear, informed Syria that an Israeli attack was imminent. The Syrians called on Nasser to make good on his pledge. Even though the best part of his army was far away in Yemen, Nasser felt obliged to respond. His trusted friend Abd al-Hakim Amer, commander of the armed forces as well as vice president of the republic, assured him that the Egyptian military was prepared. Nasser probably calculated that war would not be necessary; just the threat of having to fight on two fronts ought to be enough to dissuade the Israelis from attacking Syria. International pressure from the United States and the Soviet Union (he thought) would prevent things from getting out of hand. He moved Egyptian forces into Sinai where UNEF forces stood between the Egyptians and Israelis. The Jordanians and Saudis jeered at him for hiding behind the UN troops, and he needed to do something to signal pressure on Israel, so he requested the UN secretary general U Thant to withdraw *some* of them; U Thant responded by withdrawing them *all*, something Nasser definitely did not anticipate. Somewhat hesitantly the Egyptian army took up the vacated positions, and Nasser announced the reimposition of the naval blockade on the Gulf of Aqaba, threatening Israel's supply of oil from Iran. On 30 May, Jordan and Egypt arranged joint military command. Israel began mobilizing for war.

The intentions of Egypt and Israel preceding the 1967 War have been interpreted in widely different ways. Nasser's rhetoric was bellicose—"We are burning like hot coals in expectation of the battle"—but he insisted that Egypt would not strike the first blow, and his actions were more ambiguous than his words. Even as he imposed the naval blockade, which never had substance, Egyptian diplomats at the UN were seeking a compromise to get around it. When the war began, Nasser was not on the verge of attacking Israel. By the same token, some assert that Israel acted purely in self-defense against a lethal, encircling alliance of implacable enemies, while others hold that the Israelis' plans were expansionist from the beginning. One thing is certain: on the morning of 5 July, Egypt was not on the verge of attacking Israel. It was Israel that struck first.

Egypt was totally unprepared. Within the first hour of the war, its air force was destroyed, mostly as the planes sat on the runways. It is said that the Egyptians did not even have their radar turned on. Deprived of air cover, the Egyptian army was helpless, exposed to a relentless air assault as it retreated across Sinai under a rain of napalm and pinpoint strikes. There was relatively little left for the Israeli army to do as it quickly advanced to the east bank of the Suez Canal. On other fronts, the Israelis took the entire West Bank, including East Jerusalem, from Jordan and captured the Golan Heights from Syria. When Egypt accepted the UN Security Council's call for a cease-fire on 8 June, it had lost all of Sinai; twenty thousand Egyptian soldiers were dead and at least another five thousand captured or missing; and almost its entire air force had been wiped out along with other heavy losses in matériel such as tanks and artillery. The calamity was made all the worse for Egypt by nonsensical reports of extraordinary victories that were broadcast throughout the collapse.

Nasser was devastated. He may have been sincere when he addressed his nation on 9 June, although the event could not have been scripted better. Taking responsibility for the defeat, he told the Egyptian people that he was no longer worthy of leading them and that he was resigning the presidency. His place would be taken by the prime minister, Zakariya Muhi al-Din, one of the original Free Officers. The response was instantaneous. People filled the streets chanting, "We want Nasser!" A vast throng numbering in the hundreds of thousands, and including Muhi al-Din, converged on Nasser's neighborhood in the Cairo suburb of Heliopolis, demanding that he remain in office.

The outpouring of popular support was gratifying, but it also imposed the heavy burden of finding some way out of the mess. Nasser's primary concern, as always, was to remain in control. Despite their support for him, the Egyptian people were dismayed when they learned just how bad the defeat had been and demanded an accounting for it. Student unrest was unusually tumultuous. Nasser partially assuaged public anger at the failings of the military by sacking some thousand officers—an action that enabled him to get rid of dissident elements. Nasser's long-time associate Abd al-Hakim Amr, to whose failings he had so long turned a blind eye, finally fell. According to official reports, he committed suicide after being placed under house arrest; according to rumor, he was murdered. When continuing resentment erupted into labor and student demonstrations, the first since the Naguib crisis in 1954, Nasser confronted the demonstrators personally and made liberalizing concessions in his 30 March Program of 1968. When all was said and done, however, Nasser was still unwilling to go far with political liberalization, and things remained much as they had been before. Although his political stature was certainly diminished by what he called the *nakba* or 'setback' of 1967, Nasser emerged from a catastrophe that could easily have ended any political leader's career with his authority largely intact.

Even so, it was a difficult time. Egypt teetered on the brink of bankruptcy. With the Suez Canal closed, there were no hard currency receipts from that source; tourists stopped coming; half of Egypt's oil production was in Israeli hands; crops were bad. Subsidies from Saudi Arabia, Kuwait, and Libya kept the Egyptian economy afloat. Meanwhile, Nasser's health continued to deteriorate. Seriously ill, he had to go to Moscow for extended medical treatment during the summer of 1968; the country was told he had a bad case of flu. In September of the following year, he had a serious heart attack that forced him to take six weeks away from work. He returned to renewed student protests, much better organized and more intense than before. This time he responded firmly with a crackdown.

At the Khartoum Conference of Arab countries following the defeat in June 1967, the participants pledged themselves to act jointly against

Israel and not to negotiate one-on-one with it. "No war, no peace, no recognition" was the approach. Egypt was promised money to offset losses for canal closures, and by agreeing to withdraw from Yemen it ended the financial hemorrhage there. But when Nasser, hard-pressed by continuing military clashes with Israel, asked the Arab nations for material aid and genuine solidarity in his struggle at another summit in Rabat in December 1969, he received virtually nothing, forcing him to turn to the Soviet Union for help. It came at a price. For the first time, Soviet military personnel were stationed in Egypt. By 1970, Egypt's material losses had been made good, and then some.

Since direct negotiations with Israel were out of the question, Nasser turned to international diplomacy. The most that was accomplished was UN Security Council resolution 242, which called for Israel to withdraw from the territories it had taken in the 1967 War, for recognition of every state to existence within securely recognized borders, and for a solution to the refugee problem. When that brought no tangible results, Nasser launched his War of Attrition in March 1969, calculating that Israel would be worn down by ongoing clashes along the Suez front that would compel it to maintain an unsustainable level of combat readiness. But although Egypt could conceivably hold its own in artillery duels across the canal, Israel could hit the Egyptian positions with air strikes and conduct bombing raids deep into Egyptian territory. The towns of Ismailia, Port Said, and Suez were devastated; a million people had to be evacuated.

Egypt came away the worse from the War of Attrition, but it brought increased international involvement in a settlement. In 1969, Lyndon Johnson was succeeded as president of the United States by Richard Nixon, who wanted a "more evenhanded policy" in the Middle East. The Rogers Peace Plan, named for Nixon's secretary of state, was an initiative broadly based on resolution 242. It was attractive to Nasser because it offered the eventual prospect of return of lost territories without war and the immediate relief of a much-needed cease-fire with Israel. He accepted the Rogers Plan on 23 July 1970. The cease-fire was implemented two weeks later; the War of Attrition was not renewed.

As one crisis was soothed, however, another was ignited. The Palestinians viewed Nasser's acceptance of the Rogers Plan as a sellout of their cause. Radical Palestinian terrorists stepped up their activities, using Jordan as their principal base of operations. After they hijacked several airplanes and destroyed them in Jordan, King Husein ordered full-scale military attacks on the Palestinian headquarters and several of their civilian camps in his country. Fighting was intense and loss of life extensive in what came to be known as Black September. Syria prepared to intervene in support of the Palestinians, an action that could have destroyed Husein's government and brought Israel and the United States into the conflict.

In this foreign policy crisis, the last of his career, Nasser in some measure lived up to his role as Arab leader. He convoked an Arab summit meeting in Cairo on 27 September. It is doubtful that anyone else could have accomplished what he did in preventing the ghastly confrontation between Jordan and the Palestinians from oscillating out of control. But the strain was too much. As soon as the meeting was finished on 28 September, he suffered a fatal heart attack. More than four million people filled the streets of Cairo for the funeral of Gamal Abd al-Nasser, the first truly native Egyptian ruler of Egypt in more than two thousand years.

19 Sadat

On the death of Nasser, Anwar al-Sadat became president of Egypt. In and out of political trouble and prison during the early part of his career, Sadat was one of the original Free Officers. During the Nasser years, he never fell from Nasser's favor, nor did he ever waver in his loyalty, to such an extent that he became widely regarded as a yes-man. He was rewarded with a number of high-level posts, culminating in his selection as vice president in December 1969. But it is thought that Nasser did not intend Sadat to be his successor, and many political insiders expected that he would not last long in the presidency, or at best that he would be the figurehead of a collective leadership.

Sadat proved to be much more able than anticipated, both as a politician and as head of state. The highest levels of government were filled with Nasserites, many of whom considered themselves more worthy to rule than Sadat, who may have lulled them into a false sense of security by initially retaining them in their positions; but the challenges and responses were not long in coming. When Sadat showed signs of too much independence, his opponents attempted to force his hand by resigning en masse. If they thought Sadat could not do without them, however, they were mistaken, for he merely accepted their resignations and replaced them with his own people, strengthening his position.

Sadat's most formidable opponent was Ali Sabri, a former prime minister and one of Sadat's vice presidents. More importantly, Sabri held the key post of chairman of the Arab Socialist Union, Egypt's sole political party, a highly organized institution that was central to the functioning of the regime. Sabri also was the leader of the ruling circle's left wing, of which Sadat was particularly suspicious. But Sabri's efforts to undermine Sadat within the ASU were skillfully countered by Sadat, who had once been its chairman and understood its inner workings well. Then, in May 1971, when Sadat felt the time was ripe, he launched his Corrective Revolution. He dismissed Sabri and had him arrested for treason. The following December, Sabri and ninety others, including senior ministers and the former heads of the armed services and the *mukhabarat*, were tried and convicted of attempting to overthrow the state. Sentences were stiff. Sabri was condemned to death, although Sadat commuted the sentence to life imprisonment and eventually pardoned and released him, but not before he had served ten years in prison. However insubstantial Sadat may have appeared at the beginning, he had two important cards in his hand. First, he was the president, and most Egyptians were willing to accept that constitutional and institutional fact of life rather than sail into uncharted political waters. The presidency also gave him powers of coercion that no other political figure could match. Second, Sadat took care to secure the support of the military, and at the end of the day, that was what mattered.

Having firmly established his authority, Sadat moved to lessen the sense of oppression and arbitrary rule that overlay Egypt. The process of sequestration, by which individuals could have their personal property taken from them on mere suspicion of disloyalty, was suspended. Some sequestered property was returned, and some compensation was paid. In a highly publicized gesture, Sadat burned recordings and transcripts of wiretapped telephone conversations. Nasser's elaborate internal security apparatus was dismantled. The process was partial and selective; no one was naive enough to think that the *mukhabarat* had ceased to function, nor did it; and Sadat was to demonstrate repeatedly that he could be very heavy-handed when it suited his purposes. But the change during the Sadat years was unmistakable as people began to speak their minds and associate more freely. The Egyptian press was still subservient, but not nearly to the same degree as before, and foreign journalists were no longer censored.

Without fanfare, indeed almost unnoticed, a process of de-Nasserization was put into motion. The prolific Egyptian cinema generated films indirectly critical of the old regime—and suggesting that things had changed for the better. The images of Nasser that had made him seem omnipresent began to disappear, to the point where he became conspicuous by his absence. The most important Egyptian monument named after him is Lake Nasser, the reservoir behind the High Dam; there is no major Nasser City (although a suburb of Cairo does bear that name), and his statues do not stand in prominent locations in Cairo. Even Sadat, once his most obsequious yes-man, was quietly critical, saying in 1975, "Abdel Nasser was a human being, so it is not belittling him to say that he did right things and he did wrong things."

Diminishing Nasser was part of a policy to enhance Sadat. Although his institutional power equaled, and sometimes exceeded, that of Nasser, Sadat was painfully aware that Nasser's authority rested not so much on institutions (he had no less than six constitutions during his sixteen years of undisputed power) but on personality. Nasser was a hard act to follow—an appropriate metaphor for Sadat, who had once wanted to be an actor and entitled his autobiography *Acteur manqué*. In effect, Sadat created two roles for himself and made sure they received maximum exposure. One was that of an unaffected countryman, the father of the village, the village being the Egyptian nation. But in the other role, he reveled in pageantry, seeking dignity and majesty by wearing ever more elaborate uniforms. It is said that the one he was wearing on the day he was killed was so over the top that people gasped when they saw it. These roles were contradictory, and ultimately they were unconvincing. In the short run, the Egyptian people relaxed and enjoyed the change from the high tension of the Nasser years, but in the long run they became tired of Sadat and eventually annoyed with him—and with his wife, Jehan, who also quickly developed an inordinate craving for the limelight, in stark contrast to her predecessor, Tahiya Nasser.

Another early change came in the area of religious policy, where Sadat lent encouragement and even support to conservative Islamic groups, including the Muslim Brotherhood. His strategy was to use them as political counterweights against the Left and the Nasserites, whom he thought posed the most serious challenge to him. He underestimated how quickly the Muslim organizations would grow in strength and stridency, and indeed contribute to his personal demise. By 1975, militant Muslim groups were winning student union elections at universities, prompting him to dissolve the student unions; in July 1977, Muslim terrorists kidnapped and murdered the minister of *waqfs*. Continuing social problems, especially among the less privileged strata of society, provided a fertile field for Islamic propaganda, as did Egypt's large conscript army, which was targeted for proselytizing by the Muslim Brotherhood. Sadat's security apparatus remained in control, but his unleashing of the religious Right had far-reaching consequences.

What was most notable about Sadat's presidency at the beginning, however, was its outward continuity with Nasser's policies. Pan-Arabism was still apparently high on the agenda. When a military coup brought Muammar Qaddafi to power in Libya in 1969, talks of another union of Arab nations began to circulate. Just two months after Nasser's death, it was announced that Libya, Sudan, and Egypt would begin planning a union of their nations. Sudan soon withdrew from the scheme, but Syria took its place so that a proposed Federation of Arab Republics was announced on 17 April 1971. Strong opposition to this from Ali Sabri and others was one of the ostensible reasons for the Corrective Revolution. Qaddafi was offering much, a full organic union with Egypt, and under Egyptian leadership. Set to go into effect on 1 September 1973, the Federation of Arab Republics never came to pass as relations went sour between Qaddafi and Sadat, who resented Qaddafi's meddling in Chad and Sudan and was outraged by assassinations of Qaddafi's political opponents who had taken refuge in Egypt. Eventually Egyptian–Libyan relations deteriorated into a short border war in 1977 and a prolonged period of vigilant hostility. Less sensational but more significant was Sadat's change of Egypt's official name from the United Arab Republic, which it had remained after the union with Syria was dissolved, to the Arab Republic of Egypt in May 1971. In retrospect, this was a signal that Egypt was moving toward putting its own interests first after decades of sacrifice in pursuit of the shimmering mirage of pan-Arabism.

By far the most pressing international concern was Israel, whose occupation of Sinai created a situation that was intolerable both politically and economically. Here too Sadat appeared to follow Nasser's lead by renewing the cease-fire but warning that significant progress had to be made. Hoping for increased involvement from the United States, he floated a proposal for reopening the Suez Canal in conjunction with a partial Israeli withdrawal, the first step to implementing resolution 242. The United States did not respond, and the Israeli prime minister called Sadat's proposal "an insult to our intelligence." Rebuffed, Sadat spoke of 1971 as the "Year of Decision." His repeated message was unequivocal. In his national address that year on the anniversary of the July Revolution, he promised, "We shall not allow 1971 to pass without deciding the issue, whether through peace or war—even if it means sacrificing one million lives." Yet 1971 came and went with no decision, Sadat's feeble explanation being that events had been enveloped in an international "fog." His strong declarations became matters of disbelief and derision, inadvertently providing camouflage for action when it finally came.

It appeared that Sadat would also follow Nasser's example in maintaining close relations with the Soviet Union—indeed, it was difficult to see how he could do otherwise. The Soviets were his source of arms; more than fifteen thousand Russian military personnel were stationed in Egypt, some of them pilots flying combat missions against the Israelis; Russians were to be found everywhere in the Egyptian government, including its most sensitive ministries; Moscow was Egypt's leading trading partner. Where else could Egypt turn? The country did not even have diplomatic relations with the United States, which was perceived as the staunch supporter of Israel. When Egypt and the Soviet Union signed a fifteen-year alliance in 1971, Egypt seemed more reliant on its communist ally than ever. Addressing the National Assembly in early May 1972, Sadat declared, "I shall take strong measures against people who criticize Egypt's major ally, Russia, rather than Cairo's enemy, the United States."

Therefore it came as a complete surprise to everyone in Egypt, the Soviet Union, and the West when Sadat ordered most of the Russians to leave on 18 July 1972, giving them two days to pack up and go. "We've done it, we've done it—we've got them out!" he shouted excitedly to his ministers. Sadat's popularity within Egypt soared. The Egyptians had never liked the Russians. Western analysts were perplexed: why had he done this without exploiting the opportunity to extract diplomatic gains from the United States? It seemed like an impulsive, irrational move. But there was much more to Sadat's decision than mere whim, for he had concluded that the Russians were not going to give him the increased level of armaments he needed to confront Israel and that they were neither willing nor able to provide the necessary diplomatic support for Egypt to recover its lost territories. Yet it was generally concluded that the expulsion of the Russians made war with Israel much less likely, since Egypt would be weaker without Russian support; few realized that Sadat was throwing off a constraint that hindered him from going to war.

In fact, he had little choice left. Bilateral negotiations with Israel were out of the question, and the options of the War of Attrition and international diplomacy had been exhausted. Israel was not just intransigent about withdrawal from Sinai; it was establishing settlements there and talking about many more. Time was running out. The military burden was unsustainable, particularly without revenue from tourism, the Suez Canal, or Sinai oil. Suspension of US wheat shipments meant that Egypt had to purchase grain on the world market with hard currency, of which it had precious little left. The Egyptian military was strained to breaking point by maintaining a high state of combat readiness. When Sadat decided to go to war, he was playing his last card in a gamble that would cost him everything if it failed.

Throughout 1972 Sadat often said that military action against Israel might be necessary, but people had heard that many times before; besides, he also spoke of his desire for peace. The two sentiments seemed contradictory. He was deadly serious about both. Having beefed up his military arsenal as much as possible before breaking with the Soviets, Sadat met several times during 1973 with Hafez al-Asad, who had recently come to power in Syria, to plan joint military action against Israel. Strict secrecy was maintained. Their former ally in 1967, Jordan's King Husein, was informed, as was Saudi Arabia's King Feisal, whose financial and diplomatic support was critical, but no one else. Qaddafi of Libya probably would have joined enthusiastically, but he was regarded as too unstable. The attack was set for the early morning of 6 October 1973. By a remarkable conjunction, this was both Yom Kippur, the Day of Atonement, one of the most important Jewish holidays of the year, and the anniversary of the Battle of Badr, in which the Prophet Muhammad and his Muslim followers won their first victory over their Meccan adversaries. That year, 6 October also fell within the Islamic month of Ramadan, the month of fasting, a time more associated with lethargy than decisive action. The major reason for choosing the date, however, was probably the fact that the moon would be nearly full, aiding the Egyptians when they crossed the Suez Canal.

This time it was the Israelis who were caught by surprise. Israeli intelligence did not detect the oncoming assault until just before it was delivered. There was not even time to alert the soldiers on the front. The Bar Lev Line, which the Israelis had constructed along the east bank of the Suez Canal, was a formidable barrier, more than twelve meters high in places, but it was lightly held. Well-trained Egyptian soldiers paddled across the canal in inflatable rafts under cover of a devastating artillery barrage and precision attacks by the Egyptian Air Force under the command of Hosni Mubarak. Israeli defenses were over-run and their tanks knocked out by bazooka teams. When the Israelis attempted to establish the air supremacy that had been decisive for them in 1967, they ran into a forest of surface-to-air missiles. High pressure pumps washed away the steep banks of the canal and high mounds of sand that the Israelis had erected as anti-tank barriers. (The European supplier had been puzzled why the Egyptians suddenly wanted to buy so many. Egyptian fire brigades needed them, was the answer.) Egyptian engineers quickly spanned the canal with pontoon bridges. Before the end of the first day of the war, more than five hundred tanks and five Egyptian divisions had firmly established themselves on the east bank at a depth of about ten kilometers into Sinai.

In the north, the Syrians also broke through the Israeli lines, recapturing much of the Golan Heights they had lost in 1967, but instead of invading Israel, they switched over to the defensive. Even so, the Israelis, fearing the close approach to their heartland and the restive Palestinian population in the occupied territories, first concentrated their forces against the Syrians, conducting air strikes throughout Syria and driving the Syrian army out of the newly retaken areas in fierce fighting. Not until 10 October were the Israelis able to devote most of their resources to Sinai, where heavy tank fighting began. This raises the interesting question of why the Egyptians had not advanced farther, seizing the strategic passes in the middle of the peninsula, and relieving some of the pressure on their Syrian allies. When an effort was finally made in that direction, it came too late, and the Israelis easily repulsed it at heavy cost to the Egyptians. Sadat's basic objective had been limited: to achieve enough military success and hold enough territory so that he could negotiate internationally from a position of strength. He was only just able to do so.

During the first days of the war, things had gone much better than the Egyptians could reasonably have expected. On 17 October, however, a small Israeli force led by Ariel Sharon, the future prime minister, slipped across the canal and established itself on the west, where a gap had opened between two Egyptian armies while reserves had been depleted by the belated advance into the interior of Sinai. Instead of responding firmly and quickly, as the situation demanded, the Egyptian command delayed. The Israelis established a bridgehead, hastily constructed an earthen crossing, and rushed men and tanks across so that they were actually superior in force on the west bank of the canal, well behind the main Egyptian forces on the east bank. An Israeli thrust south toward Suez effectively cut off the main Egyptian army in Sinai.

Meanwhile, the international situation was becoming extremely dangerous. Although the United States held back during the opening days of the war, hoping the Israelis would be inclined to a settlement, President Richard Nixon finally agreed to a massive infusion of military aid to Israel, prompting an OPEC oil embargo against the West. The Soviet Union countered the US action by pouring arms into Syria. When Soviet nuclear-tipped missiles were detected passing through the Turkish straits, Nixon responded by ordering a worldwide nuclear alert. But neither superpower wanted a nuclear confrontation. Acting in concert, the United States and the Soviet Union compelled Israel, Syria, and Egypt to accept a UN-sponsored cease-fire on 23 October.

By the time the cease-fire was put in place, the Egyptian military situation had deteriorated, but the October War was acclaimed throughout the country as a great military success. Jubilant soldiers returned to heroes' welcomes—and with some justification, for they had fought well, at least partially erasing the dismal record of 1967. Without the October War, Sadat's subsequent diplomatic accomplishments would have been difficult, if not impossible. October 6 became a major Egyptian national holiday. Sadat celebrated it every year with a great military parade. He was presiding over one of them when he was murdered.

The October War also achieved Sadat's goal of bringing international diplomacy into his quest for regaining Sinai. Even so, the road was rocky. America's Henry Kissinger arranged a separation of the opposing forces in early 1974 in which the Israelis withdrew a few kilometers from the east bank of the canal, beginning a step by step approach similar to the one Sadat had proposed before the war. Following Nixon's visit to the Middle East in June, when he received an enthusiastic welcome, diplomatic relations, severed since 1967, were restored, and the United States resumed aid to Egypt. In his shuttle diplomacy the following year under President Gerald R. Ford, Kissinger arranged for the Israelis to withdraw midway into the peninsula to the passes of Gidi and Mitla. Sadat agreed to limit military forces on his side of the line and renounced war as a means of settling the Arab–Israeli conflict. The Suez Canal reopened in June 1975. Even so, much remained to be settled between Egypt and Israel, which still held fast to the eastern portion of Sinai; the ongoing problem of Palestine was unaddressed; and Sadat incurred severe criticism from the Arab world for agreeing to as much as he did.

In the aftermath of the October War Sadat launched an initiative on the economic front that was just as breathtaking and consequential in its own way as the military one. Here, too, the action was prompted by dire necessity. The state-owned, state-managed economy that Nasser had put into place had demonstrably failed to live up to expectations. Its most tangible results were a bloated bureaucracy and a stifling of initiative; internal capital was altogether inadequate to meet Egypt's needs, and foreign investment was almost nonexistent. Economically, the country was living hand to mouth, and even that could not be sustained. Yet Egypt's growing population required major economic expansion.

Law 43, enacted in 1974, initiated the *infitah*, or 'opening.' A complex of policies rather than just one, the primary objectives of the *infitah* were the mutually reinforcing ones of encouraging the private sector and attracting foreign investment through extensive economic liberalization. The timing appeared impeccable. The need was compelling. Sadat's authority had been enhanced by the crossing of the Suez Canal the previous October, so now he could lead what came to be called the 'economic crossing.' And surely the oil-producing Arab nations, having just quadrupled the price of crude oil, would want to park some of their money in an Arab nation, especially one offering good terms and abundant cheap labor. Beirut was declining as the preeminent banking center of the Middle East; Cairo could replace it. And then there were the prospects of increased contact with the West. The reopening of the Suez Canal was on the horizon. With peace restored, tourists would flock to Egypt. A much higher level of Western spending in Egypt, governmental as well as private, could be anticipated. Nasser's socialism had caused Western investors to shun Egypt; a change of course would lure them back. These were reasonable expectations.

The effects of the *infitah* have been profound. Much of Egypt has been transformed by it. But many of the hopes it engendered have never been realized, and far from solving all of the old problems, it has created new ones. Looking at the results in the mid-1980s, a decade into the *infitah*, the costs and benefits were definitely mixed. Sadat intended that the Open Door Policy should attract foreign investment, and to some degree it did. But most of the money went into tourist hotels, travel agencies, soft drink companies, and the like. The proportion invested in basic industry or agricultural projects was much smaller than anticipated. In many cases, the *infitah* actually reduced internal industry and commerce by encouraging large-scale importation of foreign consumer goods that drove locally produced goods from the market. A small fraction of the population seized the opportunities and grew wealthy, forming a *nouveau riche* class that became known as 'fat cats.' In general, the Westernized elite and most of the middle class probably improved their material condition, but that of the majority, perhaps 80 percent of the population, scarcely changed for the better, and for some conditions worsened, especially as they were constantly taunted by visible reminders of a lifestyle beyond their reach. Unmet expectations create explosive political and social situations. This may account in part for the rise in religious fundamentalism that became obvious during the 1980s.

Conditions would have been much worse had it not been for the vastly increased level of labor migration that came with the *infitah*'s further relaxation of immigration and emigration controls. Here too the impact on society was profound. During earlier times Egyptians were exceedingly reluctant to migrate away from the Nile; ties of village and family were much too strong. The intensity of Egyptian homesickness was legendary. But by the mid-1980s, labor migration to oil-rich Arab countries had become a way of life for more than three million Egyptians and an indispensable part of the Egyptian economy. The wages they earned amounted to several times more than all the wages paid in Egypt. Their remittances became Egypt's greatest source of foreign exchange, more than the combined earnings of the next two, tourism and the Suez Canal. On the average, each migrant sent home (and continues to send) enough money to support a family of six, vastly increasing their purchasing power. And when s/he returned to Egypt, usually after three years or so, it was usually with savings of many thousands of dollars, a lump sum greater than could have been earned in ten or twenty years of employment in Egypt. But most of that money was not mobilized into internal investment capital; instead, it was spent on consumer goods supplied by foreign concerns. Meanwhile, a shortage of skilled labor developed in Egypt, as Egyptians went abroad to take jobs for which they were often overqualified while underqualified personnel replaced them at home.

The state economy was not dismantled and continued to absorb a great deal of capital that could have been invested elsewhere. Yet it steadily lost money, arousing criticism on the one side that economic liberalization had not extended far enough, and counterclaims from the other side—and not just from irredentist Nasserites—that insufficient attention had been paid to reforming the defects within a socialist system that still had something to offer. A further drain on resources resulted from Egypt's policy of heavily subsidizing basic necessities. The most important of these was for bread—called *aish*, or 'life' in Egypt—which imposed a double burden on the government because it had to purchase wheat from abroad and then furnish it to the public at an artificially low price. But many other things were subsidized—rice, sugar, lentils, bottled gas, to mention just a few. Public spending for them in the mid-1970s amounted to about five hundred million pounds a year. Foreign investment was not flooding into the country anywhere near the levels Sadat had hoped. Had it not been for aid from wealthy Arab countries, the Egyptian treasury might well have foundered during the mid-1970s, but even that source did not respond to Sadat's heavy hints that an increased level of support should be forthcoming.

By the beginning of 1977, Egypt was in danger of losing control of its financial destiny. The burden of foreign debt was crushing. The International Monetary Fund (IMF), to which Egypt looked for salvation, was imposing stringent conditions: Egypt had to put its economic house in order, and the place to begin was the subsidies. In the austerity program presented on 17 January, the government sought to soften the impact as much as possible. In announcing a 50 percent cut in the subsidies, the most basic items were spared, and the level of support for the others was reduced, not eliminated. To make the bitter pill more palatable, the cuts were to be accompanied by a 10 percent increase in the salaries of public sector employees.

The public had been suspicious for some time. Though not strictly true, reports said that the price of bread would double. One must live among the poor in Egypt to know what a difference a few piasters can make, even today. In 1977, the per capita annual income was about LE 100, roughly $35–$40, and the official minimum wage was just LE 12 per month. When the subsidy cuts were announced, riots exploded in Cairo and Alexandria, the worst in twenty-five years. Shops were ransacked, especially those containing imported goods; Sadat's offices at the Abdin Palace were even attacked. Angry crowds chanted, "Sadat dresses in style, while we live seven to a room." (Sadat's selection as one of the world's ten best-dressed men by the Italian Chamber of Haute Couture did nothing to endear him to the Egyptian masses.) Jehan Sadat, whose increasingly high public profile was arousing resentment, was also the object of abuse. The people shouted, "Nasser! Nasser!" The army had to be called in to restore order. The official death count, probably underestimated, from the three days of violence was over 150. The subsidy cuts were hastily rescinded on 19 January—although the pay raises were left in place, making the financial situation worse than it was before the cuts were announced.

Perhaps it was the failure on the domestic front that prompted Sadat to seek another international breakthrough. The situation in regard to Israel remained serious. Recovering the rest of Sinai and establishing a peace that would ease Egypt's military burden were obviously high priorities, yet the Israelis had resisted further concessions, and the outlook appeared to become bleaker still when the hardline Likud coalition took power in Israel after the May 1977 elections. The new prime minister was Menachem Begin, a former Zionist terrorist who had been responsible for the 1948 Deir Yasin Massacre in which some two hundred—the number varies according to who is telling the story—Palestinian civilians, mostly old men, women, and children, were slaughtered. His intransigence on the Palestinian issue was blatantly obvious in his invariable habit of referring to the West Bank, taken by Israel during the 1967 War, as "Judea and Samaria." A Palestinian state, he said, was impossible, for it would only be a base for terrorism. Nor did he have anything good to say about Egypt. In the United States, Henry Kissinger, the secretary of state with whom Sadat had developed a warm working relationship, had been replaced following Jimmy Carter's victory in the 1976 presidential election. If there was an inauspicious year to press for a conclusive peace between Egypt and Israel, 1977 appeared to be it.

But Sadat had repeatedly proved himself capable of surprises, and he delivered a big one toward the conclusion of a speech to the National Assembly on 9 November 1977. In pursuit of peace with Israel, he said, "I am ready to go to the ends of the earth. Israel will be astonished when it hears me saying now, before you, that I am ready to go to their own house, to the Knesset itself, to talk to them." The Egyptian public was stunned—as were Sadat's closest advisers, to whom he had given no intimation of what he was going to say. His foreign minister resigned; Arab governments reacted with dismay; many at home urged him not to go. But most Egyptians, though regarding Israel as the enemy, were willing to see what Sadat could accomplish. Attention shifted to Jerusalem, where Prime Minister Begin said he would welcome Sadat's visit. Some observers felt a strong sense of unreality as Sadat was received at David Ben-Gurion Airport with all the proper honors of a visiting head of state.

Though no great orator, Sadat made an outstanding speech before the Knesset, the Israeli parliament. He reiterated his demands for withdrawal from the occupied territories and the Palestinian people's right of self-determination, and insisted that there could be no separate peace, but his presence went far toward meeting the Israelis' longstanding insistence on "direct negotiations," and he was willing to recognize the existence of Israel.

Yes today I tell you, and I declare it to the whole world, that we accept to live with you in permanent peace based on justice. We do not want to encircle you or be encircled ourselves by destructive missiles ready for launching, nor by the shells of grudges and hatreds.

I have announced on more than one occasion that Israel has become a *fait accompli*, recognized by the world, and that the two superpowers have undertaken the responsibility for its security and the defence of its existence. As we really and truly seek peace we really and truly welcome you to live among us in peace and security.[39]

Sadat's journey to Jerusalem was a big gamble, but if the Israelis were willing to make concessions comparable to his, the risk would be more than justified.

When he returned to Egypt, Sadat received an enthusiastic welcome from the Egyptian people, who were tired of the confrontation with Israel. Had he gone to Jerusalem without the October War's successes, however qualified, the Egyptians probably would have repudiated him and the army might have revolted. As it was, he appeared to be making his overture from a position of strength, and there was the prospect of an honorable conclusion. Sadat's move also captured the attention of Washington, where President Jimmy Carter's new administration was preparing a major Middle East peace initiative. But despite Sadat's repeated declarations that there would be no separate peace and that the rights of the Palestinian people would be upheld, the reaction of Arab governments was almost uniformly hostile. Libya's Qaddafi and the Palestinian Liberation Organization's Yasser Arafat were scathing; Syria held a national day of mourning when Sadat went to Jerusalem. Sadat's responses were intemperate, to say the least: he referred to the Middle Eastern leaders who criticized him as "mice or donkeys." Over the following months it was made clear that if Egypt held firm, a large amount of economic aid could be expected from the oil-rich Arab countries; if Egypt broke ranks, it would have to pay a heavy diplomatic price in the Arab world. But it appeared unlikely that things would ever reach that point.

There had been widespread assumption that Sadat's concessions were so compelling that the Israelis would have to respond in like manner. Israel's prime minister Begin saw things quite differently, however. Sadat's gestures had been a free gift that bestowed de facto recognition of Israel's right to exist and drove a wedge in the Arab front against Israel. Begin had gained much without even trying. Why should he give anything in return? After meetings in Alexandria and Ismailia— that latter being the first occasion that an Israeli head of government visited Egypt—it became obvious that the Israelis not only intended to maintain the status quo in the West Bank and Gaza Strip but also to strengthen Israeli control of it, denying the Palestinians any political rights. As for Sinai, Israeli settlements there would be maintained. An Israeli diplomat even boasted of his intention to retire in one of them. If anything was to be accomplished, the Egyptians would have to make yet more concessions, something Sadat was unwilling, indeed unable, to do. In an interview in January 1978 he admitted, "Begin has offered nothing. It is I who have given him everything. I offered him security and legitimacy and got nothing in return." Sadat ordered his negotiating team in Israel to return home. Subsequent Egyptian efforts were rebuffed by the Israelis. In June 1978, Sadat told his soldiers in Sinai that they might be called on to "complete the battle of liberation." Begin retorted that Sadat had reneged on his recent pledge that "there would be no more war."

The impasse was broken by the United States in August. Determined that the opening provided by Sadat should not be wasted, and perhaps concerned about his plummeting ratings in domestic political polls, President Jimmy Carter invited Begin and Sadat to join him in a summit meeting at the presidential retreat at Camp David. This was highly risky. Experts assumed that Carter had some preliminary deal in place; he did not, but he was betting that face-to-face meetings in rural Maryland could produce results. Sadat accepted in hopes that the United States, whose relations with Israel were at an all-time low, would apply pressure for a settlement. Begin was probably more reluctant, and signaled in advance that his position would not change, but he could hardly refuse the invitation. As it turned out, he emerged the clear winner.

At first it seemed that the deadlock was complete as the parties sparred for over a week in early September 1978. The breakthrough came only at the last moment as the pressure that Sadat had hoped would be applied to Begin was applied to him instead. Another Egyptian foreign minister, Ibrahim Kamil, resigned as a result. What exactly was agreed? Within a day of its conclusion, Israeli accounts diverged from those of the Americans and Egyptians, but as Carter understood it, they had hammered out an arrangement by which a fully autonomous self-governing Palestinian authority was to be established in the West Bank and Gaza Strip, and resolution 242 was to be implemented. This could take place within a transitional period of as long as five years, during which time the Israelis would build no new settlements in the occupied territories. On the Israeli–Egyptian front, the Israelis were to withdraw from Sinai and dismantle their settlements; Egypt would allow unhindered passage to Israeli vessels and cargoes through the Suez Canal and waterways such as the Straits of Tiran. Diplomatic relations would be established between the two countries. The formal treaty was scheduled for signing in three months' time. Carter was hailed as a peacemaker. Sadat again returned to a joyous reception in Egypt. Almost every Arab and Middle Eastern government denounced the accord, but world opinion was overwhelmingly favorable. Sadat and Begin were jointly awarded the Nobel Peace Prize.

Almost immediately the Camp David Accords began to unravel. The first problem was the settlements. Begin claimed he had agreed only to "freeze" the establishment of new settlements for the three months until the treaty was signed on 17 December; meanwhile, existing settlements would be "thickened." Furthermore, the Israeli government announced a program for establishing eighty-four new settlements. That put Sadat in an impossible position. If he established diplomatic relations with Israel without securing definite Israeli agreements about the West Bank, Gaza Strip, and Golan Heights, then he would be making the 'separate peace' with Israel that he had pledged not to make. He demanded a definite linkage and timetable; the Israelis refused. In December, Begin was alone in collecting the Peace Prize at Oslo. Sadat, who arguably deserved the award more, declined to attend. The 17 December signing of the peace treaty did not occur. The fundamental differences were too great.

The gap widened during the following months. The Israelis gave no ground and even demanded that Egypt guarantee continued oil sales to Israel, since its Iranian supply had been severed by the overthrow of the Shah of Iran in early 1979. This was to replace the oil from the fields in Sinai that the Israelis had been operating at full capacity since capturing them in 1967. Sadat refused, but he bent yet further on the matter of linkage with a pitiful proposal that Egypt at least establish a "liaison office" in the Gaza Strip. The Israelis would not have even that because it might become the basis for a Palestinian state. Desperate to salvage a peace treaty, Jimmy Carter traveled in person to Jerusalem and Cairo, a gamble even riskier than Camp David, but he probably felt there was nothing to lose. Begin knew that he was in the driver's seat now. The concessions had to come from the United States and Egypt. Carter was willing to make them, and through pressure and promise of reward, he persuaded Sadat to go along.

According to the treaty that was finally signed on the White House lawn in Washington on 26 March 1979, Egypt and Israel would exchange ambassadors immediately after the first stage of Israeli withdrawal from Sinai, a process to be completed over the next three years. The Gaza liaison office would be one of the issues to be discussed in negotiations over Palestinian autonomy. The United States paid the bills and provided the financial incentives. The cost of the Israeli withdrawal from Sinai, about three billion dollars, would be paid by the United States. If Israel could not obtain oil from Egypt, the United States guaranteed its supply for fifteen years. Two billion dollars in military aid was assigned to Egypt. In addition, the US began economic aid to Israel and Egypt that amounted to two to three billion dollars to each nation every year. Those programs continue to the present.

The Palestinians accused Sadat of selling them out, of making a separate peace, and Israel's subsequent actions lent substance to their accusations. When the treaty was presented to the Egyptian parliament, the prime minister, Mustafa Khalil, tried to put the best possible face on it and emphatically denied that it was a separate peace. On the contrary, Khalil claimed, Israel would evacuate Jerusalem and the occupied territories whereupon the Palestinians would establish their state. Begin refuted that in a speech to the Knesset the very next day. Referring contemptuously to "Dear and honorable Dr. Khalil," he asserted that Jerusalem was "the eternal capital of Israel" and that "a state called Palestine will never be established." The commitment of autonomy applied only to the Palestinian people, not to the territories, where firm control was to be retained, and new settlements would be established. "Israel will never return to the borders of 4 June 1967," Begin asserted. To emphasize the point, the Israelis announced ten new settlements in the occupied territories the day before the treaty was signed. This of course was a deliberate affront to the Egyptian government, which was far too committed to back out of the treaty, but it also served to drive the wedge deeper between Egypt and the rest of the Arab world by underscoring the fact that Egypt had indeed made a separate peace, one that gave the Palestinians nothing.

The reaction of most of the other governments of the Middle East was expected to be strongly negative, but neither Egypt nor the United States anticipated its full ferocity. The Arab League suspended Egypt from membership and moved its headquarters from Cairo to Tunis. The Organization of Arab Petroleum Exporting Countries expelled Egypt from its membership. Most Arab countries severed diplomatic relations with Egypt. Saudi Arabia withdrew promised military aid. Sadat was widely regarded as a traitor. The prospects for a comprehensive peace within the Middle East did not appear to be advanced at all; Egypt might be safer, but many Arab leaders considered that it had made the situation even more dangerous for everyone by breaking ranks. Their apprehensions soon appeared justified in June 1980, when the Knesset passed a law declaring that Jerusalem was "whole and united" and that it was "the eternal capital of Israel." In December 1981 came the de facto Israeli annexation of the Golan Heights. When the Israelis launched their massive invasion of Lebanon in 1982, culminating in a devastating artillery bombardment of Beirut, Egypt denounced the action but made no move to apply military pressure on Israel's southern border that might have given the Israelis pause about making heavy commitments in the north. All the while, Israeli settlement in the occupied territories continued apace. The Palestinian 'autonomy' talks went nowhere.

There was also much criticism of Sadat within Egypt, to the limited extent that expression of opposition was possible. And this came from all across the political spectrum, from the Muslim Brotherhood to the Nasserists; even the four surviving Free Officers wrote a manifesto against the treaty, saying that Israel had gotten everything from it and Egypt nothing. Sadat promptly moved to mask the dissent by having the Assembly ratify the treaty in an overwhelming vote of approval, with only thirteen members voting against it—and then he dissolved the Assembly and ensured that all but one of those thirteen were defeated in the new elections. The issue was then submitted to the Egyptian public in a national referendum. According to official results, 90 percent of the electorate went to the polls and voted 99.95 percent in favor of it. In other words, just five thousand of Egypt's forty million people voted against the treaty. That was preposterous; informed observers were certain that only a tiny fraction of eligible voters bothered to participate, and that of those who did, far more than 0.05 percent voted no. But the government's electoral overkill actually masked an important reality: a substantial majority of Egyptians probably wanted to end the long confrontation with Israel. There was widespread feeling that Egypt had sacrificed far more than its share in spending, fighting, and dying for the Palestinians. As for the united Arab front, that had brought more bane than benefit. The treaty was another signal that Egypt was to put its own interests first, and that was a course of which most Egyptians approved. It seemed worth a try. They certainly did not want another war.

Outside of Egypt, it is often assumed that Anwar Sadat signed his death warrant by going to Jerusalem—sacrificing himself for peace, as it were. But Sadat was one of those twentieth-century leaders whose reputations stood much higher in other parts of the world, especially the United States, than in their homelands. Sadat did offend many Egyptians, but less by his peace with Israel than by many other actions, and especially by his autocratic style of government. Nasser had largely done as he pleased, but he always found ways to connect with the Egyptian people, to convey at least the illusion of participation and shared goals, in good times and bad. Yet Sadat, for all his affectation of being a common man, "a man of the soil" in his words—which almost no one believed—became altogether out of touch with the people during his last years and did much to alienate them. "I killed the pharaoh," said one of the soldiers who assassinated him.

It is ironic that it should have been so, because at heart Sadat was less authoritarian than Nasser. The parliamentary elections of 1972 and 1976 were increasingly free of government control. To be sure, there was never doubt that the government's party would win easily, but many constituencies were fiercely contested, issues were aired, and a significant minority of non-government candidates elected. The parliament of 1976 has been accurately described as "the most independent and issue-minded since 1952." No friend of the monolithic Arab Socialist Union, which had been a Nasser creation and Nasserite stronghold,

Sadat divided that super-party into three competing 'platforms,' and eventually replaced it with his new National Democratic Party. In 1977, riding high on the upsurge of popularity following his trip to Jerusalem, he permitted increased activity by independent political parties. The Wafd reemerged with many of its old leaders and liberal platforms still in place. A leftist National Progressive Party also captured attention. They were permitted to advocate their policies in a freer press. But when they showed signs of developing into an articulate, effective opposition, Sadat closed them both down through one of his many national referenda, this one banning "atheists" and politicians who had been active before 1952 from politics. The 1979 parliamentary elections were closely controlled. Even so, and right up to his death, Sadat liked to speak of Egypt as "an island of democracy."

It was much the same with the press, where Sadat experimented with increased freedom, but when his policies and conduct became controversial, he insisted that freedom of the press could not extend to "irresponsible criticism." Several newspapers that became obnoxious to him were forced to stop publication; overly critical journalists were removed from their posts. Sadat zigzagged between liberalization and restriction of the Egyptian press throughout his years as president, but the Law of Shame, passed on 29 April 1980, came as a shock. Among its many offenses were vague crimes such as "broadcasting or publishing gross or scurrilous words or pictures that could offend public sensibilities or undermine the dignity of the state" and "allowing children or youth to go astray by advocating the repudiation of popular, religious, moral, or national values or by setting a bad example in a public place." Those kinds of restrictions could cover almost any kind of thoughtful expression. Processes for prosecution and conviction were extraordinarily swift and direct; penalties were severe. "We have been tolerant and will continue to be tolerant," Sadat said, "but let no one provoke me."

Sadat also alienated Egyptians by his support for the United States, which reached the point where it seemed to many Egyptians that he was more closely identified with the United States and the West than Egypt. He was unlucky when his friend Jimmy Carter was defeated for reelection in 1980 by Ronald Reagan, but he exploited the adamant Cold War stance of the latter by extracting increased military aid. He welcomed American military presence in Egypt. Sadat even spoke of his personal willingness to join NATO. In September 1981 he expelled the Soviet ambassador and several members of the embassy staff, and he ordered one thousand of the Soviet technicians who were still in Egypt to depart, a move that served little constructive purpose other than to signify his closer alignment with the United States. Another pro-Western act was offering safe haven to the deposed Shah of Iran, who had been cast adrift by the United States. Sadat did the United States a great favor by enabling its former ally to pass his last months in relative dignity and safety, but it earned him little credit in Egypt or the Middle East. When the Shah died, he was buried in the Rifai Mosque, next to the medieval madrasa of Sultan Hasan, at the foot of the Citadel. Sadat became a genuine world-class hero in the West, where *Time* magazine had already featured him as its "Man of the Year." It was almost as if he was building a constituency abroad rather than in his own country.

Sadat may have thought he was maintaining close ties with his fellow Egyptians through the series of referenda that he imposed on the country to signify approval of his policies, with their usual 99+ percent approval ratings—although the one in support of the Law of Shame plunged to an unusually low 98.56 percent. He also may have been under the illusion that his frequent television addresses to the nation put him in touch with his people, but these rambling exercises, often hours in length, in which he frequently seemed to lose his place and even his train of thought, became tiresome at best. So did his wife's televised MA thesis defense at Cairo University—where she had not fulfilled all of the degree requirements—which was broadcast nationwide and rerun several times.

Sadat belatedly realized that his most serious danger was not from the liberals or the Left, but from the militant religious Right. From his early days in power, Sadat had moved away from secularist policies by actively encouraging Islam. Calling himself "the pious president," he was probably sincere in his religiosity, although in this also he increased his disconnect with the public because many thought he overdid it. He certainly had practical purposes in mind, intending to use conservative religious political sentiment as a counterweight to his leftist and Nasserite opponents. Realizing that things had gone further than he wished, he reacted with a mixture of coercion and appeasement. The Muslim Brotherhood, toward whose activities he had long turned a blind eye, was proscribed. Other radical religious organizations were dissolved, and their mosques were taken over by the state. But he also sought to strengthen mainstream Muslim support for the government. In the summer of 1980, Sadat permitted the parliament to amend the constitution, making *sharia*, religious law, the basis for all legislation, an unwelcome development for Egypt's large Coptic Christian minority. Increases in subsidies and price controls were instituted at about the same time.

After a series of violent and sometimes deadly Muslim–Coptic clashes in the summer of 1981, and intimations of plots by radical Islamic groups, Sadat took sterner steps. During the first week of September, the government suddenly jailed more than 1,500 people. Most of them were thought to be Muslim militants, and many of them were, but the roundup reached all across the political spectrum, including the well-known journalist Muhammad Hasanein Heikal and the feminist leader Nawal al-Saadawi. Also included in the sweep were 160 Copts. The Coptic patriarch Shenuda III was put under house arrest in a monastery at Wadi Natrun and effectively dismissed as pope. The main Coptic newspapers were shut down. Like Nasser, Sadat constantly worried that there was a plot against him. This time he was right.

On 6 October 1981, the eighth anniversary of the crossing of the Suez Canal, Anwar al-Sadat sat in great state on the reviewing stand in Heliopolis before the pyramid-shaped Tomb of the Unknown Soldier, watching the military parade, seventeen kilometers long, pass before him. It had been going on for nearly two hours, and most eyes had shifted to the skies to watch a display of aerial acrobatics, but Sadat saw a truck stop in front of the stand and a team of soldiers run toward him. He thought it was a prearranged salute and rose to return their greeting. They riddled his body with bullets and threw hand grenades into the stand, killing him and seven others.

The contrast between Sadat's and Nasser's funerals could not have been greater. When Sadat was laid to rest the streets of Cairo were almost empty, apart from heavy security forces. The prevailing attitude of the Egyptian people could probably best be described as indifference. Internationally, the response was deeply divided. Many Western nations felt that Sadat's passing was a tragedy, that a great man had been lost. President Ronald Reagan delegated his three presidential predecessors to represent the United States at the funeral. But just two representatives of

Arab nations—Sudan and Oman—were present. The mood in countries like Syria, Lebanon, and Libya was one of jubilation at the death of the man whom they called a traitor.

Only with the passing of time is it possible to assess the accomplishments of Anwar al-Sadat and his predecessor Gamal Abd al-Nasser. Nasser created a revolution; Sadat consolidated that revolution and reconciled the Egyptian state to the realities of a post-revolutionary era. His separate peace with Israel can be faulted in many details, but it relieved Egypt of the burden of decades of military confrontation and recovered the territory it lost in the 1967 'setback,' no small achievements. Many difficulties remain in the Arab–Israeli conflict, but Sadat left Egypt's relationship to it much better than it was when he came to power. He was far-sighted enough to realize that Egypt's dependence on the Soviet Union was a dead-end street and move away from it well in time, even at the cost of tilting too much in the other direction. Likewise, his far-reaching economic reforms have not lived up to expectations, but they created a situation where Egypt could interact with the world economy instead of being largely isolated from it, as it was when Nasser died. And even though Sadat's political liberalization was more an ideal than a reality, the ideal never vanished, and it laid a foundation for a more pluralistic system that will provide Egypt with more options in future years, if the country decides to take them. Perhaps the greatest measure of Sadat's achievement was that the task he bequeathed to his successor Hosni Mubarak was the workaday one of management, not the necessity for revolution, innovation, and bold initiatives.

20 Mubarak and Beyond

ccording to established constitutional procedure, the vice president, Hosni Mubarak, who had been slightly wounded in the attack on Sadat, was nominated as president by the National Assembly and confirmed by election a week after Sadat's assassination. Born in 1928 in the Delta province of Minufiya, Mubarak graduated from the Air Force Academy in 1950. He is therefore the last of the revolutionary generation of military political leaders. He was, however, too young and too junior to be deeply involved in the Free Officers' movement, and was not one of the inner group that staged the coup in 1952 and exercised such great influence during the early years of the republic. Experienced as a fighter pilot and in bombers, which he commanded in the Yemen War, he rose rapidly, partly through exceptional ability and partly because of the opportunities for upward mobility that opened as many officers identified with the old regime were replaced. Following the 1967 'setback,' and new purges of the officer corps, Mubarak was made commandant of the Air Force Academy in 1967 and Air Force chief of staff in 1969 at the unusually young age of forty-one. His effective service in the October War, previously noted, earned him promotion to the rank of air marshal.

It was, however, a surprise in 1975 when Sadat appointed Mubarak vice president in place of the old Free Officer Husein Shafei. Mubarak had not been conspicuous in political circles, and he came from the Air Force, which was less active in politics than the Army. Although Sadat spoke of the need for "a new generation to step forward to the country's leadership," some have speculated that he, like Nasser, chose a low-key individual who would not pose a threat to him and whom he may not have intended to be his successor. If so, Sadat, again like Nasser, underestimated his man, for Mubarak was hardworking and served a careful apprenticeship as vice president, traveling, attending, and observing, often taking notes as he went. When the unexpected moment came on 6 October 1981, he was ready for the job.

Mubarak is a study in contrast with his predecessor. Sadat loved publicity and was so fond of photographers that sometimes he had them follow him into the bathroom. Mubarak keeps photographs to a minimum, and his appearances are not pompous occasions, nor has his wife, Suzanne, played the ostentatious first-lady role that Jehan Sadat enjoyed. In place of Ruthenian uniforms and designer clothing, Mubarak wears unmemorable business suits. His official portraits depict a pleasant, easygoing man—until one notices his eyes, which are intent, clever. This projection of a calm, almost plodding personality is also an astute change of political tone. Egyptians joke about their unexciting president, but few would willingly return to the flamboyant days of Sadat.

The succession was smooth, but Mubarak's first concern was security. The plot against Sadat was more extensive than it initially appeared. And although Sadat's roundup had put many Islamic extremists behind bars, others remained in operation. Declaration of a national state of emergency—which has never been lifted—gave the presidency even more sweeping power than it already had, including arbitrary arrest, imprisonment, and military trials. Mubarak used his authority firmly, suppressing an uprising in Asyut later in October with a death toll of eighty-seven and jailing another two thousand people around the country. On the other hand, he had to recognize that Sadat's sweeps had been too indiscriminate and very unpopular, therefore he made a highly publicized gesture of releasing most of the inmates, especially prominent figures like Nawal al-Saadawi, bringing some of them directly from prison to the presidential palace for a reception. The public trial and subsequent executions of Sadat's assassins in April 1982 did not provoke renewed opposition. Even so, Mubarak's difficulties with Islamic militants were far from finished.

In foreign affairs, as in other aspects of government, Mubarak's approach was to continue and adjust the policies he had inherited from Sadat. Relations with the United States remained close and became even more deeply entrenched, but Mubarak has been less impulsive in his embrace of the West. Early on, he moved to improve relations with the Soviet Union—for which he is said to have had a dislike dating from his studies there at the Frunze Military Academy. That enabled him to confront pressing problems such as Egypt's massive debt to the Soviet Union while appearing less of a pawn in America's geopolitical game. On the other hand, his rapprochement with Egypt's communist former patron was not so strong as to leave Egypt isolated when the Soviet Union went into decline during the 1980s and collapsed in the early 1990s. By then, Egypt's Western economic and political ties were firmly established. Joint military exercises between Egypt and the United States have been ongoing since 1981, and American military and financial aid to Egypt has been on a massive scale. It is estimated that Egypt received more than $50 billion in US aid between 1975 and 2004, and when indirect aid and non-governmental sources are factored in, the total is much higher. Only Israel receives more assistance from the United States. The American embassy in Cairo, one of the largest in the world, is the most important in the Middle East.

The thorn in the side of Egypt's foreign relations was Israel, but Mubarak's work in that regard was simplified by the fact that the Israeli withdrawal from Sinai was far advanced by the time of Sadat's death, and it was completed within seven months of Mubarak's assumption of the presidency. The Egyptian–Israeli Peace Treaty has survived all vicissitudes for three decades and looks likely to hold in the future, but many of the expectations it raised have never been realized. There is virtually no support for it today among the Egyptian people or media, and both the Israelis and the Egyptians refer to the situation as a 'cold peace.' At first, fairly large numbers of Israelis took advantage of the opportunity to visit Egypt (but not the other way around, although the failure of the Egyptians to reciprocate could be assigned to lack of comparable disposable income for travel, as well as aversion to Israel). After the first *intifada* in Palestine during the late 1980s and the terrorism in Egypt during the 1990s, some of which was directed against Israeli targets, Israeli tourism in Egypt diminished to insignificance. Egypt withdrew its ambassador from Israel in 1982 in protest over the invasion of Lebanon and suspended the Palestinian autonomy talks provided by the peace treaty, but the ambassador returned in 1986.

Many developments in Israel, such as the 1982 invasion of Lebanon and the *intifada*s have created deep resentment within Egypt, where most people would probably be happy to see the Camp David Accords thrown over, but almost no one would want a return to confrontation with Israel. Things have come a long way. As for the Palestinians, the minimal concessions that Egypt extracted on their behalf in its separate peace with Israel have accomplished nothing for them, but with the passing of time it is apparent that no other nation in the region has effectively advanced their cause. Just as the active participation, indeed intervention, of the United States was necessary to bring about the treaty between Egypt and Israel, the only nation that probably can do much to help the Palestinians is the United States. Meanwhile, Egypt has pointed the way for other nations to come to a better working accommodation with Israel. Jordan signed a treaty with Israel in 1994, and other Arab nations have established de facto relations with the Jewish state.

Mubarak's most impressive foreign policy accomplishment has been rescuing Egypt's relations with the Arab world from the nadir they reached after Sadat concluded the treaty with Israel. Tragically, Sadat's assassination eased the way by removing the man whom so many Arabs had come to regard as a traitor to the Arab cause. Mubarak did not carry the negative political baggage that Sadat did, and he was much more conciliatory and patient than Sadat. The Iran–Iraq War, which began in 1980 and festered through most of that decade, also helped improve Egypt's standing in the Arab world. The Saudi prince Talal bin Abd al-Aziz visited Egypt in January 1984, the first Saudi state visit since 1977. Following the conclusion of trade agreements, diplomatic relations with Jordan were also resumed in late 1984. During the years 1987 to 1990, diplomatic relations with all Arab nations were restored. Egypt was readmitted to membership in the Arab League in 1988, and the League's headquarters returned to Cairo in 1990. The Organization of Arab

Petroleum Exporting Countries also accepted Egypt back into its fold. However acrimonious Egypt's relations with other Arab countries had become, the rupture never went to extreme limits. The way to deal severe, lasting damage to Egypt would have been for Arab host countries to expel the millions of expatriate Egyptian workers on whose wages the Egyptian economy was highly dependent. That never happened.

Egypt's relationship with the United States was put to the test in 1990, when a crisis arose over Iraq's claims on the neighboring, oil-rich nation of Kuwait. Recognizing the gravity of the situation, Mubarak actively mediated between the two countries and declared that there would be no Iraqi invasion of Kuwait. When that prediction proved false, he condemned the invasion and provided diplomatic and military support for the United Nations position and the subsequent First Gulf War led by the United States, ultimately committing forty thousand Egyptian soldiers to the coalition's forces. This was not popular within Egypt, where numerous public protests demanded the return of the troops. Religious extremists, responding to Saddam Husein's calls to overthrow the government, caused a great deal of trouble, while Egypt's financial condition suffered as thousands of Egyptian workers fled Iraq and Kuwait. The 2003 invasion of Iraq did not receive Egyptian support, and the government allowed popular demonstrations against it.

Mubarak's low-key, even self-deprecating style is also evident in internal affairs. Although he has been heard to say that Egypt is ungovernable, the fact that he is the longest serving leader of Egypt since Muhammad Ali is testimony to his political skill and to the strong political stability Egypt has enjoyed since 1952. Three powerful presidents have ruled, brushing aside challenges to their authority, with overwhelming acceptance by the Egyptian people, even when public opinion would almost certainly have preferred to move in different directions. Ismail Fahmi, foreign minister until he resigned rather than go to Jerusalem with Sadat, described "the way things work in Egypt." He explained, "Once a leader is in power, people continue to support him without much bickering or questioning. They take it for granted that their ruler is a committed nationalist and knows best what is good for the country. The result is that the leader in Egypt, as in many countries, can take major decisions without worrying about public opinion."[40]

Although Mubarak was reelected in 1987 with over 97 percent of the vote, and went on to win three more presidential elections with similar majorities, his presidency has had bumpy moments. The most serious political disturbance came during 25–27 February 1986 when security police conscripts, who were paid LE 6 per month, rioted because of a rumor that their three-year terms of duty were to be extended by another year. Several tourist hotels were burned down; dozens of people were killed and more than three hundred wounded. Order was restored only after the army was called into action and 1,300 people arrested.

Egypt's economy has presented persistent problems for the government during the Mubarak era. An especially difficult year was 1986 with a severe recession, decreased revenues from the Suez Canal and oil exports, and an influx of returning Egyptian workers from Arab countries whose economies were also experiencing slowdowns. Labor unrest increased noticeably. Inflation ran as high as 25 percent. Increases in wages fell far behind rises in the cost of living. By 1987, Egypt was approaching a crisis in repaying its foreign debt, the interest on which consumed half of its annual foreign exchange. This forced it to negotiate with the World Bank, the International Monetary Fund, and Western governments to reschedule payments. Some relief was provided, but at a cost. The Economic Reform and Structural Adjustment Program, concluded in May 1991, called for internal reforms: higher taxes, removal of consumer subsidies, elimination of price controls, elimination of foreign trade restrictions, labor policy reform, and privatization. Some, though by no means all, of these measures were implemented. Interestingly, there was little comment about the historical parallels with the situation in the late nineteenth century, when Egyptian economic policy slipped out of the hands of Egyptians.

The most serious challenge to the Mubarak regime came from Islamic extremists, as Sadat's cultivation of conservative religious elements to counter his left-wing political opponents bore bitter fruit. Mubarak's attitude toward the Muslim Brotherhood during the first decade of his rule has been described as one of "grudging toleration," but in 1993 he launched a major assault on the organization, denouncing it as "illegal," and accusing it of having "ties to extremist groups." It has been plausibly suggested that the move was not prompted by terrorist associations but by growing popular acceptance and legitimation, reaching levels where the Brotherhood could express serious, mainstream opposition to the government. However that may have been, hundreds of suspects were jailed and tried in military courts after successive rounds of arrests.

The extremists' assault on the government was spearheaded by al-Gamaa al-Islamiya, which grew out of various militant student organizations active during the 1980s. Closely allied with Gihad, a group involved in the assassination of Sadat, it was led by Sheikh Omar Abd al-Rahman, now serving a life sentence in the United States for his role in the bombing of New York's World Trade Center in 1993. By 1992, the Gamaa was engaging in violent terrorist activities, primarily calculated to discourage tourism, both to remove the foreign element from Egypt and for the more practical end of harming the government by depriving the economy of lucrative revenues.

As the Gamaa escalated its terrorist activities over the next two years, tourism in Egypt was indeed devastated. It was an eerie experience to travel in Upper Egypt, as this writer and his son did during 1994, and witness the dearth of tourists. One day when we went to the Valley of the Kings, usually swarming with tourists, we were the only two visitors there. On another occasion, when we sought refuge in one of Aswan's most luxurious tourist hotels after several weeks of arduous field work, we were the only guests. Our footsteps echoed in the empty halls when we retired to our room at night. At least eighty people were killed in terrorist violence during 1994 and more than fifty extremists condemned to death.

An assassination team attempted to kill Mubarak when he attended the Organization for African Unity summit meeting in Ethiopia in 1995. High-ranking government figures were targeted; a cabinet minister narrowly escaped death at the hands of a suicide bomber within a block of the central government offices (the Mugamma) in downtown Cairo. The bomber succeeded only in blowing up himself and some innocent bystanders, but a chill ran through governing circles when a senior counterintelligence officer died in a gunfight just outside his home. His true identity and function were tightly held state secrets, suggesting extensive infiltration by dissident elements.

Tourism recovered fitfully during the 1990s, only to be discouraged by sensational acts of terrorism, including a deadly attack on a tourist bus in Cairo in 1997. The climax of violence came later that year in the massacre at Hatshepsut's temple at Deir al-Bahari, in which fifty-eight tourists were ruthlessly gunned down, and numerous Egyptians were killed and wounded as well. But things had gone too far. Most Egyptians detested the violence and were alienated by the financial hardships they suffered because of terrorist activities. After Deir al-Bahari, the violence diminished. The Egyptian government could claim credit for imposing nationwide security, penetrating the clandestine militant societies (it is not easy to keep secrets in Egypt, where social and family ties are so numerous and close) and bringing the accused to trial, imprisonment, and execution. But there was a change in the attitude of the militants as well. The Gamaa, whose ranks had been thinned by arrests and executions, called for a cease-fire in 1999. That, however, was by no means the end of Islamic extremism in Egypt. Four of the 9/11 hijackers who destroyed the World Trade Center in 2001 were Egyptian. Ahmed al-Masri ('Ahmed the Egyptian') has a five million dollar price on his head for alleged complicity in the bombings of the United States Embassies in Dar al-Salaam, Tanzania, and Nairobi in 1998. The Egyptian surgeon and professor Ayman al-Zawahiri, who was arrested in connection with the assassination of Sadat but later freed, is a prominent member of al-Qaeda. With the reaction to the US invasion and occupation of Iraq, more problems should be anticipated.

Almost all Egyptians strongly disapprove of the methods of the Islamic extremists, but there can be little doubt that religious attitudes have undergone major changes in Egypt during recent years. Anyone whose acquaintance with Egypt extends over the past several decades has noticed the growing strength of mainstream Islam, manifested in much more regular observance of Friday prayers, stricter observance of Ramadan, the month of fasting, and many aspects of daily life. The most visible change is the increase in head veiling among women. This might take the form of a simple headscarf, but it is often expressed with a *hijab* that covers not only the hair but also much of the face. Full face veiling, though still rare, is also on the rise. There was increased pressure during the 1980s for women to retreat from the workplace into the seclusion of their homes, threatening many hard-won achievements in the long struggle toward gender equality in Egypt, but the essential contribution of working women to family economies, combined with their determination to pursue careers and maintain financial independence, have prevented that. Islamic groups have demonstrated ability to offer emotional and often material support during times of increasing economic and social stress. Their effective responses in providing aid after the severe earthquake in October 1992 put the government's much slower reaction to shame. But thus far the apparent increase in religious sentiment has not manifested itself in organized political activity.

Clashes between Muslims and Christians have become more frequent, and although the apex of violence was reached and passed in 1981, Christians complain of being deprived of a share in Egyptian political life commensurate with their contributions to society and their numbers. Coptic demography has long been controversial in Egypt. Official figures for Egypt's Coptic Christians in 1976 were approximately two and a half million, but many Copts claimed that the correct figure was as high as eight million, and the latter was likely to be closer to the truth, yet no Copts were elected during the parliamentary elections of that year, nor in 1995. None was among the Revolutionary Command Council of the Free Officers in 1952, and Christians have largely been marginalized in the republic's political and administrative system. No Copt has held the most important cabinet portfolios of defense, foreign affairs, or the interior. Suspended by Sadat in 1981 and reinstated by Mubarak in late 1984, Pope Shenuda III has maintained a forward policy of defending Coptic interests since his election in 1971. Copts have generally been supportive of Mubarak, seeing him as a defense against Islamic extremists. When he exercised his constitutional right to appoint ten members to the National Assembly in 2005, Mubarak included four Copts as well as five women.

Of Egypt's Jews, a vital part of the nation's social fabric for over two thousand years, very few remain, and those few are almost invisible. Many departed during the events associated with the founding of the state of Israel; others were compelled to leave following the War of the Tripartite Aggression. This latter-day exodus is doubly tragic because it not only deprived the country of a valuable social resource but also came at a moment when Egyptian Jews were on the verge of achieving something approaching parity with the status enjoyed by Egypt's Muslim and Christian populations.

The government's approach to democratic processes continues to be one of oscillation between liberalization and control. The state-oriented National Democratic Party always wins easily, but some other party activity has been tolerated. The New Wafd, for example, displayed notable vitality and versatility, though at the expense of alienating its Coptic supporters, by forming an alliance with the Muslim Brotherhood—a point of departure for both, because it meant the Wafd's abandonment of secularism and the Brotherhood's appearance in regular political activity. In the election of 1984, the National Democratic Party won 391 out of 488 contested seats in the National Assembly, but the Wafd captured fifty-seven, making it the strongest opposition party. The government has, however, taken active measures to prevent the resurgence of the Wafd.

The parliamentary elections of 1995 were particularly notorious for fraud and violence. The National Democratic Party won its usual large majority, but Egypt's Supreme Constitutional Court ruled that the elections were not properly supervised. Mubarak subsequently passed an electoral reform law and promised that the next elections would be free and fair, declaring "the National Assembly elections will mark a new departure, affirming that Egypt is a democratic state." The elections of November 2000 were indeed freer and fairer than previous ones, but Muslim Brotherhood candidates and supporters were hindered and harassed, and even physically blocked from entering polling stations, prompting complaints that the elections were "clean on the inside and dirty on the outside." The opposition parties got a combined total of just thirty-four seats against 388 for the National Democratic Party and its allies. By marginalizing the opposition parties, the government has left a large space for the Islamicists, who could become a potent political force if they organize.

Until 2005, Egypt's presidents were elected by referenda in which it was possible only to vote yes or no on the candidate appointed by parliament. In September of that year, however, Egypt held its first ostensibly contested presidential election, although selection of candidates was highly restricted. According to official results, Mubarak won with 88.6 percent of the vote, though unofficial estimates gave his chief rival, Ayman Nour of the Ghad ('Tomorrow') Party, as much as 13 percent, with another 7 percent going to the New Wafd's Numan Gomaa. While there is little doubt that Mubarak won the election, accusations of ballot-stuffing, intimidation, and other electoral irregularities were too widespread to ignore, as was low voter turnout. Many Egyptians claimed they were most effectively voting by not voting.

Nour's arrest and sentence to five years' imprisonment three months after the election left a lingering impression that democratic institutions were not yet flourishing in Egypt.

Egypt's remarkable political stability since 1952 has rested primarily on the office of the presidency and the willingness of the Egyptians to accept presidential authority. There are no other institutional or constitutional foundations of comparable strength. But this does not necessarily assure continuity. When Mubarak momentarily appeared to suffer a collapse while addressing the National Assembly in 2003, a pall fell over the city as police and the army took control of the streets, bringing everything to a stop. People wondered what would happen next. Unlike his predecessors, Mubarak has never named a vice president, leaving the succession open. Various constituencies exist. Many upper and middle class Egyptians would like to see things remain much as they are. If the majority of people had their way, Egypt would become a more theocratic state. Then there is the army, which has maintained a relatively low profile over the years but is still quite capable of deciding Egypt's political fate.

The economic outlook for Egypt is mixed. Although the 1991 financial reforms were implemented reluctantly, and their extent may be exaggerated, the state-owned sector of the economy diminished during the 1990s while the private sector greatly expanded. National incomes have risen. Breathing space was provided by the rescheduling of the debt, which was reduced when the United States wrote off a large portion of it as a reward for Egypt's participation in the First Gulf War. Other Western creditors followed suit, reducing foreign debt to a manageable level. Tourism survived the assault on it during the 1990s and is stronger than ever, although its maximum potential has not been realized, despite the hordes that overwhelm some places. Renewed terrorist attacks on Red Sea resorts in 2004 and 2005, though killing over a hundred people and injuring many more, did not cause the precipitous declines in tourism that followed such incidents during the previous decade. The Suez Canal continues to be one of the world's major transportation arteries. At its peak during the 1980s, it accommodated more than twenty-two thousand ships per year. Traffic lessened somewhat during the 1990s but should recover with expansion of the canal that will enable fully laden supertankers to pass through it. At the beginning of the twenty-first century the canal was earning well over three billion dollars annually. Though overshadowed by some of its Middle Eastern and African neighbors, Egypt also produces and exports a significant amount of petroleum. Growing domestic consumption has cut into exports, but those losses are offset by the large increases in the price of oil in world markets. Meanwhile, Egypt's reserves of natural gas have proved to be much more extensive than previously thought, so that the country began exporting liquefied natural gas in 2005. Levels of foreign aid have been constant.

But many of the basic problems associated with implementation of the Open Door Policy remain, including the growing gap in affluence between those who have benefited from the changes and those who have remained poor, and the potentially explosive gap between rising expectations and hard reality. According to international standards, the percentage of the Egyptian population living in poverty increased from 20–25 percent in 1990 to more than 45 percent in 1997. The real wages of most workers have steadily declined over the past several decades. Unemployment has risen sharply, with published figures running between 9 and 10 percent, but those are underreported and almost certainly should be adjusted upward by at least an additional 5 percent. The direness of the situation is further masked by widespread underemployment and low wages, compelling many individuals to find supplementary work and even full-time second jobs in order to support their families. Reported inflation rates are well below the galloping levels of the 1980s, but the most casual survey of working neighborhoods shows that food prices have increased to distressing levels, consuming the greater part of household budgets. Continued subsidies of selected critical items such as bread and gasoline— to the severe disapproval of the international financial community— prevent widespread public protests. Remittances from workers abroad, as many as four million, continue to be a major, possibly essential, component of the Egyptian economy. Mubarak has corrected some of the most blatant abuses of the Open Door Policy by punishing corruption and encouraging local production rather than importation, but the fundamental difficulties remain unaddressed.

Any improvement in Egypt's overall economic situation is in danger of erosion by its rapidly growing population. At the beginning of the twentieth century there were approximately ten million Egyptians. By the end of the monarchy in 1952 the population had risen to more than twenty-two million. In 2000 it was nearly sixty-eight million, with a million more being added every ten months. As President Mubarak acknowledged in 1991, "the overpopulation stands in the way of development. It affects the standard of living for millions of Egyptian families, and it limits the government's abilities to increase the services for its citizens." Compared to some other countries in the region, Egypt's birth rate is not particularly high, and there are indications that family planning programs may be having at least marginal impact, but much more needs to be done. Meanwhile, the economy must grow faster, and with benefit for all sectors of society, in order to maintain and improve standards of living.

Egypt's demographic growth is most obvious in the metropolis, Cairo, whose population has swelled to some sixteen million, severely straining the urban fabric of a city that was designed to accommodate far fewer inhabitants. The increase in Cairo's traffic has been staggering during the past thirty years, on a scale that would have brought many major cities to absolute gridlock, but things have continued to move along, in part because of the marvelous spirit of Egyptian cooperation, as well as huge numbers of traffic police and ample labor to see to such things as parking. Congestion is being ameliorated (though some would say worsened) by major highway construction. The Cairo Metro, built by the French, opened in 1987 and is being progressively extended. The city's antiquated sewage system was largely replaced—and only just in time—by an American–British consortium during the 1980s and 1990s. All things considered, Cairo's exponential growth has not been attended by many of the usual ills of urbanization. The crime rate, for example, is remarkably low for a large city.

The most astonishing reversal of Egypt's relationship with the rest of the world has aroused little comment. During the Nasser years Egypt ceased being a net food producer and became a net food importer. The country that once provided food not only for itself but also for many others could no longer feed itself. By the end of Sadat's presidency, Egypt was importing more than half of its grain. Even with aid from the United States, this cost Egypt about two billion dollars per year. The towering grain elevators on the Red Sea port of Safaga are monuments to dependence on foreign sources of food. The situation has improved somewhat during the past two decades, but is nowhere near self-sufficiency. The amount of arable land added by the construction of the High Dam has been more than wiped out by urbanization. It is painful to see, as one does every day in southwestern Cairo, some of the richest agricultural land in the world steadily vanishing under close-packed apartment buildings—sometimes made of brick taken from that land—knowing that the fields just beside them, farmed until the last moment, will soon suffer the same fate. Such development would be better located in the desert.

As Egypt's population continues to expand, the nation must confront the limits of its most vital resource, the water of the Nile, for although Egypt consumes the lion's share of the water, it contributes none to it, while the nations upriver, whose populations are growing even more rapidly than Egypt's, will inevitably take greater portions of it for themselves while exerting increasing control over the river's flow. For most of recorded history, Egypt has been the only significant agricultural country in the Valley of the Nile, therefore it effectively had the river's water all to itself. During the late nineteenth and early twentieth centuries, sensitivity to Egypt's need to ensure access to sufficient quantities of Nile water increased, based on careful calculations by British hydraulic engineers during the early stages of the British occupation. But lack of hydraulic controls upstream meant that Egypt continued to receive the river's full flow without impediment. Also, British imperial domination of virtually the entire Nile basin guaranteed a unified policy toward the river that ultimately favored Egypt. When the Nilotic nations became independent during the 1950s and 1960s, a much more complex diplomatic situation developed.

The Nile Waters Agreement of 1959 between Egypt and Sudan is of fundamental importance in the allocation of the river's water. It was based on the average natural flow at Aswan, which was calculated at eighty-four billion cubic meters per year.* According to the 1959 agreement, Egypt was allocated 55.5 billion cubic meters; Sudan was apportioned 18.5

---

* Although the Nile is the longest river in the world, it carries a much smaller volume of water than other rivers draining similar-sized catchment areas, in large part because so much of its length runs through desert without tributaries or rainfall. The Amazon, by comparison, has an annual discharge of 5,518 billion cubic meters, and that of the Mississippi is 562 billion cubic meters.

billion cubic meters; and another ten billion cubic meters were assigned to evaporation and seepage at the projected reservoir behind the High Dam. This was highly acceptable to Sudan, whose allocation was greatly increased over that of the previous agreement in 1929, which had given it less than 5 percent of the water. But it was also favorable to Egypt because Sudan, hindered by economic and political problems and by deteriorating agricultural infrastructure, never used its full allocation; so the rest flowed downstream to Egypt as a free gift. Egyptian leaders acted as if water resources were unlimited, especially with the construction of the High Dam. Sadat spoke loosely of diverting Nile water to Jerusalem as a good-will gesture, words deeply resented by many Egyptians.

In fact, even as the High Dam was being completed, many engineers were warning that Egypt was living beyond its hydraulic means, with increasing demands for irrigation, hydroelectric production, and personal and industrial consumption. By 1980, if not earlier, the ratio of water to population in Egypt was alarmingly low. Estimates at the end of the twentieth century projected that by 2025 the amount of renewable freshwater per person would be less than one thousand cubic meters, the level at which a country is considered to be water deficient. Meanwhile, significant changes have been occurring upstream. Sudan is likely to use more of its share of the water in coming years, and its construction of the enormous Meroë Dam near the Fourth Cataract will have great impact on the Nile's flow. Also, the other riparian nations, all excluded from the 1959 agreement, are demanding a share of the water that flows through and in some cases originates within their borders. The claims of Ethiopia, which contributes 84 percent of the Egyptian Nile's water, must be taken especially seriously.

Even so, Egypt continues to place greater burdens on the river. Begun in 1997 and scheduled for completion in 2020, the Toshka Project, Egypt's largest engineering undertaking since the High Dam, will redirect approximately 10 percent of Egypt's allocated 55.5 billion cubic meters per year from Lake Nasser into the Western Desert as far as Kharga and Dakhla Oases, effectively creating a second Nile Valley by irrigating 1.5 million feddans of land. Besides increasing agricultural production, the New Valley is intended to provide homes for millions of Egyptians, relieving pressure on the overcrowded Nile Valley. Criticism of the Toshka Project includes doubts that sufficient water will be available, but the

Egyptian government insists that it can be supplied from Egypt's present allocation. The success of the Toshka Project, and the maintenance of Egypt's overall hydraulic viability, will depend on careful management and favorable climatic conditions, as well as astute diplomacy.

Looking ahead, it is obvious that the twenty-first century will present Egypt with some of the greatest challenges it has confronted during all the millennia of its eventful existence. It is difficult to imagine just how the country will meet them, but the resilience and capability of the Egyptian people have been proved time and time again, and the country retains enormous untapped potential. When one stands on the Muqattam Hills, where the heretic caliph al-Hakim used to go on his solitary nocturnal donkey rides, and looks out across the sprawling city, the silver band of the Nile, and the pyramids and the desert beyond, it is tempting to believe that *maat* somehow still suffuses the land, and that the order will continue, as it has since the time of Osiris.

Notes

1 Miriam Lichtheim, *Ancient Egyptian Literature*, 3 vols. (Berkeley: University of California Press, 1973–80), vol. 1, 189.
2 Jaromir Malek, *In the Shadow of the Pyramids* (Norman: University of Oklahoma Press, 1986), 40–42.
3 Malek, 118.
4 Stela of Irtisen, The Louvre. Translation by the author.
5 Lichtheim, vol. 2, 176–77.
6 Herodotus, *The Histories*, trans. Aubrey de Sélincourt (Harmondsworth: Penguin, 1972), 188.
7 Flavius Josephus, *Contra Apionem*. Translation by the author.
8 John H. Taylor, "The Third Intermediate Period," in Ian Shaw, ed., *The Oxford History of Ancient Egypt* (Oxford: Oxford University Press, 2000), 337.
9 Herodotus, *The Histories*, trans. Walter Blanco; Walter Blanco, and Jennifer Tolbert Roberts. eds. (New York: W.W. Norton, 1992), 85–86.
10 Garth Fowden, *The Egyptian Hermes: A Historical Approach to the Late Pagan Mind* (Princeton: Princeton University Press, 1986), 21–22.
11 Alan K. Bowman, *Egypt after the Pharaohs* (Berkeley: University of California Press, 1986), 169.
12 Polybius, *The Histories of Polybius*, trans. Evelyn S. Shuckburgh, 2 vols. (London: Macmillan, 1989), vol. 1, 453.
13 Polybius, vol. 2, 405–406.
14 Bowman, 218.

15 From Kircher, *Oedipus Aegyptiacus*, quoted in Francis A. Yates, *Giordano Bruno and the Hermetic Tradition* (London: Routledge and Kegan Paul, 1964), 417–18.

16 Lionel Casson, *Ships and Seafaring in Ancient Times* (London: British Museum Press, 1994), 123–24.

17 Eusebius of Caesarea, *History of the Church*. Translation by the author.

18 Tim Vivian, "St. Antony the Great and the Monastery of St. Antony at the Red Sea, ca. A.D. 251 to 1232/1233," in Elizabeth S. Bolman, ed., *Monastic Visions: Wall Paintings in the Monastery of St. Antony at the Red Sea* (Cairo: American Research Center in Egypt, 2002), 7.

19 Pierre Chuvin, *A Chronicle of the Last Pagans*, trans. B.A. Archer (Cambridge, Massachusetts: Harvard University Press, 1990), 68.

20 André Raymond, *Cairo: City of History*, trans. Willard Wood (Cairo: The American University in Cairo Press, 2001), 74.

21 Francesco Gabrieli, *Arab Historians of the Crusades* (Berkeley: University of California Press), 297–98.

22 Bernard Lewis, *Islam from the Prophet Muhammad to the Capture of Constantinople*, 2 vols (New York: Oxford University Press, 1987), vol. 1, 84–85.

23 Peter M. Holt, *The Age of the Crusades* (London: Longman, 1986), 126.

24 André Raymond, *The Glory of Cairo: An Illustrated History* (Cairo: The American University in Cairo Press, 2002), 269.

25 H.R. Trevor-Roper, *Historical Essays* (London: Macmillan, 1957), 24–25.

26 Ibn Battuta, *Travels in Asia and Africa 1325–1354* (London: Routledge & Kegan Paul, 1929), 50.

27 Sir John Maundeville [pseud.], *The Voiage and Travaile of Sir John Maundevile, K*^{t} (London: J. Woodman, D. Lyon, and C. Davis, 1725), 63–64.

28 Robert L. Tignor, ed., *Napoleon in Egypt: Al-Jabartī's Chronicle of the French Occupation, 1798*, trans. Shmuel Moreh (Princeton: Markus Wiener, 1993), 36.

29 Afaf Lutfi al-Sayyid Marsot, *Egypt in the Reign of Muhammad Ali* (Cambridge: Cambridge University Press, 1984), 83.

30 Edward William Lane, *Description of Egypt*, Jason Thompson, ed. (Cairo: The American University in Cairo Press), 105.

31 Samuel W. Baker, *Ismailia: A Narrative of the Expedition to Central Africa for the Suppression of the Slave Trade*, 2 vols. (London: Macmillan, 1874), vol. 1, 22.

32 Florence Nightingale, *Letters from Egypt: A Journey on the Nile, 1849–1850*, ed. Anthony Sattin (London: Parkway, 1987), 19.

33 William Makepeace Thackeray, *Notes of a Journey from Cornhill to Grand Cairo, by way of Lisbon, Athens, Constantinople, and Jerusalem: Performed in the Steamers of the Peninsular and Oriental Company*, (London: Champan and Hall, 1846), 278–79.

34 Lucie Duff Gordon, *Letters from Egypt*, Sarah Searight, ed. (London: Virago Press, 1986), 335.

35 Evelyn Baring, Earl of Cromer, *Modern Egypt*, 2 vols. (New York: Macmillan, 1908), vol. 1, 567.

36 Ronald Storrs, *The Memoirs of Sir Ronald Storrs* (New York: G.P. Putnam's Sons, 1937), 88.

37 Abbas Hilmy II, *The Last Khedive of Egypt: Memoirs of Abbas Hilmi II*, trans. and ed. Amira Sonbol (Cairo: The American University in Cairo Press, 2006), 97.

38 Hassan Hassan, *In the House of Muhammad Ali: A Family Album, 1805–1952* (Cairo: The American University in Cairo Press, 2000), 128.

39 Moustafa Ahmed, ed. *Egypt in the 20th Century: Chronology of Events* (London: MegaZette Press, 2003), 458.

40 Anthony McDermott, *Egypt: From Nasser to Mubarak, A Flawed Revolution* (London: Croom Helm, 1988), 56.

Recommended Reading

Baines, John, and Jaromir Malek. *Atlas of Ancient Egypt* (rev. ed.). Cairo: The American University in Cairo Press, 2002.

Bolman, Betsy (ed.). *Monastic Visions: Wall Paintings in the Monastery of St. Antony at the Red Sea*. Cairo: American Research Center in Egypt, 2002.

Bowman, Alan K. *Egypt after the Pharaohs*. Berkeley: University of California Press, 1986.

Doxiadis, Euphrosyne. *The Mysterious Fayum Portraits: Faces from Ancient Egypt*. Cairo: The American University in Cairo Press, 2000.

Fahmy, Khaled. *All the Pasha's Men: Mehmed Ali, His Army and the Making of Modern Egypt*. Cambridge: Cambridge University Press, 1997.

Goldschmidt, Arthur, Jr. *Modern Egypt: The Formation of a Nation-State*. Boulder: Westview Press, 1988.

Hewison, R. Neil. *The Fayoum: History and Guide* (3rd ed.). Cairo: The American University in Cairo Press, 2001.

Hölbl, Günther. *A History of the Ptolemaic Empire*. Translated by Tina Saavedra. London: Routledge, 2001.

Holt, P.M. *The Age of the Crusades: The Near East from the Eleventh Century to 1517*. London: Longman, 1986.

———. *Egypt and the Fertile Crescent 1516–1922: A Political History*. Ithaca: Cornell University Press, 1986.

Hunter, Robert F. *Egypt under the Khedives, 1805–1879*. Pittsburgh: University of Pittsburgh Press, 1984.

Kamil, Jill. *Christianity in the Land of the Pharaohs*. Cairo: The American University in Cairo Press, 2002.

Lehner, Mark. *The Complete Pyramids*. London: Thames and Hudson, 1997.

Lewis, Naphtali. *Life in Egypt under Roman Rule*. Oxford: Oxford University Press, 1983.

Malek, Jaromir. *In the Shadow of the Pyramids: Egypt during the Old Kingdom*. Norman: University of Oklahoma Press, 1986.

Midant-Reynes, Béatrix. *The Prehistory of Egypt: From the First Egyptians to the First Pharaohs*. Translated by Ian Shaw. Oxford: Blackwell, 2000.

Petry, Carl F. (ed.). *The Cambridge History of Egypt*. 2 vols. Cambridge: Cambridge University Press, 1998.

Reif, Stefan C. *A Jewish Archive from Old Cairo*. Richmond, Surrey: Curzon Press, 2000.

Sampsell, Stefan C. *A Traveler's Guide to the Geology of Egypt*. Cairo: The American University in Cairo Press, 2003.

Shaw, Ian (ed.). *The Oxford History of Ancient Egypt*. Oxford: Oxford University Press, 2000.

Tignor, Robert L. *Modernization and British Colonial Rule in Egypt, 1882–1914*. Princeton: Princeton University Press, 1966.

Trigger, B.G., B.K. Kemp, D. O'Connor, and A.B. Lloyd. *Ancient Egypt: A Social History*. Cambridge: Cambridge University Press, 1983.

Vatikiotis, P.J. *The History of Egypt* (3rd ed.). Baltimore: Johns Hopkins Press, 1985.

Winter, Michael. *Egyptian Society under Ottoman Rule 1517–1798*. London: Routledge, 1992.

Image Sources

Bevan, Edwyn. *A History of Egypt under the Ptolemaic Dynasty*. London: Methuen & Co., 1927.

Colvin, Auckland. *The Making of Modern Egypt* (2nd ed.). New York: E.P. Dutton, 1906.

Coste, Pascal. *Architecture arabe*. Paris: Firmin Didot Frères, 1839.

Frith, Francis. *Lower Egypt, Thebes, and the Pyramids*. London: W. Mackenzie, 1862?

de Guerville, A.B. *New Egypt*. New York: E.P. Dutton, 1906.

Hassan, Hassan. *In the House of Muhammad Ali: A Family Album, 1805–1952*. Cairo: The American University in Cairo Press, 2000.

Hay, Robert. *Illustrations of Cairo*. London: Tilt and Bogue, 1840.

Lane, Edward William. *An Account of the Manners and Customs of the Modern Egyptians* (3rd ed.). London: C. Knight, 1842.

Lepsius, Richard. *Denkmäler aus Aegypten und Aethiopien*. Berlin: Nicolaische Buchhandlung, 1849–1856.

Nicol, Norman D. *Sylloge of Islamic Coins in the Ashmolean: Volume 6, The Egyptian Dynasties*. Oxford: Ashmolean Museum, 2007.

Penfield, Frederic Courtland. *Present-Day Egypt* (rev. ed.). New York: Century Co., 1903.

Roberts, David. *Egypt and Nubia: from drawings made on the spot*. London: F.G. Moon, 1846–1849.

Index

Abbas Hilmy I Pasha, 235–36, 239
Abbas Hilmy II, Khedive, 261–62,
    267–71
Abbasid Caliphate, 170–72, 184, 194
Abdallah ibn Saad ibn Abi Sarh, 167–68
Abdallah ibn Saud, 226
Abdallah ibn Saud Wahhabi, 226–27
Abd al-Aziz (Umayyad governor), 170
Abd al-Latif, 201–202
Abd al-Rahman, Omar, 347
Abdin Palace, 238–39, 250, 284, 328
Abercrombie, Sir Ralph, 222
Abu Bakr, Caliph, 173
Abu Mena, 156
Abu Qir, Battle of, 220
Abu Simbel, 33, 300
Abu Sir, 39
Abu Zabal Hospital, 231
Abydos, 15, 18, 20–21, 46, 53, 55, 76
Abyssinia. See Ethiopia.
Acre, 185, 186, 194, 195, 221, 233
Acteur manqué, 319
Actium, Battle of, 122
al-Adid, Caliph, 184
al-Adil Sayf al-Din, 187

al-Afdal Shahanshah, 180, 182
Afrika Korps, 283–86
Agathocles, 110–11
Ahmed, Imam, 310
Ahmed Pasha, 209
Ahmose I, 61, 65, 84
Ain Jalut, Battle of, 191, 193
Ain Shams, Battle of, 222
'Aja'ib al-athar fi-l-tarajim wa-l-
    akhbar, 217
al-Akhbar, 307
Akhenaten, 69–75, 76
Akhetaten. See Amarna.
Alam Halfa, Battle of, 285
al-Alamein, Battles of, 285–86
Albanian soldiers, 222, 224, 226
Aleppo, 185, 190
Alexander the Great, 11, 89, 96–98,
    101, 103, 108
Alexander Severus, 140
Alexandria, 7, 97, 100–103, 106, 107,
    111, 112, 116, 117, 118–19,
    120, 122, 124, 125–29, 131,
    132, 133, 137, 141, 142, 145,
    146, 150, 125–29, 141, 163,

166–67, 183, 187, 198, 210, 224, 229, 251, 331
Allenby, Lord Edmund, 275
Ali, Caliph, 169–70, 173
Ali Bey al-Kebir, 216–18
Ali Mubarak, 239
Allenby, Lord Edmund, 275, 279
Amalric, 183–85
Almagest, 128
Alparslan, 180
Amarna, 70–74, 76
Amarna Letters, 71, 73
Amasis, 92
Amenemhet I, 48–49
Amenemhet II, 50, 56
Amenemhet III, 47, 50, 52, 56–57
Amenemhet IV, 57
Amenhotep I, 65
Amenhotep II, 68
Amenhotep III, 68–69, 76, 137
Amenhotep IV. *See* Akhenaten.
Amenirdis I, 87
Amer, Abd al-Hakim, 301, 305, 306, 311, 312, 313, 314
American Civil War, 238
Amin, Mustafa, 307
Ammianus Marcellinus, 129
Ammonius Saccas, 128–29
Amonmessu, 78
Amqa, Battle of, 75
Amr ibn al-As, 165–67, 170
Amratian culture. *See* Naqada I.
Amun and Amun-Ra, 32, 63, 70, 75, 80–81, 84, 97, 131, 138
Amyrtaios of Sais, 93
Amyrtaios of Sais, the younger, 95
anachoresis, 115, 134, 142
anchorite movement, 147
Anglo-Egyptian Condominium, 264, 290, 295
Anglo-Egyptian Civil Service, 265, 271
Anglo-Egyptian Treaty of 1936, 280, 281, 284, 288, 289, 290, 295
Ankhesenpaamun. *See* Ankhesenpaaten.

Ankhesenpaaten, 74-75
*ankh*s, 70, 71, 148
Ankhtifi, 44, 46
anona, 135
Antigonus Gonatus, 99
Antinoopolis, 133, 139
Antinous, 139
Antioch, 194
Antiochus III, 109, 111
Antiochus IV Epiphanes, 112–13
Antoninus Pius, 140
Antonius, Marcus, 117, 118, 119–22, 138
Antony, St., 151–53
Aphrodite, 108
Apollonius of Rhodes, 103
Apries, 91–92
Apuleius, 139
aqueduct of Cairo, 172
Arab League, 304, 334, 344
Arab Legion, 305
Arab Republic of Egypt, 320
Arab Socialist Union, 308, 318, 335–36
Arabian Nights, 171, 231
Arabic language introduced to Egypt, 169
Arafat, Yasser, 330
Archaic Period. *See* Early Dynastic Period.
Archimedes, 102
Archimedian Screw, 102
Arian Heresy, 145, 155
al-Arish, 221
Aristarchus of Samothrace, 103
Aristotle, 129
Aristotelianism, 128–29
Arius, 145, 155
army, modern Egyptian, 230–32, 236, 254, 258, 261, 263
Arsenal at Alexandria, 229, 233
Arsinoe II, 100, 108
Arsinoe III, 109–11
Arsinoe IV, 119

art and architecture, ancient Egyptian, 14, 15, 17, 18, 19, 21, 30–31, 48, 51–53, 55, 64, 67, 71–72, 76, 77, 84, 89, 90, 95; Roman, 132, 138–39; Coptic, 147, 156; Tulunid, 171; Fatimid, 176; Mamluk, 200, 204, 211; Turkish, 211–12, 226; orientalist art, 243
Artaxerxes III Ochus, 95
al-Asad, Hafez, 322
Ascalon, 182, 183, 185
Asclepius, 108
al-Askar, 171
Assassins, 180, 181
Assembly of Delegates, 249, 250, 251, 268
Assurbanipal, 90
Assyria, 73, 89–91
astrology in Roman Egypt, 128, 147
Athanasius, St., 145, 152, 155
Aswan, 4, 26, 48, 51, 87, 136, 168, 221, 347, 354
Aswan Dam, 5, 257
Aswan High Dam, 77, 130, 297–301, 302, 319, 354–55
Asyut, 13, 55, 342
Atbara, Battle of the, 263
Aten, 70–74
Auchinleck, Claude, 283, 285
Augustine, St., 129
Augustus, 120–23, 125, 127, 130, 133, 138
Aurelian, 141
Avaris, 60, 61, 63
Awibra Hor, 57
Ay, 74–75
Aybeg al-Turkumani, 190
Ayyubid dynasty, 183–90
al-Azhar, 175
al-Aziz, Caliph, 175, 176, 177

Bab al-Futuh, 179, 180, 200
Bab al-Nasr, 180
Bab Zuweila, 175, 180, 191, 200, 205

al-Babayn, 183
Babylonia, 69
Babylon (Egypt), 124, 163, 166
Babylon (Mesopotamia), 97
Babylonian Captivity, 91
Badarian culture, 13–14
Badr, Battle of, 322
al-Badr, Muhammad, 310–11
Baghdad, 171, 180, 184, 190
Baghdad Pact, 296, 297
Bahariya Oasis, 6
Bahr Yussuf, 50
Baldwin IV, 185
Bank Misr, 277
al-Banna, Hasan, 287, 294
baqt, 168, 193
Bar Lev Line, 323
Baring, Evelyn. See Cromer, Lord.
Barjawan, 177
Barclays Bank, 302
Barquq, 198–99, 200
barrages, Nile, 228, 257, 300
Barsbay, al-Zahiri, 199–200, 202
Bashmuric revolt, 169
Bastet, 32
Bay, Chancellor, 78
Baybars, 191–94, 200
Baybars al-Jashnikir, 195–96
Bayn al-Qasrayn, 175
al-Bayyumi, Muhammad, 278
Begin, Menachem, 329, 331, 333
Behnesa, 131
Beirut, 334
Beit al-Wali, 77
Ben Ezra Synagogue, 177
Ben-Gurion, David, 289
Benghazi, 283
Beni Hasan, 50–51
Benjamin of Tudela, 177, 201
Bent Pyramid, 35
Berber soldiers, 176, 179
Berenike (town), 7, 99, 139
Berenike II, 108
Berenike III, 116

Berenike IV, 117–18
Bernal, Martin, 130
Bernard the Wise, 201
Bes, 32
Beyezid II, 204
beylicate, 213–17
Bilbays, 78, 183, 184
Bin Abd al-Aziz, Talal, Prince, 344
Birket Qarun, 6, 104–105
Black Athena, 130
Black Death, 197, 203, 210
Black Saturday, 290–91
Black September, 316
Blemmyes, 141
Bocchoris, 88
Book of the Dead, 21
Boyle, Sir Harry, 254–55
British Commonwealth in the Second
    World War, 282, 284, 286
British Egyptian Treaty, 295
British Museum, 223
British occupation of Egypt, 251–75;
    also 275–95
Bruce, James, 217
Bubastis, 32, 86, 87
bubonic plague, 197, 203, 221, 231,
    240. *Also see* Black Death.
"bull mosaic" pendant, 53
Buried Pyramid, 23
Busir, 171
Byblos, 48, 73, 81
Byzantine Empire and Egypt,
    143–66, 168, 179, 181, 187
Byzantium, 143

Caesar, Julius, 117–20, 125
Caesarion. *See* Ptolemy XV Caesar.
Caesarium, 125, 157
Cairo, 1, 174–76, 184–85, 200–202,
    210, 220–22, 241, 325, 353–54
Cairo Arab summit meeting,
    September 1970, 316
Cairo Conference, 286
Cairo University, 277, 290, 337

Caisse de la Dette Publique, 248,
    250, 254, 255, 256, 263
Caligula, 135, 137
Callimachus of Cyrene, 103
Cambyses, 92–93
Camel Corps, 272
Camp David Accords, 331–32, 344
du Camp, Maxime, 243
cannibalism, 179
Canopus Decree, 107–108, 120
canon, ancient Egyptian artistic, 30
Capitulations, 244–45, 247–48, 255,
    280, 281
Caracalla, 126, 140
caravanserais, 212
Carchemish, 91
Carter, Howard, 75, 278
Carter, Jimmy, 329–33, 336
Carthage, 112–13
cartouches, 29, 67, 70
Casaubon, Isaac, 130
catacombs of Alexandria, 132
Cataracts, First 4–5, 25, 26, 41, 51,
    58, 125, 257; Second, 5, 51, 61,
    85, 300; Third, 58; Fourth, 65,
    85, 87; Fifth, 99
Catechetical School of Alexandria,
    150, 154
Catherine, St., 151
Cecil, Lord Edward, 254
cenobitic monsticism, 153
census of 1848, 234
Chakmak al-Zahiri, 200
Chalcedonians, 159–60, 164
Chaldeans, 91–92
Chiang Kai-shek, 286
Chamoun, Camille, 305
cholera, 231, 263
Chosroes II, 163–64
Chou En-lai, 296, 297
Christianity, 128, 143, 265; under
    Muslim rule, 168–70, 176, 178,
    193, 196. *Also see* Coptic Orthodox
    Church, monasticism, etc.

Christodoulos, 179
chronology and periodization of
    Ancient Egypt, 11–12, 49, 83,
    89, 90
Church of the Holy Sepulcher, 178
Church of the Holy Virgin at
    Musturd, Cairo, 155
Church of the Holy Virgin at Gebel
    al-Teir, 155
Churchill, Sir Winston, 286
Cilicia, 121
cinema, 278, 304, 319
Citadel, 184, 198, 209, 212, 221,
    225–26, 234, 337
City of God, 129
Civil Service. *See* Anglo-Egyptian
    Civil Service.
Claudius, 127, 128, 135, 137
Clement of Alexandria, 154
Cleopatra I, 111–12
Cleopatra II, 112–14
Cleopatra III, 114
Cleopatra VI, 117
Cleopatra VII, 105, 115, 118–22
Cleopatra's Needles. *See* obelisks.
cleruchs, 106
Clot Bey, 231
Coele Syria, 98, 111, 112, 121
coffee and coffee shops, 212
Colossi of Memnon, 69, 138–39,
    140, 156
Commission on the Sciences and
    Arts, 222–23
Commonwealth Cemetery at al-
    Alamein, 286
Communist Party of Egypt, 287
Condominium. *See* Anglo-Egyptian
    Condominium.
Constantine, 143, 151, 155, 159
Constantinople, 143, 159–61, 165, 187
Constantius, 157
Constitution of 1923, 275, 279
Constitution of 1956, 301, 304
Constitution of 1964, 308

Coptic Museum, 124, 156
Coptic Orthodox Church and Coptic
    Christians, 145–61, 163, 166,
    168–69, 176–77, 178, 193, 196,
    338, 349–50
Coptic language and script, 148–49, 169
Coptos, 141
Corrective Revolution, 318, 320
Corpus Hermeticum, 129–30, 158
corvée, 27, 34, 40, 47, 124, 228–29,
    232, 238, 240, 245–46, 272
cotton, 228, 238, 246, 257, 272, 297, 303
Council of Chalcedon, 160
Council of Clermont, 181
Council of Constantinople, 159
Council of Ephesus, Second, 160
Council of Nicaea, 155
Crassus, Marcus Licinius, 117–18
Credit Lyonnais, 302
Crete, 69, 233
Crimean War, 236
Cromer, Lord, 253–68, 269
Crusades, 181–90, 194–95, 198;
    Peoples' Crusade, 182; First
    Crusade, 182; Second Crusade,
    182; Third Crusade, 186; Fourth
    Crusade, 187; Fifth Crusade,
    187; Seventh Crusade, 188;
    Crusade of Alexandria, 198, 210
Cyprus, 98, 111, 112, 116, 117, 119,
    121, 125, 127, 199
Cyrenaica, 91–92, 98, 99, 111, 114,
    115, 121, 125, 127, 156, 283
Cyril I, 145, 158
Cyrus (prefect of Egypt and patriarch
    of Alexandria), 164–66
Cyrus the Great, 92
Czechoslovakia, arms purchase
    from, 296

Dahshur, 35, 53, 56
daily life and social organization in
    ancient Egypt, 37–38, 55–56,
    105–106, 133–36

Dakhla Oasis, 6, 125, 130–31, 355
Damascus, 167, 185, 190, 216
Damietta, 187, 188, 190, 191
Darfur, 264
Darius I, 93
Darius II, 95
Dead Sea Scrolls, 146
debt, nineteenth-century, 234, 236, 247–51, 253, 254; twentieth-century, 309, 328, 343, 346, 351
Decius, 141, 150
Deir al-Bahari, 46, 48, 52, 67, 84, 154, 347–48
Deir al-Medina, 64, 78–79, 80, 84, 154
Deir Yasin Massacre, 329
Delta, 3–4
Demotic Chronicle, 107
demotic script, 29, 106, 108, 148–49, 157
Den, 21
Dendera Temple, 109
Desaix, Antoine, 221
Description de l'Égypte, 223, 242
Desert, Eastern, 5–6, 7, 47, 125, 136–37, 152
Desert, Western, 6, 7, 8–9, 76, 125, 141, 148, 355
Dimiana, St., 150–51
Dinshawi Incident, 266–67, 268, 269
Dio of Prusa, 127–28
Diocletian, 136, 141–42, 150–51
Diodorus Siculus, 101, 105
Dionysus, 108, 110, 121
Dioscurus, 160
Divine Adoratrices of Amun, 87, 90
Djer, 20–21
Djoser, 21–23
Druse, 179
Dual Control, 249–50
Dufferin, Lord, 253
Dulles, John Foster, 297–98, 303
Dunkirk, 282
Dunlop, Douglas, 259

Early Dynastic Period, 19–23
earthquake of 1992, 349
Eastern Cemetery of Cairo, 204
Economic Development Organization, 302
Economic Reform and Structural Adjustment Program, 346
economy. ancient Egyptian, 26–27; Ptolemaic, 104–105; Roman, 135–36; Mamluk, 193, 203; Ottoman, 210; under Muhammad Ali, 228–29; under British occupation, 256–58; modern Egyptian, 277, 297, 302, 306–309, 325–28, 351–52
Eden, Anthony, 298–99
Edfu Temple, 109
Edict of Milan, 151
education, 228, 231, 235–36, 239, 254, 258–59, 269–70, 277, 301–302
Edwards, Amelia, 242
Egypt Exploration Society, 242
Egyptian–Israeli Peace Treaty, 333–35, 343
Egyptian University. *See* Cairo University.
Egyptology, 241–42, 278
Egypt's Awakening, 278
Eisenhower, Dwight D., 299, 303, 309
Eisenhower Doctrine, 303, 305
election, 1924, 276; 1929, 279; 1936, 280; 1938, 281; 1950, 290; 1972, 335; 1976, 335, 349; 1979, 334–35, 336; 1984, 350; 1987, 346; 1995, 349, 350; 2000, 350; 2005, 350; plebiscite of 1956, 301; plebiscite of 1964, 308; referendum on Law of Shame, 337
Elephantine Island, 26
emigration, 326–27, 345, 346, 352
Entente Cordiale, 266

Eratosthenes of Cyrene, 102, 128
Esarhaddon, 90
Esna Temple, 109
Etheria, Lady, 156
Ethiopia, 157, 239, 280, 282, 355
Ethiopian Christian Church, 157
Euclid, 102
Eulaios, 112
Euphrates, 61, 65
Eusebius, 150
Ezekiel, 95

Fahmi, Ismail, 345
Fahmi, Mustafa, 255, 261
Fakhr al-Din, 189–90
Falluja, 289
Farafra Oasis, 6
Faraj, al-Nasir, 199
Farouk, 276, 280–81, 284, 289–92
Fatimids, 172–84
Fayyum, 6, 44, 50, 56, 57, 60, 104–105,
    132, 133
Fayyum Portraits, 131–32, 156
Federation of Arab Republics, 320
Feisal, King, of Saudi Arabia, 322
Ficino, Marsilio, 130
First Intermediate Period, 43–47, 52
First Persian Period, 92–95
First Triumvirate, 117
First World War, 270–72
five-year plan, 306
Flaubert, Gustave, 243
Ford, Gerald R., 325
Fourteen Points, 274
France and Egypt, 217–18, 219–23,
    298–99. Also see Crusades.
Frederick II, 187
Frederick Barbarossa, 186
Frith, Francis, 243
Free Officers, 291–93, 306, 313, 317,
    334, 341, 342, 349. Also see
    RCC.
Fuad, 272, 275–76, 278–80
Fuad I University. See Cairo University.

Fuad, Ahmed, 292 n.
Fustat, 167, 171, 174, 175, 177, 178, 184

Galen of Pergamum, 102, 129
Galerius, 141, 151
Gallienus, 150
Gallipoli, Battles of, 271
Gallus, Cornelius, 125
al-Gamaa al-Islamiya, 347–48
Gaza, 185, 289, 296, 298
Gaza Strip, 331–33
Gazira Palace, 260
Gazira Sporting Club, 260
Gebel Barkal, 85, 88
Gebel Dokhan, 136
Gebel al-Silsileh, 136
General Assembly, 268
genizah, 177
Genghis Khan, 190
Geographia, 128
Gérôme, Jean-Léon, 243
Gerzean culture. See Naqada II culture.
Geta, 126
Ghad Party, 350
Ghali, Boutros, 268
al-Ghuri, 200, 205
Gidi Pass, 325
Gihad, 347
Gilf al-Kebir, 6
Gladstone, William Ewart, 253, 256,
    262
Glubb, Sir John, 305
Gnosticism, 146
Golan Heights, 312, 313, 323, 332,
    334
The Golden Ass, 139
Gomaa, Numan, 350
Gordon, Charles George, 256, 262
Gordon, Lucie Duff, 242, 247
Gorst, Sir Eldon, 261, 268–69
governmental and political organization.
    ancient Egyptian, 26–27,
    30–31, 39–41, 46, 61–63,
    80–82, 94–95; Ptolemaic, 100,

103–105, 107–108, 115; Roman, 123–25, 133, 140–43; early Islamic, 167–68; Fatimid, 176; Ayyubid, 184–85, 186–87; Mamluk, 193–94; Ottoman, 207–10, 212–16, 218, 224, under Muhammad Ali, 227–34; Khedive Ismail, 239–40; British occupation, 254–55, 265. For the twentieth century, see specific politicians or organizations.
grain shipments to Rome and Constantinople, 134–35, 143, 161, 163
Great Crisis, 179
Great Depression, 276
Great Humiliation, 284
Great Insurrection of 1711, 215
Great Pyramid, 35–36, 38, 171
Greco-Roman Museum, 126
Greek language in Egypt, 105–106, 132, 148, 169
Greek mercenaries, sailors, and traders in Late Period Egypt, 91, 92, 95
Greek War of Independence, 230, 232
Gulf of Aqaba, 7, 312
Gulf of Suez, 7
Gulf Wars, First and Second, 345, 351
Guy of Lusignan, 185

Habachi, Labib, 278
Hades, 108
Hadrian, 138, 139–40
Hajji, al-Salih, 198
Hakare-Ibi, 43
al-Hakim, Caliph, 175, 176, 177–79, 356
Halfaya Pass, 283
Harem Conspiracy, 78
Harar, 239
Harb, Talaat, 277, 278
Hariese, 87
Harun al-Rashid, 171
Hasan, al-Nasir, Sultan, 196–98

Hasan Pasha, 218
Hathor, 32
Hatshepsut, 52, 63, 65–67, 78, 154, 347
Hattin, Battle of, 185
Haussmann, Georges-Eugène, 241
Hawara, 50, 52, 56, 132
Hawara Channel, 6
Hay, Robert, 243
Hecataeus of Abdera, 103
Heikal, Muhammad Hasanein, 338
Hekanakhte, 55
Heliopolis, 51 n., 125, 166, 338
Helwan steel works, 302
Heptastadion, 101
Heraclius, 164–66
Herakleopolis and Herakleopolitan kingdom, 44–46, 87
Herihor, 82
Hermes, 129
Hermes Trismegistus, 129–30, 158
Hermeticism, 129–30, 147
Hermopolis Magna, 32, 87
Herod Agrippa, 135
Herodotus, 1, 56, 93–94, 131, 146
Herophilus of Chalcedon, 102–103
al-Hiba, 84
Hibis Temple, 93
Hicks Pasha, William, 256
Hiera Sikaminos, 125, 142
Hierakonpolis, 15, 18
hieratic script, 28–29
hieroglyphs, 20, 28–29, 77, 108, 124, 130, 148, 159, 223
High Priest of Amun, 80–82, 84–87
Hijaz, 185, 216, 227
al-Hikma, Dar, 175
Hims, Battle of, 194
History of the Church, 150
Hitler, Adolf, 281, 283, 285
Hittites, Kingdom of the, 73, 75, 76, 77, 79
Holocene Period, 8–9
Holy Family, 147, 155

Holy Trinity, 147–48
Horace, 121
Horemheb, 74–76
Horus, 29, 32, 33, 108, 139, 147
Hôtel d'Orient, 244
Hülegü, 190–91
Huni, 23
Husein, King, of Jordon, 305, 316, 322
Husein, Sadam, 345
Husein, Taha, 288
Hyksos, 57, 59–61, 65
Hymn to the Aten, 71, 72–73
Hypatia, 158–59

Ibn al-Athir, 187
Ibn Battuta, 202
Ibn al-Furat, 174
Ibn Khaldun, 200–201
Ahmed ibn Tulun, Ahmed, 171–72
Ibn Wasil, 188, 189
Ibrahim, Hafez, 278
Ibrahim Kahya, 215–16
Ibrahim Bey, 218, 220
Ibrahim Pasha (vizier of Suleiman I),
    209, 215
Ibrahim Pasha (viceroy of Egypt
    1604–1605), 213
Ibrahim Pasha (Muhammad Ali's
    son), 226–27, 232, 233
Ikshidid dynasty, 172, 174
*iltizam*s, 192, 208
Imhotep, 22
Inaros of Heliopolis, 93
independence, Egyptian, 273–75
industrialization, 229, 235, 257–58,
    277, 297, 326
Ineb-hedj. *See* Memphis.
Ineni, 65–66
infitah, 325–27, 352
Institute of Egypt, 222
Instruction of Amenemhet I, 54
Intef II, 46
International Monetary Fund (IMF),
    328, 346

intifada, 344
Ipuwer, 44–45
Iran-Iraq War, 344
Iraq, 288, 289, 296, 304–305, 306, 345
irrigation, 17–18
Irtisen, 53
Isis, 33, 108, 121, 138, 146, 147, 159
On Isis and Osiris, 138–39
Islam, advent of, 164–65
Ismail, Khedive, 236, 238–41, 245–49
Ismail Bey, 218
Ismail Pasha (Muhammad Ali's son),
    227
Ismailia, 245, 288, 290, 315, 331
Ismailis, 173, 180
Israel, ancient Kingdom of, 86
Israel, modern nation of, 288–89, 296,
    298–99, 302, 311–15, 320–25,
    328–35, 339, 343–44, 349
Italy, against Egypt during the
    Second World War, 282–83
Itjtawy, 48, 52, 58
Iuput, 86

al-Jabarti, Abd al-Rahman, 207, 217,
    220, 221
Jaffa, 186, 221
al-Jamali, Badr, 174, 179–80
Janus, 199
Japan and the Second World War, 284
Jawhar, 174
Jeddah, 216
Jerusalem, 73, 86, 91, 180, 182,
    185–86, 329–30, 334, 345, 355
Jews, Egyptian, 91, 102, 127, 128,
    146, 158, 164, 168–69, 176–77,
    178, 193, 349
Jewish Revolt, 127, 134
Johnson, Lyndon B., 309, 315
Jordan, 288, 296, 304, 310–11, 312–13,
    316, 322, 344
Josephus, Flavius, 11, 59–60
Josiah, 91
Judah, Kingdom of, 86, 89, 91

Julian, 151
Julian Calendar, 120
Julius Alexander, Tiberius, 127, 138
July Laws of 1961, 305–307
June 1967 War, 311–13, 315, 339, 341
Justinian, 159, 161

al-Kab, 13, 44
Kafur, 172, 174
Kalabsha, Temple of, 130
al-Kamil, 187–88
Kamil, Husein, Sultan, 271–72
Kamil, Ibrahim, 331
Kamil, Mustafa, 262, 267, 269
Kamose, 61
Karnak Temple, 50, 51, 63, 67, 68,
    76, 80, 86, 109
Kashta, 87
Kennedy, John F., 309
Kerma, 58
Khaba, 23
Khababash, 96
Khafra, 35, 38
Khair Bey, 208–209
Khalifa, the, 262–64, 265
Khalil, al-Ashraf, 195
Khalil, Mustafa, 333
Kharga Oasis, 6, 93, 355
Khartoum 2, 4, 236, 239, 256,
    262, 263
Khartoum Conference, 314–15
Khasekhemy, 21
Khemet, 53
Khonsu 32, 63, 131
Khrushchev, Nikita S., 299
Khufu, 35–36, 38
Khumarawayh, 172
Khusraw Pasha, 222, 224
Kings, First Book of, 86
kingship in ancient Egypt, 26–28
Kiosk of Trajan, 131
Kipchak Turks, 188, 194
Kircher, Athanasius, 130
Kissinger, Henry, 325, 329

Kitchener, Herbert, Lord, 263–64,
    269, 271
kiswa, 193
Kiya, 72, 75
Kléber, Jean-Baptiste, 221–22
Kom al-Dik, 126
Kom Ombo Temple, 109
Kordofan, 227
Krak des Chevaliers, 194
Kulthum, Umm, 278
Kush, Kingdom of, and Kushites,
    57–58, 60, 61, 85, 87–90,
    99, 130
Kutuz, 190–91, 193
Kuwait, 314, 345
al-Kuwatli, Shukri, 305

Labor Corps, 272
Labyrinth, mortuary temple of
    Amenemhet III, 52, 56, 138
Lactantius, 129
Laenus, Gaius Popillius, 113
al-Lahun, 50, 53, 104
Lake Nasser, 5, 300, 319, 355
Lampson, Sir Miles, 281, 284
land ownership and land reform in
    modern Egypt, 240, 276, 290,
    297, 307
Lane, Edward William, 242
language, ancient Egyptian, 29–30
Late Period, 22, 29, 30, 89–96
Latin kingdom of Jerusalem,
    182–87, 194
Law 43. *See infitah.*
Law of Shame, 336, 337
Lawata Berbers, 179
Layer Pyramid, 23
League of Nations, 280, 281
Lebanon, 304–305, 334, 339, 344
Legislative Assembly, 269–70
Legislative Council, 268, 269
Leisure of an English Official, 254
Lenaios, 112
Leontopolis, 87

Lepidus, M. Aemilius, 120
de Lesseps, Ferdinand, 237–38, 246
Lewis, John Frederic, 243
Library of Alexandria, 101, 103, 119,
    128, 158, 166–67
Libya and Libyans, 21, 49, 76, 78, 79,
    85–86, 280, 282–84, 314, 320,
    322, 330, 339
Libyan Desert. See Western Desert.
Libyan Palette, 18
Life of Baybars, 192, 212
Lighthouse of Alexandria. See Pharos.
Likud coalition, 328
al-Lisht, 48–49
literature, ancient Egyptian, 53–55,
    68, 72–73
Lloyd George, David, 275
Longinus, 129
Louis IX, 188, 190
Lower Egypt, 4
Lucius Domitius Domitianus, 141
Luxor Temple, 63, 68, 77, 109, 142

Maadi, 16
maat, 26, 38, 45, 67, 356
Macarius, 153
Macedonia, 99, 113
machimoi, 106
McMahon, Sir Henry, 271–72
Macmillan, Harold, 299
Mahdi, the, 240, 255–56, 262, 263–64
Maher, Ahmed, 287
Mahfouz, Naguib, 278
Mahmud II, 233
Mahmudiya Canal, 228, 229, 232
al-Mahrussa, 249, 292
Mai, 81
al-Malik al-Mansur, 199
al-Malik al-Zahir. See Chakmak al-
    Zahiri.
Malikshah, 180–81
Mamluks, 188–205; recruitment,
    training, and advancement,
    192–93, 202–203; neo-Mamluks,

208–209, 213–20, 223–26;
    Bahri Mamluks, 188, 190, 191,
    193, 195; Burgi (Circassian)
    Mamluks, 195, 198, 199
Mamun, Caliph, 171
Mandulis, 130
Manetho, 11, 19, 23, 41, 42, 43, 44,
    59–60, 65, 76, 87, 88, 103
Manichaeism, 147
Manners and Customs of the Modern
    Egyptians, An Account of, 242
Mansura, 188, 190
Manuel the Augustulis, 166
Manzikert, Battle of, 180
al-Maqrizi, Taqi al-Din, 174, 198
Marcian, 160
Marj Dabiq, Battle of, 205, 208
Mark, St., 146
Marsa Matruh, 282
martyrs, Christian, 150–51
Marwan I, 170
Marwan II, 171
Mary, Virgin, 147
al-Masri, Ahmed, 348
mastabas, 20, 27, 36, 42
Maundevile, John, 202
Maurice, 161
Mecca, 165–66, 193, 209, 216
Medes, 91
medicine in Greco-Roman Egypt,
    102–103, 129; Muhammad Ali's
    medical reforms, 231
Medina, 165, 167, 193, 209
Medinet Habu, 79
Mediterranean, 7
Meidum, 31, 35
Meketaten, 71
Meketra, 55
Melchites. See Chalcedonians.
Memnon, 137–38
Memphis, 19–20, 32, 43, 44, 61, 62,
    74, 87, 88, 89, 90, 92, 97, 101
Memphites, 114
Menas, St., 156

Menes, 11, 17
Menkaura, 35, 38–39
Menkheperre, 85
Menou, Abdullah Jacques, 222
Mentuhotep II, 46–48, 52
Mentuhotep III, 48
Mentuhotep IV, 48
Merenre, 41
Merenre II, 42
Merimda, 16
Meritaten, 74
Merneptah, 78
Meroë Dam, 355
Meroë, Kingdom of, 99, 125
Mesehti, 55
Mesopotamian stimulation of ancient
    Egypt, 16–17, 28
Metro of Cairo, 353
Middle Egypt, 4
Middle Kingdom, 46–58
midwives, 231
Minshat Abu Omar, 16
Minufiya, 341
Misr Group, 277, 278
Mitanni, Kingdom of, 65, 67, 68, 69, 73
Mithra, 146
Mithradates, 116
Mitla Pass, 325
Mixed Courts, 247–48, 280
Monastery of the Holy Virgin at al-
    Qusiya, 155
monasticism, 151–54, 156–57,
    160–61, 169
Mongols, 190–91, 194
Monophysite Controversy, 159–60, 164
Mons Claudianus, 136–37
Mons Porphyrites, 136
Montgomery, Bernard, 285–86
Montreux Convention, 281
Montu, 52, 63
Mosque of Amr ibn al-As, 167
Mosque of Baybars, 194
Mosque of al-Hakim, 179
Mosque of Ibn Tulun, 171

Mosque of Muhammad Ali, 212, 234
Mosque of Sinan Pasha, 211
Mosque of Suleiman Pasha, 211 n.
Mosque of Sultan Hasan, 197–98, 337
Moyne, Lord, 288
Muawiyah, Caliph, 170
al-Muazzan Turan-Shah, 189–90
Mubarak, Hosni, 323, 339, 340–53
Mubarak, Suzanne, 342
Mugamma, 347
Muhammad (Prophet), 164–65, 168,
    322–23
Muhammad, Pasha, 213
Muhammad Ahmed. See Mahdi.
Muhammad Ali Pasha, 216, 217, 222,
    224–34, 235, 244, 295, 345
Muhammad Bey Khusraw, 227
Muhammad ibn Abu Bakr, 170
Muhammad ibn Tughj, 172
Muhammad Said Pasha, 236–38, 246
Muhi al-Din, Zakariya, 309, 313–14
al-Muizz, Caliph, 172, 174, 176
mukhabarat, 307–308, 318
Mukhtar, Mahmud, 278
multazims, 192, 209
mummification and funeral practices,
    33–34, 131–32
Muqaddimah, 201
Muqattam Hills, 178, 356
Murad Bey, 218, 220–21, 223
Murray, John, 244
Murray's Handbook for Travellers in
    Egypt, 244
Musa Pasha, 214
Museum of Alexandria, 100, 102–103,
    128, 139, 141, 154
Muslim Brotherhood, 287, 294, 308,
    309–310, 319–20, 334, 337,
    346–47, 350
Muslim conquest of Egypt, 165–66
Mussolini, Benito, 282, 285
al-Mustadi, Caliph, 184
Mustafa Pasha (sixteenth-century
    Ottoman viceroy), 209

Mustafa Pasha (seventeenth-century Ottoman viceroy), 214
al-Mustali, Caliph, 180
al-Mustansir, Caliph, 179–80
Mut, 32, 63
al-Muzaffar Hajji, 196
Mycenae, 69
Myos Hormos, 7, 99
mystery religions, 146

Nabta Playa, 8–9
Nag Hammadi, 146, 154
Nag al-Medamoud, 52
Naguib, Muhammad, 289, 291–94, 295, 314
al-Nahhas, Mustafa, 279–81, 284, 286–87, 290–91, 294
Napata, 87, 88, 89
Napoleon III, 241, 246
Napoleon Bonaparte, 202, 219–21, 223
Naqada, 15, 17
Naqada I culture, 14
Naqada II culture, 14–16
Naqada III culture, 16–19
Narmer, 18–19
al-Nasir Muhammad, al-Malik, 192, 195–96, 200
Nasser City, 319
al-Nasser, Gamal Abd, 287, 291–316, 319, 321, 326, 328, 335, 338, 339, 342
Nasser, Tahiya, 319
National Democratic Party, 336, 349–50
National Party, 269
National Progressive Party, 336
National Unity Party, 301, 308
nationalist movements and nationalism, 107, 155, 160, 249–51, 259, 262, 265–69, 272–74, 280, 286
NATO, 337
Naukratis, 92, 95, 97, 133
Navarino, Battle of, 232, 233
Nebuchadnezzar II, 91–92

Necho II, 91, 93
Nectanebo I, 95
Nectanebo II, 95
Neferrohu, 44
Nefertem, 32
Nefertiti, 71–74
Neferure, 65–66
Nelson, Lord, 220
Neolithic Age, 8
Neoplatonism, 128, 146
Nepherites I, 95
Nepherites II, 95
Nero, 125, 127, 131, 138, 146
Nestorius, 145
Netjerykhet. See Djoser.
New Kingdom, 61–82
New Stone Age. See Neolithic Age.
New Testament, compilation of, 154
New Wafd, 349–50
newspapers and press, 231, 262, 277–78, 304, 319, 336, 338
Nezib, Battle of, 233
Niankhptah, 31
Nicene Creed, 145
Nicopolis, 124, 125
Nightingale, Florence, 242
Nikiu, Bishop of, 166
Nile and Nile Valley, 1–5, 7–9, 279, 295, 354–56
Nile Hilton Hotel, 276
Nile Waters Agreement of 1959, 354–55
Nitiqret, 42
Nixon, Richard M., 315, 324–25
Nizam Jedid, 230–32
Nizam al-Mulk, 181
Nizar, 180
Nobel Peace Prize awarded to Sadat and Begin, 332
Nofret, 31
non-aligned movement, 296
Norden, Frederick Lewis, 217
Northern Pyramid, 35
Nubar Pasha, 247

Nubia, 5, 25–26, 41, 44, 48, 49, 50, 51, 57–58, 61, 62, 65, 73, 76, 77, 81, 85, 87–90, 99, 114, 130, 142, 168, 193, 226, 117, 263, 300
al-Nuqrashi, Mahmud Fahmi, 287
Nour, Ayman, 350–51
Nur al-Din, 183–84

obelisks, 51 n., 125, 138
Octavia, 121–22, 131, 137
Octavian. *See* Augustus.
October War, 322–25, 330, 341
Old Kingdom, 6, 25-42
Old Stone Age. *See* Paleolithic Age.
Oman, 339
Omdurman, Battle of, 263
OPEC (Organization of Petroleum Exporting Countries), 324
Open Door Policy. *See infitah.*
Opera, 241
Operation Crusader, 283
Opet festival, 63, 74
Oracle of the Potter, 107
Organization of Arab Petroleum Exporting Countries (OAPEC), 334, 344–45
Organization for African Unity summit meeting 1995, 347
Origen the Christian, 129, 150, 154
Origen the Pagan, 129
orthodoxy, Christian, 154–55
Osiris, 25, 33, 108, 138-139, 147, 356
Osorkon II, 86
Osorkon V, 87
ostraka, 29, 64
Ottoman Empire, 203, 204–205, 207–18. Also pertinent are chapters 14, 15, and 16.
Oxyrhynchus, 131, 132, 140, 153
"Ozymandias," 77

Pachomius, St., 153
Paleolithic Age, 8

Palestine War, 288–90
Palestinian issues, 311, 315–16, 325, 329–35, 344
Palestinian Liberation Organization, 330
Palmyra, 141
pan-Arabism, 295–96, 303–305, 310–12, 320
pan-Islamism, 262
pan-Ottomanism, 262
Panhellenic Games, 100
Panion, Battle of, 111
papyrus, 21, 25, 28–29, 39, 54, 104, 132, 139
Papyrus Westcar, 39
Paris Peace Conference, 273–74
Parthian War, 121
Pelusium, 92, 166
Pepy I, 41
Pepy II, 41–42
Pepynakht Heqaib, 41
Peribsen, 21
persecution of Christians, 149–51
persecution of pagans, 157–59
Persian Empire and Egypt, 92–96, 163–64
personal piety, 31
Peter the Hermit, 182
Peter I of Lusignan, 198
Petrie, Sir Flinders, 13, 16
petroleum and natural gas, Egyptian production of, 314, 322, 332, 346, 352
Petronius, 125
pharaoh, meaning of term, 26
Pharos, 101
Philae Temple and island, 109, 131, 142, 159, 257
Philip Augustus, 186
Philippi, 120
Philo, 124, 127, 128, 154
philosophy at Alexandria, 128–29, 158
Phocas, 161
photography, 243

Piankh, 81–82
Pinudjem I, 82, 85
Pinudjem II, 85
Pi-Ramesses, 63, 84
Piye, 87–88
Plato, 128
Plotinus, 129
Plutarch, 32–33, 138–39
Pococke, Richard, 217
Polybius, 110
Pompey, Gnaeus, 116–18
Pompey's Pillar, 126, 141
population, ancient Egypt, 55–56,
    105; Coptic Egypt, 161;
    Ottoman, 210; nineteenth cen-
    tury, 240; twentieth century,
    276–77, 352–53
Port Said, 245, 315
Portland Vase, 136
Portuguese intrusions into the
    Mamluk Empire, 203
postal service, 239
Praxagoras of Cos, 102
Predynastic Egypt, 13–19
printing press at Bulaq, 231
Probus, 141
Protectorate, 271–75
Psammetichus I, 90–91
Psammetichus II, 91
Psammetichus III, 92–93
Psusennes I, 85
Psusennes II, 86
Ptah, 22, 32
Ptahhotpe, 31
Ptolemaeus, Claudius, 128
Ptolemaia festival, 108
Ptolemais, 133, 141
Ptolemaic Egypt, 97–122
Ptolemy I Soter, 97–99, 101, 102,
    103, 105, 108
Ptolemy II Philadelphus, 99, 100,
    102, 103, 104, 108
Ptolemy III Euergetes, 99–100, 103,
    107–108

Ptolemy IV Philopater, 107, 109–10
Ptolemy V Epiphanes, 108, 110–11,
    223
Ptolemy VI Philometor, 111–14
Ptolemy VII Neos Philopater, 112 n.,
    114
Ptolemy VIII Euergetes II (Physcon),
    98 n., 112–14
Ptolemy IX Soter II (Lathyrus), 116
Ptolemy X Alexander I, 115
Ptolemy XI Alexander II, 116
Ptolemy XII Neos Dionysus
    (Auletes), 116–18
Ptolemy XIII, 118–19
Ptolemy XIV, 119–20
Ptolemy XV Caesar (Caesarion),
    119–20, 122
Ptolemy Apion, 115
Pulcher, P. Clodius, 117
public health, 231, 240
Punic Wars, 112–13
Punt, 67
Pydna, Battle of, 113
pyramid complexes and temple cults
    and endowments, 36–37, 52
pyramid construction, 22–23, 34–36,
    38–39, 40–41, 48–49, 52, 56,
    57, 88, 99
Pyramids, Battle of, 220
Pyramids of Giza, 27, 35–36, 38, 138,
    197, 201–202
Pyramid Texts, 28, 41
Pyrrhic War, 112

Qaddafi, Muammar, 320, 322, 330
Qadesh, 77
al-Qaeda, 348
Qaitbey, 203–204
Qaitbey, Fort, 101
qaimaqam, 214
Qalawun, 194–95
Qasim, Abd al-Karim, 305
Qasr al-Aini Hospital, 231
Qasr Ibrim, 125

Qasr al-Sagha, 57
al-Qatai, 171–72
Qattara Depression, 6, 285
Qift, 6
quarries and quarrying, 4, 23, 31, 36, 47, 49, 50, 76, 136–37
Qeytas, 214
Qur'an, 34, 164
Qurqumas, 200
Quseir, 6
Qutb, Sayid, 294, 310

Ra, 39. *Also see* Amun and Amun-Ra.
Rabat Arab summit conference, 315
al-Radi, Caliph, 172
Radio Cairo, 278, 296, 304
Radjedet, 39
al-Rahmaniya, Battle of, 218
railroads, 236, 239, 258, 263
Rahotpe, 31
Ramesses I, 76
Ramesses II, 33, 76–78, 84
Ramesses III, 78–80, 85
Ramesses XI, 81–82, 85
Ramesseum, 33, 77
Ramessid era, 79–82
al-Ramla, 185
Raphia, Battle of, 110
Rashid, 223, 225
RCC, 293–97, 301, 349
Reagan, Ronald, 336, 338
Red Pyramid, 35
Red Sea, 7, 91, 99, 125, 127, 136, 142, 176, 199, 203, 204, 209, 227, 238, 351, 353
religion, ancient Egyptian, 22, 26, 31–34, 39, 70–75, 107–109, 130–31, 138–39, 146–47, 157–59
Reserved Points, 275, 278–79
Revolution of 1919, 273–75, 279
Revolution of 1952, 291–92
Revolutionary Command Council. *See* RCC.

Rhakotis, 97, 102
Rhodes, 100, 208
Rhomboidal Pyramid, 35
riasa, 215, 216, 218
Richard the Lion-Heart, 186
Ridwan Bey al-Faqairi, 214
Ridwan Kahya, 215–16
Rifai Mosque, 337
Rigoletto, 241
riots, 1977, 328, 346
Roberts, David, 243
Rogers Peace Plan, 315
Roman Empire and Egypt, 123–43
Roman Republic and the Ptolemaic Empire, 109, 111, 112–22
Romance of Abu Zeid, 212
Rommel, Erwin, 283–86
Roosevelt, Franklin D., 286
Rosetta Stone, 29, 108, 223
Rushdi, Husein, 270

Saadist Party, 287
*sabil-kuttab*s, 211, 226
Sabri, Ali, 318
sacrifice, human 20–21
al-Sadat, Anwar, 286, 291, 309, 317–39, 341, 342, 343, 344, 347, 348, 349, 355
Sadat, Jehan, 319, 328, 337
al-Saadawi, Nawal, 338, 342
Safaga, 353
Safavid Empire, 204–205
Said Pasha. *See* Muhammad Said Pasha.
St. Antony's Monastery, 152, 153, 156
St. Paul's Monastery, 153, 156
Saint-Simonians, 237
Sais, 87, 88–90, 92–95
Salah al-Din, 183–86
Salamis, Battle of, 94–95
Salar, 195–96
al-Salih Ayyub, 188–89
Salisbury, Marquis of, 262, 263
al-Sallal, Abdallah, 310–11

Sand Sea, 6
Saqqara, 20–21, 22, 39
saqiya, 104
Satire on the Trades, 28
Saud (king of Saudi Arabia), 304
Saudi Arabia, 296, 304, 310–311, 314,
    322, 334, 344
Savary, Claude Étienne Savary,
    217–18
Sayings of the Fathers, 152
schistosomiasis, 300
Scorpion, 17
Scorpion Macehead, 18
scribes, 27–28, 53–55, 62, 64, 106, 169
Sea Peoples, 79
Second Intermediate Period, 59–61
Second Persian Period, 95–95
Second World War, 280–87
Sekhemkhet, 22–23
Sekhmet, 32
Seleucid dynasty in Syria, 98, 99, 110,
    111–13, 114, 116
Selim I, 204–205, 208
Selim III, 221, 225
Seljuk Turks, 180–81, 183
Semiramis Hotel, 260
Semna, 51
Senenmut, 66
Sennacherib, 89
Sennar, 227
Senwosret I, 49–50, 51 n., 53
Senwosret II, 50, 56
Senwosret III, 47, 50–52, 52, 56
Septimius Severus, 138, 140
Septuagint, 103
Seqenenre Tao II, 60–61
sequestration, 299, 302, 307, 318
Serapeum, 101, 103, 108–109, 119,
    158, 166
Serapis, 108-109, 138, 158
serekhs, 29
Seth, 33, 139
Sethnakht, 78
Seti I, 76, 84

Seti II, 78
Severan dynasty. *See* Septimius
    Severus, Caracalla, and
    Alexander Severus.
Shabaka, 88–89
Shaban, al-Ashraf, 198
shabtis, 21
shaduf, 104
Shafei, Husein, 342
Shah of Iran, 337
Shajar al-Durr, 189–90
Shamir, Yitzhak, 288
Sharawi, Hoda, 274
sharia, 338
Sharm al-Sheikh, 298
Sharon, Ariel, 324
Shawqi, Ahmed, 288
Shebiktu, 88
Sheikh Abd al-Qurna, hill of, 64
al-Sheikh Ibada, 139
Shenuda III, 338, 349
Sheykh, 199
Shelley, Percy Bysshe, 77
Shenute, St., 153
Shepenwepet I, 87
Shepheard's English Hotel, 244, 260,
    290
Shepseskaf, 38–39
Shia Islam, 173, 178, 184
The Shipwrecked Sailor, 54
Shirkuh, 183–184
Shoshenq I, 85–86
Shoshenq II, 86
Shupiluliuma, 75
Sicily, 180
Sidi Barrani, 282
Sidqi, Ismail, 279
Sinai, 7, 47, 76, 313, 320, 322–25,
    328, 331–33
Sinai, Mt., 151
Siptah, 78
Sitt al-Mulk, 179
Siwa Oasis, 6, 92, 97
Slatin, Rudolf, 264–65

smallpox, 231
Smendes, 84
Smenkhkare, 74
Sneferu, 23, 35, 37, 38
Sobek, 32
Sobekhotep III, 57
Sobekneferu, 57
Socrates, 128–29
Sohag, 13
Solomon, 86
Sosibus, 110–11
Sosigenes, 120
Sossianus Hierocles, 150
Sothic Cycle, 140
Soviet Union, 296, 298–99, 303, 315,
    321–22, 324, 337, 343
Speos Artemidos, 67
Sphinx, 109
Stack, Sir Lee, 279, 287
state of emergency, 342
Step Pyramid, 22–23
Stern Gang, 288
Storrs, Sir Ronald, 260
Strabo, 124
Straits of Tiran, 332
Sudan, 227, 230, 235, 239–40,
    255–56, 262–65, 275, 279,
    280, 282–83, 288, 290, 295,
    320, 339, 354–55
Sudanese soldiers, 176, 179
Suez, 7, 315, 324
Suez Canal, 7, 236–38, 245–46, 251,
    253, 271, 275, 280, 282, 285,
    288, 290, 298–99, 313, 314,
    315, 321, 322, 323–27, 332,
    338, 346, 351–52
Suez Canal Company, 237–38, 246,
    248, 268, 298
Suez Crisis, 298–99, 302
Sufism, 193
Sukarno, 296
Suleiman I, 208–10
Sulla, 115–16
Sunni Islam, 173, 178, 184

Supreme Constitutional Court, 350
Sweet Water Canal, 245
Synagogue, Cairo, 260
Syria, 47, 304–306, 312–13, 316, 320,
    322–24, 339
Syrian War of Muhammad Ali, 233
Syrian Wars of the Ptolemies, 99,
    109–10, 111, 112–13

Tabennesi, Monastery of, 153
Taharqa, 88, 90
al-Tahtawi, Rifaa, 228, 231, 236, 239
Takelot I, 86
talatat, 72
Tale of the Eloquent Peasant, 54
Tale of Sinuhe, 54
Tamerlane, 199, 201, 204
Tanis, 84
Tantamani, 90
Tanzimat reforms, 236
Tauret, 32
Taz, 192
Tefnakht, 87, 88
telegraph, electric, 236
telegraph, semaphore, 229
telephone introduced, 258
Tell al-Fara'in, 16
Tell al-Kebir, Battle of, 251
Templar crusading order, 194
temples and temple cults and endow-
    ments in ancient Egypt, 64,
    80–81, 107–108, 130–31, 133.
    Also see specific temples such as
    Abu Simbel.
terrorism, 269, 279, 287, 288, 315–16,
    320, 329, 344, 346–48, 351
Teti, 41
Tetrabiblos, 128
Tewfiq, Khedive, 250–51, 254–55,
    261
Thackeray, William Makepeace, 243
Thebes, 32, 44, 46, 48, 52, 55, 58,
    60, 62–64, 67, 70, 74, 76, 80,
    85, 87, 89, 90, 124, 138, 308

Theocritus, 103
Theodosius, 157–59
Theon, 158
Theophilus, 157–58
Third Intermediate Period, 83–9
Thomas Cook, 244
Thoth, 22, 29, 32, 129, 131
A Thousand Miles up the Nile, 242
Tiye, 69
Tobruk, Battles of, 283, 284
Tomb of the Unknown Soldier, 338
Tomb of the Warriors, 46
Tombs of the Nobles. *See* Sheikh
   Abd al-Qurna.
Toshka Project, 355–56
tourism, 137–38, 139, 171, 242–44,
   260, 308, 314, 322, 326, 327,
   344, 346, 347–48, 351
Trajan, 127, 131, 135, 136
travelogues, 156, 202, 242, 243
Treaty of Amiens, 222
Tree of the Virgin in Heliopolis, 155
Tripartite Aggression, War of the,
   298–99, 311, 349
Tripoli (Lebanon), 182, 190, 194
Tripoli (Libya), 283
Tughril, 180
tulba, 213
Tulunid dynasty, 171–72
Tumanbey, 205
Tura, 36
Turan-Shah. *See* al-Muazzan Turan-
   Shah.
Turf Club, 260, 290
Turkish language and culture, 211
Turkish soldiers, 176, 179
Turks. *See* Ottoman Empire and
   other Turkish references.
Tusun Pasha, 225–26, 235
Tutankamun, 72, 74–75, 84, 278
Tutankaten. *See* Tutankamun.
Tuthmosis I, 61–62, 65, 84
Tuthmosis II, 65, 84
Tuthmosis III, 29, 65–68, 84

Tuthmosis IV, 68
Tuthmosis (sculptor), 71
Twosre, 78
Tyre, 186

U Thant, 312.
Ubayd Allah ibn al-Habhab, 170
Ugarit, 79
ulama, 224, 241
Umar, Caliph, 166, 173
Umm Diwaykarat, Battle of, 264
Ummah Party, 269–70
Ummayad Caliphate, 167, 169–71
Unas, 39, 41
UNESCO, 300
United Arab Republic, 304–306, 308,
   310, 320
United Nations, 287, 289, 298–99,
   311–13, 345
United Nations Educational,
   Scientific, and Cultural
   Organization. *See* UNESCO.
United Nations Emergency Force,
   311–12
United Nations Security Council
   resolution 242, 315, 321, 332
United States, 284, 296, 297, 299,
   302–303, 309, 321, 322, 324,
   325, 329–31, 333, 336–37,
   343, 344, 345, 348, 351, 353
Upper Egypt, 4
Urabi, Ahmed, 250–51
Urban II, 181
Urban III, 186
Userkaf, 39
Userkara, 41
Uthman, Caliph, 167, 169, 173

vaccination, 231
Valerian, 150
Valley of the Kings, 29, 63, 64,
   67, 75, 76, 78, 79, 82, 84,
   278, 347
Vanished Army, 92–93

Verdi, Giuseppe, 241
Via Hadriana, 139
The Voiage and Travaile of Sir John Maundevile, K^t., 202
veiled protectorate, 255, 271
Venice, 187
Vespasian, 127, 138
"Voice of theArabs," 310
Volney, Constantin, 217–18
Voyage around the Red Sea, 136

Wadi Hammamat, 6, 15, 17
Wadi Natrun monasteries, 153, 179, 338
Wadi Qena, 6
Wafd, 273–74, 276, 277, 279, 280, 281, 286–87, 290, 297, 336, 350. *Also see* New Wafd.
Wahhabis, 225–27, 230
Walls of the Ruler, 49, 57
Walter the Penniless, 182
*waqf*s, 209, 228, 240, 320
War of Attrition, 315, 322
*wekala*s, 212
Wenamun, 81
West Bank (Palestine), 313, 331–32
White Monastery, 153
Wilkinson, John Gardner, 241–42, 244
William of Tyre, 184
Wilson, Woodrow, 274

Wingate, Sir Reginald, 264, 271–72, 273, 275
Wisdom Literature, 54
Wolseley, Garnet Joseph. *See* Wolseley, Viscount, 251, 256
women, status of, 348
World Bank, 346
World Trade Center, 347, 348
writing, development of, 27–28

Xerxes I, 93

Yalbogha, 197–98
Yarmuk, Battle of, 165
Yemen, 185, 227, 233, 304, 310–11, 315, 341
Yom Kippur, 322
Yusuf (son of Barsbay), 200

Zab, Battle of, 171
Zafaran, 151
Zaghlul, Saad, 269–70, 272, 273–76, 277, 278–79
al-Zahir, Caliph, 179
Zangi, 183
Zanzanza, 75, 76
al-Zawahiri, Ayman, 248
Zawyet al-Aryan, 23
Zenobia, 141
Zeus, 108–109
Zionism, 288, 297